Priesthood
in a
New Millennium

Moberly

Priesthood in a New Millennium

TOWARD AN UNDERSTANDING OF ANGLICAN PRESBYTERATE IN THE TWENTY-FIRST CENTURY

R. DAVID COX

CHURCH PUBLISHING
New York

Library of Congress Cataloging-in-Publication Data

Cox, R. David.
  Priesthood in a new millennium : toward an understanding of Anglican
presbyterate in the twenty-first century / by R. David Cox.
     p. cm.
Includes bibliographical references and index.
  ISBN 0-89869-388-8 (pbk.)
  1. Anglican Communion—Government. 2. Church polity. 3.
Priesthood—Anglican Communion. I. Title.
  BX5008.5.C69 2003
  262'.143—dc22

                                                                2003020652

Church Publishing Incorporated
445 Fifth Avenue
New York NY 10016

www.churchpublishing.org

5 4 3 2 1

Contents

Acknowledgments

When I spoke with diocesan clergy on Maundy Thursday, 1997 on the nature of priesthood, little could I predict that a few simple thoughts would turn into a massive study. I was grateful for the responsiveness from my colleagues then, and ever since, for I have had nothing but support from the clergy and laity of the Episcopal Church, in the Anglican Communion, and beyond.

Early blessing—practical and otherwise—came from my parish, R. E. Lee Memorial Church, Lexington, Virginia, through continuing education and sabbatical time, a generous grant from its Gadsden Endowment, and the consistent encouragement of the *laos* in Lexington. I am especially grateful for my two assistants at that time, the Rev. Mark Lattime and the Rev. Deacon Katherine Tupper Gray. The Leyburn Library of Washington and Lee University as always provided its excellent resources.

When the pursuit of my Ph.D. through the Graduate Theological Foundation took me to Oxford, Kellogg College provided welcome hospitality, and the staff of the Bodleian Library managed to be both consistently helpful and universally cheerful in making available its vast resources. I found a similar reception at the Church of England Records Centre in London.

Two theological centers excited my incentive. In providing the six weeks of a Woods Fellowship, the Virginia Theological Seminary in Alexandria opened its arms and its substantial collections in Anglican materials in its Bishop Payne Library. I am grateful to Dean Martha Horne; to Associate Dean William Stafford who saw to it that his former pupil could at last finish his education, and his assistant, my longtime friend Kathleen van Esselstyn; to the students who shared their thoughts, lives, and aspirations, notably over breakfast; and to the faculty and staff, especially of the library.

Harvard Divinity School provided the intellectual opportunity of a lifetime through a Merrill Fellowship in the spring term of

2001. I am grateful to Dudley Rose and Laura Ruth Jarrett, to my fellow fellows Jean Larson-Hurd, Peter Laarman, and George Thomas, and to Charles Merrill for funding this unparalleled opportunity for clergy. I reveled in the vast resources of Harvard's libraries. I savored a course at Episcopal Divinity School with a friend of two decades, Ian Douglas, whose ideas on mission pepper this paper, and made good use of EDS's fine library. Harvard's Memorial Church and the Rev. Professor Peter J. Gomes afforded sanctuary and warm community, notably in the daily services and weekly teas. As for hospitality, my son Trevor, a senior at Harvard College while I did my work in Cambridge, generously included me in so much of his collegiate life.

Three weeks in Uganda in 1998 began my work with an international perspective to priesthood. I am grateful to my son Andrew for his companionship; to the Rev. Canon Mabel Katah-weire for inviting and shepherding us and for sharing her insights; and for the chance to participate in clergy refresher courses in Namugongo and Kabale. Clergy were most receptive, including the archbishop, the Most Rev. Livingstone Mpalanyi-Nkoyoyo; the Rev. Canon Dunstan Bukenya, acting principal, and the faculty of Bishop Tucker Theological College/Uganda Christian University; the acting principal and faculty of Bishop Barham Divinity School in Kabale, Kigezi; and the diocesan bishop and his wife, George and Laura Katwesigye.

The people of the Diocese of Bradford, England, make returning there always a pleasure. Christopher and Jill Wright have been marvelous hosts and perspicacious observers of the clerical condition from a lay view. Bishop David and Mrs. Mary Smith, the Rev. Canon Christopher Lewis, the Rev. Adrian Botwright, and two exchangees to Southwestern Virginia, the Rev. Janet Sharp and the Rev. Eric Kyte, all added their perceptions. I am particularly grateful to my erstwhile counterpart in our diocesan parish-to-parish link, the Rev. Stephen Treasure, for his and Heather's friendship and candor.

Innumerable conversations and interviews have guided and sometimes corrected my thinking. Along with those listed above and in the bibliography, I recall helpful talks in Oxford with the Rev. Dr. Jane Shaw of New College who chaired my thesis committee, the Very Rev. Robert M. C. Jeffery of Christ Church, Ms. Sarah Ogilvie, and the Rev. Dr. John Macquarrie; in Uganda, with clergy and laity who directly focused my attention on the concept of the "elder"; the Rev. Mauricio Andrade of the Episcopal Church of Brazil; in Cambridge, Massachusetts, with James L. J. Nuzzo, M.D., who shared challenging comments from having read the manuscript, and at the Society of Saint John the Evangelist, Br. Paul Wessinger SSJE and Br. Brian Bostwick SSJE; and with the Rev. Dr. John Martiner over breakfasts on Cape Cod. In Lexington, countless friends, colleagues, and parishioners have lent their insights on the topic or on the production of a work like this, including notably Dr. Alexandra Brown and Dr. Edwin Craun. The Rev. Dr. Rowan Greer, my teacher of many years, also added valuable observations.

My tremendous appreciation goes to those who helped to shape the manuscript: the Rev. Dr. Jackson Hershbell, now of Lexington, Johnny Ross of Church Publishing, Cynthia Shattuck, and the Rev. Deacon Vicki Black. My daughter Meredith undertook the odious task of helping to check quotations, bless her heart. The Rev. Lauren Stanley brought her journalist's eye to the task of proofreading.

I am grateful to two parishes in the Diocese of Virginia, St. Michael's in Arlington, and Emmanuel Church at Brook Hill, Richmond, for permitting me the time to complete this work while I served as their interim rector. Delivering the Alfred St. John Matthews Lectures in Lent, 2002 at St. John's Church, McLean, Virginia helped in honing and testing the theses of this book; my thanks go to the congregation, its rector, the Rev. Edward O. Miller, Jr., and his colleagues. During my time in Richmond, my retreat and resource has been the William Smith Morton Library of Union-PSCE, which, for a Presbyterian school, contains Anglican holdings in abundance. Two people warrant my deepest thanks. One is the Rev. Canon Vincent Strudwick, my ordinarius at Oxford, whose hearty sponsorship and constant advice gave motivation to persevere and direction to forge ahead.

The other is my wife Melissa, whose patience under the afflictions that I imposed, whose gracious latitude when I went off to some other school or yet another library, and above all whose partnership for thirty years, I appreciate beyond measure.

Abbreviations

BIBLICAL ABBREVIATIONS

Unless otherwise specified, all biblical references are from the *New Revised Standard Version.*

OT: Old Testament/Hebrew Scriptures

NT: New Testament/Christian Scriptures

KJV: *King James Version*

RSV/NRSV: *Revised Standard Version/New Revised Standard Version*

NEB/REB: *New English Bible/Revised English Bible*

NIV: *New International Version*

JB: *Jerusalem Bible*

NAB: *New American Bible*

STANDARD REFERENCE WORKS

DNB: *Dictionary of National Biography*

OED: *Oxford English Dictionary*

TDNT: *Theological Dictionary of the New Testament*

OTHER FREQUENTLY USED ABBREVIATIONS

BCP: *The Book of Common Prayer*

MP: R. C. Moberly, *Ministerial Priesthood*

PECUSA/ECUSA: [Protestant] Episcopal Church in the United States of America

NAAD: North American Association for the Diaconate

Notes on Style

Although I follow an American style of spelling and punctuation, the only alteration made in quotations (other than to correct obvious typographical errors) is to change "inverted commas" to American-style quotation marks. While the style of many quoted authors and documents is to capitalize the word "church," I do not, unless it refers to a specific ecclesial body ("the Church of Wales"). The term "catholic" is problematic, as it can refer to the tradition of the church throughout the ages (as in "holy catholic church"), which I will imply by using the lower case; the denomination led by the papacy, which I will invariably refer to as "Roman Catholic"; a wing, party or inclination within Anglicanism that goes by several specific names and which I will designate either specifically (Anglo-Catholic, Liberal Catholic) or generically as "Catholic" using the upper case.

Introduction

CHANGING IMAGES OF PRIESTHOOD

Once upon a time, the Anglican priest conformed to a particular image in the popular mind, a stereotype fired by the imaginations of authors of ecclesiastical fiction. The twentieth-century stereotype was not terribly different from its nineteenth-century predecessor, of which the clergy in Anthony Trollope's Barsetshire series (which includes *Barchester Towers*) are the most memorable. A sufficient number of clergy conformed to the caricature of an older, often kindly but rather bumbling parson, with his foibles and eccentricities along with his occasional ambitions for higher office. Although contemporary novelist Susan Howatch might place the priest in a college or cathedral setting, usually he was a country parson, whether in mysteries by Agatha Christie, novels by Barbara Pym, or more recently as the character "Father Tim" in the popular Mitford series by Jan Karon. This cleric was invariably male until the 1970s, when the decision to open priesthood to women allowed the *Vicar of Dibley* to break the male clerical monopoly on British television in the 1990s. But although these clergy portraits did arise from some grounding in life, fewer and fewer clergy actually fit the stereotype, especially as the century progressed. "Once it was clear what shape the good priest's life should have," wrote Rowan Williams ten years before he became Archbishop of Canterbury. "But it's not so clear now."[1]

If any life in the priesthood approximates the standard "shape," as Williams calls it, it has been mine. Located one state north of Jan Karon's fictional Mitford and a few miles south of where Gail Godwin's Father Melancholy had his church, Lexington, Virginia, is a small town with a nineteenth-century feel. The

---

[1] Rowan Williams, *A Ray of Darkness* (Cambridge, MA: Cowley Publications, 1995), 157–158.

parish where I served as rector until recently had around six hundred fifty baptized members, plus a substantial number of students from two colleges. It maintains a traditional pattern of staffing, with two stipendiary clergy along with part-time musicians and an educator. When I was there, a deacon and four or five other priests happened to live locally and assisted in parochial ministry. It is the sort of place where parish calling can still be done, often on foot. Perhaps because of its small-town ethos, its Southern ambiance, or the abiding prominence of churches in the community, clergy have tended to be more notable figures in Lexington than elsewhere. It was easy to define the priesthood I was exercising in terms of what I did: celebrating sacraments, teaching, visiting, preparing couples for marriage or individuals for baptism or confirmation, administering the parish, and sharing in the councils of the church.

Stephen Treasure, a priest of the diocese of Bradford in the Church of England, would not match that pastoral stereotype, however. He and his family left a working- and middle-class congregation in 1998 to assume the incumbency of a newly yoked parish of St. Oswald's and All Saints, Little Horton, where few work at all. The city of Bradford itself does not evoke the nostalgic postcard view of English life, and it probably never did. Once an industrial center peopled by textile workers drawn from all over Europe, its mills closed down decades ago, restoring the air quality but spoiling the economy. More recent immigrants from Asia have created a culture in West Yorkshire as much Muslim as Christian, or in the vicinity of St. Oswald's, vastly more Muslim, Sikh, and Hindu than Christian. The vicarage is about the only item that on first glance fits the traditional stereotype—a rambling stone house of Edwardian vintage, with room after room of lofty proportions. Empty for years, it was used only as a surface for graffiti artists and a target for slingshot sharpshooters.

Stephen Treasure volunteered for what he knew would be a tough assignment. His primarily Asian neighborhood had been classified as the second most economically deprived area in all of England. With few Christians in the area, St. Oswald's Church drew maybe twenty people on a good Sunday. As for All Saints, built as Bradford's most fashionable church nearly one hundred fifty years before, its steeple still dominates the Bradford skyline, a spiritual counterpoint to the mill chimneys—and almost as defunct. For years it was hard to see the splendid stone inlays and oaken carvings because the electric wiring had failed. The congregation of thirty or forty abandoned the stunning apse, with its glorious Victorian windows, for a plain cubicle erected in the back of the nave.

Yet in each of those places the worship of God continues. The sheer presence of the Treasure family, not to mention the refurbishment of the vicarage, represents a rekindled commitment by the Church of England to a local community. The renewal of Bible studies and classes, of church socials and mission projects, along with the services of worship signify a ministry that proclaims the gospel, administers the sacraments, and works for the well-being of people both in body and in soul—which is at the heart of even the most nostalgic view of the church. At the center of that effort is the priest. Alongside his pastoral duties, Treasure is leading a £2 million project to transform the grand old building into a "community advice and education centre" that will house rehearsals for the local arts festival and community college, a parent-and-toddler group, a post-natal support group, and in due course a nursery and theater. But it remains, at heart, a place of worship: already, Sunday services have returned to the chancel.

Phyllis Hicks does not fit the traditional priestly image, either. In fact she is not yet a priest, but, if all goes well, will be raised up as one amid her fellow Monacan Indians whom she will be ordained to serve. Saint Paul's in Bear Mountain sits nestled in the Blue Ridge Mountains of Virginia, a parish about as different from All Saints, Little Horton, as can be imagined. In 1908 Episcopalians established a mission to this Native American tribe that was largely ignored and marginalized by the surrounding Anglo community. In the days of racial segregation the children were forced to attend the "Negro" school, but the African-American population did not accept them any more than the whites did. Finally a school all their own was built, and a church, then a community center.

Throughout this time their small congregation was served by a priest of the diocese. By the end of the century it was the Rev. "B" Lloyd who would drive up the mountain from his home in Blacksburg a hundred miles away. Aware of the provisions whereby the Episcopal Church allowed small and isolated congregations to raise up ordained leadership from among themselves, he encouraged the Monacan parish to pursue this "Canon 9" approach.

Phyllis Hicks seemed the natural choice as someone long active in the Bear Mountain congregation and in the diocese, with, as her community discerned, potentially priestly gifts.

If we move from Appalachia to Africa, we find that on that continent, Anglicanism is now enjoying its most dramatic growth anywhere in the world. The Church of Uganda alone numbers two or three times more than the whole Episcopal Church in the United States. In 1904 the name of Jesus Christ had hardly been spoken in the Kamwezi area of Kigezi in Uganda's southwestern corner; by now, the average Ugandan parish numbers in the thousands, subdivided into as many as eight or ten different congregations. While an English parish might nominally include as many, in Uganda they all come to church—or so it seems. In 1998 I joined Bishop George Katwesigye for his visitation to the Kamwezi Archdeaconry where, from its five parishes, he confirmed about two hundred in an assembly of ten thousand people. For a priest to minister to his share of that throng, he must rely on lay readers in each congregation and give them what training and oversight he can. Visiting congregations that may lie miles apart means that, unless blessed with a bicycle, he walks a great deal.

Mabel Katahweire is one of Uganda's priests. For many years she taught seminarians at Bishop Tucker Theological College in Mukono, outside Kampala. In time, she herself was ordained, and continued her ministry in education. When she was the provincial secretary for education, she held the highest office of any woman in the Church of Uganda. Simon Mwesigwa also pursues a priestly calling in education. Recently ordained and well below thirty, he was assigned as chaplain to a secondary school in Central Uganda. He simmers with excitement over communicating the gospel to the young, especially the bright minds who yearn to move beyond milk to solid food. Craving more education for himself, too, he prepares for further work through studies at Makerere University.

As these snapshots of various clergy suggest, the meaning of priesthood at the dawn of a new millennium will be shaped by a variety of factors. First is the dramatic change in the nature of the Anglican Communion itself. Any notion of priesthood must apply to the archdeacon of Kamwezi in Uganda, the dean of the cathedral in Hong Kong, the priest in the mission station in the outback of Australia, the "local priest" in Alaska, the provincial secretary of the Episcopal Church of Brazil, the chaplain of a school in Nigeria,

a rector in Virginia, and a vicar in Bradford, England. Having
spent some time in Uganda and Hong Kong as well as England, I
am extremely conscious of the point Titus Presler makes in light of
the shift in world Christianity's center of gravity from north to
south, which "requires us to shift our thinking away from a Euro-
American assumption that defining Anglicanism is a Euro-Ameri-
can responsibility and privilege."[2] This internationalism, moreover, adds a rich complexity to the various strands of Anglican
piety, worship, churchmanship, theological perspective, and sociological reality, all inevitably reflected in its ordained leadership.[3]
Any attempt at definition has the wide cultural and ecclesial diversities of increasing globalism to take into account.

Another dramatic new circumstance is the altered relationship
between church and society, in which the church in many parts of
the world plays a decidedly lesser role in its society than formerly.
Timothy Sedgwick, in introducing his study of ministry, calls this
"as fundamental and radical as the change brought about in the
fourth century with the establishment of the Christian church as
the state religion of the Roman Empire."[4] The cleric's role within
society shifts as a result.

A theology of priesthood should also cover a growing diversity
of priestly ministries. In the early twentieth century clergy almost
exclusively served in parishes or cathedrals, academic settings, or
as diocesan assistants. At its conclusion, along with the more
familiar roles, priests serve as substance-abuse counselors, pastoral therapists, hospital or prison chaplains. The Rev. John Dan-
forth, a priest of the Episcopal Church, was elected to three terms
in the United States Senate. In Hong Kong I met an ordained
banker. Practical considerations enter into the conversation about
priesthood, too, since how clergy lead their lives and how the people
of the church regard their clergy have evolved as well. As Gregory
Dix pointed out, the idea may influence the practice but so too the

---

[2] Titus Presler, "Old and New in Worship and Community: Culture's Pressure in
Global Anglicanism," *Anglican Theological Review*, 82, no. 4 (Fall 2000), 711.

[3] Cf. Perry Butler, "The History of Anglicanism from the Early Eighteenth Century
to the Present," *The Study of Anglicanism*, eds. Stephen Sykes and John Booty
(Minneapolis: Fortress, 1988), 28–47.

[4] Timothy F. Sedgwick, *The Making of Ministry* (Cambridge, MA: Cowley
Publications, 1993), v.

xviii   Priesthood in a New Millennium

practice affects the idea. Although the clergy may have the same
function now as they did five hundred or fifteen hundred years
ago, their mode of exercising it has changed.[5] Nevertheless, we
will find a remarkable continuity in *what* priests do even if not in
how they do it.

What is it that all priests share? The anthropologically minded
might speak of the priest as the one who stands before God on
behalf of people and vice versa, a mediator between the human
and the divine. Most parishioners, I suspect, would respond in
more functional terms: "The priest presides at the Eucharist"; the
priest is "the rector of the parish," "the one who baptizes, marries,
counsels, and visits the sick," "the one who stands at the altar
wearing odd clothes," "the man or woman of God" and the like.
Manuals of priestly functions abound, advising clergy on how to
do their job, but far fewer confront the ontology of the priest. It
seems easier to describe what the priest *does* than what the priest
is. But what priests *do* spans an increasingly wide spectrum, the
nature of their service varying with the assignment and the context
in which it takes place. The nature of priesthood lies, I think, in
what their church ordains them to *be.* They are called and ordained
to be *priests*—presbyters, to use the technical name, a word derived
from the Greek for "elders"—within the community of faith.

There may always have been confusion over what the clergy
are and do. If so, the concern has increased. As the New Testament
professor William Countryman writes, "Fifty years ago, the role
and purpose of ordained ministry seemed clear in the Western
world. Since then the task has become more problematic, both for
the public at large and for the churches—and, indeed, for the clergy in particular."[6] To reform our understanding of priesthood, he
adds, the whole church must be involved. I am not so certain,
however, that the situation *was* so clear fifty years ago. "In our
days very many lay-people and some priests have no clear idea of
what the priesthood means nor what is rightly to be expected of a

---

[5] Gregory Dix, "The Ministry in the Early Church," in Kenneth E. Kirk, ed., *The
Apostolic Ministry* (London: Hodder & Stoughton, 1946), 185–189.

[6] L. William Countryman, *Living on the Border of the Holy: Renewing the
Priesthood of All* (Harrisburg, PA: Morehouse, 1999), 111 (cf. xii), 135.

[7] Raymond Raynes, *Called By God (What It Means to Be a Priest)* (London:
Church Literature Association, c. 1945), 19.

priest," an English priest wrote in 1945.[7] John Tiller, in examining the state of the English clergy, concludes that serious confusions began appearing in the 1960s, though signs were evident since World War I in light of ever-shifting and often declining roles, status, influence, definitions, and the growing participation of the laity. He remarks that *Crockford's*, a directory of English clergy, noted in the 1980s that increasing ecumenical agreement on the nature of priesthood has not been accompanied by a similar clarification of what the job entails, producing a "crisis of confidence."[8] But some of those same agreements revealed deeper confusions. It was observed at the time of the aborted Methodist-Anglican reunion in England in 1969: "Acute questions are now being raised about what a man in priest's orders exists to do and to be, and there is at present much confused debate."[9] In more recent studies of priesthood, Robin Greenwood noted that few have taken much trouble to articulate a theology of ministry; and Gordon Kuhrt finds persistent references to someone "preparing for the ministry" or "going into the ministry" when for a century theologians have underscored the unity of the *whole* church and, increasingly, the ministerial role each Christian plays within it.[10]

Reformulating conceptions of priesthood, however, may not be an easy task. For one thing, no common theological basis seems to exist. Both seminarians and experienced priests study the functions of priesthood in the books they read, but rarely works that address the ideas behind it. Some read Charles Gore, or Richard Hanson's *Christian Priesthood Examined*, and occasionally R. C. Moberly's *Ministerial Priesthood*, which was recommended to me. Michael Ramsay's *Christian Priest Today* is popular and remains a solid choice, but it reflects the presumptions of fifty years ago. I believe there is a fundamental Anglican understanding of priesthood, but it is not easily discerned, and the lack of an identifiable

---

[8] John Tiller, *A Strategy for the Church's Ministry* (London: CIO Publishing, 1983), 96–97.

[9] Church of England, Advisory Council for the Church's Ministry, Ministry Committee, *Ordained Ministry Today: A Discussion of its Nature and Role* (Westminster: Church Information Office, 1969), 7.

[10] Robin Greenwood, *Transforming Priesthood: A New Theology of Mission and Ministry* (London: SPCK, 1994), 29; Gordon Kuhrt, *An Introduction to Christian Ministry* (London: Church House Publishing, 2000), 7.

common perspective explains the sometimes baffling diversity of views in our attempts to explicate the priesthood of the ordained while at the same time trying to grasp the ministry of all.

This, then, is a book about an idea—the idea of priesthood. It is not a full-fledged doctrine of the church or of ministry. Nor is it a history of Holy Orders: readable summaries can be found in Urban Holmes, *The Future Shape of the Ministry*; R. P. C. Hanson, *Christian Priesthood Examined*; M. A. H. Melinsky, *The Shape of the Ministry*; and James Monroe Barnett's *The Diaconate: A Full and Equal Order*. Neither is this a full-blown history of the idea, since I limit myself to the past century or so. Furthermore, I trace the idea primarily, almost exclusively out of *Anglican* thought, even though this voluntary limitation does not always give a full picture because of ecumenical influences. Trying to discuss the Liturgical Movement or revolutions in church architecture without reference to Roman Catholic insights or the enormous impact of Vatican II may seem as foolish as ignoring the wealth of biblical and theological scholarship of European Protestantism. However, I am more interested in how these influences affected the Anglican mindset, more in what was heard and passed along rather than what was originally said. I believe that as we refresh our own Anglican understanding of the idea of priesthood and orders, we may relate to other denominations more effectively, or dispute with them more clearly. We can find a commonality within our own house, vast though it now is. We may better understand each other, too, in the various manifestations of vocation and ministry to which Jesus calls each one of his people—layperson, bishop, priest, deacon—together as one in a priesthood of all.

Here a problem of language arises. I will argue for seeing clergy as inherently part of the baptized community. How then can we speak in a way that distinguishes the ordained from the non-ordained while retaining their commonality? To refer to "clergy" and "laity" or "lay persons," as canons and catechisms often do,[11] implies an almost absolute separation that has for centuries undermined concepts that unite all Christians, without distinction, in

---

[11] Norman Doe, *Canon Law in the Anglican Communion: A Worldwide Perspective* (Oxford: Clarendon Press, 1998), 160 (n.b. fn. 5); The Episcopal Church, *The Book of Common Prayer* (New York: Church Hymnal Corp., 1979) [afterwards, US BCP], 855.

the whole Body of Christ. I will use the Greek term *laos* to refer to the "whole people of God," and adopt the canonical definition of "laity," "lay persons" and their equivalents as those who are not ordained.[12]

This book is in two parts. Part One gives the background for where we find ourselves today. I will begin with the Church of England in the 1870s, the essay of J. B. Lightfoot entitled *The Christian Ministry*, and the scholarly work of two of his contemporaries, followed by the reactions of Charles Gore and R. C. Moberly. Moberly's concept of the ministerial priesthood within the Body of Christ seemed to catch the imagination of subsequent theologians and archbishops. At first, the discussion was mostly confined to the English church. As Moberly's sense of the presbyter as a representative of Christ and his church found its way into canon law, prayer books, liturgies, and the statements of successive Lambeth Conferences, first Episcopalians in the United States and then other Anglicans across the Communion began to add their voices and insights to a nascent theology of the priesthood and of the church as a whole.

Part Two develops my own perspective on where we are and where we are heading as regards the changing understanding of bishops, priests, deacons, and the people of God.[13] Theology stands at the heart of the endeavor, and changes in theology will inevitably affect how clergy and people see themselves. To take one example, in the twentieth century the vision of a church comprising the entire people of God took even greater hold and tended increasingly to minimize distinctions between clergy and laity, redefining the relationship among them. The theological ponderings of ministry and mission itself reflect a broadening of Anglicanism. Whereas a hundred years ago those who had their thoughts published and read were predominantly if not exclusively British, American writers now take at least an equal share in the discussion, with those of other provinces adding their voices. In the future,

---

[12] "Originally in the New Testament,...[the adjective "lay"] meant 'one of the people of God' and included all members of the Church. As a general term, it had come by the third century to mean 'one of the people of God' who was not a clergyman. But by the fifth century it meant 'profane'" (James Monroe Barnett, *The Diaconate: A Full and Equal Order* [New York: Seabury, 1981], 112); cf. Dix, "Ministry in the Early Church," in Kirk, ed., *Apostolic Ministry*, 285.

African and Asian theologians will likely become prominent. As for this work, while striving to incorporate as globally Anglican a perspective as I can, I recognize that inevitably my own context as an Episcopalian and American shapes my point of view.

Understanding priesthood depends not so much on what happened or what was said but on how these events and views were assimilated. The late nineteenth and early twentieth centuries were rich with extensive studies of the earliest church, for example, and rife with authors who produced incredibly long books to explain what they thought it was like. For our purpose, what matters is not so much the accuracy of their history, but the degree to which their history entered Anglican consciousness. So this is not so much a history of priesthood as an institution but rather a contemplation of priesthood as a concept. By recovering a sense of "presbyterate" within the priesthood shared by all Christians, the ministry of the ordained may take on new significance for the dawning age—always in light of the greater ministry of the church which is the Body of Christ.

It may be a more vital task than might at first appear. In the 1970s, when the dictator Idi Amin was devastating Uganda, the plea went out from that ravaged country for clergy shirts and clerical collars. What an odd request: of all things, why paraphernalia for clergy? The answer came back, "So that when Amin's soldiers round us up to be killed, we'll know who our priests are."

We still need to know who our priests are.

---

[13] Bishops will not receive a chapter of their own, however. Although evolutions in the episcopate may warrant a thorough study, I do not believe that they bear as strongly upon presbyterate as the changes in ideas of priests, deacons, and laity.

I
Priesthood in the Late Nineteenth Century

In the latter days of Queen Victoria's England, certain theological scholars took a new look at the ancient church, reconsidered it in their own day and, in applying it to their own times, revived a concept of a representative and ministerial priesthood. As a new century dawned, that concept took on a focus and power that spread well beyond England to wherever Anglicans worshiped.

The ideal had originated long before that a priest was both a servant of Christ and of his church. Since the seventeenth century, George Herbert had epitomized the Anglican pastoral vision of one who represented both Lord and community through the ministry and service he offered. A courtier of promising talent who abandoned the glitters of London for a Wiltshire country parish, Herbert said his prayers, tended his ecclesial flock, wrote sublime poetry and, in 1633, died at forty: a perfect life to idealize, but his writings made him even more so. *A Priest to the Temple; or the Country Parson*, first published in 1652, set forth an exemplar of a well-read divine, temperate in all things, constant in duty to his God and his people alike. His near contemporary, Izaak Walton of *The Compleat Angler* fame, described how farmers in their fields "would let their Plow rest when Mr. *Herbert*'s Saints' Bell rung to Prayers, that they might also offer their devotions to God with him."[1] In saying his prayers, Herbert was praying *for* the whole congregation. Rather than functioning as a substitute for his people, he provided a unifying voice, twice a day, for the prayers they offered as they separately paused quietly throughout the village. In visiting the sick, he as the "parson," the "person" who embodied the parish—the words share an etymological heritage[2]—would figuratively bring the whole congregation with him in all its collective concern. Herbert represented his people. At the same time, he saw himself as an agent of God. "A pastor is the Deputy of Christ for the reducing of Man to the Obedience of God," he began *The Priest to the Temple*, "reducing" meaning to bring back from error. Pastoral duty and pastoral dignity were one, which is "to do that which Christ did." He held the authority of Christ as his "Vicegerent."[3]

Because the Church of England was by law established, the parson was expected to hold, and wield, a degree of the authority that comes from an earthly king as well. In duties that accumulated over time, he recorded births, marriages, and deaths, which, given his pastoral connection, is logical enough; but when a stamp tax was levied on every name in the parish register, the priest took on the added chore of tax collector too. He was becoming an officer of the law, a magistrate; by 1816, clergy comprised more than a third of Oxfordshire's justices of the peace.[4] That he had studied at Oxford or Cambridge made him a natural candidate for teacher, not only of religious subjects. Educating the young thus became a responsibility. So did his parishioners' physical welfare,

---

[1] Izaak Walton, *Life of George Herbert* (1670), q. in John N. Wall, introduction to George Herbert, *The Country Parson, The Temple* (New York: Paulist Press, 1981), 7. Walton's portrait, of course, is idealized (and the italics are his). Cf. also Monica Furlong, *The C of E: The State It's In* (London: Hodder & Stoughton, 2000), 260–261, or Arthur Middleton, *Towards a Renewed Priesthood* (Leominster: Gracewing, 1995), esp. ch. 2. Cf. Michael Hinton, *The Anglican Parochial Clergy: A Celebration* (London: SCM Press, 1994).

[2] *Oxford English Dictionary*, 2nd ed. (Oxford: Clarendon Press, 1989), s.v. "Parson," "Person." Both derive from the Latin, *"persona."*

[3] Herbert, *The Country Parson*, 55; cf. also 82: "The Country Parson is in God's stead to his Parish."

[4] Anthony Russell, *The Clerical Profession* (London: SPCK, 1980) 142, 151–152.

for his pastoral role made him a logical almoner. But when it came to relationships with the mass of laity, the roles collided: he represented them, but also the king. He gave them alms, but took their tithes. His educational experience helped them to learn, but also elevated him above the farmers and villagers to the social plane of the local squire. By the eighteenth century, the clerical stereotype depicted "an occupational appendage of gentry status." The image was not altogether fair, for it could overshadow the often devoted and frequently low-paid cleric, who might rely on farming his glebe to make ends meet when tithes fell short.[5]

But many a clerical image, and not a few realities, were about to change.

THE CRITICAL CENTURY

The nineteenth century in England was a time of exceptional ferment as its society and its theological mind were transformed. A rural flight that emptied the countryside and poured people into cities; the process of industrialization that helped lure them there; the social problems that resulted; the abundance of scientific discovery and intellectual interest spurred by the Enlightenment; an Evangelical revival; the Romantic movement in the arts that revived attention in medieval culture; the dominance of a British commercial and political empire: all these, and more, had their effects on every part of British society, including its church, including its clergy. How priests functioned, were trained, and fit into the life of the larger community changed far more between 1800 and 1900 than between 1900 and 2000. By 1870, a very different kind of priest had emerged, and this was the kind that prevailed to the present.[6] Accordingly, from about 1870 until the close of the century, theologians struggled to define the nature of that priest, in light of the radical evolution in society, in the church, and in scholarship itself.

---

[5] Russell, *Clerical Profession*, 6; C. K. Francis Brown, *A History of the English Clergy, 1800–1900* (London: Faith Press, 1953), 18–35. As an example of this stereotype, cf. Henry Fielding's Mr. Thwackum in the novel *Tom Jones*.

[6] Russell, *Clerical Profession*; Brian Heeney, *A Different Kind of Gentleman: Parish Clergy as Professional Men in Early and Mid-Victorian England* (Hamden, CT: Archon, 1976).

The ideal of a representative and ministerial priesthood, inherent in the seventeenth century, took on a new and modern form with vigor. The picture of the clerical life developed from that of the country gentleman in holy orders to a more complex portrait of a person who was at once a holy man of God and also a professional, with little leisure, high responsibility, and lofty standards to uphold. But that image was merely an inset within the far grander sweep of an England in the midst of momentous change—change that would inevitably affect its established church, change that would also influence the way the Anglican Communion was taking shape. Three of these trends in England especially influenced the clergy's position: the move to the cities, the evident decline of church attendance, and the shift in the clerical role.

In the second half of the nineteenth century, England's population grew by about three million each decade, all in and around cities. Meanwhile, the rural population declined from half the people of England and Wales to one-fourth. A growing middle class often chose to live in newly expanding suburban areas made viable by improved transportation. Many in the working class had no choice; they were forced into cheap new housing estates outside the city centers as these areas were being commercialized. But in neither area were there any churches. When it awoke to the need for them, the Church of England struggled mightily to build more structures and recruit more clergy. It was not altogether successful. Despite the new edifices and faces that filled them, there was a sense that the established church was declining in its effectiveness and position, especially with the working class.[7]

Not surprisingly, the ramifications of these sociological developments bore heavily upon church and clergy. No longer was the village parson, ensconced in his formidable rectory, the quintessence of clerical life, not when depopulated villages undermined his pastoral purpose and financial support. The action was in the

---

[7] Owen Chadwick, *The Victorian Church*, 2nd ed., Part II (London: Adam & Charles Black, 1972), 218–222, 160–163. Robin Gill suggests that church building may have been *too* successful, so that a relatively static number of churchgoers were spread out into too many, and overlarge, new buildings, which gave the impression of decline. See Robin Gill, *The Myth of the Empty Church* (London: SPCK, 1993).

clergy of other stripes

cities—but few clergy were. Those who did minister to the new urban throngs were often of Tractarian sympathies, laboring selflessly among the poor. Other clergy, of other stripes, also labored selflessly, often because they had no choice: pay was frequently poor, and in the cities or new towns they had no glebe to farm when tithes failed to come in. Low levels of clerical remuneration became a chronic complaint, the more so as numbers of parishioners decreased—and that decline further lowered clerical prestige.[8] Some parishes seemed to thrive as places of revival with plenty of parishioners to support them, and there were the old sinecures of deaneries and archdeaconries to lift clerical spirits and incomes. Still, striking inequities and discouraging prospects dogged those clergy who were unable to win the lottery of preferment or benefice.

"Professionalization" was one response. "[T]he clergy were anxious to regard themselves and be regarded by society as a professional body with specific functions and duties," writes Anthony Russell, all in contrast with a century before.[9] Higher standards, better training, greater collegiality, more adequate pay, and even a touch of prestige were marks of a "professional" status akin to that of doctors, lawyers, and other respected Victorians.

Accordingly, how clergy were trained became a growing concern. At the century's start, Oxbridge graduates, plus a few from Trinity College, Dublin (which also supplied most Church of Ireland clergy), produced nearly all the candidates for ordination. What they learned differed little from what any other Oxbridge students learned—and would not explicitly include theology. A don complained in 1868, "Theology has not begun to exist as a science among us," and feared it would continue to be "an extraneous appendage tacked on to the fag-end of every examination in every

---

[8] Chadwick, *Victorian Church*, II, 160–161, 222–223.

[9] Russell, *Clerical Profession*, 6. The degree to which the nineteenth century marked a decided professionalization of the clergy, the point of Russell's book, is disputed by Rosemary O'Day, "The Clerical Renaissance in Victorian England and Wales," in *Religion in Victorian Britain*, ed. Gerald Parsons (Manchester: Manchester University Press, 1988), I, 184–212. She perceives a reassertion, in light of a newly urban and industrial society, of characteristics that jelled in the wake of the Reformation; indeed, other professions drew characteristics from clergy.

remuneration

other subject." He was too pessimistic, for by the 1870s, universities offered specific degree programs in theology. However, a more fundamental change was afoot. "Graduates" diminished as a percentage of ordinands as years wore on, meaning that ever-increasing numbers of clergy were being trained outside of the traditional university system.[10] Starting in 1817, American Episcopalians had begun to organize institutions to train clergy, sometimes for geographic convenience, sometimes for nurturing a particular style of churchmanship.[11] A decade or two later, English bishops began to do the same. They created diocesan schools for ordinands,[12] sometimes in the cathedrals (thereby deflecting criticism that the ancient piles were underused and scandalously wasteful). Sometimes they had partisan intent. Bishop Samuel Wilberforce in 1854 modeled Cuddesdon, just across the road from his Oxfordshire palace, on Roman Catholic seminaries in Europe.[13] Not to be outdone by "rankest semi-popery," Evangelicals founded Saint Aidan's, Birkenhead in 1856, and St. John's Hall, Highbury near London in 1863.[14] Others wanted their theological colleges to

---

[10] F. W. B. Bullock, *A History of Training for the Ministry of the Church of England in England and Wales from 1875 to 1974* (London: Home Words Printing and Publishing, 1976), xvi. Trinity College, Dublin was in some respects ahead of Oxford and Cambridge, but in its connection to the church it was significantly behind. Cf. Alan Acheson, *A History of the Church of Ireland 1691–1996* (Dublin: Columba Press, 1997), 90, 148, 214–215. Mark Pattison, q. in M. A. H. Melinsky, *The Shape of the Ministry* (Norwich: Canterbury Press, 1992), 252.

[11] E.g., General Theological Seminary (New York City, 1817), Virginia Theological Seminary (Alexandria, 1823), Nashotah House (Wisconsin, 1842), Berkeley Divinity School (Connecticut, 1854, now affiliated with Yale), University of the South School of Theology (Sewanee, TN, 1868). American non-sectarian—if largely Protestant—colleges were also establishing specific divinity schools, such as Harvard (1816) and Yale (1822). Many an Episcopal diocese, such as Kentucky, also created its own school for training clergy.

[12] Bullock, *Training, 1875 to 1974*, xviii–xix. Diocesan colleges include Durham (1831, later a university), Chichester (1839), Wells (1840), Lichfield (1857), Canterbury (1860), Salisbury and Exeter (1861), Gloucester (1868), Lincoln (1874), and Ely (1876). Melinsky, *Shape*, 253.

[13] Russell, *Clerical Profession*, 46. Also see Brown, *English Clergy*, Appendix B (240–249), and Melinsky, *Shape*, 253.

[14] The Evangelically oriented Church Missionary Society in 1825 had opened an institution at Islington to train missionaries who were members of its society and were not university graduates. See F. W. B. Bullock, *A History of Training for the*

address some need in church or society. Bishop Christopher Wordsworth opened Lincoln Theological College in 1873 with two students and the future Archbishop of Canterbury Edward Benson as its head. Wordsworth meant it to be a working laboratory to address the "spread of sceptical opinions among us" even in ancient colleges; the "weakness of the foundations of religious belief in the upper and middle classes of society; the attempt to build up systems of education on the quicksand of creedless ethics; the spread of immorality and licentiousness."[15] In the 1890s the Society of the Sacred Mission started an experiment at Kelham in training clergy from lower social classes. Whatever the motive for founding theological colleges, church officialdom by 1908 recognized that its own schools, rather than the old universities, were better for preparing ordinands.[16] This mode for theological education became the Anglican standard worldwide, as institutions appeared around the globe to train clergy in their local areas.[17]

With professional training came standards for ordination akin to those measuring prospective doctors or lawyers. By 1884 all but two English bishops had accepted a "deacon's examination" patterned on a general theological examination that originated in 1874,[18] concerning theoretical knowledge but also the practice of pastoral care. GTE

Ministry of the Church of England in England and Wales from 1800 to 1874 (St. Leonards-on-Sea: Budd & Gillatt, 1955), 31.

[15] Vincent Strudwick, *Christopher Wordsworth, Bishop of Lincoln 1869–1885* (Lincoln: Honywood Press, 1987), 26–27 (q. from Wordsworth's visitation address of 1879).

[16] David Dowland, *Nineteenth-Century Anglican Theological Training* (Oxford: Clarendon Press, 1997), 69, cf. ch. 5 (n.b. esp. quotations from *The Report to the Archbishop of Canterbury on the Supply and Training of Candidates*, cited in ibid., 132), though see ch. 6 for a fuller discussion of advantages and disadvantages of each, largely a distinction between general education in theology and professionally oriented training. The point was made at least as early as 1862: see Bullock, *Training, 1800 to 1874*, 100–102.

[17] E.g., Codrington College in Barbados, which began an advanced program in 1829; what became Queen's College, Newfoundland in 1842, and a variety of schools in Canada as early as 1789; Moore College in Liverpool, near Sydney, Australia in 1856, with other attempts—not always successful—in Bermuda, Hong Kong, Melanesia, New Zealand, India, Ceylon, South Africa, and West Africa. Bullock, *Training, 1800 to 1874*, 149–158.

[18] Melinsky, *Shape*, 253; Bullock, *Training, 1875 to 1974*, xx.

did was changing dramatically as older roles like
e gave way to new demands of industrialized life.
e, the urge to professionalism intensified the spir-
clergy held, especially as pastor and priest. As a
lamented in 1872, "It is undeniably more difficult
to meet a clergyman's responsibilities now" than just twenty years
before.[19] The load was too great for one person to bear, exceed-
ingly so in city parishes with tens of thousands of parishioners.
The old tradition of a Mr. Herbert doing all things for all people
in the village church no longer worked. Calls went forth for more
clergy to meet a chronic shortage, to oversee the newly built
churches and to staff the overwhelmed old ones. The novel concept
of team ministries was developed to care for the masses within a
congregation, teams of clergy but also laity, and among the latter,
men but also women.[20] Anthony Russell concludes:

> The contradiction in the range of clerical functions, the
> increased autonomy of the professional body, the desire
> to re-establish representative organs, the proliferation of
> clerical journals and periodicals, the anxiety to exclude
> unworthy persons and the concern at maintaining high
> standards, and the establishment of the theological col-
> lege may all be regarded as demonstrative of the grow-
> ing acceptance by the clergy of the professions as a new
> reference point for the development of their role.[21]

Many clergy aspired to professional status—or even higher,
given the divine nature of their calling. The loftiness of such a calling was one measure of self-understanding. A second measure
divided them among themselves according to theological perspective and liturgical practice. The differences showed forth in so simple a manifestation as what they wore. Attire separated clergy
from laity, but also distinguished one sort of cleric from another.
As an American learned in 1894:

---

[19] Henry Parry Liddon, *Clerical Life and Work* (London: Longmans, Green, and
Co., 1903), 243.

[20] Chadwick, *Victorian Church*, II, 243.

[21] Russell, *Clerical Profession*, 47.

> The high churchman is close-shaven, with a collar, high vest and a long coat...the low churchman, with whiskers and neckerchief, is neatly attired in customary suit of solemn black, desiring to appear, and appearing, more as the minister than the priest; while the broad churchman disports himself in a straw hat and short jacket...sometimes adorning his countenance with a huge moustache and looking like a dragoon on furlough.[22]

Appearance revealed a deeper difference in fundamental outlook, which lasted well beyond 1900. Borrowing Russell's distinction, was the presbyter a "priest" or was he a "clergyman"? The one term underscored the spiritual aspect of the role within the Christian community; the other placed the cleric alongside the doctor, lawyer, or other professional whose own role was increasingly specialized and professionalized.[23] Haberdashery and terminology also both signified the degree to which a priest saw himself as one of, or distinct from, his people.[24] On those issues, Anglican clerics differed.

They were more united, however, in perceiving themselves increasingly as religious specialists within a steadily more specialized, secularized, and downright busy society.

> Both the Evangelicals and the Tractarians had sought to emphasize the spiritual and consecrated nature of the clergyman's role. No longer was the role legitimated principally by appeals to its social utility, but in terms of the spiritual and sacramental nature of the Church. If, in the eighteenth century, the clergyman had been a member of the leisured class free to indulge his interests in gentlemanly sports, the administration of the county, together with scholarly and social pursuits, the typical mid-nineteenth-century clergyman was a man without leisure. At a time when the tempo of life was quickening, the clergy were required to be energetically engaged in the sacred duties of their calling.[25]

[22] Q. in Brown, *English Clergy*, 218.

[23] Russell, *Clerical Profession*, 3, 233.

[24] Chadwick, *Victorian Church*, II, 254

[25] Russell, *Clerical Profession*, 233.

Thus, in the course of a hundred years, clergy came to see themselves differently, to relate to their people in new ways, and to accentuate the more pastoral aspects of ministry. This transformation was being matched and sustained by an intellectual reevaluation of ordained ministry, which began about 1870 and found a synthesis on the eve of the twentieth century.

THE SHIFT IN THEORY

With a transformation in the life of the church came new ideas that both reflected and fueled the changes in the church's life. In politics, old concepts of establishment had eroded with the advent of Nonconformists, Roman Catholics, and eventually Jews into Parliament. The Church of England's roof did not collapse but its foundations were shaken enough for many to demand something steadier on which to stand. The Oxford Movement, in particular, looked to apostolic succession as a means of expressing an even firmer, more ancient grounding than its status as a state church would provide. Rather than the authority of the nation, as Owen Chadwick observed, the church could possess "a divine authority whatever the State may do, even if the State should be represented by an indifferent or a persecuting government; that the authority of the bishop or the vicar rests not upon his national or his social position, but upon his apostolic commission."[26]

That was in England. But the faith of England's church had already spread beyond the British Isles, tucked in the spiritual baggage of colonists seeking new lives and of missionaries seeking new converts. Dominions within the empire could establish the church precisely as at home, at least in law; but bishops who were lords of state would be anathema to Americans, who associated them with the crown they so recently had rejected. Episcopalians in the United States had to find a basis other than establishment for episcopacy and, thus, priesthood. Having a church founded on apostolic commission was as useful in their situation as it was for Tractarians in theirs.

---

[26] Owen Chadwick, "The Mind of the Oxford Movement," in *The Spirit of the Oxford Movement: Tractarian Essays* (Cambridge: Cambridge University Press, 1990), 3.

A swirl of ideas was blowing fresh if not always welcome air into the studies of Oxbridge theologues and local vicarages alike. Whether from science or politics, technological advance or popular culture, intellectual developments were forcing reappraisals of fundamental aspects of Christian life. When Victorians began reading Dickens's *A Christmas Carol* next to a trimmed evergreen (which Prince Albert introduced to England), they were—knowingly or not—trading their earlier preoccupations with Christ's passion for contemplations of Jesus' incarnation. This in turn contributed to the theological ruminations of the incarnationalist school of *Lux Mundi*, as we shall see.[27] When ancient texts were being discovered or reprinted, like the little manual of ethics and liturgy from a second-century church called the *Didache*,[28] readers inevitably began to consider the origins of the church in a new light. But when the tools and methods developed in the natural sciences started to be applied to biblical and religious study, great could be the controversy—especially if the results were tainted with the evolutionary theories of Charles Darwin. In 1860 a group of Anglicans, influenced by German ideas and aware of Darwin, published a volume of *Essays and Reviews*. The authors, including the future Archbishop of Canterbury Frederick Temple, invited new views of biblical interpretation, the creed, and the very nature of the church. One writer alleged that biblical creation stories might not constitute scientific truth. Another, Benjamin Jowett of Oxford, asserted that while the Bible requires a faithful approach, it can be studied with the same tools as other works of literature.[29] People were shocked. Heresy trials followed for two of the writers (who were eventually vindicated). Even stone cried out: On an old baptismal font in Coventry Cathedral were figures symbolizing the

---

[27] See Chadwick, *Victorian Church*, II, 469.

[28] For a discussion of the effects of these influences on the church, see Chadwick, *Victorian Church*, II, 1–97. Found in 1873, this "Teaching of the Twelve Apostles" overflows with hints about how a second-century church in Egypt or Syria led its life. For a restrained view, see Charles Gore, *The Ministry of the Christian Church*, 2nd ed. (London: Rivingtons, 1889), 276–278 including 277, n. 2.

[29] William L. Sachs, *The Transformation of Anglicanism* (Cambridge: Cambridge University Press, 1993), 138–140; a recent scholarly edition is Victor Shea and William Whitla, eds., *Essays and Reviews: The 1860 Text and Its Reading* (Charlottesville: University Press of Virginia, 2000).

deadly sins. Each held an appropriate emblem, some of which were defaced or missing. Victorians replaced one of them with a representation of "Heresy," shown reading from an open book. Its title: *Essays and Reviews.*[30]

Reactions to *Essays and Reviews* proved mild compared to those that greeted John William Colenso's commentaries on Romans (1861) and the Pentateuch (1862–70). Not only did he question Moses' authorship of the first five books of the Old Testament, but he also challenged literal truths of creation and flood stories and long-held views of the nature of Christ's atonement. Even more galling, he was a bishop.[31]

England was used to being the center of an economic and political empire and also a budding Anglican Communion. But never before had her church dealt with so global a fracas. Colenso was British but his diocese was in Natal, South Africa. His initial critics were Canadian, though plenty more inhabited the British Isles; and the Canadians were the ones agitated enough to petition the Archbishop of Canterbury to do something, anything, like calling bishops together to talk about how to maintain unity in the face of such a disaster. So out of a remarkably complex, bitter, persistent, and international controversy emerged the first Lambeth Conference in 1868, beginning the tradition of Anglican bishops' gathering from throughout the Communion. Crisis induced the recognition that Anglicanism was growing beyond England and that daughter churches were starting to influence, rather than merely respond to, the mother.

Intellectually, the church was expanding its horizons. On the surface, outside influences seemed nonexistent. Despite a resurgence of biblical, historical, and theological work on the Continent, rarely did British ecclesiologists cite them. In fact, several writers were studying German critics, at least, with care.[32] A surprisingly influential force on English Anglicans were the Non-

---

[30] F. R. Barry, *The Relevance of the Church* (London: Nisbet & Co., 1935), 26–27.

[31] Sachs, *Transformation*, 142–143.

[32] Fenton John Anthony Hort, *The Christian Ecclesia* (London: Macmillan & Co., 1908), 3. Lightfoot cites the scholars Mosheim (p. 13), Rothe, *Anfänge etc.*, Bauer and Ritschl, 32 n.1, and Rothe, 40, but the surprise is how rarely he does so. Moberly extensively responds to French writers in his appendix concerning

conformists. One, the Free Churchman William Milligan, was quoted at length by the two key Anglo-Catholic writers whom we will encounter, Charles Gore and Robert Campbell Moberly, betokening a growing awareness of other denominations' thinking.[33]

For the most part, English Anglicans talked to English Anglicans, and, on the subject of the church and its priesthood, the conversation occurred within a small circle of Oxbridge scholars. Most notably, J. B. Lightfoot, Edwin Hatch, F. J. A. Hort, R. C. Moberly, and Charles Gore shared their research, aired their opinions, and sometimes vented their spleens—though their habit of dying, one after another, just after publishing their key books rather truncated the conversation, and leaving the last word to the remarkably enduring Gore. In what they produced, they manifested the academic presuppositions of their day. The literary and historical approach to the Scriptures that came to characterize twentieth-century work was only just beginning to appear. Colenso's strident view of the Pentateuch, for example, found no parallel in these authors. For them, Peter and Paul wrote the letters attributed to them (except maybe Hebrews). The Acts of the Apostles constituted reliable history.[34] Jesus said what the gospels say he said.[35] A "pre-critical" Bible, especially a pre-critical New Testament,

---

Apostolicae Curae, but otherwise confines himself almost exclusively to fellow Britons. Hort maintained a "considerable" correspondence with scholars in Germany, Holland, and the United States, where his work, he felt, may have been better known than in his homeland (Arthur Fenton Hort, *Life and Letters of Fenton John Anthony Hort* [London: Macmillan and Co., 1896], II, 369). Hatch, too, was appreciated in continental circles, his Bampton Lectures being translated into German by no less than Harnack. The interest did not seem to be mutual. As William Sanday recalled, Hatch "knew and appreciated what was done on the Continent, but he was himself essentially English both in the character of his mind and in method" (*Memorials of Edwin Hatch* [London: Hodder and Stoughton, 1890], xvi, xx, xxi). See Chadwick, *Victorian Church*, II, 69–72.

[33] Both Gore and Moberly quote Milligan approvingly, e.g., Gore, *Ministry*, 346–347; Robert Campbell Moberly, *Ministerial Priesthood*, 2nd edition (repr. London: SPCK, 1969), 34, 72, 97, 248, 251.

[34] Hort, however, inserts "Ephesians" within inverted commas, implying yet not explaining some question of audience, though not authorship (cf. *Ecclesia*, 138–144). As for the pastoral epistles, he is aware of challenges to "their authenticity and integrity" but concludes that they are Paul's own writings (171). Hort's pre-critical view is the more striking for his prominence as a NT Greek scholar.

[35] E.g., Hort, *Ecclesia*, 18–19.

formed the primary source for their study. Their intellectual ferment caused them to plumb it and contemplate it anew, trying to exact precise meanings of key words—Greek scholars that several of them were—but without pushing beyond acceptable boundaries.[36] They were also historians, deeply fascinated by the earliest church, particularly of the first three centuries. What Ignatius wrote, or the *Didache* prescribed, attracted their scrutinizing (if also uncritical) attention. Michael Ramsey, who became 100th Archbishop of Canterbury, looked back on the era of 1889 to 1939—which these authors began—when

> Anglican theology had its own marked characteristics. There was the emphasis upon the Incarnation, the striving after synthesis between theology and contemporary culture which the term "liberal" broadly denotes, the frequent shift of interest from dogma to apologetics. But if these were the more dated characteristics, there were also the more permanent ones, seldom absent from Anglican divinity in any age: the appeal to Scripture, and the Fathers, the fondness for Nicene categories, the union of doctrine and liturgy, the isolation from continental influences.[37]

THE REEVALUATION OF MINISTERIAL FOUNDATIONS

As Americans of the mid-twentieth century had their baseball cards, pictures of players along with a thin slab of pink bubble gum, so a hundred years before Victorians in England had their ecclesiastical equivalent. *Cartes de visite*, they were called, and, without the bubble gum, pictured luminaries like John Keble, E. B. Pusey, John Mason Neale, and Thomas Thelluson Carter. These priests were all part of a "catholic revival" in the Church of England and beyond: Keble and Pusey, with John Henry Newman, in the initial leadership of the Oxford Movement; Neale, Carter, H. P. Liddon, and later Moberly and Gore in the next generations.

---

[36] E.g., Hort, *Ecclesia*, on *"Ecclesia,"* lecture I, 1–21, or "apostle," lecture II, 22–41.

[37] A. Michael Ramsey, *An Era in Anglican Theology: From Gore to Temple* (New York: Charles Scribner's Sons, 1960), 2, viii.

Although the movement itself, and its chief organ, the *Tracts for the Times*, paid little attention to ecclesial structures or the nature of priesthood, its efforts to reconsider the basis of the Church of England as an apostolic entity guaranteed that, sooner or later, one or another of its adherents would turn to such topics. When they did, it was equally guaranteed that an equal and opposite reaction would result. And so it happened.

THE INITIAL DEBATE

A long-lived parish priest (1808–1901), T. T. Carter had studied at Oxford under Pusey before the movement began, but was enthralled by the *Tracts for the Times* when they appeared. He tried gradually to instill their ideals in his parish at Clewer, near Windsor, where he founded a "house of mercy for fallen women" and a sisterhood. He also espoused their principles in his profuse writings.[38]

In his *Doctrine of the Priesthood in the Church of England*, Carter proposed the idea of a "ministerial priesthood," which consists of a "mediation, or ministerial intervention between God and man."[39] Alongside that, he posited a second priesthood, which begins with baptism and is "the inheritance of all the faithful." The "ministerial priesthood" communicates "the fruits of the Atonement" by "outward means and a human agency," while the "Priesthood of the individual Christian" allows the believer to receive these fruits. Carter tried to skirt the pitfalls of vicarious priesthood, in which the priest stands as an intermediary of salvation, by asserting that saving grace, like both priesthoods, comes from Christ. He also pleaded for a "higher view of congregational worship" as an expression of the people's priesthood.[40]

---

[38] John Shelton Reed, *Glorious Battle: The Cultural Politics of Victorian Anglo-Catholicism* (Nashville: Vanderbilt University Press, 1996), 52, 215; *Dictionary of National Biography* (London: Oxford University Press, 1882), 2nd Suppl., v. 1, 319–321.

[39] T. T. Carter, *The Doctrine of the Priesthood in the Church of England*, 3rd edition (London: J. Masters and Co., 1876; first published 1857), 98–100, 106. Although Carter was an early proponent of the concept, he may not have been the first to expound it.

[40] Carter, *Priesthood*, 147–149, 153.

rep. of christ to world   *ministerial priesthood*

Carter would seem to resemble a guest at a proper tea party who voices, too early, too crudely, bold ideas that clash with the civility of the occasion. His concept of an individualized priesthood of each believer received no support then and hardly a mention thereafter, and that of the ordained was too high by far. But without ever being credited, if credit was even due, Carter's understanding of a "ministerial priesthood" in which the ordained becomes a "representative of Christ to the world" were adopted and adapted by a rising generation of catholic-minded writers.[41]

Carter's viewpoint was certainly too much for J. B. Lightfoot. The shining star in a constellation of scholars that included B. F. Westcott and F. J. A. Hort, together they were known as the "Cambridge School," after the university where they taught. With others such as Edwin Hatch of Oxford, they investigated New Testament exegesis, textual criticism, and the history of Christian origins. While some explored the gospels in search of the "historical Jesus," others delved into ecclesial history: How did the church emerge? In what sense is it "apostolic"? Who ran it, and on what authority? Inexorably, their search would extend into the origins of orders as well: What is the nature of the various orders? And what is a priest? Dogma was not their primary concern; someone like Hatch would write long articles on the derivation of orders or ordination, letting historical chips fall where they may. But the Cambridge School's influence was powerful, especially upon those in the ecclesiastical, theological middle such as A. P. Stanley of Westminster Abbey.

Joseph Barber Lightfoot (1828–89) towered over them all. Fellow of Trinity College, Cambridge, Bishop of Durham from 1879, he pursued scholarship that was conservative enough in its conclusions to influence the English church yet sufficiently academic in its method to treat German critics fairly.[42] When he published a commentary on Philippians in 1868, he appended an essay on the

---

[41] Reed, *Glorious Battle*, 135, re Carter's novel idea of Convocation's authority over church *and* crown; Carter, *Priesthood*, 159. It is unclear how much influence Carter wielded. Moberly does not cite him, nor Gore, it seems; yet Carter publicly defended *Lux Mundi* and was an honorary canon at Christ Church, Oxford, suggesting that he was well known personally and through his multitudinous publications.

[42] Chadwick, *Victorian Church*, II, 69.

Christian ministry, later reprinted in his *Dissertations on the Apostolic Age* and as a separate work. In that article he sought to define the essence of ministry as it emerged in the early history of the church, but his conclusions differed sharply from Carter's. God's kingdom "interposes no sacrificial tribe or class between God and man, by whose intervention alone God is reconciled and man forgiven. Each individual member holds personal communion with the Divine Head."[43] If Carter's view of priesthood was excessively "high," Lightfoot's was so "low" that he seemed to dispense with orders altogether. This was not altogether true, but he forced his readers to dig to find the value of priesthood.

He was followed by others who took the same approach, adopted a similar view, and left a similar impression. One was the scholarly priest Edwin Hatch (1835–89). In 1880 he presented the prestigious Bampton Lectures at Oxford, issued the next year as *The Organization of the Early Christian Churches.* Seven years later, he published for a general audience *The Growth of Church Institutions,* in which he traced the development of such familiar notions as the diocese, bishop, parish, tithes, and chancel. Aiming "to be not controversial, but historical," he emphasized these notions' rootedness in Roman society and governance.[44] With the same goal as Lightfoot, Hatch adapted as "historical science" the same methods he saw used in scientific inquiry into the natural world. Like continental scholars with whom he corresponded, he also applied biblical criticism to survey the early church: "[T]he developments of these sciences in our day has been a necessary preliminary to the study of Christianity."[45]

---

[43] J. B. Lightfoot, *The Christian Ministry* (London: Chas. J. Thynne & Jarvis, Ltd., 1927), 1.

[44] Edwin Hatch, *The Growth of Church Institutions* (New York: Thomas Whittaker, 1887), v.

[45] Claude Welch, *Protestant Thought in the Nineteenth Century* (New Haven and London: Yale University Press, 1985), Vol. II (1870–1914), 172, 179. Edwin Hatch, *The Organization of the Early Christian Churches* (London: Longmans, Green and Co., 1918), 2–12, cf. 19; "The Religious Tendencies of our Time" (1888), *Memorials,* 318–319. Hatch's historical approach may be most evident in the four articles he wrote for *A Dictionary of Christian Antiquities,* ed. William Smith and Samuel Cheetham (Hartford: J. B. Burr, 1880): s.v. "Orders, Holy" (1469–97), "Ordinal" (1497–1501), "Ordination" (1501–21), and "Parish" (1554–61).

What did those sciences reveal? For Hatch, they showed that Christians came together for mutual financial support. As human "associations," these "Christian assemblies" resembled other fellowships of their era, excepting only, but brilliantly, that churches cared for the poor. Borrowing from Jewish precedent, they took collections to relieve human needs within the church and beyond. To oversee this effort, Christians adapted the structures of Graeco-Roman groups for those officers called *episkopoi*, and these (Hatch thought) turned into bishops. These bishops needed helpers, called "deacons," to distribute the corporate charity.[46] Those who were presbyters resembled heads of families or elders in a tribe, or presiders over local Jewish courts, or a council of elders supervising a Gentile community. By Hatch's reconstruction, when the emperor Constantine legalized Christianity and the church began to grow rapidly, a single presbyter functioned to lead "the ministry of the word" and "the ministry of the sacrament."[47] Hatch uncovered evidence that laity could teach, preach, baptize, exercise discipline, or even celebrate Eucharist. Though leaders possessed certain rights, their rights were not exclusive. Indeed, when clergy claimed sole ownership of these powers, the Montanist[48] reaction reiterated the priority of spiritual gifts over official rule. Nonetheless, the ordained officialdom gradually diminished lay rights. Ordination, a parallel to admission to civil office, became the means of appointing individuals to churchly office. Clergy received state-sponsored privileges that segregated them from laity all the more.[49]

---

[46] Hatch, *Organization*, Lecture II, 26–55.

[47] Hatch, *Organization*, Lecture III, 56–81. Note, however, the leap from a ministry of governance/oversight to that of word/sacrament.

[48] Montanism grew up in the late second century as an apocalyptic movement, which expected the speedy outpouring of the Spirit upon the church. It was rigorous in its ethical demands, distinguishing the "Psychics" or "animal men" from its own members who were "Pneumatics" or "Spirit-filled." It won over the North African theologian Tertullian. Cf. F. L. Cross, *The Oxford Dictionary of the Christian Church* (n.p.: Oxford University Press, 1977), s.v., 934; also Gore, *Ministry*, 189–193.

[49] Hatch, *Organization*, Lecture V, 113–142; Lecture VI, 143–168.

Hatch's reading of ecclesial history, so much more sociological than Lightfoot's, also came across as more a matter of civics and business administration than of divine inspiration. Two consequences resulted. Of one Hatch was aware: When, in the centuries following those of the early church, people separate themselves from "the main body of Christians" in order to restore what they consider "in their own practice the uncorrupted simplicity of primitive usage," he wrote in *Church Institutions*,[50] there is in fact no such thing. Yet that consequence, so useful a point for those who wish to protect some established system (like the Church of England), produced an unintended but inevitable corollary. If matters were not so simple for those who might wish to restore a radical simplicity of primitive usage, neither were they so simple for anyone else. The absence of clear roots equally affected those establishments that traced their heritage to those now-questionable roots. No one could base an exclusive ecclesiology of orders upon the precedent of the earliest church, neither the radical reformer (or Nonconformist), nor the conservative traditionalist (or Anglican).

Scholars of Bible and history had muddied the clear waters of simple certainty, and many in the church did not like it at all.[51] In their distress, they perceived that Hatch—though a man of deep piety and author of the hymn "Breathe on me, breath of God"[52]— had pursued a "scientific" method that packed faith and theology into a closet. In distinguishing "history" from "exegesis," he had foresworn examining evidence from the New Testament. In cleaving "Christian faith" from "the organization of the Christian churches," he had equally resolved to avoid doctrine.[53] To those who considered the church to be in itself an article of faith—which is an article that his most ardent critics stoutly affirmed—he had attempted the impossible, and was doomed to fail.

---

[50] Hatch, *Church Institutions*, 3.

[51] Hatch, *Memorials*, xxiv, xxviii. E.g., the Bampton Lectures evoked a firestorm of controversy. Cf. Gore's scathing critique in his review, "Hatch's Bampton Lectures," *Church Quarterly Review*, 12 (1881): 409–452, e.g., 410.

[52] Chadwick, *Victorian Church*, II, 469.

[53] Hatch, *Organization*, 23.

Another scholar, in another series of lectures, took the discussion in a still different direction. Fenton John Anthony Hort (1828–92) was Lady Margaret professor at Cambridge. Well known for his Greek edition of the New Testament, which he published with Westcott, Hort was also one of the producers, along with Westcott and Lightfoot, of the Revised Version of the Bible. In his 1888–89 lectures at Oxford, published in 1897 as *The Christian Ecclesia*, Hort asserted that apostles held sway in the early church but with an authority more moral than formal. Christ, he suggested, did not commission them to run a churchly government but instead to bear witness to him, especially by preaching and healing. By that witness they garnered "an ill-defined but lofty authority in matters of government and administration"; nonetheless, according to Hort, theirs was "a claim to deference rather than a right to be obeyed."[54]

Like Lightfoot, Hort supposed that "elders" (a term he used consistently for *presbuteroi*) were no new phenomenon but rather a Christian version "of the ordinary Jewish elders" who governed the synagogue.[55] These elders exerted oversight without holding a title of oversight: their episcopate was a function, not an office. Like Hatch, Hort saw similarities between the church's structure and that of Graeco-Roman society. He departed from Hatch and Lightfoot, however, in underlining the role of the Holy Spirit in setting these elders apart to fulfill their function within the *ecclesia*.[56]

Hort's approach is primarily a functional one. Apostolic authority was needed to provide supervision "till the newly appointed Elders should have gained some really effective influence under the difficult circumstances of their new office." Then these elders/presbyters could function as overseers. Between the terms *episkopos* and *presbuteros*, Hort perceived no formal difference. "'Elder' is the title, 'oversight' is the function to be exercised by the holder of the title within the Ecclesia." Deacons, he thought,

---

[54] Hort, *Ecclesia*, 84–85. Note Moberly's vigorous dispute of the point in *Ministerial Priesthood*, 135.

[55] Hort, *Ecclesia*, 62, 100; see 194.

[56] Hort, *Ecclesia*, 98–99, relying especially on Acts 20:28; see also 227, 230.

constituted a distinct office as ministers to needy members.[57] But he also alleged that the structure of functions, and who exercises them, varied from place to place, and from time to time: the situation in Crete differed from that in Ephesus, and from one decade to another.[58] Monolithic, the early church was not.

In responding to Hort, his critics charged him with looking through a microscope not only when it was necessary, but even when he needed a telescope. The quality may be marvelous for the textual critic, less so for the historian.[59] His book consists of one vignette of early Christians after another, without the unity of a cohesive theme. Yet his very methodology significantly contributed to portraying a diversity of life in the early church that defied simplistic assumptions. In the end, he could stand back from the data he so carefully scrutinized and warn of the "futility of endeavoring to make the Apostolic history into a set of authoritative precedents." From his functional view, Hort agreed with Hatch in cautioning against trying to replicate past models.[60]

Nineteenth-century contemporaries took their warning to heart. Arthur Penrhyn Stanley was one. As dean of Westminster Abbey, he stood at a pinnacle of ecclesial establishment. When he wrote a little book on *Christian Institutions* a year before his death, he indicated the degree to which the observations of scholars like Lightfoot and Hatch (whose just-delivered Bampton Lectures were the talk of the church) were being assimilated by those in high positions. These well-placed members of the clergy would, in turn, convey these points to an even wider audience.

---

[57] Hort, *Ecclesia*, 176, 190–191 (cf. 193, re Titus 3:1ff, 5:17ff, and the terms *episcopoi/diakonoi*), 209–210 (cf. Hatch, *Organization*, 50).

[58] Hort, *Ecclesia*, 190–198. In Philippians, Paul (Hort says) implied two contrasted functions of oversight and service, giving evidence "that the community of saints was indeed an organized body, needing and possessing government on the one side and service on the other" (212–213).

[59] Chadwick, *Victorian Church*, II, 49.

[60] Hort, *Ecclesia*, II, 232–232; cf. Hatch, *Organization*, 217, who agreed that, even if some office could be restored, it would lack the unique dynamics and relationships of a now long-past era: "The attempt artificially to restore an ancient institution is futile."

It is certain that the officers of the Apostolical, or any subsequent, Church were not part of the original institution of the Founder of our religion.... It is certain that they arose gradually out of the preëxisting institutions either of the Jewish Synagogue, or of the Roman Empire, or of the Greek municipalities, or under the pressure of local emergencies. It is certain that throughout the first century, and for the first years of the second...Bishop and Presbyter were convertible terms, and...were the rulers...of the early Church. It is certain that as the necessities of the time demanded...the elevation of one Presbyter above the rest..., the word "Bishop" gradually changed its meaning, and...became restricted to the chief Presbyter of the locality. It is certain that in no instance were the Apostles called "Bishops" in any other sense than they were equally called "Presbyters" and "Deacons." It is certain that in no instance before the beginning of the third century the title or function of the Pagan or Jewish Priesthood is applied to the Christian pastors.[61]

Stanley's certainties indicate the degree to which old assumptions had broken down under the weight of new scholarship. No more could "bishop" be uncritically equated with "apostle"; no longer could the Ordinal's confident statement that the three distinct orders of ministry were present at the church's creation be assumed; no longer could *any* form of orders be assumed. At the same time, Stanley, himself a one-time professor of ecclesiastical history at Oxford, expressed great trust in the research itself, an early sign that a faith based on tradition was yielding to one that relied on science and scholarship.

"Catholics" Respond

But Stanley's certainty did not convince those of more catholic persuasion, who trusted neither the scholarship nor what it purported to find. With a zeal for an apostolically founded, divinely commissioned ecclesial ideal bequeathed by their Tractarian forebears, clerics like Henry Parry Liddon, Charles Gore, and Robert Campbell Moberly rebutted with vigor, and with a certainty to match.

---

[61] Arthur Penrhyn Stanley, *Christian Institutions* (New York: Charles Scribner's Sons, 1881), 207–208.

Liddon (1829–90), disciple and biographer of Pusey, champi-
oned the ordained ministry as a witness to the truth of the "reconciliation between God and man, achieved by Christ," and the
grace that makes it possible. For such a devout sacramentalist as
he, Christian ministry was an effective tool, "itself a means whereby the grace or invigorating force of Christ, conveyed by His Spirit, and reaching man by the certificated channels of His approach,
[that] makes us 'one with Christ, and Christ with us.'"[62] Therefore, ministry—in any denomination—requires a call of God. But
the need for a "Divine warrant for their momentous work" leaves
the ordained open to the danger of "sacerdotalism," the clerical
conviction that they are celestially special, favored, or removed
from the rest of humanity, or its corollary, which is the feeling
among laity either that clergy are just that or that they believe they
are. About this chronic concern, Liddon observed that, within
"the original equality of man with man," distinctions inevitably
emerge, whether of wealth or knowledge or political power. "A
ministerial order illustrates and consecrates the general law" by
serving as one human means of conveying God's blessing. While
not the only means, it serves as a counterpart to other human
agencies that, like the state, purport to further the common
good.[63]

In the religious realm, what justifies any distinction? Nothing
can. Liddon endorsed a priesthood of all, perhaps more strongly
than any we have seen: "If Christian laymen would only believe
with all their hearts that they are really priests, we should very
soon escape from some of the difficulties which vex the Church of
Christ." Unlike the first Christians, "penetrated through and
through by the sacerdotal idea," laity of his day had absorbed no
such notion. "But if this can be changed; if the temple of the layman's soul can be again made a scene of spiritual worship, he will
no longer fear lest the ministerial order should confiscate individual
liberty. The one priesthood will be felt to be the natural extension

---

[62] Henry Parry Liddon, *Sermons Preached Before the University of Oxford,* 2nd
ser., Sermon X (London: Rivingtons, 1879), 189–190 (quoting the Exhortation
from *The Book of Common Prayer* communion service).

[63] Liddon, *Sermons,* 193, 194, 197. Lightfoot was another who was deeply dis-
turbed by the "sacerdotalism" he perceived about him, as we shall see in the next
chapter.

and correlative of the other."[64] A strong laity cannot only coexist with clergy; working together, they may thrive together.

If Liddon showed himself ahead of his time regarding the laity, he dragged his heels on other theories and methods of his day. Liddon was irate when his young successor at Pusey House, Charles Gore, took up a few of them. Gore (1853–1932) edited *Lux Mundi* (1889), a book of essays that Liddon deemed close to heresy. In exploring the ramifications of Christ's incarnation, the volume provided a theological parallel to Christmas carols and Yuletide trees, all of which diverged pointedly from the long-established emphasis on atonement. Perhaps more disturbing, the essayists dared to take seriously the newly developing critical views of the Old Testament. They allowed scientific methods of study to apply to Scripture, which rankled Liddon no end. He complained to Gore, "I hold all Criticism to be mischievous, while you hold it to be generally illuminating and useful."[65] Yet Liddon was sedate compared with what others had to say. Gore's leadership of the "Holy Party" of catholic-leaning scholars, his apparent blessing of theories of evolution, his role in starting a monastic community, and above all his editing of *Lux Mundi* all provoked protests when he was appointed Bishop of Worcester in 1902. Eventually, his effectiveness there, then at Birmingham and Oxford, along with his writings, earned him respect as a "religious genius" and helped him to make "Criticism" of the Bible acceptable. Often consulted by Archbishop Randall Davidson, a large influence on the young William Temple, Gore was credited with "transform[ing] Tractarianism from a near fundamentalist and high Tory movement still on the margins of Anglican life into something central to the Church."[66] But that lay in the future.

---

[64] Liddon, *Sermons*, 198–200. Liddon does not spell out his thought precisely as to how what appear to be two priesthoods relate to each other, but that is not his purpose—rather, he intends to underscore the importance of the laity within a priesthood of all believers.

[65] Liddon to Gore, Oct. 29, 1889, in John Octavius Johnston, *Life and Letters of Henry Parry Liddon* (London: Longmans, Green, and Co., 1904), 365. Liddon claimed to be "miserable" about the last pages of Gore's essay (ibid., 367).

[66] Adrian Hastings, *A History of English Christianity 1920–1990* (London: SCM Press, 1991), 82–83. See James Carpenter, *Gore: A Study in Liberal Catholic Thought* (London: Faith Press, 1960), 7–10 and 27–41. The standard biography remains G. L. Prestige, *The Life of Charles Gore* (London: William Heinemann, 1935).

Liddon may have worried unnecessarily about his protegé. When Hatch's Bampton Lectures appeared, Gore panned them as representing the worst of the critical method. Hatch was so busy being critical that he was not being faithful, Gore asserted, and thereby Hatch missed crucial items of evidence—such as the Scriptures themselves. Like Liddon, Gore inherited two Tractarian teachings on the church. One was the apostolic succession of bishops. Newman had confidently written in Tract VII, "Every link in the chain is known, from St. Peter to our present metropolitans." The second was the doctrine of the "visible Church." In Newman's bold phrase, the church is "the gift which Christ let drop from Him as the mantle of Elijah, the pledge and token of His never-failing grace from age to age."[67] So when Hatch appeared to liken the early church to some ancient Ladies' Aid Society, and without any reference to the Bible, Gore exploded over what he deemed to be a travesty of legitimate criticism.[68] Not only had Hatch forgotten the New Testament, but also he had forgotten his history. The New Testament alone, Gore claimed, refutes the notion that the episcopate derived from diaconal service. "Really, in the name of sobermindedness," he sputtered, "we feel bound to protest against what we are tempted to call the insult to our intellect."[69] Henry Scott Holland wrote his friend Gore to advise ever so gently that perhaps he had been too harsh on poor Hatch, but Hatch had tread on both of Gore's sacred principles. Criticism, whether of the Bible or of history, was a legitimate enterprise. But the endeavor relied on facts, and those facts had to be correct. Then those facts needed interpretation; they needed a theological framework and, even more, a vision.[70]

---

[67] Q. in John R. H. Moorman, "Charles Gore and the Doctrine of the Church," *Church Quarterly Review* 158 (1957): 130, 131.

[68] Gore, "Hatch's Bampton Lectures," 409–411. It should be noted that Hatch omitted a "discussion of the ecclesiastical polity of the New Testament, *because I believe that polity will be best understood by the light of subsequent history*" (*Organization*, 20, emph. added). His was the critical principle, well accepted today, that the NT may reflect a *later* reality rather than contemporaneous history.

[69] Gore, "Hatch's Bampton Lectures," 418.

[70] Prestige, *Gore*, 45, 127.

church

Gore

Gore aimed to combine facts with vision. The church arose as a visible society out of Christ's incarnation, Gore wrote, founded by Christ, with his authority and thus able to claim "divine institution." As a human society, the church necessarily exists in the world, so the world about it will inevitably influence it. Historical realities cannot be escaped. Consequently, the church's Jewish background and Graeco-Roman surroundings each would have its effect on the church. Both Hort and Hatch had a point. Nevertheless, the church arose as a deliberate design of Christ, Gore asserted. Jesus' calling of disciples, his bestowing of rites, and his claiming to be the Messiah of a new kingdom all pointed to clear intentionality.[71] While the church is not to be equated with the kingdom of God, the church does represent that kingdom on earth as a visible society which is the Body of Christ. The church embodies the same principle as the "Word made flesh" in sacraments and in visible organization bound together by apostolic order and historical continuity: "The church exists to perpetuate in every age the life of Jesus, the union of manhood with Godhood."[72] It is "prophetic" in that "it is to speak for God by definite commission and inspiration: it is to be the divine teacher of its own members and of the nations."[73] The church is also "priestly." Out of Christ's high priesthood, by which his sacrifice won the fullest reconciliation of God with humankind, "[t]he church is the priestly body" because it fully enjoys his reconciliation and serves as the instrument by which the world may be reconciled to God. Within the church are those entrusted with a special "ministry of reconciliation." However, "the whole body is priestly," all together, without a discrete priestly class, in which each may stand before God and the world in a priestly function, offering "itself to all men as the example and the instrument of reconciliation with God."[74]

---

[71] Gore, *Ministry*, 8–10; cf. Carpenter, *Liberal Catholic Thought*, 216.

[72] Charles Gore, *The Incarnation of the Son of God*, Bampton Lectures for 1891 (New York: Charles Scribner's Sons, 1891), 237–239.

[73] Charles Gore, *Orders and Unity* (New York: E. P. Dutton & Co., 1909), 60–61. He will cite Moberly's much longer exposition of the point.

[74] Gore, *Orders and Unity*, 65–66. Gore then addresses the "kingly" aspect of the church.

ministry
of
reconciliation

The church's express priesthood—those entrusted with the ministry of this reconciliation—emanates from this basis in Christ. From the outset, in its worship, discipline, and mission "the church was continually exercising its priesthood" even though it used no priestly titles. The titles came later, Gore wrote (disagreeing with Lightfoot), first to bishops and then to presbyters, but the concept of priesthood emanated from Christ himself. His priesthood "was so unlike the conception of the sacrificing priest, whether Jewish or pagan." That is, "the sense in which Christ was a priest" cannot be found in his offering sacrifice (although he offered himself on the cross) as Jewish or pagan priests had done with animals. Rather, Christian priesthood derived from Christ is a "ministerial priesthood," which is never mechanical but always within the context of pastoral effort—"the office of teaching and guiding and feeding human souls in order to present them perfect in Christ Jesus."[75]

R. C. Moberly (1845–1903) continued the hybridization of theology and history that Gore began. Moberly was born in 1845 to a cleric of High Church sympathies and a career on the rise. George Moberly, then headmaster of Winchester School, had left Oxford on the eve of Tractarianism and largely avoided its controversies, though Keble was a neighbor and friend. As Bampton Lecturer in 1868, he upheld the lay role as crucial to the church,[76] a pioneering point his son would later pursue. From 1869 to 1885, he was Bishop of Salisbury.[77] Moberly the younger spent nearly all his life in Oxford, as student, then teacher, then head of a school for training clergy for missionary work. He left Oxford for fourteen years to lead the theological college in his father's diocese and then to serve a parish in Chester, only to return to Oxford to become the Regius Professor of Pastoral Theology in 1892.[78] His

[75] Gore, *Orders and Unity*, 160–166.

[76] George Moberly, *The Administration of the Holy Spirit in the Body of Christ*, 2nd ed. (Oxford and London: James Parker & Co., 1870), xi, 194, 204, 244. His thought is not nearly so systematic as his son's, nor as far reaching, yet the son's debt to the father is clear.

[77] "Moberly, George," *Dictionary of National Biography* (Oxford: Oxford University Press, n.d.), XIII, 535.

[78] "Moberly, Robert Campbell," *Dictionary of National Biography*, 2nd suppl. (London: Smith, Elder & Co., 1912), II, 624–625. See also the biographical sketch, "Robert Campbell Moberly," *Church Quarterly Review* 58, no. 115 (April 4, 1904): 74–93.

Atonement and Personality (1901) was called "perhaps the most original and profound study of the Atonement in modern Anglican theology" and is still considered his major work.[79]

The High Churchmanship of his day influenced him strongly. In his contribution to *Lux Mundi*, Moberly expressed a central tenet of the volume in his article on "Incarnation as the Basis of Dogma." As a person of history, Jesus' life, death, and resurrection root every doctrine concerning him in historical fact. His being divine *and* human means that the creed describes acts directly involving God. Consequently, Moberly argued, credal statements about the church, the communion of saints, forgiveness, the resurrection of the body, and the life everlasting are all "essential parts of the understanding of the doctrine of the Holy Ghost" in that they constitute "the very essence and meaning of the work of the Incarnation" after the ascension.[80] The life of the church, then, becomes a necessary implication of incarnational dogma.

Moberly's supreme contribution to Gore's theoretical line was *Ministerial Priesthood: Chapters (Preliminary to a Study of the Ordinal) on the Rationale of Ministry and the Meaning of Christian Priesthood* (1897), which originated as collegiate lectures at Christ Church. They may not have gone over well. "His mannerisms of elocution, and the hesitating involved style which was an unfortunate result of his scrupulous fastidiousness" made him a less than popular speaker.[81] His writings too were, and are, difficult to read. His friend and colleague William Sanday observed his propensity for "circumlocutions" and preference for two negatives to a positive: "I do not think that I have ever known such punctuation as that in Dr. Moberly's writings."[82]

---

[79] Cross, *Oxford Dictionary*, 925, s.v. "Moberly, Robert Campbell," *DNB*, 625. See also William Sanday, "Robert Campbell Moberly," *Journal of Theological Studies* 4 (1903): 481–499; W. H. Moberly, "Robert Campbell Moberly," *Journal of Theological Studies* 6 (1905): 1–19; Henry Scott Holland, "Robert Campbell Moberly," *Personal Studies* (London: Wells Gardner, Darton & Co., Ltd., n.d. [1905]), 272–279. No biography appears to have been written.

[80] *Lux Mundi: A Series of Studies in the Religion of the Incarnation*, ed. Charles Gore (London: John Murray, 1904), 180 (cf. 170–182).

[81] "Robert Campbell Moberly," *Church Quarterly Review*, 75, though cf. Sanday, "Robert Campbell Moberly," *JTS*, 481, re flashes of "arresting" sermons.

[82] Sanday, "Robert Campbell Moberly," *JTS*, 488, 490.

His thought, however, was another matter. In writing *Ministerial Priesthood*, Moberly confronted several challenges. One was to draw out the implications of his *Lux Mundi* essay and posit a divine commission first for the church, then for its clergy. He wanted, as well, to place the laity as integral members of what Protestants cherished as the "priesthood of all believers." He strove to avoid clericalism while being "catholic," and to skirt antisacerdotalism while being "reformed." Even as Rome was proposing to castigate Anglican orders as "null and void," demanding a defense of the legitimacy of English clergy, Moberly endeavored to articulate a positive Anglican vision of church and priesthood. Such a view should take seriously the ideal and the real, the "inward" and the "outward," and the connection they hold for each other, in particular regarding ministry. He hoped, further, to avoid a stereotypically Roman Catholic belief, which he considered to be mechanically sacerdotalistic and also a stereotypically Nonconformist understanding of ministry, which he saw as resting merely on delegation of authority or duty.[83]

Slowly, patiently, sometimes painfully for the reader, with constant reference to the Bible and the earliest Christian writers, Moberly built his case upon seven points: the church is one; it outwardly signifies an inward reality; its ministry arises from the entire people of God; it holds a divine commission; it is varied in its orders from the outset; those orders developed further in the life of the early church; and, most important of all, its priesthood represents that of Jesus Christ himself and that of his Body the church. His ideas, as the next chapters explore, created a motif that dominated thinking well into the twentieth century.

---

[83] Cf. W. H. Moberly, "Robert Campbell Moberly," *JTS*, 9.

[handwritten margin notes: "priesthood", "striking changes in 19c"]

A LAST WORD FROM THE CRITICAL CENTURY

The very idea of the Anglican priest underwent a striking change in the nineteenth century. He started off in 1800 as a leisured "English Gentleman in Holy Orders"[84] but by 1900 was a busy professional, a specialist in the spiritual. As early as mid-century, Liddon observed, "Much more is expected in the way of personal exertion and ministerial efficiency."[85]

Yet if he were no longer merely an agent of the nation at prayer, he was more than a professional. Anglo-Catholics and Evangelicals alike stressed a spiritual nature to Christian ministry.[86] Even though to A. P. Stanley ordained ministry may have been merely "a Divine afterthought," it is divine nonetheless "because it belongs to the inevitable growth of Christian hopes and sympathies, of increasing truth, of enlarging charity." But ordained ministry is human, too, "because it arose out of, and is subject to, the vicissitudes of human passions, human ignorance, human infirmities, earthly opportunities."[87]

Humanness here has two implications. First, Christian ministry is placed within humanity, specifically the redeemed humanity of the entire people of God. So, for example, as Lightfoot and Liddon each noted from their respective positions, the laity do matter.

Second, as the Bible came to be seen as a human document, subject to critical examination, so did the church and its institutions. The same scholarship into ancient documents that questioned biblical certainties also clouded the origins and meanings of the church. Those who upheld Reformation principles of the authority of Scripture and of the early church—whether Evangelicals in their way, or neo-Tractarians in theirs—faced a problem, then, for the studies made the object of study less lucid and thus less authoritative. Hort cited "the futility of endeavouring to make the Apostolic history into a set of authoritative precedents, to be

---

[84] The phrase is B. K. Cunningham's, q. in Bullock, *Training, 1875 to 1974*, xvii.

[85] Liddon, *Clerical Life and Work*, 243.

[86] E.g., Liddon, *Clerical Life and Work*, 162–163; Russell, *Clerical Profession*, 233–239.

[87] Stanley, "The Clergy," *Christian Institutions*, 218–219.

1806 - Engl. gentleman in Holy Orders,
n 1900 busy prof, specialist in spiritual
Priesthood in the Late Nineteenth Century 31

rigourously copied without regard to time and place, thus turning
the Gospel into a second Levitical Code." But the burden returned
to the church to understand itself anew in every era, not so much
in prescription by the past as in conversation with it. "The Apostolic age is full of embodiments of purposes and principles of the
most instructive kind: but the responsibility of choosing the means
was left for ever to the Ecclesia itself, and to each Ecclesia, guided
by ancient precedent on the one hand and adaptation to present
and future needs on the other. The lessonbook of the Ecclesia, and
of every Ecclesia, is not a law but a history."[88]

The century's last word went to Moberly, whose *Ministerial
Priesthood* set forth a vision for the twentieth century to contemplate and, to some degree, pursue. But the questions had been
posed that the next era would ponder: What is the authority of the
Bible? How much does it tell of historical origins, and what influence does that history hold? Whatever happened to deacons?
What is the role of the layperson within the *laos*, the people of
God, initiated at baptism and expressed in worship and work? In
consequence, what then of the presbyter in his, and later her, relationship with church and society alike? In their confidence in God
and church, history and theology, and certainly themselves, the
Victorians had little notion of the debates and confusions that
their questions would bring.

Bible human document
subject to crit. exam.
church too a human inst.

---

[88] Hort, *Ecclesia*, 232–233.

II
The Idea of the Ministerial Representative

From this heated nineteenth-century dialogue began to emerge a concept of ordained service that is ministerial in nature and function and representative in quality. From reconsiderations of the church and, increasingly, of Christ incarnate, the scholars and theologians shaped new articulations of orders, and the relationship of those who are ordained to the vast majority of Christians. Moberly's was the most fully developed. He envisioned the church as a divine society, which revealed heaven to earth and which embraced all Christians without discrimination, with a ministry distinguished by pastoral devotion and costly service. The power of his vision—certainly not his turgid prose—propelled his ideas to the forefront of Anglican thinking. What Gore and he espoused was adopted, extended, and eventually given the official stamp of approval by thinkers and writers of a new century. Before seeing how this theory was embraced, we should consider what it was.

THE THEOLOGY OF MINISTERIAL PRIESTHOOD

THE INCARNATION AS THE BASIS OF ECCLESIOLOGY

While Victorians decorated those Christmas trees that Prince Albert had introduced, the average person among them seemed to be thinking more deeply of Jesus' incarnation. Theologians certainly were. Ecclesiologists, especially of the catholic school,

marveled at the doctrine of the Word-made-flesh as a key to understanding the church as the Body of Christ, one means whereby the
incarnate One may abide on earth. The church becomes an outward and visible sign of a vivid inward reality of unity between
God and humanity.

While Lightfoot and others made almost no use of the doctrine, Gore and Moberly started emphasizing the importance of
the Incarnation with their *Lux Mundi* essays—and never stopped.
Gore claimed that the church intentionally reflected the Incarnation. Jesus' calling of disciples, bestowing of rites, and claiming to
be the Messiah of a new kingdom all indicated to Gore a clear
dominical design. Never coextensive with the kingdom of God, the
church nevertheless represents the kingdom on earth as a visible
society, which is the Body of Christ.[1] Just as Jesus in his flesh
embodies the divine Word, so the church expresses and communicates "the spiritual and the divine through what is material and
human" in its sacraments, visible organization, apostolic succession, and historical continuity. As a "visible, material, human society,"
the church "exists to perpetuate in every age the life of Jesus, the
union of manhood with Godhood."[2] Moberly's *Lux Mundi* essay
made much the same point. Since Jesus' humanity makes him a
person of history, his life, death, and resurrection root all doctrine
concerning him in historical fact. His divinity means these events
are also acts directly involving God. The church by extension
perpetuates the Incarnation through its creed, sacraments, and
ministry.[3]

The idea of the church, then, flows out of incarnational
dogma. The Christmas tree implies the cross, to be sure; Moberly

---

[1] Gore, *Ministry*, 216. (Note that some editions of this work, including what
Moberly used, are entitled *The Church and the Ministry*.) The thought was put
more boldly by the Oxford church historian William Bright (1824–1901): "The
Church began in a clergy." (Q. by Kirk in *Apostolic Ministry*, 30, who also cites
F. D. Maurice: "So that if we called the four Gospels 'The institution of a Christian Ministry,' we might not go very far wrong, or lose sight of many of their
essential qualities" [p. 30, n. 4].)

[2] Gore, *Incarnation of the Son of God*, 237–238.

[3] In Gore, *Lux Mundi*, esp. 170–182. See discussion of *Lux Mundi* in chapter 1,
above.

highlights Jesus' sacrifice and atonement as crucial to understanding the ministerial nature of priesthood. Incarnation, though, remained a prime ingredient in developing ecclesiology.

PLATONISM, THE SACRAMENTAL PRINCIPLE, AND THE CHURCH'S UNITY

In explaining how an earthbound church can function as an incarnational sign of heaven, Moberly relies on the Platonist tradition that is woven through Anglican theology. Simply put, Platonism accepts the existence of ideals, which are represented, however crudely, by external realities. The chair on which I sit, for instance, represents the "ideal" chair despite its warped seat and canes cracking from ever-increasing weight. Looking at the chair, for all its flaws, one can glimpse in limited fashion the eternal and abiding perfection that is every furniture designer's dream, the ultimate in seating.

Platonism was an attractive philosophy for Anglicans, especially Incarnationalists like the *Lux Mundi* school. They affirmed that Jesus, in his divine yet still earthly life, death, and resurrection, discloses the full reality of the Godhead. They also found Platonism useful in defining such notions as sacrament, church, and ordained ministry, so that these can be understood as nothing less than outward signs, which represent divine mysteries and genuine realities.[4] Moberly uses the dynamic of "outward" and "inward" to define the church as more than that which abides on earth. It represents a unity that exists in heaven but can only be perceived partially here and now. For all the church's present divisions, a deeper unity nonetheless prevails. The church outwardly if imperfectly reveals an inward and perfect reality.

His explanation was well-timed. Christians had become acutely aware of their divisions. Though the ecumenical movement as an organized effort lay two decades in the future, theologian after theologian held in mind the prospect of some more basic fellowship than was then evident. Moberly surely did. For him, the church is one because God is one: As unity prevails in the Trinity, so it abides fundamentally in the church. Quite the opposite of an

---

[4] Cf. Ramsey, *Era*, 164.

historical "accident" (as Hatch called it), this unity is "a necessary element in the meaning of the life of the Church." If the church on earth falls short of the ideal, what Moberly calls the "idea" of the church remains "fundamental and constant" regardless of what is "realized in fact," simply because the church is of God. Its unity is not "acquired by degrees from below" but is "revealed as inherent from above."[5] That revelation is an unfolding one; Moberly did not expect the church to have sprung full-blown from the head of Jesus but understood it as a phenomenon developing from him, and continuing to develop.[6] And so, Christian unity "is in Scripture direct and complete. It is there as an ideal, not implicit only but expressed, not in the early aspirations of the Church only, but in that which was divinely set before the Church, before as yet the Church had begun to be."[7]

How can Moberly insist that the church is one when, on earth, it so clearly is not? Again, because the church is of God. Any failure results not from any defect in the ideal, but from imperfect Christians failing to *realize* the ideal by not making it real, or by not recognizing its divinely based reality, since "the unity which it represents, whether more perfectly or less, is the essential unity of the One God."[8] Putting his Platonism and sacramental principles

---

[5] Moberly, *MP*, 2.

[6] Moberly cites neither Darwin nor Newman, two great influences on the nineteenth-century mind. But his thought is not inconsistent with either a Darwinian notion of evolution or the idea of the development of doctrine such as Newman proposed and, in a different way, as Adolph von Harnack was publishing in Germany in Moberly's day. He does, however, distinguish between the "emergence" of episcopate and its "evolution" (*MP*, 216), contending that "evolution" implies a time in which episcopate derived from the church and its presbyterate "from below," as opposed to being delegated by the apostles. See Welch, *Protestant Thought*, II, 172. Moberly shows no familiarity with Harnack's, and indeed his approach of unfolding doctrine differs from Harnack's, who has more in common with Hatch's while Moberly's more closely resembles Newman's.

[7] Moberly, *MP*, 7.

[8] Moberly, *MP*, 20–22 (cp. *Lux Mundi*, 181). How Moberly differs from Hatch was hard to see at the time, and since. Sanday suggested the difference was more in emphasis than in principle. The two men's ideas in retrospect do not seem necessarily inconsistent, much less mutually exclusive, except that Moberly does wish to underscore divine initiative in ecclesiastical development. Hatch's entire intent was different, which Moberly took as disagreement.

to work, Moberly attests that the church that we see can at best signify the greater reality that it can never fully capture. Still, because the church is divinely conceived as well as humanly composed, it will always express an ideal that transcends the actual facts of its existence. Is it unified? Outwardly, no; but earthly reality does not negate divine ideal. On the contrary, "the imperfect outward will represent, will aspire towards, will actually in a measure express, that perfect ideal which is waiting still to gain, in outward expression, its consummation of reality." My chair cannot aspire to be anything more than it is; but human beings can, especially Christians, and so can the church. Despite a seemingly hopeless contrast between real and ideal, the Body of Christ becomes a veritable outward and visible sign of an inward and spiritual reality.[9]

THE REPRESENTATIVE QUALITY

Moberly employs the same principle to explain the "representative," starting with the church itself. What one sees in the church is no mere human institution but a representation of a reality of God. Lightfoot altogether dismissed such a possibility: "The ideal conception and the actual realization are incommensurate and in a manner contradictory."[10] Moberly posits just the opposite, that the earthly church already embodies in some measure that which will be attained ultimately. He asserts, "The Church militant does not merely *represent* the Church triumphant," if what is meant by "representing" implies (as Lightfoot stated) that the church we know on earth will be abolished and discarded to be replaced by the kingdom of heaven. As Simon-bar-Jona grew by grace to become the one known as St. Peter, so too the church is being transformed; it "shall be found to *be* the Kingdom; the Kingdom of Heaven is already, in the Church, among men." No mere symbol, the church is a foretaste of the reality it shall become.

Thus the church discloses a transcendent reality. "[I]t does not represent—but it *is*—the Kingdom of God upon earth."[11] The bod-

[9] Moberly, MP, 31–36. See the definition of "sacrament" in the Catechism, 1979 BCP, p. 857; Moberly does not use this terminology.

[10] Lightfoot, *Christian Ministry*, 2.

[11] Moberly, MP, 37–38, 40 (italics in original). Moberly uses the term "representative" in opposite senses in proximity (35, 37); he evidently means to avoid the connotation of "representative" as something that symbolizes or hints at a reality

ily manifests the spiritual. For now, the spiritual relies on the bodily. Sacraments, ministries, holy times, and holy places, far from
being the transitory devices that Lightfoot considered them, all
give bodily substance to spiritual reality.[12] For Moberly, they constitute elements of God's message. Though surely not the
"essence" of the church—which is the "Spirit of the Incarnate"
alone—they matter as "God's own appointed and imperative conditions and methods." God *can* work beyond them but *does* work
through them. "If God is not in any way bound to His own
appointed methods of grace, yet we are." Sacraments and ministry
become essential not for God's sake, but for ours, "to authorize
and enable us."[13]

The Church Is the Body of Christ

Lightfoot and others had rejected so close an association of the
earthly church with anything beyond. Gore and Moberly valued it
deeply. Paul's metaphor of Christ's Body explains, for Moberly,
what the church *is*, and also what it is *not*. Additionally, this "matter of quite capital importance" aids mightily in defining the basic
relationships Christians have with each other, specifically relationships between clergy and laity.

Because, in scriptural language, the church is the Body of
Christ and Temple of the Holy Ghost, the outward "fabric"
expresses a "Presence, the Body of a Spirit." The church must
therefore be vastly more than the clergy. Rather, this "spiritual
Body" consists of "the whole corporation...into which Christian
Baptism primarily admits" and confirmation bestows "full

but rather to connect intimately, organically, and permanently what we see on
earth with the reality that abides in God.

[12] For Moberly, Lightfoot erred in this very matter, by suggesting that the church
is merely a convenience without lasting significance. He also wandered astray in
conceiving of the church in what Moberly calls "a wholly individualistic form."
Lightfoot had declared, "Each individual member holds personal communion
with the Divine Head" (*Christian Ministry*, 1). While true enough, that, joined
with his understanding of the church as a "practical necessity" rather than a
"divinely ordered principle of life," had the effect of disproportionately magni-
fying the inward so as to undervalue the outward (*MP*, 46; note his excursus,
46–56.)

[13] Moberly, *MP*, 60–63.

exercise of that spiritual franchise or privilege of Divine citizenship (in real sense, even of Divine priesthood)." In one fell swoop, Moberly dismisses those like Carter who would segregate clergy and laity into separate castes. He affirms the priesthood of all, but not the priesthood of each, for "the corporate life precedes and transcends the individual." He vouchsafes the membership of each yet protects the ministry of the whole. Spiritual privilege, divine access, life in God, and the powers, functions, and gifts of this Body "are essentially the possession of all, not of some."[14]

Moberly's voice added to a heated conversation at the time. Popular religion and efforts to professionalize the clergy were tending to separate the ordained from the laity. Yet theological justifications of the division (such as Carter's) smacked of Roman Catholicism to many. Lightfoot was one who took umbrage. In upholding the unity of all Christians before God without discrimination, however, Lightfoot may have overstated his case. Christ's kingdom "has no sacred days or seasons, no special sanctuaries, because every time and every place alike are holy. Above all it has no sacerdotal system," he wrote. "It interposes no sacrificial tribe or class between God and man, by whose intervention alone God is reconciled and man forgiven. Each individual member holds personal communion with the Divine Head."[15] To be sure, given earthly practicalities, "appointed days and set places are indispensable to [the Church's] efficiency." It could not fulfill its purposes "without rulers and teachers, without a ministry of reconciliation, in short, without an order of men who may in some sense be designated a priesthood." Yet no clique standing between God and his people is needed because the ideal Christian priesthood encompasses *all*, without exception or specific designation. Lightfoot dreamed of "a priesthood coextensive with the human race."[16]

---

[14] Moberly, *MP*, 66, cf. 68. Note, though, his agreement with Carter re baptism (cf. Carter, *Priesthood*, 148).

[15] Lightfoot, *Christian Ministry*, 1.

[16] Lightfoot, *Christian Ministry*, 2, 3–5. See p. 7: "As individuals, all Christians are priests alike."

At least on one point, Liddon had agreed with Lightfoot: There should be no divisions among Christians. He endorsed a priesthood of all, perhaps more strongly than any:

> To the first Christians this lay priesthood was a reality. A Christian layman in the Apostolic age conceived of himself as a true priest. Within his heart there was an altar of the Most Holy, and on it he offered continually the sacrifice, the costly sacrifice of his will, united to the Perfect Will of Jesus Christ.

This, Liddon avowed, was the idea of priesthood that had fired the fervor of the first Christians. If recovered, it would fire Christians again. Thus inspired, clergy and laity would do better than merely coexist; together, they would thrive.[17]

Because of his Pauline theology of the Body, Moberly heartily agreed with Liddon about the laity. He did more, extending it to explicate relations within the church. As all Christians are part of the Body of Christ, all share the church's work of "ministry" in the generic sense. Those who hold orders—the "ministers specifically ordained," that is, the clergy—relate to the whole as organs relate to a natural body, neither mediating "between the Body and its life" nor conferring life on the Body, but "working organically for the whole Body."[18] Far from standing between the majority of Christians and their God, the ordained are "specifically representative" for distinct purposes and processes of the life of the whole entity. A body without eyes cannot see through the nose, nor does the eye see at the behest of the ear. An ability to see comes with life itself, and that ability comes by means of the eye. But for "Church ministers" to be "organs" does not imply that the Body or its components can fill the role of minister. Nor does the Body confer authority *on its own* to minister, any more than it can cause an ear to kick a football; that is neither the ear's purpose nor identity.[19] To function effectively, laity and clergy must work as one, each group in its own appropriate ways. The Eucharist especially exemplifies

---

[17] Liddon, *Sermons*, 199–200 (cf. chapter 1, above).

[18] Moberly, *MP*, 68.

[19] Moberly, *MP*, 68–69; see G. Moberly, *Administration*, 60; Hatch, *Organization*, Lecture V, 113–142.

how they may do so. Eucharist involves "functions of the whole body. 'We bless the cup of blessing,' 'we break the bread'"[20]; and it is necessarily corporate, always transcending individuals (contra Lightfoot) yet never removing clergy from those they represent (contra Rome). However, at the same time that Eucharist embraces everyone, it relies on those who are duly commissioned to preside, offer, and distribute. Thus—according to Moberly via a quotation from his father—ordained priesthood is "strictly representative in its own proper being, yet receiving personal designation and powers, not by original derivation from the body which it represents, or continual reference to it, but by perpetual succession from a divine source and spring of authorizing grace."[21]

Moberly, then, sought to define a vital tension that Anglicans have struggled to maintain. The Body of Christ is one, and each member a part of it, entitled to all of its rights and responsibilities especially in a relationship with God through Christ; however, paradoxically, a "ministry" divinely summoned "represents the whole Body and (under whatever sanction) wields, ministerially, authority and powers which, in idea and in truth, inherently belong to the collective life of the Body as a whole." He cannot, however, imply that just anyone may so minister.[22] To return once again to the formula popular since the Reformation, he must acknowledge the priesthood of *all* believers without conceding the individual priesthood of *each* believer. Yet he must also stress the essential unity between the ordained priesthood and the corps of the faithful. Leaving aside the problem of how God and the Body do the authorizing, Moberly concluded that "ministry" represents the whole Body, without each being a "minister."

Moberly pursued his distinctions in the conviction that previous authors had failed to make them as they really needed to do. Hatch tended to lump all early Christians together in one category of status. In his picture, the laity were on the same spiritual footing as their "officers," distinguished only by the Holy Spirit

[20] Moberly, *MP*, 71, emphasis in quotation.

[21] Moberly, *MP*, 70, quoting George Moberly (*Administration*, 60, 61), who, in discouraging "continual reference" to the Body that priesthood represents, may not entirely fit into his son's case.

[22] Moberly, *MP*, 72–73.

through its bestowal of gifts, which were potentially available to any and all. Later theologians largely—but to Moberly's eye uncritically—adopted Hatch's conception.[23] While admiring Hatch's "exaltation of the ideal of lay life," Moberly pointed out his undue license in interpreting history and Scripture, which, along with being incorrect, also upset the careful balance between lay and ordained roles within the larger Body. To this, Moberly reiterated his idea of

> ministers, as organs of the whole Body, specialized for certain particular functions, which are necessary for the life of the whole; in function, so far, distinct; not dependent simply upon any act or will of the whole for their functional empowerment and authority; yet being none the less, even in their most distinct functional activity, organs representative and expressive of the living capacity or inherent prerogative of the whole.[24]

If Hatch did not make enough distinctions, Lightfoot made them too carelessly. He started off satisfactorily enough, Moberly thought, regarding the early Christian priest as "the mouthpiece, the representative of a priestly race." To the degree that Lightfoot understood this "priesthood of the ministry" to spring from the priesthood of the whole Body,[25] Moberly agreed. But Lightfoot equated "sacerdotal ministry" not with "representative," but with "sacerdotalism," an ecclesiastical aberration that effectively set the priest apart, above, and isolated from the Christian Body as a whole. At Eucharist, according to Lightfoot's characterization, the sacerdotal priest was seen to offer a sacrifice of praise and thanksgiving *on behalf of* the congregation and not *by* the congregation. If true, the Eucharist became an act of the clergy, not of the congregation; the priest was set apart from the faithful as a veritable substitute for them. The distinction was one of a vicarious priesthood more characteristic of Roman Catholicism than of the representative quality of the early church. Lightfoot, being leery of

---

[23] Moberly, *MP*, 73–74, quoting Hatch, *Organization*, 121–122; cf. Barnett, *Diaconate*, 13.

[24] Moberly, *MP*, 75.

[25] Lightfoot, *Christian Ministry*, 119, q. by Moberly, *MP*, 76.

clerical power, would have none of it. But in the process of rejecting a concept he abhorred, he asserted that "the minister is a priest
in the same sense that each individual member of the congregation
is a priest."[26]

Lightfoot's conclusions stunned Moberly. Their differences
were subtle; both argued for a "representative" ideal rather than
a "vicarious" one that gave the priest power to stand in the place
of God and the congregation. But where Lightfoot saw the
ordained as ultimately dispensable, Moberly did not; when Lightfoot claimed that, in a pinch, any Christian can take on the duties
of the ordained, Moberly quickly realized the unsettling implication: that any Christian can celebrate the Eucharist—pinch or no.
Lightfoot, in short, failed to realize that an ordained priesthood
was as crucial to the church as a liver is to the human body and
that no femur or wrist can take its place. The problem grew from
Lightfoot's original distinction of "sacerdotal" as opposed to
"representative." If the words are not contradictory but consistent
with each other, the issue is resolved. Laity and clergy share in the
Body as one, yet each is integral to the other—which is precisely
what Moberly propounded.[27]

Moberly reached the diametrically opposite conclusion that, as
orders developed in the early church, Christians did not understand the distinction between clergy and laity *until* clergy were
identified with ministry. What is "official" and "visible" and, ultimately, "episcopal" reveals what is "invisible," "spiritual," and
representative of the whole Body. He cited Justin Martyr, who
referred, long before the individualized term "priest" was used, to
the priesthood that belongs to the Christian people, offering sacrifice supremely through the Eucharist, led not "by any miscella-
neous Christians at random," but by one who headed the Christian community. Christians collectively embody the earthly priesthood, which in turn is expressed through those authorized as that

---

[26] Lightfoot, *Christian Ministry*, 124–135. Lightfoot derives his vicarious/repre-
sentative distinction from F. D. Maurice's major work, *The Kingdom of Christ*.
Originally published in 1838, its second edition is the more common and is probably what Lightfoot used. Cf. *The Kingdom of Christ*, ed. Alec R. Vidler (London:
SCM Press, 1958), 144–150.

[27] Moberly, *MP*, 77–78.

collective priesthood's instruments.[28] That authorization comes most clearly in ordination.

Like any ordinance of God, ordination involves both a divine act and "a natural and secular need." It embraces a divine call and human activity, for "the general Church body has a responsible work of preparing for and concurring with the Divine act." It is mutual:

> Though ministerial appointment is certainly not human in place of being Divine, yet neither is it Divine quite apart from being human also. The Church as a whole has its selecting and consentient voice; and even what is most distinctively Divine in ordination is still conferred through the Church.[29]

In sum, Moberly warned against overemphasizing the mutual priesthood so as to extinguish any difference between clergy and laity; but he cautioned equally against the opposite extreme of exaggerating the distinction between priest and people. Any "indelible character" conferred at ordination does not refer to the "moral quality of the individual man." It implies instead "a status, inherently involving capacities, duties, responsibilities of ministerial life" as distinct from "the secret character of the personal self." "Character" applies more to what the priest *does* than to what the priest *is*. Furthermore, there can be no double moral standard, one for clergy, one for laity. "[W]hat is essentially right or wrong for

---

[28] Moberly, *MP*, 87–88, citing Justin (c. 100–c. 165), *Dialogues with Trypho,* 116–117. The use of "priest" to refer to an individual did not begin appearing in Christian terminology for about another century after Justin. Justin "greatly fortifies our characteristic position that the minister is so the representative of the community that what he does they do, and what they do they do through him."

[29] As *MP*'s subtitle suggests, Moberly wrote with an eye to revisions in the English Ordinal. Here was one point where revision was needed, for the then-current rite muddied the place of the church at large, and laity in particular: "So far as the general or lay voice is concerned, the circumstances of popular election and public approbation have at many times in the Church presented to view much more emphatically than they nowadays do the aspect of the priesthood as representative of the congregation" (Moberly, *MP*, 89). See also Gore, *Ministry,* 85–88. Moberly's position on issues of lay-clergy relationships, such as lay presidency of the Eucharist and the distinction, if any, between priest and people, holds implications we will postpone for chapters 6 and 11.

either, is so of necessity for both."[30] One is no holier than the other. To think otherwise breeds the concept of priesthood as *vicarious*, not simply representative, but *in the place of* the people as a whole. "That the priest was holy, while the layman was not; that the priest performed God's service in the layman's stead; that the priest propitiated God on the layman's behalf; that, when the layman's time came, the priest could come in and make right his relation with God—here was indeed a distorted development of ministerial theory." Like Lightfoot, Liddon had termed the conception of vicarious priesthood "an unchristian one" and challenged the laity to realize their priesthood.[31] Moberly readily concurred. "The word laity...is a far nobler word than people imagine." Far from connoting negativity, like "lay doctor" or "lay lawyer," it implies an awe-inspiring heritage.

> [T]o Israel of old, to be "the People" of God was the height of positive privilege: and to be a layman means to be a member of "the People"—not as in modern phrase contrasted with privilege, nobility, government, &c., but as in the mouth of a devout Israelite,—"the people," ὁ λαός—in contrast with the nations, the Gentiles, the heathen. It is the word of most positive spiritual privilege, the glory of covenanted access to and intimacy with God.[32]

The priest, in the end, remains one of the community of the faithful. With that statement, Moberly opened the door to a new century of understanding the nature of the people of God and its leaders.

---

[30] Moberly, *MP*, 91–92.

[31] Moberly, *MP*, 93; 96–97, q. from Liddon, *Sermons*, 198–199. Moberly's father anticipated this emphasis in his Bampton Lectures, both in lauding the "personal priesthood" of each Christian, and the connection that each has with the larger Body, to the benefit of all: "[T]he inherent priestliness of the whole body helps, in a way that cannot be dispensed with, the official priestliness of the organic priesthood, and that the organic priesthood, in various departments of its exercise, is requisite, as to produce, so also to maintain and keep up in its full strength and under its deep occasional needs, the priestliness of each single member of the entire body" (G. Moberly, *Administration*, 227).

[32] Moberly, *MP*, 98.

THE COMMISSION OF THE ORDAINED

But what is the origin of specific ministry? Do those who are ordained minister as a result of human assignment, or does some greater agency appoint or even anoint them? In the language of the day, is their commission from "below," within an earthly frame, or from "above," from God?

Much of the theory and practice at that time answered in favor of the divine. The ultra-High Churchmanship of a Carter conceived of a divinely ordained "commission of the ministry" that is a "consecrated channel of communication" by which heaven and earth become one; otherwise, he asserted, absolution would have no power, and Eucharist no sacramental effect.[33] Some clergy acted as though they were God's gift to church and nation, regardless of what party they claimed. Lightfoot was one who reacted perhaps too strongly against any divine right of clergy. Liddon strived for a more balanced perspective, which led him to a surprisingly ecumenical concession; he understood *any* call to *any* clerical ministry, of *any* denomination, to emanate from God.[34] Moberly expanded substantially on the idea. To be "the People" of God may be "the height of positive privilege," but some within it are designated for particular service. Whence comes the specific ministry? To avoid implying a "Spirit-endowed" ministry "on behalf of those who are not," he extends his representative theory:

> Christian ministry is the instrument which represents the whole Spirit-endowed Body of the Church; and yet withal is itself so Spirit-endowed as to have the right and the power to represent instrumentally. The immense exaltation—and requirement—of lay Christianity, which in respect of its own dignity cannot be exaggerated, in no way detracts from the distinctive dignity of the duties which belong to ministerial function, or from the solemn significance of separation to ministry.

On the one hand, he affirms that God blesses all, laity no less than clergy. On the other, a distinction persists: "We insist that some, and not all, have the right, as organs and instruments, to

---

[33] Carter, *Priesthood*, 99–100, 106.

[34] Liddon, *Sermons*, 193 (cf. chapter 1, above).

represent the Church, and wield ministerially the powers that are inherent in her."[35]

What makes the difference? Where ministry is concerned—remembering that Moberly construes "ministry" as ordination—"the work is God's work, and the authority to undertake it must be God's authority." That is, God initiates ministry. As it was under the Old Covenant, so it is under the New. It can be valid only with adequate commission, and that is a "commission understood to proceed from God." Even if the initiative to pursue ministry may be granted to the individual—note that for the moment the collective Body is peripheral—the ministry takes its character, authority, guidance, and very meaning from the Spirit.[36] While such commissioning may "be accompanied by, or even may require, as a regular preliminary, acclamation or acceptance from below," whoever is commissioned receives his warrant "not from below but from above"—"from God essentially and not man." Only then can the commission genuinely authorize and empower. Unlike those who saw the difference between "ministry and laity" as one "merely of secular or politic convenience," Moberly considered it part of the divine schema.[37]

How then are such individual ministers commissioned in the earthly sphere? Moberly reviews three possibilities: (1) divine appointment, individually perceived; (2) an individual perception affirmed by appointment of the church or one of its components but without any specific or required method of transmission; (3) commission by one or more who themselves have received authority to transmit such a commission—in short, apostolic succession. Each has points in its favor, though the final is the "familiar Church view."

---

[35] Moberly, MP, 98, 99 (contrast 1979 BCP Catechism, that the laity "represent Christ and his Church" [855]).

[36] Moberly, MP, 100, 102–103; Hooker, Eccl. Pol. V.lxxvi.8. Hooker too is thinking specifically in terms of ordination and claims that this is something Jesus himself did.

[37] Moberly, MP, 104, 105. Although the specifics of how the commission is conveyed—e.g., by bishops—is not addressed, he does write, "It never can be conferred by those who have not authority to confer it."

(1) *Divine appointment, individually perceived:* While open to the abstract possibility of individual call, Moberly doubted its practical viability. One reason is sacramental, for "inward acts through outward" and "Spirit through Body." Although both testaments provide precedents of those receiving direct divine calls— Amos in the Old, Paul in the New—the *church* still laid hands on Paul to entitle his mission to Gentiles. In any case, individual appointment poses dangers given "the fancies of a man's own brain about himself or his own inspiration." A call from the corporate is standard.[38]

(2) *Individual perception, corporate appointment:* Might that commission be affirmed by a church "or some portion thereof"— but without "ministerial succession or sacramental method"? This problem is more subtle. Surely the church may appoint its officers? Yes; but how, and through whom? Can laity ordain a priest or bishop, for instance? Tertullian in the early third century implied they could,[39] but subsequent Christian tradition suggested otherwise. Here Moberly puts his "ministerial principle" to work, "that whilst it is always the corporate Church which acts through its representative instruments, it is only through instruments, empowered to represent, that the corporate Church does act." No individual may act on the church's behalf unless the church gives permission. A portion of the church lacks the right to commission, unless it is authorized to do so by the whole.[40]

(3) *Apostolic succession:* That authorization is incorporated in the "traditional view as to the 'ministerial' transmission of ministry." The Articles of Religion affirmed the necessity of lawful call by lawful authority.[41] Moberly reasons, "Those only are duly commissioned who have received commission from such, before them,

---

[38] Moberly, *MP*, 105–110. On Paul's commissioning, see Moberly's note, 125.

[39] Cited in Moberly, *MP*, 112.

[40] Moberly, *MP*, 111.

[41] Article XXIII: "It is not lawful for any man to take upon him the office of public preaching, or ministering the Sacraments in the Congregation, before he be lawfully called, and sent to execute the same. And those we ought to judge lawfully called and sent, which be chose and called to this work by men who have public authority given unto them in the Congregation, to call and send Ministers into the Lord's vineyard."

as were themselves commissioned to commission others." It began
with the apostles who, in Moberly's view, in turn constituted bishops and deacons in "a continuous succession of ministerial
office." Transmission of commission validates ministerial office.[42]
Even if episcopate did evolve from presbyterate, as scholars were
suggesting (a point he did not concede), Moberly argued that the
evolution occurred within a church of apostolic commission that
gave its leaders the authority to transmit authority. The principle
of an "apostolic church" abides. As Gore noted:

> The Church's doctrine of succession is thus of a piece
> with the whole idea of the Gospel revelation, as being
> the communication of a divine gift which must be
> received and cannot be originated,—received, moreover,
> through the channels of a visible and organic society;
> and the principle...lies at the last resort in the idea of
> succession rather than in the continuous existence of
> episcopal government.[43]

Both scriptural and historical authority affirm a dependency
upon "a continuity of orderly appointment and institution, received
in each generation from those who themselves had been authorized
to institute by the institution of those before them," transmitted
ultimately from those who "too were 'Apostles,' 'sent' by Him
who, even Himself, was 'sent' to be the Christ."[44] These representatives, Moberly maintained, are apostolic.

VARIETIES OF (ORDAINED) SERVICE

"It is evident unto all men diligently reading holy Scripture
and ancient Authors, that from the Apostles' time there have been
these orders of Ministers in Christ's Church; Bishops, Priests and
Deacons." So declared the Ordinal.[45] By the end of the nineteenth

---

[42] Moberly, MP, 114, 115 (paraphrasing 1 Clement). Although Moberly clearly
favors an "apostolic succession" point of view, he does not inherently necessitate
apostolic ordination—the tactile "contagion" principle—but rather only the
passing along of commission. But see 1 Clem. 37–44, which he quotes at length.

[43] MP, 123 n. 2, q. Gore, Ministry, 63.

[44] MP, 125. The word "apostle" derives from the Greek verb "send."

[45] The Book of Common Prayer, 1662 (Cambridge: Cambridge University Press,
c. 1968), 553.

century, it was not nearly so evident. Lightfoot, Hatch, and Hort each in his way had questioned how the various orders came to be. In so doing, they undermined the assumption that the apostles had appointed deacons to serve, bishops to oversee, and "elders" (*presbuteroi*) to do whatever they did, which was murky enough. As Dean Stanley liked to point out in his assessments of the early church researches of his time, all we know assuredly about the roles of early bishops, deacons, and priests is what their roles were *not*. For him, the only certainties were uncertainties.[46]

Unsurprisingly, Gore and Moberly dissented in their readings of New Testament and ancient church writers. Not only did they dispute the scholarship, but they also disagreed with any theological position that would deracinate contemporary ministry from apostolic origins. Moberly's view of the earliest church employed the "background of apostolate, unquestioned, supreme, everywhere" based on the principle of "mission from Christ." Evidence points toward a "quasi-apostolic rank, jurisdiction, and prerogative" in those, like Timothy and Titus, who are nonetheless "apostolic" without being apostles themselves. From the outset, presbyters were appointed "everywhere" as rulers, teachers, and representatives of the local communities of Christians. Deacons emerged immediately, probably among Hellenistic Christians in Jerusalem, evidently including women as well as men, but without clear distinction "between the 'officer' and the 'servant' aspect of ministry." Finally, a "great variety of special spiritual graces" pervading the church of the New Testament era gave their recipients almost apostolic prominence but not in a formal sense of office or order—and indeed sometimes counterproductive to order.[47]

Moberly's image of the earliest church managed to run afoul of both sides of the prevailing argument. On the left were the scientifically inclined historians who followed the advice of Hatch: the "divine plan must be inferred not *a priori*, from a conception of what He was likely to do, but *a posteriori*, from the investigation of what He has actually done."[48] Moberly, they charged, was

---

[46] Stanley, *Christian Institutions*, 207–208. See chapter 1, above.

[47] Moberly, *MP*, 167–169.

[48] Hatch, *Organization*, 215.

doing the opposite by reading the realities of a later period back into an earlier one. Consequently, when Moberly borrowed church practices prevalent in the second century to describe those of the New Testament period, he was, in effect, writing a history every bit as suspect as the histories he hoped his own work would debunk. Furthermore, alleged his critics, Moberly was coloring his history with his theology—a case of "eisegesis," to borrow a word that had only just been coined in Moberly's day to describe those who interpreted Scripture through their own biases. The Anglican bishop W. E. Collins, himself a church historian, used *Ministerial Priesthood* as an example of "the way in which historical work is not to be done," accusing Moberly of letting presuppositions determine his conclusions rather than letting historical fact influence theory. Even Moberly's friend Sanday tended to agree that he had crossed the fine line that separated historical scrutiny from theological partisanship.[49]

Meanwhile, from the right came criticism from those who—unquestioning of the Ordinal's assertions—were the inheritors of preconceptions of the previous century. To them, Moberly was the avatar of doubt, shockingly undermining the established order.

But Moberly was doing his job as an academician. As such, he was applying the tools of his trade to his scholarship, which in this case meant employing the "state-of-the-art" techniques of biblical and historical criticism, techniques that were to some degree derived from the natural sciences. As a theologian, he was responding to those like the don we encountered in chapter 1 who, three decades earlier, complained that theology was not yet considered a science at Oxford and might never be respected as one. Finally, as a person of faith, Moberly was determined not to set his convictions on the shelf in the process of doing his job—as he blamed Hatch for doing—but rather to let the theological science

---

[49] William Edward Collins, *The Study of Ecclesiastical History* (London: Longmans, Green & Co., 1903), 68–69; W. Sanday, *The Conception of Priesthood in the Early Church and in the Church of England* (London: Longmans Green, and Co., 1898), 5–34. Sanday contrasted Hort's and Moberly's historical approaches, noting—as he did between Moberly and Lightfoot—the extensive common ground they shared. See also John Bascom, "Reason and Faith," *The Dial* 24, no. 284 (April 16, 1898), 262: "The view which has much logical force within itself seems, however, to be constructed in oversight, if not in contempt, of the actual stages of growth in the world."

he was advancing inform and infuse his faith. Yet his personal and professional approach took him into the middle of the battle between "science" and "religion," alongside others who were trying to mediate between factions. Together they drew the fury of the warring factions but managed nonetheless to find a *via media* in the use of tools borrowed from science to explore the Bible, history, and theology, an approach that Anglican thinkers of the next century would pursue. And, while Moberly's attempt to preserve definitive apostolic roots cannot be called a complete success, still his vision of orders and ministry within the Body of Christ seemed to capture the imagination of Anglican leaders who followed him.

With that, we turn to the presbyteral order and what may be Moberly's greatest contribution: his development of the idea of a ministerial priesthood.

MOBERLY AND THE MINISTERIAL PRIESTHOOD

Moberly originally intended to write a study of the development of the Anglican Ordinal. He envisioned his long prolegomenon in *Ministerial Priesthood* to be merely an introduction to the ordination rites and their liturgical background. His readers, then and since, may be grateful that he did not spend several hundred more pages getting to his basic point; but, for whatever reason, he dropped the larger project to proceed to his conclusion. His haste to publish may have been provoked by his need to refute the well-meaning but misleading notions of Lightfoot or, more likely, to rebut the bull of Pope Leo XIII that denied the legitimacy of Anglican orders.[50] Whatever the cause, Moberly dropped his plan to examine the medieval precursors to the Ordinal and proceeded to his conclusions about the ministerial character of priesthood. First, though, having explored at length the situation of the early church, he had to bring the story into his present, and consider the controversy that surrounded the nature of ministry—a controversy that had marked the Reformation as well as his century, and ours.

Priesthood: Two Wrong Views

As Moberly looked back to the era of the Reformation, he noted two formidable and opposing concepts. One—derived from

---

[50] See the preface to the first edition, *MP*, iii–iv.

a popular Roman Catholic way of thinking directly traceable to
the Counter-Reformation and the Council of Trent, though never
raised to the level of official doctrine—saw the priest as an intermediary who stood between God and the people, offering sacrifice
more in the heritage of pagan religion or Old Testament tradition
than in Christian heritage. It was this concept of a sacrificing
priesthood that had thoroughly offended Lightfoot. Moberly was
no less repelled. He asserted that this view produced "outward
observance" rather than "spirituality," and made "the Priesthood...mechanical, and the Sacraments material, to an extraordinary degree."[51] The disconnection between formal, outward
observance and inward reality (a concern of his first chapter) was
one problem that worried Moberly. A second was how disconnected the concept of priesthood was from pastoral ministry.
Roman ordinations of priests marked them as empowered to offer
sacrifice; more prominence to teaching and pastoring was given in
rites for consecrating bishops than for ordaining priests.[52]
Anglicans might quickly notice that, in the Roman Catholic priestly
ordinations,

> there is no emphasis whatever upon what we mean by
> service to, or self-sacrifice for, the people. There has
> been no attempt to develop, by so much as a single
> word, the correlative idea of priestly "intercession," or
> indeed any form whatever of self-expenditure. There is
> no solemn responsibility for the flock...not a word of
> anything like what we mean by "pastoral" devotion, or
> responsibility, or suffering.[53]

---

[51] Moberly, *MP*, 221; see 53. This council of Roman Catholic bishops met in
1546–47, 1551–52, and 1562–63.

[52] Moberly, *MP*, 226–227. "The one thing which stands out at last so conspicu-
ously that it seems to be the very thing which 'priesthood' distinctively signifies,
is the *'potestas offerre sacrificiuum'* [the power or authority to offer sacrifice] or
'placabiles hostias' [appeasing sacrifice]" (227, italics mine).

[53] Moberly, *MP*, 228. It should be recalled that Moberly deals with official and
liturgical statements that create an understanding or idea of priesthood. He does
not consider the practice of priesthood, which often involved the clergy in hero-
ic martyrdoms or intense pastoral concern, as he admits (286, n. 1).

Moberly's third critique concerned whether the Eucharist was (in his words) "the Church's divinely ordered ceremonial method of self-identification with the sacrifice of Christ" or a sacrifice in itself, as if it were a New Testament fulfillment of Old Testament parallels. Since the Reformation, Anglicans concurred with the first point but strenuously disputed the second. To Moberly (again like Lightfoot before him), whether expressed in theological nuance or in popular language, that latter concept of sacrifice constituted "the one differentiating conception and definition of 'priesthood'"[54] in Roman Catholicism.

What Moberly characterized as "terrible excesses of irreligious churchmanship on the Roman side" produced another excess: "virulent antichurchism on the Protestant side." In the name of personal religion and spiritual truth, "genuine enough in its original impulse, but ignorant to an extreme degree," Nonconformist reformers were "eager to sweep away, in one great destructive flood, all ordinances, outward and historical, whatsoever; as if the inward would best express itself without an outward."[55] "Unbridled Protestantism" overreacted by obliterating all mention whatsoever of sacrifice and priesthood.

Against both of these extremes, Anglicans tried to find a middle way, to which they gave expression in *The Book of Common Prayer.* They perceived that the nomenclature of sacrifice, sacrament, and priesthood was not wholly wrong, but that, in the centuries

---

[54] Moberly, *MP*, 229–230, 231–232, 233. The point of comparison/contrast of Eucharist with OT sacrifice bears particular noting. Moberly writes, "To call the Eucharist 'the Church's sacrifice' (in the sense e.g. of the Church's identification with the sacrifice of Christ) is one thing: to call it '*verum sacrificium*' may point only a most legitimate contrast between it and the Old Testament sacrifices which were certainly not '*vera*': but to call it (under anathema) '*proprium sacrificium*' either is, or certainly may seem to be, another" (232). The comparison/contrast with OT sacrifices gives rise to popular (mis)understandings not only of Eucharist but also of priesthood: Those who offered OT sacrifices were (primarily) priests; thus those who offer the *true* sacrifice, that of the New Covenant— i.e., the Eucharist—must also be considered priests. Hence presbyters slowly evolve from being councilors to the bishop, to leaders of local congregations, who in leading eucharistic worship turn into "priests."

[55] Moberly, *MP*, 222, cf. ch. II. It should be noted that Moberly speaks not of the extreme continental Protestantism of Zwinglians or Anabaptists, but of the English reformers; however, he notes that the Council of Trent responded more to German Protestantism than to the English variety (223).

preceding the Reformation, both concept and expression had "so far fallen out of due proportion as, if not to contradict, yet at least to jeopardize, the right balance of Christian truth." Though tempted to scuttle the language of priesthood (like calling presbyters "priests"), the English reformers deliberately retained it.[56] This tension—whether to retain or retire the problematic language—abided into Moberly's day. Lightfoot, for instance, had worried so over the connotations of the terminology that he had wondered if "it might have been better" to drop the language of priesthood when the Reformers had the chance.[57] But to Moberly's way of thinking, this was Lightfoot's falling once again into the trap of defining "sacrifice" and thus "priests" in the Roman way. If Lightfoot honestly considered priests as a "sacrificial caste" that forms "an exclusive priesthood" with "sacerdotal privileges,"[58] then he was reading "priesthood" through Roman glasses, or with reactionary Protestant blinders, instead of from a classic Anglican view.

Moberly tried to profess just such a classic Anglican view through his theory of representation. Christian ministry does not posit a "substituted intermediary" between God and people, but rather a "representative and organ of the whole body, in the exercise of prerogatives and powers which belong to the body as a whole" but which are exercised through its own organs "duly fitted for the purpose."

> What is duly done by Christian ministers, it is not so much that *they* do it, in the stead, or for the sake, of the whole; but rather that the whole does it by and through them. The Christian Priest does not offer an atoning sacrifice on behalf of the Church: it is rather that the Church through his act that, not so much "offers an atonement," as "is identified upon earth with the one heavenly offering of the atonement of Christ."[59]

---

[56] Moberly, *MP*, 234–239.   representation   not substituted intermediary

[57] Q. in Moberly, *MP*, 239, from J. B. Lightfoot, *Dissertations on the Apostolic Age* (London: Macmillan and Co., 1892), 235.

[58] Moberly, *MP*, 241. Lightfoot knew better, Moberly says, for he had disclaimed a "sacerdotal system" for the church (*Christian Ministry*, 1). Of the two possible meanings for "priesthood," Lightfoot chose the wrong one.

[59] Moberly, *MP*, 241–242. √

priesthood is an outward that is perfectly expressive of an inward," and that which is inward is given utterance by the outward. From this reality all ceremonies and rituals take their meaning. Any priesthood that relies on outward alone is a mere shell of true priesthood—whether it be Jewish or, he warns, Christian.[64]

As Christ is, so his church also must be: as he is prophet, or king, or priest, so the church is prophetic, royal, priestly. The people of God, then, altogether constitute a priestly people. Denigrating priesthood demeans the laity no less than the ordained. Exalting the "priesthood of the ministry" exalts "the priesthood of the body as a whole."[65] It ought not to be torn down, but built up!—for the sacrificial priestly character of the church arises from "her identification with the priesthood and sacrifice of Christ." His outward "enactment is but the perfect utterance of a perfect inwardness" of holiness and love. So too the church's priesthood combines outward with inward: "by outward enactment ceremonially, and by inwardness of spirit vitally." Eucharistic worship identifies the church on earth with the sacrificial oblation of its Lord, not as a one-time offering on Calvary nor as a repeated act, but as an "eternal presentation of Himself in heaven in which Calvary is vitally contained."[66]

Moberly would raise the church's understanding not only of priestliness but of Eucharist and, indeed, of Christ's eternal activity. In heaven Christ presents himself; on earth he is being formed in the life of his church. The church truly becomes, and is becoming, the Body of Christ.[67] As such, the church reflects the two priestly attributes of Christ. One dimension is Godward: "from her proceeds the aroma of perpetual offering to God"; the other is worldward: "her arms are spread out perpetually to succour and intercede for those who need the sacrifice of love." This latter direction concerns both those who are outside of the church in

---

[64] Moberly, MP, 249–250. Moberly does not speak in psychological or individual spiritual terms, but rather in the Platonist/theological sense he outlined in his chapter II—by which the outward and visible is intimately related to inward and spiritual realities, as supremely the church is to its Lord.

[65] Moberly, MP, 251–254.

[66] Moberly, MP, 254–255.

[67] Moberly, MP, 255.

missionary and evangelical purpose, and also those within it, in mutual service, fellowship, and nurture. The two directions are of a piece. Both emanate from the same priestly service to God. Both involve and include the entire Body of Christ. Both are reflected in Eucharist, in the Godward "sacrifice of praise and thanksgiving," and in what Moberly calls "sacrifice taking practical form." This outwardly directed "intense 'for-other-ness'" has been

> characteristically exemplified, all the world over, in great things and in small, in the self-sacrificing minis-trations of Bishops and Pastors, in the tender, self-devo-tion of fathers or mothers, comrades or brothers, wives or sisters, or teachers, or nurses, or neighbours, or strangers, yes or even, with a certain reflected fidelity, in outsiders, Samaritans, enemies.

This is the priesthood of all Christians, "the inherent privilege of the members of the body of Christ."[68]

Moberly provided the theological rationale for an understand-ing of ministry that the next century would embrace. His hypoth-esis consists of several elements. One is the innate and intimate relationship between all aspects of the church's life; social out-reach, evangelism, pastoral care, and worship (especially Eucharist) all constitute the offering of the Body to its Lord. Another is his emphasis on the unity of the Body, which gives deeply honored place to those who are not ordained as well as those who are. "The ministry of the laity" can find justification in Moberly's thought.

Yet another is a rationale of the priesthood of the church, which all share. As the church's priesthood follows from Christ's, so the ordained priesthood derives from the church. "What the one is, the other is." As the church at large identifies "ceremoni-ally" through eucharistic worship with the eternal sacrifice of Christ and "spiritually" through the sacrificial love of devoted ser-vice, so do the ordained. "For the priesthood of the ministry is nothing distinct in kind from the priesthood of the Church."[69]

---

[68] Moberly, MP, 255–257.

[69] Moberly, MP, 257–258. It bears reiteration that Moberly's terminology of "ministry" refers to the ordained, not to the whole. It will be a later generation that expresses "ministry" in broader terms as applying to the entire Body, but Moberly's thought is consistent with this point even if his language is not.

One final element is an understanding of the clergy and the laity. There is little ontological difference between the two.

> The ordained are priestly only because it is the Church's prerogative to be priestly; and because they are, by ordination, specialized and empowered to exercise ministerially and organically the prerogatives which are the prerogatives of the body as a whole. They have no greater right in the Sacraments than the laity: only they, and not the laity, have been authorized to stand before the congregation, and to represent the congregation in the ministerial enactment of the Sacraments which are the Sacraments—and the life—of both alike.

There is, however, a distinction in function and authority. Priestliness of the whole Body does not permit just anyone to exercise the rights of that corporate priesthood on his or her own. "Those who stand before the congregation, either as its representative organs to Godward, or as the accredited ministers of God to it, must be authorized and empowered to do so."[70] Ordination matters. By comparison, a citizen of the United States who visits Great Britain or Zambia, in a way, represents the United States. Through his acts or statements, others may form opinions of his homeland based upon their observations of him. But in no sense may the visitor speak officially on behalf of the people or President of his nation: that is the role of the ambassador and others duly appointed and commissioned for the task. Yet the traveler is no less a citizen of the United States, with all the rights and privileges thereof.[71] Each Christian may be baptized as a citizen of heaven and will to some degree represent the Body of Christ without in turn receiving the power to represent the church officially, corporately, or ceremonially. That authority is given at ordination.

Unity within the Body will not be served "by exalting the ministry at the expense of the laity," even less by dropping the terminology of priesthood. On the contrary, the status and purpose of

---

[70] Moberly, *MP*, 258.

[71] This analogy is limited by the fact that the ambassador is delegated by another human being, the President, and while she owes allegiance to the "higher authority" of the Presidency, the dimension is human, lacking the "vertical" aspect of divine commission.

the laity expand "by insisting, in no metaphorical sense, upon the sacred character and solemn responsibility of the priesthood of the Christian Church as a whole, and (apart from its ministerial and executive sense) of every individual lay-member of the Church."[72] Moberly opens the way for a deeper understanding of the place of the laity.

As for presbyterate, Moberly reiterates a classic Anglican understanding but with a catholic twist. Priests are "personally consecrated to be the representatives and active organs of the priesthood of the Church." In worship "they represent it as divinely empowered to be themselves its leaders and instruments." Apart from altar or church building or even official position, a priest is no less a priest. Having received a "personal relation to the priest-liness of the Church" conferred "once for all, and which dominates everything that he does, or is," the priest will always and everywhere be a representative—"to Godward for man, to man-ward for God." Neither an intermediary nor one who possesses what the church at large does not, the priest represents "in his own personality, with an eminent distinctiveness, that which the whole Church cannot but essentially be"—that which is in a corporate sense priestly.[73]

Because the church's priestliness involves both ceremonial and sacrificial service, so must the priesthood of its ministerial representatives. Levitical priesthood involved ceremony only, but Christian priesthood must never define itself solely by outward ceremony or sacrament. The "priestly spirit" and "priestly heart" move beyond worship alone. While this "priestly spirit" is emphatically "not the exclusive possession of the ordained ministry" but of the entire "priestly Church," its ordained representatives bear a special responsibility. Toward that end, they receive "a charisma of grace which constitutes a special call and a special capacity, for its exercise." The opportunity and the call arise inseparably from the life of the church before God and extend to the Body (and beyond). Eucharistic leadership holds the two corollaries of "over-

---

[72] Moberly, MP, 258–259.

[73] Moberly, MP, 259–260. He uses the term "personality" not in a psychological sense but in an ontological one, regarding the priest's being as representative. He was writing, of course, at a time when only males were ordained.

sight of the life of the Christian body to Godward" and pastorally of "the bearing of the people on the heart before God; the earnest effort of intercessory entreating; the practical translation of intercession into pastoral life, and anxiety, and pain."[74]

So priesthood of ministry and priesthood of laity are not antithetical or inconsistent, but correlative, complementary, and "mutually indispensable ideas." One could extrapolate from clerical ministry the "priesthood of the laity" or magnify "lay priesthood" and discover the "concentrated meaning" of those set apart "to represent the collective priesthood."[75] There is no inherent conflict, because they are at one in Christ.

The Christlike, Sacrificial Nature of Ministerial Priesthood

Having established the intimate connection of the ordained to the Body as a whole, and thus the laity, Moberly turned to liturgical, governing, and pastoral leadership. Like the mutual priesthood of the ordained and laity, these three are all of a piece. "Each in its reality requires and implies the other" not as discrete duties "but as several aspects of one," the "true priestliness" that finds its heart in the pastoral. The unity, which Moberly expresses in so many ways, applies no less to what the priest may do. In that light, "sacerdotalism" in the pejorative sense (as used by Lightfoot) may be understood as an exaggeration or even isolation of one element against the others, certainly contrary to the ideal or to the scriptural and historical tradition.[76]

---

[74] Moberly, *MP*, 261 (italics in original).

[75] Moberly, *MP*, 262.

[76] Moberly, *MP*, 263; see n. 1. Moberly then looks at why NT language does not employ sacerdotal language: first, because outward/inward were so closely connected, there seemed to be no need; second, given the associations of priestly language with Mosaic law, the terminology would have led to "inextricable misunderstanding and confusion." He then explains the emergence of priestly/sacrificial terminology as coinciding with the demise of Judaic priesthood and sacrifice and thus of any ambiguity. Not only does Moberly's scholarship seem weak—his citations are few and strained—but so may be his logic. Can another view be possible, which might have strengthened Moberly's thesis: that NT writers wished clearly *not* to adapt Jewish language? In calling a local leader *presbuteros* and not *hiereus*, the Greek term for a Levitical or pagan priest, Christians would thereby have differentiated themselves markedly from the OT blood-sacrificial system.

Eucharist, to Moberly, constitutes "the essential Christian service from the first." Through it, the church identifies with its Lord. To preside over it is the prototypical presbyteral function. Moberly finds evidence from Paul, with clues from Hebrews, all bolstered by patristic sources, that the eucharistic leaders in the earliest church were the "elders"—the presbyterate. This was the "one necessary aspect of the office." Not the *only* aspect by any means, it was nonetheless cardinal.[77]

Anglican reformers carefully expunged from the Ordinal any reference to priests "offering sacrifice." Moberly proposes what he understands to be an appropriate, scriptural, traditional understanding of the Christly nature of "sacrifice" that would express an Anglican distinction reflective of the true nature of "ministerial priesthood." Even as Pope Leo XIII was preparing to declare Anglican orders "utterly null and absolutely void" for not being sacrificial, Moberly was developing an Anglican riposte that its priesthood is indeed sacrificial, in ways that tried to answer and transcend the Roman assault on his church.

Why had the Prayer Book Ordinal omitted terms of sacrifice? Such language, he argued, had become all-encompassing of the role and understanding of priesthood. "It is one thing to admit the reality of sacrificial language; it is quite another to make it the one definition and measure of Christian ministry." The "presbyter" had become a "priest" defined in Old Testament terms as one who offers sacrifices. For Moberly, the true mark of the Christian leader is not officiating at worship, much less offering sacrifice, but following the example of Jesus, "the care of an utterly loving pastor, a shepherd who tends, feeds, nurses, rescues and is ready to die for the souls of his flock." It is an "outward representation of the sacrifice of Christ."[78] Thus the Ordinal

---

[77] Moberly, *MP*, 276, see 266–278. Moberly then disputes Lightfoot's argument against "sacerdotalism" (279–282), claiming that the language and certainly the thought were indeed present in the life of the early church, though of a kind such as he has sought to define.

[78] Moberly, *MP*, 285. "Every overemphasized truth is itself, in another aspect, untruth; and the untruth which was bound up with this over-emphasis made itself obvious in the more and more absolute overshadowing of the whole pastoral ideal" (286). Moberly concedes that he critiques the "'unreformed' Ordinal," not necessarily the "unreformed Ministry.... No doubt there have been, and are, vast numbers of most admirable Roman pastors" (286, n. 1).

fixes the eye, first and foremost, just as St. Paul in the
New Testament does, upon the thought of the self-ded-
ication and surrender, the pastoral responsibility, the
service of the flock, the cure of souls—the life-absorbing
inner and spiritual relation—in which, and of which,
"administration of sacraments" comes in as the highest
method, the culminating point of executive privilege and
power.

Though Eucharist may be "the very highest...the most glorious
and wonderful" duty of the priesthood, "yet priesthood is something more vitally inclusive than any mystery of formal executive
privilege." There remains, for example, the "'cure of souls,' whose
meaning can never be exhausted by anything in the sphere of ceremonial method"; nor does liturgical leadership outweigh "'care
of all the Churches' as a separate or higher thing." This is the
sense that "stands in the forefront of the Anglican Ordinal."[79]

Perhaps, Moberly concedes, the Reformers overreacted. Along
with deleting any and all references to priestly sacrifice, they omitted such liturgical touches as handing the ordinand a chalice and
paten in token of his responsibilities.[80] Nonetheless, Anglican
reformers made a significant and praiseworthy contribution, in
that they "restored the essential relation and harmony between
Eucharistic leadership—with all that it involves—and a right conception in Christ's Church of the meaning of ministerial priesthood as a whole."[81]

Moberly saw several implications of this right relationship
between the pastoral and priestly aspects of the presbyterate. First,

---

[79] Moberly, *MP*, 286–287. He proceeds to cite illustrations from the Ordinal.

[80] Moberly, *MP*, 288–289. So far, restoration of this practice remains largely a
vain hope, though ordinands often receive the eucharistic vessels in an extra-
liturgical gesture, and *The Alternative Service Book* does permit a priest to
receive a paten and chalice after delivery of the Bible, though no form of words
is provided *(The Alternative Service Book 1980* [London: Clowes, SPCK, Cambridge University Press, 1980], 338, n. 8). Technically, Moberly errs in part, for
in the first Anglican Ordinal (1550) the priestly ordinand received a Bible, chalice,
and bread. One may understand why Cranmer et al. wished to omit this ceremony, however, as popular devotion often considered this to comprise the matter
of the sacrament. See R. C. D. Jasper and Paul F. Bradshaw, *A Companion to the
Alternative Service Book* (London: SPCK, 1986), 432, 445–446.

[81] Moberly, *MP*, 290.

is it a mistake to refer to the pastoral as an aspect of priesthood? This was an issue of his day, arising from pronouncements—most prominently from the pope—that a pastoral heart, no matter how effective or sincere, cannot "compensate for any defect in the priestly character." That is, even the sincerest pastoral heart cannot correct a defective ordination; and on that basis Leo XIII was about to adjudge all Anglican ordinations defective precisely because they did not include the language and intention of priestly sacrifice. But Moberly recalled how gradually priestly terminology and sacerdotal titles came into use alongside—and not replacing—ideas of presbyterate. He regretted that the meanings of "priest" and "pastor" had been "divorced." Even so, the church ordains to one presbyteral order—not one order of "priests" and another of "pastors"—and in so doing "she stamps with so solemn an emphasis the 'pastoral' aspect of their 'priesthood.'" Moreover, "he who finds the whole meaning of his priesthood in the act of celebrating does not at all understand what the Christian priesthood truly means." A disabled priest who cannot officiate at Eucharist is nonetheless a priest, exercising a ministry in preaching, writing, counseling, or teaching, in organizing or visiting, or just in maintaining a priestly integrity and example in suffering. The ideal pastorate and ideal priesthood are blended together in the idea announced by Jesus, "I am the good shepherd."[82]

Here the now familiar tensions of function and being, of duty and character, of "outward" and "inward" reappear. Given humanity's "inveterate tendency" to form definitions on the basis of visible reality or function, it is no wonder that Christian priesthood is explained by what the priest *does,* primarily in ceremonial. Moberly complained, "It is so much easier to be mechanical than to be spiritual!"[83] Concentrating on outward acts misses inward realities, which is where their "true meaning and character" lie. Interpreting deeds without this inward sense misinterprets the deeds themselves. Moberly used the example of a viceroy. He signs death warrants and pardons, approves statutes, and leads great ceremonies of state. Yet to describe the job in those terms alone

---

[82] Moberly, *MP,* 290–294.

[83] Moberly, *MP,* 298.

misses his far broader powers and responsibilities. These immediate duties are outward acts that indicate "the truth of the office that he receives." They symbolize the viceroy's general responsibility and commission, both of which derive from a still higher authority. The tasks point toward what he *is*, without ever encompassing the fullness of his identity.[84]

So it is with priesthood or any ministerial office in the church. What one sees is not all there is to the office; rather, the visible duties reveal and derive from a greater commission. The "sublime function and prerogative" of presbyters arise from the demands of their office, but all of these "illustrate, and give a crowning expression to, the true essential meaning of the office, [rather] than constitute its essence in themselves." Moreover, the presbyterate cannot be defined as "what Christian lay priesthood may not do, as rather by discernment of the quickened intensity and more representative and responsible completeness" of qualities that belong to and derive from the Body as a whole: Moberly always wishes to keep the unified nature of the people of God in focus.[85] In the end, priesthood is not simply what the ordained do. Instead,

> [p]riesthood is a relation—to God, to the Church, to the world—which touches and consecrates the whole range of the personal life, so that its own technicalities, however precious, its own executive possibilities, however august, either must be understood to include the essential pastoral relation and responsibility to the "Spouse and Body of Christ," or else will fall far short of that deep and vital and mysterious reality into which those who have really been admitted who are sent out as "priests" in the Church of God.

Therein lies the truth that the Ordinal should express, for the sake of the ordained, for the sake of the priesthood as a whole, for the sake of understanding the very nature of the church.

---

[84] Moberly, *MP*, 296–297. For this reason, I have always been skeptical of clergy "job descriptions" at the parochial level. They may describe, but never fully encompass, the responsibilities that priesthood implies. For, precisely as Moberly suggests (299), the office is not so much one to be defined in terms of duties, as of relationship.

[85] Moberly, *MP*, 298.

[T]o the ideal meaning of the Church the outward of administrative priestliness must be in perfect correspondence with the inward; that objective and subjective are but conterminous aspects of one living reality; that true priesthood is pastorate, and true pastorate based on priestliness; that "cure of souls" is itself so really a sacrifice, and intercession an Eucharist, that the very ministry of the Eucharistic sacrifice fails to understand itself, if it find no corresponding utterance in the secret chamber at least, as the divine love and "cure" of souls.[86]

MOBERLY'S LEGACY

Initial responses to *Ministerial Priesthood* discouraged Moberly. In trying to synthesize and bridge the two rival theories of ordination—the sacerdotalism of Roman Catholicism and the idea of delegation of English Nonconformity—he had hoped to offer a path toward reconciliation, "an *eirenicon*," which, in good Anglican fashion, would bridge the differences within his own church if not between denominations. To his disappointment, his son W. H. Moberly would later report, "Critics of all complexions simply treated it as a High Church manifesto."[87] Some defended the late Bishop of Durham from Moberly's criticism. Lightfoot had not truly meant to equate priesthood with sacerdotalism. Moberly overstated Lightfoot's point "by subordinating the Bishop's obvious meaning to his occasional loose phraseology." Others saw emphasis alone separating the two men's thinking.[88] Still others questioned whether Moberly's historical method was all that historical; a French reviewer, noticing

---

[86] Moberly, *MP*, 299.

[87] W. H. Moberly, "Robert Campbell Moberly," *JTS*, 9. *The Church Quarterly Review* labeled *Ministerial Priesthood* a "loyal and temperate exposition of Anglo-Catholic principles" ("Robert Campbell Moberly," *Church Quarterly Review*, 85).

[88] "Apostolical Succession: The Latest Nonconformist Manifesto," *London Quarterly Review* 30, no. 60 (July 1898), 300; cp. "Robert Campbell Moberly," *Church Quarterly Review*, 85–86. William Sanday devoted an entire University Sermon at Oxford to explain the proximity of thought of Lightfoot and Moberly (*Conception of Priesthood*, see esp. 75–93).

Moberly's well-established position in Oxford and the church, deemed his work more an ecclesiastical statement than a scholarly examination.[89]

Few, though, addressed his central ideas, probably because few really absorbed them. Time was needed for Moberly's thought to sink in—an observation made by Henry Scott Holland at a conference on priesthood:

> I can never forget how, at the Round Table gathered by Professor Sanday to consider the subject of Priesthood and Sacrifice, the representatives of English Nonconformity and of Scotch Presbyterianism gave him their bowed attention.... I saw, then, how deeply his work had passed into the religious mind of England.[90]

If Scott Holland was right, what about Moberly's work had entered the mind of Anglicans? Perhaps more importantly, a hundred years later, what did he say that bears remembering as we enter a new century?

(1) Moberly's use of the imagery of the Body of Christ expressed the nature of the Christian community. The metaphor held the potential of moving the Church of England beyond its self-understanding as the established church toward a deeper spiritual awareness of itself—a goal of the original Tractarians. The concept was useful, too, as the Anglican Communion extended beyond the British Isles. Because the Episcopal Church was never "established" in the United States (however much Episcopalians thought of themselves as such), being part of a larger Body was a means to explain in biblical language how they related to each other, either domestically within the United States or more broadly to the "mother church" and her sisters. Still more, it articulated a vision of the church as a transcendent reality which, far more than a human institution, was intimately related to the divine being itself. For the individual to be part of a Body that extends well beyond parish, diocese, national church, Anglican Communion, or

---

[89] "Ce n'est pas un livre d'histoire ni de pensée indépendante" (Jean Monnier, review of MP, Revue de L'Histoire des Religions 54 [1906], 141). For a more positive review, cf. Bascom, "Reason and Faith," 261–262.

[90] Holland, Personal Studies, 277.

even earthly bounds was a concept that could greatly elevate the Christian's daily life, as well as that of the local community.

(2) Moberly used the outward/inward dichotomy to imbue every aspect of earthly ecclesial life with celestial meaning. The "outward"—even the church's organization, no matter how bureaucratically flawed—reveals the inward reality of the Body of Christ.

(3) Moberly employed the Protestant tradition of the "priest-hood of all believers" but in a "catholic" manner that linked this priesthood directly with the priesthood of Christ. His critics thought otherwise, as if his focus on the priestly (and on priests) necessarily diminished the role of the laity. Inherent in Moberly's schema, however, is a vibrant place for a lay role in the life of the church. He avoided the priestly pretensions of more extreme Anglo-Catholics, steering instead a careful middle course between a Carter and a Lightfoot while keeping an eye on the excesses of both the Roman Catholic and the Protestant positions. His emphasis on the Christian community in its nature as the Body of Christ placed the presbyter within the context of the *laos* and the ministry of the ordained within the ministry of the entire priesthood.

(4) The representative quality of leadership, notably the ordained, relates clergy to the rest of the Body in ways that the new century would develop. It places the priest clearly within the context of the community of the faithful, with authority delegat-ed from the church as Christ's Body. No mere political conve-nience of a human community, priestly authority derives from the church and thereby from Christ as an action of the Holy Spirit. At the same time, as one of the faithful, the priest shares a unity with all members that places him on the same spiritual level as all oth-ers—bishops, deacons, and most certainly laity. Yet each differs just as organs of the body vary, not only in function but in com-position; the leg with its bones and sinews would hardly be known as coming from the same organism as the eye, with its lens and cornea. Their being differs along with their function. Yet both belong to the same body: diversity amid unity.

(5) That same point also authenticates a diversity of legitimate ministries. Laity have an authentic and authorized place within the wider Body, as do deacons. How they function and interrelate and what their specific job description entails—all warrant further—

scrutiny. Moberly gave as short a shrift to deacons as did anyone else of his day, but his work sanctions them in ways that twentieth-century thinking and practice would pursue. In noting the presence of women among the deacons, he even cracks open a door for what would become an astounding change within a hundred years, the admission of women into every order of ministry.[91]

(6) Presbyterate is ministerial rather than sacrificial in nature. While priesthood is sacrificial at large, and Prayer Book eucharistic rites consistently refer to the "sacrifice of praise and thanksgiving," the essential priesthood is that of the entire Body of Christ, consistent with the sacrificial nature of its Lord. Presbyterate shares in that sacrifice, but it is more specifically pastoral. Herein lies a crucial distinction from the Roman Catholic understanding of priesthood as Leo XIII would define it at virtually the same moment. The distinction continues to characterize Anglican discussions with Rome. However, his unification of the pastoral role with the ceremonial holds enormous importance for how clergy exercise their priesthood. His is a view highly consistent with the best of the Anglican pastoral tradition.

(7) The call to ordained ministry, in particular, emanates from both the divine and the human planes. On the one hand, Moberly asserts the need for a stronger lay voice in the ordination rite if not also in the selection process.[92] On the other, he maintains the church's role as a representative of God. It is not simply the church that acts in ordination, as the more Protestant-minded would say, but rather the Spirit, who is acting through the human voice of the church. A "private" call, then, is inconceivable. There can be no ministerial summons apart from the Christian community any more than there can be ministry apart from community.

---

[91] See MP, 139. Moberly was by no means unique. Lightfoot, for one, extolled the "revival of the female diaconate" and of sisterhoods, but this was consistent with the "order of deaconesses" in the apostolic church as part of "recent developments of woman's work" in the church ("The Place of Woman in the Gospel," June 19, 1884, in J. B. Lightfoot, *Sermons Preached on Special Occasions*, vol. 13 of *Works* [London: Macmillan and Co., 1891], 226–227). He was speaking to the Girls' Friendly Society.

[92] Moberly, MP, 89.

When Scott Holland described Moberly's influence, he was not quite so broad in his praise as he might have been. Moberly's work passed deeply into the mind of the whole Anglican Communion, as the dawning century would reveal. His legacy can be seen in the writings of theologians after him and even in the revisions of prayer books that incorporated his themes and utilized the images he propounded.

III

Developing a New Anglican Ecclesiology

Moberly's vision of a Body of Christ, with a representative ministry, seemed to touch a nerve within Anglicanism. In short order, it was seized upon by theologians on both sides of the Atlantic, developed and incorporated into their work, and utilized to articulate concepts of ministry and of the church.

A CHANGING COMMUNION, 1900—1965

War and violence were bitter handmaids to the dawning century. When Britain entered the Great War, England's church went to battle too. It exhorted recruits to enlist and sent thousands of clergy to minister to them as chaplains, or "padres" as the fighting men affectionately began to call them. The conflict's horror made their pastoral ministrations all too necessary. But chaplains in the trenches were sorely hindered by two deficiencies. One was the prevailing theology of the era. Liberal Protestantism, with its cheery assumptions of human progress, offered hollow comfort to millions who confronted the dreadful forms of death that "progress" had produced. Evangelicalism, the other dominant element in nineteenth-century religion, had already lost most of its steam. After the war, Hensley Henson, no fan of Anglo-Catholics,

Liberal Prots. @ its cheery assumptions of human progress

dismissed the Evangelicals as "a moribund party...out of touch with the prevailing tendencies, social and intellectual, of the time."[1] Though on the rise within the church, the catholic wing fared only somewhat better. It was the church at large—not just its theology—that was disconnected from the general populace. Seventy-five percent of the soldiers in the field were nominally Anglican, but many considered the institution to be "the heredi- tary enemy of the working classes." Trenches, like foxholes, may have contained few atheists; but not many believers showed up for rites according to *The Book of Common Prayer*.[2]

This alienation was the second deficiency that war made apparent. Over a decade later, the 1930 Lambeth Conference loftily conceded, "We recognize that there is some truth in the impression that the clergy are often out of touch with the life and thought of the laity." To solve the problem, the bishops suggested having prospective ordinands glean some "experience of the life and work of the world at home or abroad" before receiving episcopal hands.[3] Sensing that more was needed, William Temple, as bishop of the working-class city of Manchester, pursued a mediator's role during labor turmoils of the 1920s.[4] Cyril Garbett, who, like Temple, became an Archbishop of York, published a book entitled *The Challenge of the Slums* (1933). From the postwar parochial trenches came the work of Hugh Lister, a priest who chaired a local branch of the Transport and General Workers Union and, as curate in a depressed East End parish, promoted strikes as one way to help his struggling people.[5] Efforts bore little fruit. A priest- historian later identified "the failure of every Church to reach the

---

[1] Q. in Hastings, *History*, 76.

[2] David Edwards, *Christian England* (Grand Rapids, MI: Eerdmans, 1984), III, 361; cf. 358–366.

[3] *Lambeth Conference 1930* (London: SPCK, 1930), 170.

[4] Cf. F. A. Iremonger, *William Temple: Archbishop of Canterbury* (London: OUP, 1948), ch. XXI.

[5] Hastings, *History*, 386–387. Cf. Alice Cameron, *In Pursuit of Justice: The Story of Hugh Lister and His Friends in Hackney Wick* (London: SCM Press, 1946); and David Hein, "Hugh Lister (1901–44): Priest, Labor Leader, and Combatant Officer," *Anglican and Episcopal History*, 70, no. 3 (Sept. 2001), 353–374.

working masses of an industrial society" despite trying "harder and more consistently in this matter than in any."[6]

Recrafting theology to meet an age of disillusionment was more successfully undertaken between the two world wars. On the continent, Karl Barth led what became known as "Neo-Orthodoxy," which made new uses of old Protestant concepts such as sin, evil, grace, and forgiveness. Subsequently, biblical critics like the English Methodist C. H. Dodd and the American Protestant theologian Reinhold Niebuhr demonstrated anew that careful scholarship was not inconsistent with traditional faith. They were so successful that by 1937 their admirers were proclaiming, "Thou shalt love the Lord thy Dodd and thy Niebuhr as thyself."[7]

Concurrent with revitalized theology came a renewed interest in the life of the church, which also coincided in the Anglican world with the flowering of Anglo-Catholicism. This was the group that increasingly supplied university chairs and episcopal thrones. Their great names—Lionel Thornton, Michael Ramsey, Kenneth Kirk, Gregory Dix, A. G. Hebert, and later on Eric Mascall and Austin Farrer—were known for a biblical foundation that provided a basis for whatever else they said or wrote, Ramsey in theology, Hebert and Dix in liturgy, Kirk in moral theology.

The very worship of the church, too, was reevaluated, on both sides of the Atlantic. American Episcopalians succeeded in passing a revised Prayer Book in 1928. English Anglicans failed. When Parliament twice vetoed the proposed revision, Henson was so traumatized that he wanted to cut the church-state tie altogether.[8] Hebert, undeterred, labored to change what he could on the parochial level to make worship ever more integrated with life beyond the church walls (as in *Liturgy and Society* [1937]) or more vibrant within (as in *Parish Communion* [1937], which inspired renewed appreciation for the Eucharist and more frequent celebrations of it). That Hebert was a monk also reflected the growth and increased influence of religious orders. Laypeople, too, nurtured spiritual life and interest, notably Evelyn Underhill

---

[6] Roger Lloyd, *The Church of England 1900–1965* (London: SCM Press, 1966), 25.

[7] Q. in Hastings, *History*, 297.

[8] Cross, *Oxford Dictionary*, s.v. "Henson," 637.

as a spiritual director and author, and C. S. Lewis, the Oxford don who was explicating "mere Christianity" to masses of radio listeners and readers.

Good books may have been the only abundant resource in the English church. Surely clergy were not. Numbers of ordinations continued to decline. In 1938, 4,554 curates assisted vicars; ten years later, the Church of England counted only 2,189. Because of the shortage, vicars in larger towns were in an increasingly perilous predicament, trying to maintain big parishes that could not be managed without a curate or two. Funds were nearly as scarce for parishes of any size. In smaller communities, too many clergy were

> trapped with diminished income in some vast historic vicarage with the servants gone, the curate gone, the Church school gone, only the damp rising. Even his horse was gone and he could seldom afford a car but was left with a cheap bicycle, "peddling laboriously up a country lane, with his shabby mackintosh flapping in the wind."[9]

Efforts to increase stipends, merge livings, and sell those old vicarages did not even begin until mid-century. As a result, the Church of England found itself struggling to maintain the pretenses of its past, which left it alienated from its population, and from its century.

One of those pretenses was England's being the center of Anglican energy. From Pearl Harbor into the postwar era, Britain came to rely increasingly on its American cousin, even in its culture and religion.[10] When Britons attended the Pan-Anglican Congresses in 1954 in Minneapolis and 1963 in Toronto, they found wealthy, generous, dynamic churches in North America that often put to shame the ancient, underpopulated, and threadbare, if not bombed-out, buildings at home.[11] The daughter churches were

---

[9] Hastings, *History*, 437–438 (q. from Beverly Nichols, *A Pilgrim's Progress*).

[10] Hastings, *History*, 362.

[11] John Stoward Moyes, *America Revisited* (Sydney, Australia: Church Publishing Co., 1955), 35; cf. Paul A. Welsby, *A History of the Church of England 1945–1980* (n.p.: OUP, 1984), 24, 28.

outshining their mother, and their voices would be heard more and more.

Those congresses made clear, as no Lambeth Conference ever had, that Anglicanism had become international, interracial, diverse, and much less clerical. Lay men—and women—also began to attend the congresses, sometimes attired in flowing African robes or elegant Japanese kimonos, all demolishing stereotypes of Anglicanism as an English men's club.[12] Meanwhile, as the Union Jack was lowered over erstwhile colonies and flags of newly independent nations flew in its place, the equation of the British Empire with the Anglican Communion would no longer hold. The 1958 Lambeth Conference took steps to define new relationships and create new entities, including the position of Anglican Executive Officer, which—tellingly—was first held by an American, Stephen Bayne. The Communion was entering a new era.

Meanwhile, the idea of the priest as ministerial representative was flourishing anew.

THE NEW IDEALS OF CLERGY AND LAITY

What Moberly proposed, others picked up, elaborated, included in official statements, and embedded in Prayer Book revisions. The ideal of a ministerial priesthood was becoming the official teaching of Anglicanism. We will glance at how two Americans adopted Moberly's ideas, then take four examples of English perspectives before exploring at greater depth the theological consensus that developed.

Two American Views

In discussions of orders, Americans had largely remained quiet. One of the first bishops consecrated on American soil, John Henry Hobart, declared in 1815, "Apart from its divine origin, the office of the ministry is connected with the very existence of religion. There never was, and there never can be, a religion without

---

[12] Moyes, *America Revisited*, 34.

a priesthood."[13]

But American theologians of stature were rarer than Episcopalians at tent meetings. Working primarily in seminaries rather than in universities as English writers generally did, their writings took an even more practical bent with parish ministry in mind.[14] For their inspiration, Americans looked to their English mother church, to Lightfoot and Hort and Hatch, and in due course to Gore, and then to Moberly.

Charles Henry Brent (1862–1929) is one who indicates the degree to which clergy in the field adapted Moberly's thinking. A Canadian by birth and a parish priest in Boston, Brent was consecrated missionary bishop of the Philippines in 1901 and became a leading light in the worldwide ecumenical movement. He quoted *Ministerial Priesthood* nearly as soon as it appeared, in ways that underscored the link between priest and people.

For Brent, the representative nature of priesthood and the way in which it related priest with people was pivotal. "The functional peculiarities are as few as the representative duties are many. The priestly life is mainly, though not solely, the intensification of fundamental relations with God and man...and the ideal priesthood...is but the perpetual and living reminder to the laity of what they should be and do."[15] Fifteen years later, he returned to the idea that "the clergy are not the Church." Laity are one with the clergy, "inasmuch as they form an integral part of the organism."[16] Thus, Brent advised English ordinands in 1910 that a member of the clergy should "not separate himself from, but...unite himself to his fellows, and...stimulate others likewise to exalt their commission that they too may be bond-slaves of the Lord and servants of

[13] Q. in A. H. Baverstock, "The Theology of Priesthood," in Herbert S. Box, ed., *Priesthood* (London: SPCK, 1937), 21 (from Hobart's First Charge, p. 6, q. by William Denton, *The Grace of the Ministry Considered as a Divine Gift* [1872]. Note that in this case, an English writer refers to an American bishop).

[14] Cf. David Holmes, *A Brief History of the Episcopal Church* (Valley Forge, PA: Trinity Press International, 1993), 161–162.

[15] Charles H. Brent, *With God in the World*, 1899 (New York: Longmans, Green, and Co., 1908), 130–131.

[16] Charles H. Brent, *The Inspiration of Responsibility* (New York: Longmans, Green, and Co., 1915), 100–101.

men." Their "commission does not come trickling down the ages from a distant source, with perhaps some leakage on its journey. The connection is with heaven. Your ministry is received from Jesus Christ." Yet this commission "also has its human side," coming "through, as it is for, the whole Church."[17]

Another American, Francis J. Hall (1857–1932), claimed for himself the distinction of attempting the first Anglican systematic theology anywhere.[18] Anglican tradition, lacking the central authority of Roman Catholics or great teachers like Luther and Calvin, has not been inclined to systematic thinking. Still, Hall was a surprising candidate for the honor: an Anglo-Catholic from Chicago who taught at General Seminary, not nearly so well-known or mainstream as a William Porcher DuBose. Nonetheless, in ten volumes Hall submitted "a connected treatment of the entire range of Catholic Doctrine as it is maintained in the Episcopal Church and the Reformed Catholic Tradition of the Anglican Communion." *Dogmatic Theology* became required reading for the higher-church ilk well into the twentieth century.[19]

Like Moberly, Hall envisioned the church as an assembly of saints, the visible Body of Christ, a living organism marked by sacramental life. Its ministry is appointed by the Spirit and vitally related to the Body. The outlines of that ministry emerge, however obscurely, with the clear tradition of three orders of apostolic origin and divine prescription, essential to the church's corporate life and sacramental function, and dependent upon episcopal ordination.[20] Within the organic church, all baptized Christians are "interiorly" related to each other and to Jesus their head. Those appointed to be "ministers of Christ" and the faithful likewise relate to each other in a manner "fundamentally organic and interior." In sacrament, they

---

[17] Charles H. Brent, "A Glorious Ministry," in *Prisoners of Hope, and Other Sermons* (New York: Longmans, Green, & Co., 1915), 176–178.

[18] Francis J. Hall, *Introduction to Dogmatic Theology* (1912; reprint, Pelham Manor, NY: American Church Publications, 1970) vii, 4.

[19] Hall, *Dogmatic Theology*, 122–123.

[20] Hall, *The Church and the Sacramental System* (1920; reprint, Pelham, NY: American Church Union, 1967), 44–45, 46.

are not external to the Body, as substitutionary agents for its members. They are organically one with the baptized, and in their appointed ministry act not only as agents commissioned by Christ but also, and in spite of anything they can do, as organs through which the faithful at large function as well as they.... [T]here cannot, rightly speaking, be any real coming of the Church's ministers between Christian souls and God.

Therefore, all share in the priestliness of the Body. "All the faithful function in what [the priest] is appointed to do, as well as he. He acts ministerially and the laity, participatively, but the action is corporate and organic."[21] Hall essentially repeated what Gore and Moberly had been saying and, accordingly, continued, "There is but one priesthood; and the participation in it of ministers and laymen is equally real, is equally grounded in membership of Christ's Body, and is unalterably conditioned by interior organic relations which preclude external substitution or intervention by ministers between the laity and Christ." Any difference between the priest and the layperson—and the difference is real—is not one of kind but of function and office.

> The "priest" technically so called has an official or ministerial part in it, whereas the rest participate in his priestly ministrations unofficially and personally. He is their leader and organ, but the function is as truly theirs as it is his. This function is organic, an act of the Body of Christ, and the ministerial organs are organs of the Body.

As the "machinery of the Kingdom," the church functions as "the organized and organic instrument and agency for extending the Kingdom." Because of the headship of Christ, "the Kingdom and the Church are inseparably united."[22]

In two respects, however, Hall showed his American bias. He mistrusted church-state involvement. Lacking "'coercive' jurisdiction," which properly belongs to the secular, the church will invariably suffer from alliance with the state. He warned, too, against the

---

[21] Hall, *Church*, 52–54; Hall quotes both George and Robert Moberly (54).

[22] Hall, *Church*, 62–63, 101, 105–106.

church's becoming "a synonym for the clergy, who are regarded as a self-centered and largely secularized caste."[23] Brent would have agreed.

In their understandings of church and ministry, the two gave a New World expression to the thought of Gore, Moberly, and the catholic school at large. And yet by no means did they speak for all Episcopalians.

AN ENGLISH SAMPLER

England, meanwhile, continued to produce a diversity of perspectives.

An Evangelical: W. H. Griffith Thomas (1861–1924)

Lightfoot died before Moberly took him to task. His defender appeared in the person of the Evangelical teacher and writer W. H. Griffith Thomas. In *The Catholic Faith* (1911) and his posthumously published introduction to the Articles of Religion entitled *The Principles of Theology* (1930), Thomas called Moberly's concept of "ministerial priesthood" a "contradiction in terms."[24]

The church, for Thomas, is not an organic entity but an aggregation of individuals, saved by Christ yet joined in community. Its priesthood, derived from the high-priesthood of Christ alone, is one of all.[25] No "class" of believers may exclusively claim spiritual functions, much less constitute a specific order; this is unknown, he says, in New Testament times. Indeed, no function of the "priesthood" is forbidden to any believer, "of either sex, whatever or wherever they may be."[26]

He does distinguish between "priesthood" and "ministry," though, with differences in function existing in the latter but not in the former. "Ministry" should fulfill two primary purposes: evangelism and edification. The "minister" is primarily a preacher and teacher. Christ commissioned the church to preach the gospel

---

[23] Hall, *Church*, 109; cf. Liddon, *Sermons*, 193–200.

[24] W. H. Griffith Thomas, *The Principles of Theology* (London: Church Book Room Press Ltd., 1956), 317.

[25] Thomas, *Principles*, 316; W. H. Griffith Thomas, *The Catholic Faith* (London: Longmans, Green and Co., 1911), 379.

[26] Thomas, *Catholic Faith*, 375ff., 382; cf. *Principles*, 318.

and to pronounce forgiveness; the presbyter thus serves as God's prophet—the one who brings God's word to humankind—and announces (without bestowing) God's remission of sins.[27]

By no means, then, is the presbyter a "priest" in the sense of a sacerdotal mediator who brings humanity to God, much less as one who offers sacrifice. If Lightfoot was implicitly refuting T. T. Carter, Thomas echoed Lightfoot's argument to refute the more subtle sacerdotalism he alleged of Moberly. Thomas accused Moberly of asserting a priesthood that will "act *for* the body and *through* the body, in the sense of not being *immediately* in contact with the Head,"[28] and thereby contravene the priesthood of all believers. Where Moberly would reinsert the presentation of eucharistic vessels at ordinations, Thomas rejoiced in the absence of the symbol.[29]

Yet Thomas's argument offered little help. He often contradicted himself.[30] Worse, he fell into the same trap that (in Moberly's judgment) caught Lightfoot: though he traced "presbyter" to the Greek *presbuteros* and alleged that the Prayer Book consistently used the term "priest" in that sense of "elder," he attacked ordained "priesthood" as if it derived solely from the sacerdotal (*hiereus*).[31] Although he called the Ordinal's exhortation to the new presbyter "a truly remarkable picture of pastoral life and work" and quoted the words accompanying ordination ("Receive the Holy Ghost"), he confined the presbyteral role to his categories

---

[27] Thomas, *Catholic Faith*, 382, 293–294; cf. *Principles*, 315–316, 318, 329, 321.

[28] Thomas, *Catholic Faith*, 380; cf. *Principles*, 317–318.

[29] Thomas, *Principles*, 328; cf. Moberly, *MP*, 288–289.

[30] For several examples: "The Church is an institution, intended solely for the present," but a few pages later, "The true Church, or Body of Christ, is thus invisible by reason of the vital union of its individual members with Christ..." (*Principles*, 266, 279); nonetheless, he dismisses Moberly's use of "Body of Christ" imagery as "unsafe...if not perilous" (*Catholic Faith*, 379). He lauds the pastoral nature of ministry but confines the exercise of ministry into the primary category of the prophetic (*Catholic Faith*, 294, vs. 382; see *Principles*, 315). He claims in one place that "'High' views of the Church often mean low views of Christ," but in another, "The best way of meeting [wrong views of] Apostolic succession is a high doctrine of the Church" (*Principles*, 279, 337).

[31] Compare Thomas, *Catholic Faith*, 291 and 376ff.

of evangelization and edification.[32] Little in his priestly job description is sacramental or pastoral. He also may have been lured into a danger that (some said) had caught Moberly: setting up straw men too easily knocked down. Thomas's dismissals of a *ministerial* priesthood cause one to wonder if he understood what Moberly wrote.

Thomas nonetheless agreed with Moberly on some points. Both emphasized the unity between pastor and people, as in the voice of the laity (however muted) in choosing clergy.[33] Despite his tendency to understate the sacramental, he still perceived that "[b]ehind the outward life is Divine grace, and only as grace is realised can the visible be realised and expressed in the invisible and spiritual." They concurred that, in Thomas's words, "The Christian on earth is to correspond with the purpose of the Church in God's sight."[34]

In the end, though, Thomas's picture of the church was not compelling enough to draw an admiring audience: too vague, too contradictory, too unclear as to what the clerical role should be, and therefore too muddy as to the laity's purpose too. As Robin Greenwood observed decades later, "The unquestionable verdict of history is that it was Moberly's powerful paradigm, rather than that articulated by Thomas, that received general acceptance."[35] Yet, though hidden within the shade of Moberly's ascendance, the perspective of Thomas and Lightfoot reappeared at the twentieth century's close.

An Anglo-Catholic: A. H. Baverstock and Sacerdotalism Revived

If Thomas assaulted Moberly's thesis from the Evangelical side, Alban Henry Baverstock (1871–1950) snipped at it from the Catholic side. His reaffirmation of high clericalism, far beyond Hall's, appeared in his 1917 book, *Priesthood in Liturgy and Life*, and an essay two decades later, which expanded his theology of priesthood.

---

[32] Thomas, *Catholic Faith*, 292–293, 382; *Principles*, 320–321.

[33] Thomas, *Catholic Faith*, 295–296; *Principles*, 316. Cp. Moberly, *MP*, 89.

[34] Thomas, *Principles*, 270.

[35] Greenwood, *Transforming Priesthood*, 11.

Baverstock accepted the priestliness of Christ's body in which "every member of the Church is therefore, in a true sense, a priest." A "ministerial priesthood," however, is "more than the authoritative expression...of priestly powers inherent in the whole body." Instead, the clerical priesthood "is given to a special class" and "is the glory of the Catholic Church, and essential to her existence."[36] While all the baptized constitute the "royal priesthood" of Scripture, the ordained priests are associated with Christ in his divine priesthood. "He and they alone may perform priestly functions." But it is more than what they *do* that sets priests apart from laity and deacons. As the service of God exceeds the service of man, so "priesthood differentiates the priest from the congregation as the shepherd is differentiated from the flock, the ruler from the subjects." For Moberly, priests share in governing; Baverstock defines the role as outright rulership.[37]

He softened his boldness somewhat with themes reminiscent of Moberly. The priest is representative of the church, which offers itself to its Lord; his priesthood emerges especially, not in Eucharist, but in his "self-oblation to God for man.... He is led to live in daily, hourly dependence" upon God's grace so that his life becomes, like that of Christ, a "liturgy."[38]

Although his old-fashioned, high-Catholic opinions ignored the previous fifty years' scholarship,[39] Baverstock made several helpful points about the ordained. For one, he warned against overemphasizing the "manward aspect" of Jesus' life as nine-

---

[36] A. H. Baverstock, *Priesthood in Liturgy and Life* (London: Faith Press, 1917), 25.

[37] Baverstock, "Theology of Priesthood," 21, 12; cf. *Priesthood in Liturgy and Life*, 29. The concept is not foreign to English soil, however; the term "rector," for instance, derives from the Latin *regere*, "to rule," and entails certain legal powers and privileges. Recalling 1 Peter 5:3 cautioning against elders' "being lords over God's heritage," the American Walter Lowrie suggested that "the Rector would do well to forget it" (*Ministers of Christ* [Louisville: Cloister Press, 1946], 3).

[38] Baverstock, "Theology of Priesthood," 14–15, 26; cf. *Priesthood in Liturgy and Life*, 33–34.

[39] He belittles "modern theories which impute to Our Lord some degree of ignorance," and only by critical implication cites Moberly or, for that matter, any other author we have been studying (Baverstock, "Theology of Priesthood," 10; cf. *Priesthood in Liturgy and Life*, 25).

teenth-century liberalism had done, lest "its primary, priestly character, as a life lived for God" be lost. The result, he feared, is "a humanised and degraded conception of religion" in which the church becomes an institution for human conversion rather than a temple for God's worship; a cleric then becomes a preacher rather than a priest "ministering to God," and religion "a satisfaction of man's need" rather than "a yielding to God's claim."[40] Baverstock's priest holds a job description nearly opposite to Griffith Thomas's.

For another, although he cared little about how the episcopate came to be, Baverstock treasured the bishop as a "chosen instrument of the living Lord, present with His Church." Therefore, he affirmed (as Thomas also acknowledged) that the universal, timeless unity of the church is symbolized in each diocese in the person of the bishop. The bishop, to Baverstock, is foremost a priest—one who has the "fullest expression" of priesthood because, being able to ordain, he possesses the fullness of sacramental authority (as *summum sacerdotium*) above and beyond that of the "ordinary priest" (*inferius sacerdotium*). Speaking of the "historic episcopate," Baverstock insists, "An episcopate divorced from the idea of priesthood could hardly be described as historic." Since that is not the case, but rather the bishop is "principal representative...of the great High Priest" in the diocese, the parish priest derives his authority from the bishop. The parish priest has become "the ordinary custodian in his own sphere of those sacraments which he administers." But the bishop "can do nothing, constitutionally, apart from his priests"; his powers are "constitutionally exercised synodically." To put Baverstock's point in contemporary language, the priest, whether a presbyter or bishop, acts sacramentally as a functionary of Christ (*in persona Christi*, i.e. "in the person of Christ"), but in governance acts as a representative of the church.[41]

If between bishop and priest there is a theological gully, surely between the priest and layperson is a great gulf fixed. All priesthood (which for Baverstock includes bishops as well as presbyters)

---

[40] Baverstock, "Theology of Priesthood," 8.

[41] Baverstock, "Theology of Priesthood," 17–18, 22–24.

is a divine gift resulting from a "special vocation." "The Christian cannot make himself a priest: he must be authoritatively designated and admitted to his office." The Spirit's sevenfold gifts, given to all Christians at their confirmation, said Baverstock, are imparted for special purpose at priestly ordination. For Baverstock, they have indeed become a special class, separated and distinct from the laity who, to be sure, have an exalted place,[42] but a quiet one.

Like Carter before him, Baverstock extolled the ordained priesthood to heights beyond what all but the most fervent Anglo-Catholic would aspire. But as with Carter, Baverstock received little reaction. His was an extreme view, opposite that of Thomas. And, as Thomas's ideas would reappear in later decades, so would Baverstock's. But for the moment, both were largely ignored. The mainstream was flowing too strongly in the more Liberal Catholic directions of Gore and Moberly—and away from what were increasingly antiquated ideas—to pay much notice or be bothered.

A Scholar: Burnett Hillman Streeter (1874–1937) and the Primitive Church

B. H. Streeter spent his entire career as a New Testament scholar and theologian at Queen's, his Oxford undergraduate college. Known primarily for his work in the gospels, he visited Harvard in 1928 to lecture on a new way of early church governance, an understanding that departed significantly from established views. Lightfoot had believed episcopate developed from presbyterate. On the Continent, Harnack, relying on the *Didache,* proposed that a "universal" ministry co-existed with a "local" variety, the first composed of apostles, prophets, and teachers, the latter of pres-byter-bishops and deacons. Conversely, Streeter pointed to the diversity of the early church in its doctrine and its use of Scripture, and wondered if the same diversity applied in its governance and ministry. Comparing ancient churches, he concluded that apostles had not laid down a single system of order. Like a growing organism, the first-century church adapted its organization to meet

---

[42] Baverstock, "Theology of Priesthood," 24; cf. *Priesthood in Liturgy and Life,* 32. "The greatness of the privileges conferred upon the layman can scarcely be exaggerated.... His character is priestly.... He is a King's son:... But his royalty is not that of those set to bear rule in the Church" (Baverstock, *Priesthood in Liturgy and Life,* 30).

early church complex
far too to function within one form of governance

changing needs from place to place. "Uniformity was a later development; and for those times it was, perhaps, a necessary development." Whoever, then, justified a particular ecclesial structure on the basis of early precedents could find whatever he or she wanted.[43]

Streeter was not so much original as articulate. He gave a different twist to what was becoming a familiar idea: that the primitive church was far too complex to function within one simple form of governance. He lent the prestige of a respected scholar to growing doubts about the clarity of ministerial origins.

A Bishop: Herbert Hensley Henson (1863–1947)

The story goes that Cosmo Lang, who preceded Temple as Archbishop of York, was showing Bishop Hensley Henson of Durham the archiepiscopal portrait gallery. When they arrived at Lang's own likeness, he said, "You know, Henson, I don't like it; it makes me look proud, pompous, and prelatical." Henson replied, "To which of those adjectives does your Grace take exception?"[44]

The story probably is apocryphal but characteristic of Henson. Opinionated, acerbic, independent, Henson cut an especially colorful figure on the English bench of bishops. After ordination he dropped his High Church sympathies to express a more relaxed and latitudinarian approach in the many books he produced. When the more controversial of his theories aroused opposition to his consecration as Bishop of Hereford in 1917, he seemed to renounce them. Soon translated to Durham, he served as its bishop from 1920 to 1939 and became, decades later, the model for the bishop in the highly popular novels of Susan Howatch (who used fragments of his letters as epigrams for her chapters).[45] Henson was hardly typical of his fellow bishops. Nonetheless, his sermons and his addresses to candidates for ordination hint at what one member of the hierarchy was thinking at the time.

Contrary to Thomas, Henson found the essence of the ordained commission not in preaching and teaching but rather in

---

[43] B. H. Streeter, *The Primitive Church* (London: Macmillan and Co., 1929), 261, ix.

[44] Ronald Preston, "William Temple: The Man and his Impact on Church and Society," in *Archbishop William Temple: Issues in Church and Society 50 Years On* (Manchester: William Temple Foundation, 1994), 15, n. 4.

[45] Cross, *Oxford Dictionary*, s.v. "Henson," 637; e.g. Susan Howatch, *Glittering Images* (New York: Ballantine Books, 1988).

1 Peter
pres —
elder / pastor /
shepherd

preaching and serving. These are inseparable duties that are "distinctive of Christ's religion."[46] As opposed to Baverstock's notion of rulership, Henson emphasized the terms drawn from 1 Peter for the presbyter as "elder" and as "pastor or shepherd." Lauding Lightfoot's *Christian Ministry* ("still...the most adequate and satisfying treatment of the subject"), he commended what he deemed to be New Testament teaching on apostolic witness, by which "we think of ourselves mainly as pastors, preachers, stewards, the servants of the people for Christ's sake." Henson considered his church to be "divinely guided" by its Ordinal's subordinating— without eliminating—the sacerdotal element to the pastoral[47]: Priesthood is deeply ministerial.

The ordained life at the same time is deeply practical: Henson spoke as a master to apprentices on the verge of their careers. Priesthood has all the elements of a profession, for instance. Its practice requires an "efficiency"—he means *proficiency*—equal in its way to that of a doctor, lawyer, or schoolmaster. Ministry requires adequate education, practical knowledge, the ability to win public confidence, a sense of the discipline of the office, and avoidance of unprofessional conduct. For all its pragmatism, though, ordination also represents a response to a divine summons and the gift of a divine commission. But that commission is mediated by the church, and so it necessitates a willingness to accept "the doctrine and discipline of the Church" from which the ordinand seeks the commission.[48] The Godly summons, then, must be grounded in the realities of life within the Christian community.

AN "OFFICIAL" SYNTHESIS

Just prior to World War II, there emerged a consensus of English thinking on the nature of orders, ministry, and the church. A synthesis of ideas similar to Moberly's, this consensus was evident in the writings of major theologians, bore the stamp of a major doctrinal commission, and was propounded by no less than two

---

[46] Herbert Hensley Henson, *Ad Clerum* (London: Hodder and Stoughton, 1937), 44.

[47] Henson, *Ad Clerum*, 213–216.

[48] Henson, *Ad Clerum*, 144–145 (cf. 165), 153, 157.

Archbishops of Canterbury. With that backing, it dominated eccle-siology for most of the remaining twentieth century.

Five writers contributed to, exemplified, and solidified this consensus. William Temple (1881–1944) was almost foreordained to ecclesial prominence: son of an Archbishop of Canterbury, he became in quick order an Oxford fellow, a headmaster, the rector of a posh London parish, a canon of Westminster Abbey, then Bishop of Manchester, Archbishop of York, and, from 1942 until his death, Archbishop of Canterbury. He was renowned as a seeker of synthesis, whether trying to mediate labor disputes in Manchester or nurturing the nascent ecumenical movement.[49] So accomplished was Temple in the ways of conciliation, accommodation, and compromise that a dean of St. Paul's, London, opined that had Temple chaired the Council of Nicaea, the church would not have lost the Arians. He was a figure of substance, so corpulent that he had to squeeze sideways into the pulpit of the Church of St. Mary the Virgin, Oxford, to deliver a University Sermon, and so conse-quential that he was generally deemed the outstanding British church leader of his century.[50]

Temple admired the theological work of Oliver Chase Quick (1885–1944). Professor at Durham (1934–39), then Christ Church, Oxford (1939–43), Quick brought to the consensus the independence of a scholar who carefully avoided any particular school or party within the Church of England.[51]

By contrast, Kenneth Kirk (1886–1954) was an unabashed Anglo-Catholic. His first books helped to revive interest in moral theology in the 1920s, and his 1928 Bampton Lectures, published as *The Vision of God*, was a long and learned treatise on the mystical life. He edited the essays in *The Apostolic Ministry* (1946) on episcopacy in particular and ministry in general from a High Church viewpoint.[52]

---

[49] F. A. Iremonger, "Temple," *DNB*, 6th Suppl. (1941–50), 870; Welsby, *History*, 4.

[50] Preston, "Temple," 6 (quoting W. R. Matthews); 4. For the story of the sermon, I am indebted to the Rev. Canon Reginald Fuller, who was present in the congregation.

[51] See *DNB*, 6th Suppl. (1941–50), s.v. "Quick," 702.

[52] See Eric Kemp's biographical sketch in *DNB*, 7th Suppl. (1951–60), s.v. "Kirk," 589–591.

Among Kirk's essayists was a leading liturgist of the day. Arthur Gabriel Hebert (1886–1963) was a crucial force in making the liturgical movement on the Continent widely known in England. Through his books and his efforts to make the parish communion the central focus of worship in the Church of England, he tried eagerly to reveal to average parishioners the inherent connections he saw in the Eucharist between the mysteries of divine action and the realities of daily life.

When Temple died, Geoffrey Fisher became primate, followed by Arthur Michael Ramsey (1904–88). A professor of divinity at Durham and Cambridge and author of *The Gospel and the Catholic Church* (1936), Ramsey was nominated by Winston Churchill to the see of Durham in 1952. As bishop there, and as Archbishop of York (1956–61) and Canterbury (1961–74), he provided himself time for study and writing, such that he and Temple rank among the most-published of primates.[53] His work was perhaps the most recognizable influence upon Anglican thought from mid-century into the 1970s.

Three of these five—Hebert, Kirk, and Ramsey—were associated with the church's catholic wing. However, the consensus on ministry embraced a broader span of the Church of England, as can be seen in the report of the Commission on Christian Doctrine. The two English primates appointed this commission in 1922 to thrash out what the Church of England believed, against a backdrop of controversies between Anglican Evangelicals and Catholics, and between liberal theologians and traditionalists. The task was monumental enough to take fourteen years; a final report did not appear until 1937. Given the relatively new ecumenical climate, the commission took special care to clarify its church's understanding of ministry in order to encourage budding conversations with other denominations. Two of the five, Quick and Temple, served on the commission (Temple as its chairman from 1925 onward), but rather than reflecting the views of any one individual or any one church party, the report aimed to speak for the entire church with an inclusiveness that embraced its various segments and an authority that rose above them. It carried, therefore, a veritable seal of episcopal approval as a statement of what

---

[53] Owen Chadwick, *Michael Ramsey: A Life* (Oxford: OUP, 1991), 74.

the whole Church of England believed. And, in that era, what the Church of England believed, the Communion still accepted.

What did that consensus entail?

The Role of History and Scholarship

By the end of the nineteenth century, scholars had begun to challenge assumptions of a millennium. For instance, how much should the study of the church's history, through Scripture and ancient writers, influence the church's contemporary life? For a church that counted tradition as one of the bases of its authority, this was no idle question.

Theories were lauded or deprecated, often depending upon the author's ecclesial leanings. Hall, the High Churchman, deemed inadequate the historical evidence contrary to his position. "Does modern knowledge of sub-apostolic developments in the Church afford proof that the catholic doctrine of the ministry and, in particular, of apostolic succession, is erroneous?" Thirteen pages later, he answers, "no."[54] Hall avoided trying to decipher what the apostles did. A dozen years later, Streeter, the less partisan academician, seriously doubted that their acts could be deciphered at all. The twelve did not lay down a single system of order, he claimed, but instead the church like an organism just grew, and its organization varied in form to meet various needs in various places. Intentionally or not, Streeter applied Moberly's "Body" metaphor, but with an implication that would have nonplussed Moberly: that one could find nearly whatever ecclesial structure a person could wish.[55] With that in mind, the archbishops' commission cautioned (as had Hort), "We must beware of reading back into the earliest period the systematic organization of later times."[56] By the 1940s, Kirk was interested in but not preoccupied with historical precision. As the means of grace in word and sacrament took time to develop, he explained, so did the ministry of grace—though he also

---

[54] Hall, *Church*, 137, 150.

[55] Streeter, *Primitive Church*, 261, xi.

[56] Archbishops' Commission on Doctrine, *Doctrine in the Church of England: The Report of the Commission on Christian Doctrine Appointed by the Archbishops of Canterbury and York in 1922* (1938; London: SPCK, 1962). 115.

held that all ministries essentially grew out of apostolic foundations.[57]

In the very growth of the church, Ramsey saw a theological meaning that those tracing historical ecclesial development had been ignoring. Ramsey bubbled with frustration. "What does this development mean? is it an indifferent thing? or does it rather express some truth about the Body and the Gospel of God?" Echoing Newman's *Essay on the Doctrine of Development,* Ramsey observed that the very fact of change, and what those changes were, merit careful consideration. Simply to "burrow" the New Testament to find forms of ministry to replicate in modern times, Ramsey denounced as "archaeological religion." Rather, "to seek that form of ministry which the whole New Testament creates is the more evangelical way. And our view of the ministry had better be evangelical than archaeological."[58] Ramsey contended that the attempt to discern what the Bible conveys about ministry should *mean* something for the church. For him, Scriptures and Fathers spoke as clearly to his century as they did to theirs; and the more that moderns study them, the more moderns may learn. It was a solid Anglican approach. Patristic writings may not be able to specify how to govern the church of today, but they can do something far more significant: they can guide the spiritual life of the church of today (and indeed tomorrow) as surely as they guided the church of yesterday.

The Person of Christ

Ramsey figured in a renaissance of biblical study that took a "neo-orthodox" turn away from the previously dominant liberalism. Hebert and Temple did as well.[59] "Why anyone should have troubled to crucify the Christ of Liberal Protestantism has always been a mystery," wondered Temple, who considered Jesus a "miraculous Figure making stupendous claims."[60]

---

[57] Kirk, *Apostolic Ministry*, 8–9.

[58] A. Michael Ramsey, *The Gospel and the Catholic Church* (1936; reprint, Cambridge, MA: Cowley Publications, 1990) [GCC], 68–69.

[59] Cf. A. M. Hunter, *Interpreting the New Testament 1900–1950* (London: SCM Press, 1958), 126–132. Also, Hebert's esteemed *Throne of David* (1941) pondered how Christ and the church fulfilled the Old Testament.

[60] William Temple, *Readings in St. John's Gospel* (London: Macmillan and Co., 1940) [RSJG], xxiv. Cp. Baverstock, "Theology of Priesthood," 8.

Temple and others saw in Jesus a person very different from the one known to liberal Protestants of the nineteenth century, and because this new generation recognized a different person, they recognized also a different church. "[T]hat the Gospel and the Church belong together" was a perception the biblical movement realized anew, Ramsey reflected later. Evangelicals grew more aware of the church's place in the gospel, while High Churchmen comprehended it not only as an extension of the incarnation but arising from the Bible itself as a royal priesthood. The "principle of the Incarnation" retained the prominence it had begun to win in the previous century and in turn encouraged biblical criticism and historical investigation into Christian tenets; and the renewed interest in liturgy enhanced the sense of the church as "Body of Christ."[61]

Ramsey departed from over-reliance on incarnational doctrine by using Christ's passion as his point of origin in *The Gospel and the Catholic Church*. He sought to explain doctrines of the church, orders, ministry, and sacraments "not primarily in terms of an institution founded by Christ, but in terms of Christ's death and resurrection of which the one Body, with its life and its order, is the expression." Ramsey's incarnationalism embraces the cross, such that ecclesial forms and structures themselves help to convey the gospel proclamation; they are important (among many reasons) for their "*evangelical* meaning."[62]

Hebert expanded upon this application of the Incarnation to the life of the church. "Behind the forms of Redemption we must discern the Person of the Son of God; it is He who is *The Form of the Church*." The four credal "Notes of the Church"—unity, holiness, catholicity, and apostolicity—"apply to the Church only because they first apply in all their fulness to Him." Scriptures, creeds, sacraments, and ministry—specifically episcopal ministry—are "forms" that draw their meaning from their association with Christ. "The essential Forms of the Church all bear witness to the Son, and are the means of His operation through the Spirit. The

---

[61] Ramsey, *Era*, 143–144; A. G. Hebert, *Liturgy and Society* (1935; London: Faber & Faber, 1966), 105.

[62] Ramsey, *GCC*, 7, vii, emph. in orig.

Church exists that He may reign."[63]

One vital means of revealing Christ is worship. Ramsey admired the Orthodox Christians who believed that truth and tradition "reside in the Body as a whole; they are not something clerically imposed upon the Body." In consequence, "truth is very close to life and worship."[64] Hebert went a step further. Liturgy *reveals* ecclesiology. The church as the Body of Christ

> is not merely an organization to bring together a number of religious individuals, nor yet an institution with a quasi-legal claim to validity, but a society with an organic life, such as is best described by metaphors drawn from living things—she is the Bride of Christ, she is our Mother, she is the Body of Christ, of which He is the head and we the members.... And many of us are convinced that the apprehension of these things is closely connected with the recovery of the true place of the Holy Eucharist in the life of the Church; not merely as Sacrifice, not merely as Communion, but as Sacrifice consummated in Communion.

In those prewar days, before the term "Eucharist" and frequent reception of the sacrament became common, the Holy Communion (as it was called) was rarely celebrated, and, when and where it was, served as an opportunity for personal devotion. Hebert held a different vision. He argued that a parish Eucharist with communion of the people should be "the central act of service of worship on every Sunday—that service will teach us, by our participation in it, the meaning of the Fellowship of the Body more effectively than all our books of theology." That fellowship, moreover, is characterized by a unity like that of a Body—"not a unity of uniformity, but of manifold diversity, brought together into a living unity by the reconciling work of God through Christ." Like Moberly before him, Hebert claimed that this unity is not an ideal toward which Christians are to strive, but an existing fact whose meaning is to be "progressively realized."[65]

This unity of the Body extends beyond earthly bounds. As incarnation joins God and humanity in the person of Jesus, so is

---

[63] A. G. Hebert, *The Form of the Church* (London: Faber & Faber, 1947), 17, 51, 16, 136, emph. in orig.

[64] Ramsey, *GCC*, 148.

[65] Hebert, *Liturgy and Society*, 13, 151.

the church both human and divine. "As a human society, she comes in for criticism and blame. But her very nature and structure testifies [sic] to her Divine character. Her ground-plan is that of the Celestial City." This also has urgent social consequences, for,

> in a world which treats the factory-worker as a cog in the industrial machine, the forms of the Church still proclaim him to be called to be a child of God and an heir of eternal life, and in this world a member of a fellowship that is based not on his own self-interest nor yet on other people's ideals for his welfare, but on the will of the God who made him. The Church stands as the witness, against the world, of the right of a man to be treated as a human being.[66]

Hebert and his colleagues invited the onlooker to see through the church to its Head. Ministry means something because it exhibits its Lord. Those who look may behold the divine design.

The Church

The use of worship for personal devotion was consistent with a view of the church as an aggregation of individuals. It was an institution "intended solely for the present," Thomas declared, very much along lines Lightfoot had expounded.[67] But this view, reminiscent of mainstream nineteenth-century thinking, was giving way to a different way of understanding the church. As a later commentator observed (with some hyperbole), "The age of individualism has given place to one that hungers for the secret of true community."[68] Reconsidering the church was both an exercise in Christology and in pastoral theology.

Individually, and corporately through the doctrinal commission, theologians came to vastly different conclusions from those of fifty years before—for example, that Jesus intended to create a new society and that what resulted itself constitutes a revelation of God.[69] "Christ is the whole life of the Church," Temple asserted.

---

[66] Hebert, *Liturgy and Society*, 157–158.

[67] Thomas, *Principles*, 266–267.

[68] Hunter, *Interpreting the NT*, 135.

[69] Hunter, *Interpreting the NT*, 136–137. Cf. Gore's observation (*Ministry*, 63), cited in chapter 2 above.

He later explained that the "Spirit-bearing Body" lives, however imperfectly, by the life of its incarnate Lord. As Christ's Body in the world, the church "itself is the sacrament of human nature indwelt by God." As "the direct outcome of the divine act of the Incarnation and the continuance of its principle," it is not constituted by individuals coming together, but by "their actual union in response to the divine act."[70]

The church is a historical phenomenon, but as the Body of Christ it transcends the historical and human. The doctrinal commission inserted mystical and ecumenical elements by defining the church as "an object not only of sight, but of spiritual discernment or insight. It emerges in history, but it is essentially a Fellowship, constituted by a relation between God and Man, which in the last resort must be discerned and apprehended by faith." The church, then, "is the whole company of those who share in the regenerate life."

Therefore, the unity of the church is a central characteristic of the church. Though beset by human divisions, the commission acknowledged, the church retains "a real and concrete unity underlying these divisions," which may be expressed in common outlook, practices, and such forms as credal formulations, "the articulation of the ministry," and liturgical structure.[71] L. S. Thornton, another of Kirk's essayists, wrote that Christ "is the Body in virtue of what He is. We are the Body in virtue of the fact that we are united in Him, and only so. The Church is the unity of Christians in Christ with all that this implies."[72] Some took that implication to mean ecumenical cooperation and even ecclesial reunion. O. C. Quick composed his thoughts on the creed because "misunderstandings and differences of view" regarding the church "are a principal hindrance to that Christian reunion towards which the Holy Spirit to-day is surely directing our efforts."[73]

---

[70] William Temple, "The Church," in B. H. Streeter, ed., *Foundations* (London: Macmillan & Co., 1914), 341–342; *Christus Veritas* (London: Macmillan and Co., 1949) [CV], 234–235, 167–168.

[71] *Doctrine in the Church of England*, 105–106.

[72] L. S. Thornton, "The Body of Christ in the New Testament," in Kirk, *Apostolic Ministry*, 69.

[73] O. C. Quick, *Doctrines of the Creed: Their Basis in Scripture and Their Meaning To-Day* (New York: Charles Scribner's Sons, 1951), 272.

Unity, furthermore, is broader than denomination. Every writer worked against the backdrop of what Temple called in his enthronement sermon at Canterbury "the great new fact of our era."[74] Temple began advocating ecumenism from an early age, writing in 1914, "There is, and there can be, only one Church. However multiform its organization, however varied in degree of adequacy its interpretation, still in its adherence to that one fact it is one, with a unity not made by its members but by Christ." Unity, he explained in 1940, is precious not only for "strengthening the Church as an evangelistic agent"; it is also "in principle the consummation to which all history moves." Even more than unity in ecclesial structure, what matters is "the love of God in Christ possessing the hearts of men so as to unite them in itself" just as the Triune God is one. The solution to the "hideous fact of Christian divisions" must be "through personal union with the Lord so deep and real as to be comparable with His union with the Father."[75] Reunion was Hebert's concern too, as he studied the liturgical movements in continental Roman Catholicism. From first to last, Ramsey's work likewise took into account propositions and efforts aimed at reunion.[76]

Unity is inherent, too, in priestly ministry. Temple perceived it in the act of celebration:

> Every priest who by virtue of his Ordination celebrates the Holy Communion acts not only for the congregation there present, nor for all Christian people then living on the earth, but as the organ of the Body of Christ, the ministerial instrument of Christ active in and through His Body;...the congregation at that Holy Communion service is the Communion of Saints, with which the persons present, be they few or many, are there conjoined.

---

[74] Q. from *Personal Religion and the Life of Fellowship* in *William Temple's Teaching*, ed. A. E. Baker (Philadelphia: Westminster Press, 1951), 98, and from *The Church Looks Forward* in ibid., 99.

[75] Temple, "The Church," in *Foundations*, 342; *RSJG*, 320.

[76] Hebert, *Liturgy and Society*, 7–8. Cf. Temple, *The Church Looks Forward* (New York: Macmillan Co., 1944) [*CLF*], 16; Ramsey, GCC, 7, ch. 14. A. Michael Ramsey, *The Anglican Spirit*, ed. Dale Coleman (London: SPCK, 1991), 117–151. Kirk was skeptical of the ecumenical venture of the Church of South India insofar as how the reunion scheme viewed episcopacy (cf. *Apostolic Ministry*, e.g., 3, 7).

> Here therefore as in the Incarnation itself, we find the
> eternal in the midst of time, the secret of a fellowship
> against which the gates of death cannot prevail.[77]

A minor dispute had arisen over which came first, church or
ministry. Quick wondered whether the church derives validity
from sacraments and ministry, or whether sacraments and ministry take their validity from the church. Kirk, admitting that his
essayists would tend to stress the ministry side of the question,
considered the issue of priority akin to that of chicken and egg.
One requires the other: a shepherd is no shepherd without a flock,
even as the sheep depend upon the herder.[78] The faithful rely upon
their leaders, and vice versa.

The Priesthood of All Christians   *Hebrews*

Another element of Christology captured attention: the high-
priesthood of Christ, as articulated in the letter to the Hebrews.
From his high-priesthood emanated the "priesthood of all believers."
All continued to affirm the doctrine, from Hall and Baverstock to
Thomas, who gave it primacy of ecclesiological place. In a general
priesthood that incorporates all Christians, no "class" of believers
may make exclusive claim on spiritual functions, much less constitute a specific order. This was unknown in New Testament
times, Thomas said, and everyone nodded in agreement.

But then he added, no function of the "priesthood" is forbidden
to any believer, "of either sex, whatever or wherever they may
be."[79] Suddenly the old dispute between Lightfoot and Moberly
reared its contentious head once more. The "priesthood of all
believers" could become a "priesthood of each believer considered
by himself,"[80] Kirk warned, and that was just as unacceptable to
him as Baverstock's two-priesthood theory. Ramsey took a more

---

[77] Temple, *CLF*, 25–26.

[78] O. C. Quick, *The Christian Sacraments* (London: Nisbet & Co. Ltd., 1948),
133–137; Kirk, *Apostolic Ministry*, 31–32.

[79] Thomas, *Catholic Faith*, 375–382; and *Principles*, 316, 318. With that
thought, Thomas became one of the first to advocate, however implicitly, the
ordination of women.

[80] Moberly, *MP*, 72–73 (cf. chapter. 2, above); Kirk, *Apostolic Ministry*, 49.

nuanced position altogether. He mused to his ordinands, "Unique and unrepeatable is Christ's priesthood; but if we shrink from saying that Christians are to share in it, we seem compelled to say that Christians are called to reflect it."[81]

Sacrament and Worship

Christians reflect their corporate priesthood most explicitly in their worship, and most supremely in sacramental worship. But Temple looked beyond liturgy in considering what sacraments represent. The universe itself is "the perfect sacrament extensively" as the Incarnation is "the perfect sacrament intensively." Each expresses God's will. So the sacramental concept of outward and visible signs of God's grace find their meaning in the wider span of God's action in creation and redemption. In what the church names as sacrament, "as in Incarnation, we have specific acts of God; for of course the work of Grace accomplished by means of any Sacrament is the work of God Himself and not of His ministers except as instruments; and here, too, as in the Incarnation, we have the material made into the vehicle through which the Grace is given."[82] Temple resembles Moberly in the relation of inward/outward, and in the recognition that God may choose additional forms to convey his grace. He takes Moberly's position, too, on how sacraments convey God's grace, which is both in a psychological/spiritual process, and also by "an actual conveyance of spiritual meaning and power by a material process."[83]

Worship, then, as one event where God meets his people, opens to far more than the immediate experience at hand. In that sense (as if in retort to Lightfoot), Temple declares that "all worship is representative, not exclusive."

---

[81] Michael Ramsey, *The Christian Priest Today*, rev. ed. (London: SPCK, 1987), 107. Notice his careful preference for the verb "reflect" rather than "represent," which had become the more general term.

[82] William Temple, *Christ In His Church* (London: Macmillan and Co., 1925) [*CHC*], 27.

[83] Cf. Temple, *Nature, Man and God* (London: Macmillan, 1934) [*NMG*], 482, 484; on inward/outward, cf. *RSJG*, 78; *Thoughts on Some Problems of the Day* (London : Macmillan, 1931) [*TPD*], 125; cf. Moberly, *MP*, 46–56.

We set apart certain places as sacred, not to mark other places as profane, but to represent and remind us of the sanctity of all places. We set apart certain times as sacred, not to mark other times as secular, but to represent and remind us of the sanctity of all Time. We consecrate certain food and drink, not to mark other meals as non-religious, but to represent and remind us of the fact that all our food should build us up as members of the Body of Christ.[84]

Hebert likewise found liturgy and orders revealing the vastness of God's work. He concentrated on unity: "All the essential forms of the Church are forms of its unity," he asserted.

But it is Baptism and Eucharist that most evidently set forth the truth of Christian unity: the one as the sign of our incorporation into the body of Him who died and rose again, and the other of the membership in one body of those who partake of the one bread, while the minister of the Eucharist, whether he be the bishop in the diocese, or the priest in the parish, represents in his person the unity of the Church in that place."[85]

This realization led to a new discussion of ministry and priesthood.

Ministry

"The fundamental Christian Ministry is the Ministry of Christ." The doctrinal commission was unequivocal: "There is no Christian Priesthood or Ministry apart from His." Christ shares this ministry with his church, which derives whatever it does from him. "[E]very member has his place and share according to his different capabilities and calling." In the church's work of bringing "all the various activities and relationships of men under the control of the Holy Spirit," each member has a part.

Ordained ministry takes its meaning only "against the background of this universal ministry," the commission declared.[86] What it called a "formal" or "official" ministry is a subset of that of the whole Body. Vague though its history may be, a formal ministry is nonetheless "an original and essential element in the Church."

---

[84] Temple, CV, 242.

[85] Hebert, Form, 71.

[86] Doctrine in the Church, 114.

As well, "a distinction corresponding to that drawn later between Clergy and Laity— κλῆος [*kleros*] and λαός [*laos*]—is there from the outset." Even if a direct link cannot be proven between today's bishops and earliest apostles, still "Ministry exists in succession to the original Apostolate."

Ordained ministry, therefore, is both apostolic in heritage and grounded within the church as a whole. Moberly's influence can be seen. "The Ministry does not exist apart from the Body, nor the Body apart from the Ministry." But as Moberly also proposed, roles within the Body differ. Though Christ may call some to be prophets, evangelists, or teachers, within or outside established structures, the mutually shared ministry of all "does not mean that any member may perform any function indifferently, any more than every function of the human body can be performed indifferently by any limb. Each has its own function, and the one life of the body is expressed through the due performance by each of its own function."[87]

The medium of ministry, then, conveys a multifaceted message about the church itself. The commission declared, it is "essential to the idea of the Ministry...that it is an organ of the whole Church, not of a single group or Congregation"; that is, the church is catholic. "Continuity of ministerial commission embodies in the sphere of Order the principle of Apostolicity in the sense of continuous mission from Christ and the Father"; that is, the church is apostolic. As sacrament, Scripture, and creed all proclaim the kingdom, so does the church by what it is and does through ordained leadership. Ministry is "a symbol and effective instrument of the unity of the Church"[88]; that is, the church is one. And the church entrusts this message to certain parts of the body. William Temple summarized the point:

> The Church reserves to ministers duly ordained the right to "celebrate" the Eucharist....What is secured by a universally recognised ministry is that at every "celebration" the act is that of the whole Church through its accredited minister. The Bishop, in ordaining, acts in the name of

---

[87] *Doctrine in the Church*, 115 (cf. 117 on the disagreement of scholarship on ministerial origins), 116.

[88] *Doctrine in the Church*, 119.

the whole Church; the very meaning of his office is that he represents the Church Universal in one area—his diocese—and represents that area in the Church Universal.

A priest celebrates by commission of the entire church, a principle Temple extends to each form of ministry.[89]

Representative Orders and the Church

"Tomorrow," Michael Ramsey told those he was about to ordain, "you will receive [Christ's] commission and power to bring peace to many fretting lives."[90]

Who commissions? Is it Christ? Yes; he is always the ultimate minister. But who in the church conveys this commission on Christ's behalf—the apostles or the bishops who eventually assumed the apostles' role of leadership and who might be termed a "higher" authority? Or is it the "lower" authority of the church itself, the people? Given the doctrine of episcopal ordination in Anglicanism, what then is the bishop's role, and whom does the bishop represent? The doctrinal commission, and in varying ways the others we have been following, leaned toward the "higher" while answering, in effect, "both." While pastoral authority derives ultimately from Christ through the apostles, it is also representative of Christ's Body, the church.

The doctrinal report made two assertions. First, a continuous ministry "embodies" apostolicity. That is, "[t]he commission continuously given expresses the unceasing exercise of the pastoral oversight of the Good Shepherd" for his people. Apostles governed the early Christian community with an authority derived not from election by the flock but by the call of Christ. Subsequently,

> ministers of the Church in all later generations have possessed a pastoral authority as themselves holding commission from the Lord in succession to the Apostles, and the status of ministers in this succession has been guaranteed from one generation to another by a continuously transmitted commission.

---

[89] Temple, CV, 163.

[90] Ramsey, *Christian Priest Today*, 87.

Yet, no commission, however continuous, can suffice apart from the Body.

> [W]e cannot accept a conception of ordination which is exclusively hierarchical, as though the ministerial succession alone constituted the essence of the Church apart from any continuing body of the faithful, or, on the other hand, a conception which would make the ministry representative only of the congregation, or of the whole body of the laity, or, again, a conception which represents it as having its justification only in administrative convenience. The Ministry is to be regarded as having its entire existence and significance within the life of the Body as a whole. The fact that the ministry does not derive its commission from a Church which initially had no Ministry, but derives it, within the Church, from Christ Himself, the Head of the Church, His Body, does not involve the consequence that it can perform its function apart from the Body.[91]

The report needed somehow to reconcile the tension between the "higher" and "lower" authorities. It had to acknowledge the specific apostolic role while at the same time affirming the role of the church at large. That is, it had to ensure a place for bishops at ordinations but also a place for everyone else. So it borrowed a Moberlian conception in which orders are rooted in and connected with the whole church, functioning as a representative ministry only in connection with that Body, and deriving their authority *through* the church *from* Christ its head.

Furthermore, authority in the church is expressed both by means of the corporate faithful and also the apostolic leadership. But that leadership extends beyond episcopacy. The whole "ministry" shares this apostolicity. The doctrinal report asserted the point. So did Hebert.

> [C]an the Apostolicity of the Church be regarded as residing in the Bishops of the Church exclusively? Certainly not. To begin with, in an episcopal Church the parochial Minister exercises within the limited sphere of his parish the same Apostolic Ministry which the Bishop exercises in the wider sphere of his diocese. And in the

---

[91] *Doctrine in the Church*, 119–121

> present state of divided Christendom, we are bound to
> say that an apostolic function is laid upon every pastor
> and preacher, and that wherever the word of God is
> rightly preached the Apostolicity of the Church is in
> some measure present.[92]

In short, the function or purpose of one order is never limited to that order alone. The bishop may *represent* oversight without ever holding that role exclusively. (Of this, more in chapter 6.)

Ramsey, too, argued that orders should derive from the corporate life of the church. His approach contested centuries of assumption. What he characterized as an "Augustinian" view had dominated Western Christianity. Under this doctrine, forged in the complexities of fourth-century North African schisms, a person duly anointed with a Holy Order was given authority and power to exercise that ministry, knowing that it was Christ who is always the ultimate minister of any sacrament. Someone baptized with water in the name of the Trinity was truly baptized regardless of who did the baptizing—orthodox bishop, schismatic priest, heretical deacon, or even a layperson. By the same principle, which goes by the technical term of "*ex opere operato*,"[93] Anglicans consoled countless parishioners worried over the sad state of their clergy—and therefore themselves—with the twenty-sixth of their Thirty-Nine Articles, which assured that "the Unworthiness of the Ministers...hinders not the effect of the Sacraments." But, as O. C. Quick trenchantly noted, this Augustinian precept risks segregating sacrament and order from the church's life. It implied, for instance, "that a man, who has received ordination in some hole-and-corner fashion from a wandering bishop deprived of all office and jurisdiction, is fully and validly ordained."[94]

---

[92] Hebert, *Form*, 125.

[93] The term aims to express the objective nature of the sacraments as instruments of God, independent of the subjective attitudes of either the minister or the recipient. So long as sacraments are validly administered, they confer grace regardless of the merits or qualities of the ones administering or receiving them (though right dispositions of the recipient are necessary for grace to be really effectual). That is, God's act in the sacrament overrides any defect in the "doing" of the act, or of the "doer." Cf. Cross, *Oxford Dictionary*, s.v. "Ex Opere Operato," 493.

[94] Quick, *Christian Sacraments*, 143; he found this offensive to non-episcopal denominations as it implies that the "solemn authorization" they give is no ordination at all. On the danger of separation, see Ramsey, *GCC*, 154.

Ramsey found in Cyprian (a precursor to Augustine) a patristic alternative. For Cyprian, as interpreted by Ramsey, "validity of orders depended upon their derivation from and their exercise within the one life of the whole Church." Therefore, the "first fact must be the Church's corporate family life; then come valid orders which are an organ of that whole life." Temple concurred. "[T]he whole question of Orders and Sacraments must be considered in reference to the Church's life through the ages, and not with direct reference to the gift received by any individual at any given service."[95]

Orders, then, arise from the corporate Body, or, more precisely, from Christ *through* the Body. Christ can work his grace through the church to commission sacred ministers who will represent both the divine Godhead and the earthly Body.[96] Quick perceived a double intention and purpose in each ordination:

> On the one hand a divine gift of power for spiritual work is to be bestowed by God, as it were directly. On the other hand a certain solemn authorisation to act in the Church's behalf is to be conferred, also indeed from God as its ultimate source, but by God as working through the body of the Church which is Christ's Body.

The ordained minister is "a sacramental man. On the one hand he is a man of God ministering gifts of spiritual life to his fellows; on the other hand he is *persona ecclesiae*, and the true representative of those to whom he ministers, and of whom the ecclesia is composed."[97]

How that principle operates can be seen more fully in examining the laity, and the three orders of sacred ministry.

---

[95] Ramsey, GCC, 152. As Ramsey notes, Cyprian's view has the downside of denying the baptism and orders of schismatics or any who are not part of the "catholic" community. William Temple, *Church and Nation* (London, Macmillan, 1915) [CN], 111–112.

[96] Ramsey is not consistent on the point. Over thirty years after GCC, he declared, "Both Church and ministry are gifts of the divine Lord Jesus. He appointed twelve that they might be with him, and that he might send them forth.... The apostle draws his commission and authority from Christ alone, and he uses an authority given to him when in Christ's name he ordains and commissions the presbyters" (*Christian Priest Today*, 10).

[97] Quick, *Christian Sacraments*, 141–142.

1. *Laity*

By the 1930s, Moberly's expression of the priesthood of all Christians had been accepted to the point of being quoted almost verbatim by the doctrinal commission: Given Christ's self-offering, "the whole Church, as His Body, thereafter continues to be the sphere within which His mediatorial office is exercised."

> The fundamental priesthood of the Church is thus the priesthood of the whole Body. This is the meaning of the doctrine of the priesthood of the laity, a doctrine which does not mean that laymen are individually priests, but that the laity are, as such, members of that Body which is in its entirety priestly.

What is called "priesthood"—the commission here avoids "presbyterate"—as a result is representative "not either of the hierarchy or of the laity, but of the whole Body of Christ."[98]

In explaining the commission's thought, Quick announced, "We desire to preserve absolute equality of status both in privilege and duty, but to reserve to the clergy, both as representative agents of the whole society and as special experts within it, the functions which properly belong to them in these capacities." Despite whatever Baverstock may have said, sole supreme governance was *not* one of these functions. Rather, "the laity should exercise in reality the general control which is nominally theirs" in the Church of England. "But they must do so," he reiterated, "with due regard to the special functions for which the ordained ministry exists."[99]

Quick's comment revealed anew the ongoing tension between those things that all share in common and those diverse functions, offices, and roles that God's diverse people exercise in the church. On the one side was the unity of all. Hebert the liturgist commended the full liturgical inclusion of the laity as an inherent good and unifying restoration of right, and a necessary implication of the Eucharist. The elimination of the communion of the people, sometime between the sixth and twelfth centuries in the West, "fatally impoverished" the liturgy by stilling lay voices and making them "mute spectators at a ceremonial."

---

[98] *Doctrine in the Church*, 156–157.

[99] O. C. Quick, *The Testing of Church Principles* (London: John Murray, 1919), 113.

> We to-day know what that means. One of the worst symptoms of the diseased condition of Christendom to-day is the widespread passivity of the laity. Those who call themselves Christians do not feel themselves to be members of a body through the veins of which a flow of strong life is felt: they feel isolated and lonely, in their religion as in their social life.

Ramsey agreed, chastising Roman Catholic legalism, which tended to produce "a diminished sense of the oneness of the Body.... The church becomes viewed as an institution to which men submit and within whose world-wide structure men say their prayers and live their lives, rather than as a Body which *is* its members themselves."[100]

Yet such a Body is inherently diverse: this is the other side of the tension. A genuine catholicity gathers "into its unity all sorts and conditions of men...offering up to God and consecrating all their different occupations and ways of living: government, industry, commerce, finance; education, learning, and the arts; work on the land and the life of the villages."[101] Vocational diversity exemplifies this catholicity. Like the priesthood of all believers, vocation was a favorite notion of Martin Luther, notably articulated for Anglicans by William Law and summarized by Evelyn Underhill, who in 1924 observed, "It has always been the Christian view that every bit of work done toward God is a prayer."[102] Hebert hoped not "to make all these people religious, or at least persuade them to 'come to church'" but rather to "lead them to find out how God is to be glorified in all their ways of life, so that each shall see his daily duty as a vocation; and it must integrate all these different sorts of people into a community, a commonwealth, by showing them the meaning of their lives in the light of a common purpose."[103]

In exhorting each to find a vocation, Temple avoided defining "vocation" as "ordination." On the contrary, he told Oxford undergraduates in 1931,

---

[100] Hebert, *Form*, 74–75 (see *Liturgy and Society*, 81–86) [recall Liddon's plea]; Ramsey, *GCC*, 167.

[101] Hebert, *Form*, 102.

[102] Law, *A Serious Call to a Devout and Holy Life*; Evelyn Underhill, *The Ways of the Spirit* (New York: Crossroad, 1990), 77.

[103] Hebert, *Form*, 102.

Never imagine that vocation is to the ministry alone.
Every man has his own vocation, and must try to find it.
The work which has now to be done for God in this
world is not work for the clergy alone; it is the work of
the whole Church, the whole body of the disciples of
Christ, in which every man must be finding God's will
for him, and doing that.[104]

Laity and clergy, then, have different roles within the larger
work of the church. In Temple's day, some roles open to one were
actually prohibited to the other; the layperson could not officiate
at the Eucharist, yet the priest could not serve in Parliament. But
this difference of roles could be turned to advantage, such that
"the priest will stand for the things of God before the laity—who
seek the help that a religious specialist can give them, while the
laity stand for the things of God before the world."[105]

Clergy have the task of helping the laity stand before the
world, Temple continued. They are professionals—the nineteenth-
century trend extended into the twentieth. But being "professional"
can be a mixed blessing. Temple noticed that clergy can come
across to laity as holier than they, by taking their devotional practices, for instance, too seriously. But because devotions are part of
their daily work, clergy can refer to them flippantly, as part of professional shop talk, and thereby seem irreverent to laity. Quick,
however, saw great advantages to this "professional" caste in the
"religious specialist" who serves as a spiritual director. He advocated spiritual direction as an element of every priest's ministry but
the special vocation of some, making use of psychology and other
scientific knowledge, "not [for] the production of conformity to
rules even of Christian morality, but [for] the strengthening of
souls to take charge of their own lives through communion in the
life of Him Who is their wisdom and their righteousness." In other
words, he hoped for pastoral care, informed by "scientific"
advances, that would help laity to stand on their own feet, not just

---

[104] Temple, CN, 95; William Temple, *Christian Faith and Life* (London: SCM Press, 1931) [CFL], 137.

[105] Temple, RSJG, 163; cf. *The Hope of a New World* (New York: Macmillan Co., 1942) [HNW], 106, in virtually the same words.

for themselves, but for a world desperately in need of the social reform that a spiritually enabled laity could foster.[106]

Evangelism was an arena Temple envisioned for lay action. Spreading the gospel requires everyone, "not only the minister, but minister and congregation together." Effective Christian fellowship will appeal to those seeking God, but "quarrelsome or self-complacent" congregations will not. "The presupposition of effective evangelism, and the first step towards achieving it, is a truly dedicated Church." Achieving that makes the laity central; but so does evangelistic preaching. "It is impossible for clergy and ministers alone to preach the Gospel to the detached multitudes. If they are to be reached it must be by lay witnesses. Their testimony is the more effective because it is not professional."[107]

Laity, then, are full partners in a priesthood shared by all. Theory did not always match practice or solve all difficulties, as we shall see; but the fundamental point was made repeatedly by the doctrinal commission and individual writers alike: All Christians represent Christ and his church.

2. Priesthood

What is called "priesthood" and refers to "presbyterate," the doctrinal commission said, is representative "not either of the hierarchy or of the laity but of the whole Body of Christ."[108]

A priest is the agent of the Body, Temple reminded. If Christ is truly the Word-made-flesh, "then the sign of God's calling to this priesthood is to be found in the supreme privilege of knowing the only true God and Jesus Christ whom He has sent. All Christian people are therefore members of a fellowship that is charged with a priesthood to all the world." Christ as high priest culminates the principle of priesthood.[109]

Temple then intertwined several themes: the priesthood of all; a designated priesthood that is representative in nature; the dangers of sacerdotalism and its antidote, the Augustinian perception

---

[106] Temple, *RSJG*, 163; Quick, *Testing*, 126.

[107] Temple, *HNW*, 105.

[108] *Doctrine in the Church*, 156–157.

[109] Ramsey, *GCC*, 152. William Temple, *Fellowship with God* (London: Macmillan and Co., 1920) [*FWG*], 161.

of Christ's role in any sacrament. The people of God may all be called to be his priests, he began.

> But we cannot trust ourselves without further aid to fulfil our obligation, and therefore in the Church certain men are set apart for the specific office of priesthood, not in denial of the priesthood of others, but to represent and remind them of the priesthood of that whole Body of Christ, whereof we are members.... In every right priestly act, the agent is Christ Himself; and the Body of Christ on earth is not the clergy but the whole Church, which exercises certain of its priestly functions through the organs which exist for that purpose; but the act is the act of the whole Body.

He reiterated, "We are then all of us called to be priests unto our God."[110]

Temple tended to emphasize the presbyter as representing those who comprise the Body, that is, the human element. Ramsey accentuated the divine aspect: "The apostle draws his commission and authority from Christ alone, and he uses an authority given to him when in Christ's name he ordains and commissions the presbyters."[111] Each archbishop acknowledged that the priest represents both dimensions—the earthly and the divine—and does so through his very being.

Prayer is one way the priest exercises his nature. Ramsey recalled the high-priesthood of Jesus in exhorting his ordinands to pray for the people they will serve. Given Christ's example, priesthood means

> to *meet*, to *encounter*, to be *with* someone on behalf of or in relation to others. Jesus is *with* the Father; with him in the intimate response of perfect humanity; with him in the power of Calvary and Easter; with him as one who bears us all upon his heart, our Son of Man, our friend, our priest; with him as our own. That is the continuing intercession of Jesus the high priest.

---

[110] Temple, *FWG*, 164–165; cf. *RSJG*, 387 regarding the connection with the Holy Spirit.

[111] Ramsey, *Christian Priest Today*, 10. However, "the ordained ministry serves both" Christ and church, Ramsey said, "and indeed will have authority from both" (109).

> Now we can begin to see what is our own role as men
> of prayer, as priestly intercessors. We are called, near to
> Jesus and with Jesus and in Jesus, *to be with God with
> the people on our heart.* That is what you will be
> promising when I say to you "will you be diligent in
> prayers?". You will be promising to be daily with God
> with the people on your heart.

Morning and Evening Prayer, still required of every English
cleric, puts the priest "near God, with God" with intercessions on
his heart, Ramsey added. It also roots prayer in the Scriptures and
in the church's corporate prayer,[112] all as a sign of and exercise in
community with God and with God's church.

So the concept of a *representative* priesthood cannot be separated from Moberly's concern that it be *ministerial.* Prayer is service.
So too is preaching, which, for Ramsey, concerns "all that the
Church does to convey a message about Jesus, a message whose
heart and centre is Jesus." This kind of preaching includes homilet-
ics, but extends to so much more—indeed to all of Christian life.
Spiritual direction, too, especially in the traditional Anglican
model, "sees the priest's role more as that of a physician than that
of judge."[113]

Returning to the dual nature of God's people, Ramsey advised
that we "remember that the Church is both divine and human."

> It is *human,* inasmuch as its members all share in our
> sinful and fallible human nature. Thus our "we and
> they" talk about the Church melts into our contrition. It
> is *divine,* inasmuch as the principle of its life is the risen
> Jesus and the Holy Spirit, whose presence the sins of
> Christians never prevent being somewhere at work. Let
> us then be as critical, as discontented as we may be, and
> never complacent. But our discontent, without losing its
> integrity or its sharpness, will not turn into fretting if we
> remember that it is God who judges the Church in its

---

[112] Ramsey, *Christian Priest Today,* 14–15.

[113] Ramsey, *Christian Priest Today,* 27, 47. On the "cure of souls," see also
Quick, *Testing,* 123–126. In the role of confessor, a priest becomes something of
a judge, but also a physician. "As physician he must do what he can to heal the
souls of his penitents" through absolution and through strengthening the will
toward leading a good life in the future (Hubert S. Box, "The Priest as Confessor,"
in Hubert S. Box, ed., *Priesthood* [London: SPCK, 1937], 187–188).

> human element, and after judging can raise up a faithful remnant.[114]

The priest represents and serves both.

3. Diaconate

Typically for the period, little is said of deacons, their role or place. The doctrinal commission's one mere paragraph on the subject plowed the same sparse ground:

> The diaconate originally represented the ministry of the Church to men's bodily needs, but not as though these were separable from their spiritual state. Though the original function is still emphasised in the Anglican Ordinal, the Deacon to-day exercises his office almost entirely in spiritual activities.

Those activities include the liturgical functions of reading the gospel, preaching if licensed, assisting in administering communion at the Eucharist, and, in the absence of a priest, baptizing infants. "Holding a ministerial commission, he also appropriately assists the priest in pastoral work."[115]

Omitted was any mention that deacons almost invariably took priest's orders in a year—a point Henson did not miss. Though termed by the Ordinal an "inferior office," the diaconate did secure for its recipients the full commission of Christian ministry. Precisely *how* deacons of the day represented God and church went unexplored, for, Henson lamented, the diaconate was "hardly more than nominal." Though it marked a "decisive step out of the secular into the ecclesiastical life," the "settled practice" was to treat it as "no more than a brief apprenticeship to priesthood." Henson preferred a longer period, not less than three years, which "could be made into a real apprenticeship to the priesthood."[116] New thinking on the subject would not appear for another half-century.

---

[114] Ramsey, *Christian Priest Today*, 84–85.

[115] *Doctrine in the Church*, 124. Only infants were specified; evidently the commission did not conceive of an adult convert.

[116] Henson, *Ad Clerum*, 127, 43.

4. Episcopate

When the topic turned to bishops, for once the usually circumspect Ramsey overstated the general consensus: "The apostle"—by which he meant bishop—"draws his commission and authority from Christ alone."[117]

The doctrinal commission was more tempered in its claims. Its report applied to episcopate the two themes so stressed by Moberly of the organic and the representative qualities of all ministry. Episcopacy is an "organ of continuity" like no other order "in that it early became the one recognised organ for transmitting the ministerial commission." Episcopacy "symbolises and secures... apostolic mission and authority within the Church." It guards the church against erroneous teaching. Next, a bishop "represents the Good Shepherd" as chief pastor. He serves as "a living representative of the unity and universality" of the church, personifying the wider church to the diocese and the diocese to the wider church. The bishop is the "appropriate agent" for extending, through ordination, the church's apostolic mission. These organic and representative elements coalesce in one person, and balance each other. That is, a bishop cannot represent his diocese to the church at large, the commission says, if he administers it autocratically, but only if he is "in close and sympathetic relations" with his clergy and laity. Even more pertinently, he who is shepherd remains one of the sheep.[118]

Hebert amplified the report's comment on the bishop's unifying role. Because the church's unity is of God, that unity is expressed in its structure. The bishop in each place is by virtue of his office the center of Christian unity. He represents catholicity and unity of all in Christ. By providing a link among parishes within the diocese, or between his diocese and the larger church—for example, in council with other bishops—the bishop assumes a spacial universality to his office. Through apostolic succession, "he links this generation of the Church with other generations, both of the past and of the future." As a result, his care extends beyond his

---

[117] Ramsey, *Christian Priest Today*, 10 (cf. note 111, above).

[118] *Doctrine of the Church*, 121. It reiterates, "We are convinced that the Anglican Communion has been right to regard the historic Episcopate as in a special sense the organ of unity and continuity" (122–123).

immediate flock to the well-being of the church as a whole, throughout time and space.[119] Temple could not have agreed more fully:

> [W]hen I consecrate a godly and well-learned man to the office and work of a Bishop in the Church of God, I do not act as a representative of the Church, if by that is meant the whole number of contemporary Christians; but I do act as the ministerial instrument of Christ in His Body the Church. The authority by which I act is His, transmitted to me through His Apostles and those to whom they committed it; I hold it neither from the Church nor apart from the Church, but from Christ in the Church. I was myself admitted to the episcopate by the twofold succession—succession in office and succession of consecration....
>
> This authority to consecrate and to ordain is itself witness to the continuity of the life of the Church in its unceasing dependence on its Head, Jesus Christ.[120]

Episcopate shares, then, with priesthood a representative quality of both Christ and church and indeed Christ *in* his church. It, too, is ministerial in its nature.

PRESBYTERAL PRIESTHOOD IN THE MID-CENTURY SYNTHESIS

By World War II, English theologians had attained a relatively clear and well-accepted understanding of Holy Orders generally, and presbyterate in particular. During the hard years of the war, Kirk painted a reassuring picture for his diocese as "the Church in miniature," which was like a "divinely created family."

---

[119] Hebert, *Liturgy and Society*, 155–156.

[120] Temple, *CLF*, 25. A. T. Hanson took issue with that statement, claiming that Temple here was denying a role to the church by stating that, as a bishop, he held his power to consecrate solely from Christ. That would contradict what we have elsewhere read of Temple, though his sense would have been improved by adding a key word: "I hold it neither from the Church *alone*...."

As reflected in the commission's report, Anglicans approached the entire idea of sacrifice in a different way altogether. The self-offering of Jesus on the cross was a sacrifice of the highest order, and it established Christ as the "great high priest" (as Hebrews 8 described him). The Eucharist, which commemorates the sacrifice of his death along with his resurrection, relates Christian worship to that sacrifice. As a result, admitted the commission, "[t]here was thus a priestly character implicit in the celebration of the Eucharist from the beginning." Eucharist is sacrificial and it is priestly.

The implications of that understanding of Christ's sacrifice, the connection of worship to his sacrifice, and the role of those who led this worship were interpreted differently, however. One strand of Christian tradition used the terminology of a sacrificing priesthood (the Hebrew *kōhēn*, the Greek *hiereus*, and the Latin *sacerdos*, with their cognates) to describe the eucharistic presiding officer. This usage began in the third and fourth centuries. By the Middle Ages—the commission asserted—the Christian presbyter had stepped into the role that heathen priests once had filled; the presbyter's office as celebrant was regarded as a sacrificial one, and the sacerdotal nomenclature applied to him.

According to the commission, though, Anglicans followed a different strand of tradition, one which was older and, the report implied, more biblically based than the sacerdotalist view. New Testament writers, and those who wrote in the next century or two, employed the word *presbuteros/presbuteroi* or "presbyter[s]," meaning "elder[s]," to describe the ministers who became known as "priests." This language of "elders" is not the language of sacrifice. Accordingly, Christian priesthood is not a sacrificing one, except to the extent that the corporate worship of the church is a "sacrifice of praise and thanksgiving," as Prayer Book eucharistic rites proclaim. Eucharist is a corporate enterprise, the commission reiterated; "the thankful commemoration of the Lord's Death in Holy Communion is the common act of all Christians," even though one person stands at the altar to give that act its formal expression. The priest, then, leads the eucharistic ritual

> as the appointed representative of the whole Church. But the significance of his acts is derived from the Christian revelation of God in Christ, and from that work of

Christ upon the Cross which his words and acts com-
memorate, and not from the current conceptions of the
priestly function in sacrifice, even at the highest level of
evolution which it reached.[127]

The commission was following the now familiar line of distinguishing between the sacrificial high-priesthood of Christ, the
corporate priesthood of the Body, and the representative role of
the priest/presbyter.

Finally, those ritual acts at altar or table signify what the priest
does and is in all aspects of his life. Echoing his English colleagues,
the American scholar Edward Rochie Hardy defined the priest as
a "servant of the altar" who also holds a "pastoral task of guiding
men along their way to God." Sacraments "are administered in an
atmosphere of worship, while the proper preparation of candidates for the Sacraments is an important part of pastoral care."
The degree to which the sacrament signifies a sacrifice is reflected
in the presbyter. "The dignity of the priest comes from his union
with the priestly work of his crucified Master, and is therefore only truly
realized when the priestly life is in a real sense a life of sacrifice."[128]

THE PRIESTLY CHARACTER

Clerical character had become an issue in the 1800s.[129] In formal
ways, clergy were a breed set apart. Well into the twentieth century
it was accepted that ordination committed a man totally to God
and the church. Precluded from Parliament (unless he became a
bishop with a seat in the House of Lords) and banned from secular
employment, he was expected to embody a single-minded dedication. This expectation inspired the odd phrasing of a sign posted
in the earliest years of World War II: "All persons in the above age-
groups are required to register for national service except lunatics,
the blind and ministers of religion."[130]

---

[127] *Doctrine in the Church*, 158–159.

[128] Edward Rochie Hardy, Jr., "Priestly Ministries in the Modern Church," in
The Ministry in Historical Perspectives, ed. H. Richard Niebuhr and Daniel D.
Williams (New York: Harper & Brothers, 1956), 152, 155, 151.

[129] Cf. Heeney, *Gentleman*, 12–34; Moberly, *MP*, 293–294.

[130] Q. in Daniel Jenkins, *The Gift of Ministry* (London: Faber and Faber, 1952), 7.
See chapter 10, below.

With the personal commitment came public commission. O. C. Quick ventured that, uniquely among the sacraments, orders confer authority as their essential meaning, even if they do so with "the co-operation of the whole body of the Church."[131] Holy Orders authorize the few in distinction from the many. But defining the nature of that distinction has been difficult.

The phrase "indelible character" was part of the difficulty. The doctrinal report seemed to impute to those words a combination of power and grace bestowed upon the holy-ordered. Hall distinguished between the two: the power to act rightly in the name of Christ as stewards of the mysteries of God (*gratia gratis data*), and the personal grace to exercise ministerial functions in an edifying manner (*gratia gratum faciens*). Authority and power are always bestowed, never taken on oneself; and like baptism and confirmation, Hall wrote, ordination "has a permanent and irreversible effect upon its recipient, stamping the soul with a spiritual quality and mark which forever differentiates him from those who have not received this sacrament." Indelibility of character means God's act cannot be repeated or cancelled; a priest deposed is still a priest, though deprived of authority to act as such. As for personal grace, clergy need as much as they can get; "without special help from God, Christ's ambassador may lose his own soul in the very work of saving others." Succumbing to snares does not void the sacramental act, thanks to the doctrine of *ex opere operato*. Still, Hall admitted, "ministerial unworthiness...does materially reduce, sometimes wholly destroys, his efficiency as pastor of souls and spiritual leader."[132] That is, the priest *really* needs God's grace. The doctrinal commission concurred. "We are all agreed that the effect of Ordination is to set apart for life the person ordained as a minister of the Church, to convey the commission for the ministry and to convey grace for its exercise."[133] The recipient of ordination also benefits from an "indelible character," which, as in initiatory rites, impresses the candidate as that onto a seal, and does not refer to ethical significance. That a "character" should be

---

[131] Quick, *Christian Sacraments*, 144–145.

[132] Hall, *Church*, 260–263. See Quick, *Creed*, 334, 340 for a different use of this doctrine; and chapter 10, below.

[133] *Doctrine in the Church*, 199 (cf. Kirk, *Apostolic Ministry*, 15), 125.

imprinted means, too, that any "grade" of ministry cannot be repeated: once ordained, always ordained, "whether he exercise it or not."

"Character" as an ecclesiological category, then, does not imply moral status. Clergy too often prove that they are not morally superior to laity, and often show themselves to be considerably worse. Just as clearly, scoundrelish clergy poorly serve their Lord and their church. With all the more reason then (and consistent with nineteenth-century notions), Temple commended priestly sanctity. "It is in the person of its priests that the Church must maintain that outward holiness, that separation from the world, which alone makes possible a concentration upon things divine; and without this concentration it can never become a catholic or universal body."[134] Thereby representative character becomes credible.

Ramsey had urged a form of this holiness in exhorting his ordinands to prayer. He also urged a profound humility. "All Christians are called to be humble," he remarked. "But the ordained man...leads them in the way of humility as their pastor."[135] The priest is both example and leader.

THE PERSISTENT TENSION BETWEEN CLERGY AND LAITY

Ramsey labored valiantly to reiterate the fundamental union between priest and people. "The ministerial priesthood—an indelible order as it is—is the priesthood of the one Body focused in certain organs which act for the Lord and for the Body." But he also wrote that the priest at ordination "receives grace from our Lord by an inward and an outward act of our Lord, through His death and resurrection, and through the one Body both in its world-wide existence and in its historic past which is really present in the Communion of saints." As representatives of Jesus himself, and as an expression of their corporate priesthood, the people play

---

[134] Temple, CN, 99, cf. 95: "It is not because they are more truly members of the Church than others, nor because there is a different moral standard for clergy and laity, but because in the whole life of the Church there are certain functions which are incompatible with others, just as in the State a man cannot be at the same time an advocate and a judge, or commander-in-chief and ambassador."

[135] Ramsey, *Christian Priest Today*, 14–15, 77.

a vitally important part in that process, "a single congregation ratifying the call to an individual and adopting him as its minister." Nevertheless, here "is an act of the Lord, expressed plainly and outwardly through His whole Church whereof the parts derive their power from the whole."[136]

Not even Ramsey could explain away the tension. The strain was too inherent in the fundamental principle that all may be called, but a few are chosen for special work. A divine commission, even one conveyed with full lay cooperation (more in theory, less perhaps in practice), set clergy apart from laity, especially if they received a power and grace not available to other mortals. A healthy reiteration of the "priesthood of all believers" could balance priestly prerogatives. But an extreme exponent of the corporate priesthood, Kirk warned, could slip too easily into asserting a "priesthood of each believer" in which one decides, "I need no man to stand between myself and God," and then could take the further step of rejecting the church and its ministry altogether.[137] Furthermore, the growing clerical professionalism in the nineteenth century may have improved proficiency and, with it, public confidence,[138] but the additional education and heightened status that accompanied this improvement could push the clergy upward beyond the reach of many of the laity. The aura of sanctity cultivated by many clerics may also have bred a feeling among laity that their clergy really *were* holier than they. Brent might innocently have widened the gap when he called the presbyterate a "perpetual and living reminder to the laity of what they should be and do." He cited how "[t]here are many ready to decry sacerdotalism" but suggested that few "have sufficient logic to recognize that the more completely the ministry is denuded of all but its representative character, the more fully is the layman weighted with spiritual responsibility."[139]

---

[136] Ramsey, *GCC*, 117, 83–84.

[137] Kirk, *Apostolic Ministry*, 49.

[138] Cf. Henson, *Ad Clerum*, 145.

[139] Brent, *With God in the World*, 130–131.

Some who were confronting that gap wanted the priest to become more like the layperson. In O. C. Quick's analysis, that solution would aggravate the basic problem of the twentieth-century cleric, who "has no recognized and definite position of his own." Thus, "because his real function is not recognized or understood, he exhibits that superficial clericalism which the layman finds repellent." Added to that were controversies over remuneration—whether priests should be paid comparably to laity, and if so, which: workmen or professionals. The solution for Quick lay in an appeal to the cleric's "special function in the body" and "what will best help him to perform his special task."[140]

But a "special function" did not imply an elitist position for clergy. Temple insisted that "[p]riesthood becomes evil just when it is thought of as belonging to the ordained ministry exclusively, instead of representatively."[141] Against these dangers, he proposed a double solution that he knew many would find strange.

> The first is perpetually to remember that men are called by God to the different kinds of work which He has for them to do; and we shall avoid unctuousness, which is no doubt what men most dread about a priestly caste, if we keep it perpetually in our mind that we are not personally holy because our calling is....
>
> And the other safeguard, paradoxical as it may sound, is a very complete specialised training. One of the reasons, I am quite sure, why lay people often find us rather stilted and uncongenial is because we have not secured a sufficient grasp upon what is our own special subject to feel full liberty in conversation and to speak naturally.... Precisely in the degree in which we know our own work and have full possession of what is entrusted to us, shall we obtain liberty and ease of manner, and be in general behaviour just like other people, which is what we ought most to desire.[142]

---

[140] Quick, *Testing*, 118–119, 129.

[141] Temple, *FWG*, 165.

[142] Temple, *CN,* 97–99.

In essence, like Quick, he advised an even greater sense of professionalism. Ironically, by gaining self-confidence in the clerical role, clergy could become more like everyone else. Temple's point makes sense only in light of Christian relationships that deepen with each other as they deepen in Christ.

Ramsey extended Temple's thought. "[T]here is only one kind of *person* who makes God known and realized by other people, and that is the person who is humble because he knows God and knows God because he is humble.... It is only a humble priest who is authoritatively a man of God, one who makes God real to his fellows." To develop this attitude, Ramsey suggested an obvious model: "We are to share in Christ's sorrow, and the realm in which we do this is not the realm of a special kind of mystical experience, but the realm of everyday ministry.... In and through [our own little griefs or worries] we are drawn near to Christ's sorrow. It makes all the difference."[143]

Ramsey tried to close the clergy-lay gap using Moberlian phrases common to the mid-century synthesis.

> In the Eucharist the Church is very near to the sacrifice of Christ, for the once-for-all offering is brought into the here-and-now by the memorial. While all the people participate, the priest acts in the name of Jesus in the words and actions of the Last Supper, and he represents also the Church as Catholic. So, too, the other parts of his ministry are in Christ's name: his preaching, his absolving, his caring for people in every kind of way, and his witness to the community.

He then turned the professionalizing tendencies of Temple in a Christocentric direction:

> At the same time, the ordained priest evokes and serves the ministry of the people of God, and he sees so many of the laity eager to serve and lead. While he is called to bring the expertise and the authority of his ordination into this scene, he knows that the expertise and the authority are rooted in the humility of Christ.[144]

---

[143] Ramsey, *Christian Priest Today*, 78, 92–93.

[144] Ramsey, *Christian Priest Today*, 111–112.

The fact that the next stage of theological development would repeatedly address these same issues relating to clergy and laity shows that, for all the power of Ramsey's attempts at resolution, he did not entirely succeed. Conversely, as Archbishop of Canterbury, Ramsey was instrumental in bringing to Communion-wide attention the ecclesiological vision of representative ministry.

IV
Bringing the "Body" into the Church

O ne August night in 1963, nearly a thousand delegates from every province in the Anglican Communion—bishops, priests, laity, and one deacon—processed into Toronto's Maple Leaf Gardens for the service of Evensong that opened the ten-day Anglican Congress. This assemblage was even more international than the first Congress, nine years before in Minneapolis. At this service representatives of newly minted provinces in Africa and Asia wore their native dress proudly to introduce their home churches to the Anglican scene. A congregation of sixteen thousand greeted them, and a choir of one thousand voices sang the *Magnificat* and *Nunc Dimittis* to "Stanford in C" in grand old English style. But what happened later during the actual proceedings of the Congress was even more remarkable.

For three days and into the fourth, speaker after speaker and panel after panel talked of the church's mission as it was and as it should be. Then on Saturday, August 17, as the throng settled after a mid-morning break, in a departure from the agenda, the Archbishop of York, Donald Coggan, took the podium. "The Church is not primarily a debating society; it is the Body of Christ at work in God's world and at war against God's enemies," he declared. "The Anglican Communion has its part in that work and that war." With that introduction, he read a manifesto entitled "Mutual Responsibility and Interdependence in the Body of Christ" (MRI).

The idea of this document germinated two weeks before at a preliminary conference for missionary leaders from all over the Anglican Communion. After they poured out their concerns and frustrations in the presence of American bishop Stephen Bayne, the Anglican Executive Officer, they began to imagine together what could be done. Bayne took their basic concepts to the council of primates and metropolitans; these leaders of the Communion's provinces refined and approved the ideas of MRI and forwarded it to the Congress.

When Coggan had finished reading the document, his brother primate, the Archbishop of Canterbury, Michael Ramsey, commended it: "A church which lives to itself will die by itself."[1] His words electrified the Congress. MRI caused a sensation—first in the Congress, then around the Communion. It challenged Anglicans to do many things differently: to alter radically their priorities; to work together; to commit to raising then-substantial funds (fifteen million dollars) to train leaders, construct churches and other buildings in "new areas of Christian responsibility," and to provide mission funding in those new areas; to make "a parallel commitment as to manpower"; and to urge each church to study its own mission. "Mission is not only a giving to others, it is equally a sharing and receiving," the document stated, asking that each province of the Communion examine what it can receive as well as give. Gone would be the days of givers and receivers, of "mothers" and "daughters," but instead, of "mutual responsibility and interdependence."

The Toronto Congress marked a high point in postwar Anglicanism, the likes of which we have not seen since. The gathering broadcast to one and all that the Anglican Communion had developed into a thoroughly international community. The MRI document—the centerpiece of the Congress—summed up the understandings of church and ministry that had emerged over the course of the twentieth century. In one sense it was a program that strived to educate

---

[1] E. R. Fairweather, *Anglican Congress 1963*, 124–125 (cf. "Congress Message," 264). The text of the MRI document is on pp. 117–122.

all Anglicans to the needs of the world, promote their response in mission, identify projects, share resources, and raise funds—the only coordinated program that the Communion had ever seen. It led to new ways of operating, including such innovations as the Anglican Consultative Council, a biennial gathering of delegates from each province to share information and views and to foster mutual cooperation. But MRI was, in a profounder sense, exactly what Bishop Bayne called it on that warm August day: "a theological document."[2] It promulgated the ecclesiological statement that identified the Anglican Communion with the Body of Christ: Anglicans are not the only members of it, of course, but because they are part of this Body, they must act like it. MRI asked Anglicans to do more than act differently; it also asked them to think of themselves differently—as no less than the Body of Christ.

In that sense, Toronto and MRI signified the triumph of the ecclesiology of the Body of Christ. As of August 1963, MRI and its program were set before the Communion for all to see, blessed by archbishops, primates, and delegates of every sort from all over the world. This vision of the church with a *representative* ministry within a common priesthood shared by all Christians then strongly influenced Anglicanism on two levels: on the "official" plane of Lambeth resolutions, constitutions, canons, and related official statements; and on the more everyday level of the theology, liturgy, and even the church buildings that week by week embody the concept of the church as the Body of Christ. What linked these two levels was *The Book of Common Prayer*—more precisely, the *Books* of Common Prayer, as provinces revised the liturgies they used. Prepared and authorized on the higher plane, they were slowly and sometimes painfully ratified through their ongoing use by Sunday morning worshipers, for whom nothing is *really* "official" in Anglicanism unless it appears in the liturgy. The old maxim, *lex orandi, lex credendi*, remained true: how people pray affects what and how they believe. As liturgical scholar William Seth Adams rephrased the principle, "the ritual life of a community is formative of that community."[3]

---

[2] Fairweather, *Anglican Congress 1963*, 130.

[3] William Seth Adams, "Decoding the Obvious: Reflections on Baptismal Ministry in the Episcopal Church," in Ruth A. Meyers, ed., *Baptism and Ministry (Liturgical Studies One)* (New York: Church Hymnal, 1994), 12.

In short, the representative, ministerial idea had been *received*, to use a term employed by the bishops at Lambeth in 1988, to signify that what is affirmed in word becomes a living experience of the community. As the bishops explained, conclusions reached by some forum or another gain acceptance only in time, through a "gradual and dynamic process...always open to the guidance of the Holy Spirit within the community." Until that process is completed, "there is necessarily a 'provisionality'" about decisions of synods or councils or, we may add, ideas of prelates and scholars.[4]

ANGLICAN ECCLESIOLOGY WORLDWIDE

Now the vision of Moberly, Temple, Ramsey, and their contemporaries was being incorporated into the innermost life of the Anglican Communion. The synthesis on ministry that developed in the first half of the twentieth century found its way into countless books, articles, memoranda, and regulations of the Anglican Communion around the world. Statements by the Lambeth Conferences of Anglican bishops ranked as most significant. Though Conference resolutions are advisory rather than mandatory, they give a sense of the mind of Anglican leadership at least in the moment they are issued. With increasing numbers of bishops attending Lambeth, the work increasingly falls to committees or "sections," whose reports do not bear the stamp of full conference approval but rate only slightly less in importance. Moving beyond Lambeth, constitutions and canons show the measure to which provinces and dioceses have received this consensus and are among the few evidences available from the newer regions of Anglicanism, which necessarily are less economically developed and therefore less likely to publish their perspectives.

The Ecclesiological Vision of Lambeth

When the Archbishop of Canterbury first invited all Anglican bishops to his palace at Lambeth in 1867 for "brotherly counsel

---

[4] *The Truth Shall Make You Free: The Lambeth Conference 1988* (London: Anglican Consultative Council, 1988) (section II report, ¶147), 117. Footnotes of Lambeth Conference sources, after the first citation, indicate the Conference year, the source of the citation (e.g., resolution or section/committee report), if appropriate, and page[s].

and encouragement,"[5] he created a tradition followed roughly every ten years since. Although composed entirely of bishops, these conferences are international, which has given at least some opportunity for voices from outside the Anglo-American orbit to be heard. Indeed, the international tone increased with each conference. The 1998 gathering was the largest ever (750, versus 76 in 1867), and Africans, Asians, and Latin Americans played a prominent part, with Nigerians as the third-largest group.

The Nature of the Church

From envisioning the church to figuring out how to attract more clergy and involve more laity, Lambeth Conference discussions ranged from high theology to the pragmatics of running a huge institution. Sometimes they combined the two but always with the image of the Body of Christ in mind. For instance, the principle that a person is ordained to serve the entire church and not one diocese led bishops in 1948 to encourage "the highest possible standard of training...throughout the whole *body*." The church could act more effectively as one body by exchanging information on methods of recruiting, selecting, and testing candidates; on standards for ordination; about schemes for post-ordination training. A 1958 committee on "ministries and manpower" placed ordained ministry "within the life of the whole Church and in relation of that Ministry to the priestly office inherent in the Body of Christ in the world." The committee report added: "All baptized members of the Body are called to share in its priestly function, the offering of life as a living sacrifice, acceptable to God, through Jesus Christ." In a 1988 report on women and orders, the bishops declared, "The Church is the body of Christ. We are cleansed and called into mission by baptism, empowered for mission and commissioned by the Holy Spirit."[6]

Other images, equally biblical, were equally important for what they implied about the church's mission. One section of the

---

[5] Q. in *Lambeth 1988* (section II report, ¶117), 110.

[6] *The Lambeth Conference 1948* (London: SPCK, 1948), 48 (¶85; ¶86 recommends establishing a "Central College" in Canterbury), emph. added; *The Lambeth Conference 1958* (London and Greenwich, CT: SPCK and Seabury, 1958), 2.99; *Lambeth Conference 1988* (section I report, ¶135), 59.

1978 conference declared, "The Church is both 'a holy priesthood' to offer God spiritual sacrifices, and 'God's own people' called to proclaim his wonderful deeds," which meant (as Hebert had urged) that worship and mission are major tasks of the church that can never be separated. The church as a whole serves the mission of Christ. "The pressing needs of today's world demand that there be a massive shift to a 'mission' orientation throughout the Communion," one section report urged in 1988, a commitment that would require the realignment of structures, roles, and understandings. The bishop would become the leader in mission; dioceses, congregations, and seminaries "would become instruments that generate missionary movement as well as pastoral care." Reorienting the church toward mission also demanded nothing less than "a revolution in the attitude to the role of the laity," that would "see every Christian as an agent of mission."[7]

The 1998 conference moved away from the image of the Body to adopt a more trinitarian motif. Well prior to that year's conference, an inter-Anglican commission on theology and doctrine had been formed to consider the nature of communion itself. Its report drew inspiration from the very nature of God. Unity in the Anglican Communion "derives from the unity given in the triune God, whose inner personal and relational nature is communion."[8] To describe, by any image, a people God claims as God's own is to depict Christians as participants in the divine nature; they shape the relationship of one Christian to another. The doctrine of Trinity is just such an image; it helps explain the church's very being as an "icon of the future toward which God is directing the history of the world." For the Christian, to be "baptized and to participate at the Table of the Lord is to be entrusted with Christ's one, continuing mission through the Church." With gifts bestowed upon the community by the Spirit, the church exercises a ministry

---

[7] *The Report of the Lambeth Conference 1978* (London: CIO, 1978) (section report), 54–55; *Lambeth 1988* (section report), 32; cf. Res. #45, 232.

[8] Resolution #18, *Lambeth 1988*, 216–218; *The Official Report of the Lambeth Conference 1998: Transformation and Renewal* (Harrisburg, PA: Morehouse, 1999), 22.

that finds "its motivation, its intelligibility and its integrity in the ministry of the Church's Lord, Jesus Christ."[9]

By 1998 the Communion needed every source of unity it could find. Liturgies reflecting varying cultures, differing convictions on the ordination of women, and formal agreements with other denominations that manifested diverse understandings of orders and the historic episcopal succession "strained the ability of Anglicans to maintain their unity in diversity." Finding what doctrine and structures would hold the Communion together had become a major priority. *Koinonia* was one way, creating a sense of community that "points us to the Trinitarian life of God and the mutual love and action of Father, Son and Holy Spirit."[10]

The Nature of Ministry

That Jesus is the source of ministry was the cornerstone of all deliberations at Lambeth. "Our Lord Himself shows us the crucial importance of providing leaders by the care and patience with which He trained the twelve," states an encyclical from 1930. "This ministry has been perpetuated from the first days until now." A committee on the prayer book in 1958 went further, quoting Hebert's observation that in the Eucharist, "the true celebrant is Christ the High-Priest, and the Christian people are assembled as members of His Body.... The essential ministry of the Word and Sacraments is the ministry of Christ himself."[11] A 1968 committee, with the whole conference's endorsement, took the next step:

> *All* Christians share in the priesthood of their Lord. This is the primary order of ministry in the Church to which all Christians are consecrated by baptism, and which in union with Christ they fulfill by offering the diversity of their lives, abilities, and work to God.

---

[9] *Lambeth 1998* (Virginia Report), 27, 29. One might quibble whether God's will is "inspired by" the work of the Spirit in the Church (27). Other images were by no means abandoned; for instance, a section reported that the "Pauline theology of the church as the Body of Christ provides a framework for a wholistic understanding of the way Christians receive and pass on a tradition." *1998* (section III report), 208.

[10] *Lambeth 1998* (section IV report), 227, 230.

[11] *Lambeth 1930* (encyclical letter), 30; *Lambeth 1958*, 2.85, q. from *Ways of Worship* (1951); 2.88.

start?

Baptism underlies all ministry, ordained and lay. As for presbyters, the bishops' report added, "Christ calls and empowers some to be priests of the priestly people." These must be recognized by the church as its representatives and set apart by God for special ministry at ordination. In presiding at the Eucharist, "a priest is seen as an agent of Christ, of the Church, and of the bishop." The committee added, "Vocation to God's service in the ordained ministry is never the concern of an individual alone," but is also that of the church and the bishop.[12]

The 1988 conference concentrated with particular intensity upon mission. It vigorously envisioned a corporate ministry that involves all the baptized to whom, as the Body of Christ, "the Lord of the Church gives a variety of spiritual gifts." The focus must be outward: "The primary ministry of the great majority of Christians is their service of humanity in the everyday work of the world." Since God's gifts are diverse and widely distributed, working together is crucial. Choosing and training clergy must give priority to "equipping the saints for the work of ministry." Teaching and preaching should relate to the questions of everyday life so that all Christians may pursue the common ministry, which is emphatically *for* the world.[13]

From virtually the first Lambeth Conference, bishops worried about finding enough clergy to supply a ministry that continued to expand. Fretting about it throughout the 1920s and 1930s, they called for prayer and teaching about ministry and vocation. By 1958 the bishops felt such concern about the inadequacy of clergy training for present and future missionary opportunities that they resolved to do more than pray. They called for "first-class theological teachers," especially in developing areas of the church, and for better standards of training and post-ordination education. They also proposed a distinctive order of deacons, a turnaround from the 1930 Conference that had rejected the idea, and an office of Reader to be filled by laypersons who could lead services as well as read the Scriptures.[14] The concept of *who* ministers was slowly expanding.

---

[12] *The Lambeth Conference 1968: Resolutions and Reports* (London and New York: SPCK and Seabury, 1968), 100 (cf. Res. #31, p. 38), 101, emph. in orig.

[13] *Lambeth 1988* (section report), 44–45.

[14] *Lambeth 1930* (Res. #61), 58; *1958* (Res. #81), 1.49; cf. 2.99; (Res. #83, 85–90), 1.49–51.

Calling for increased ministerial vocations was one thing, but nurturing them was another. In 1930 bishops presumed that most candidates for orders should be university graduates with some ministerial training that included at least elementary instruction in psychology, the art of teaching, social economics, and the like. They hoped to stimulate the intellectual and spiritual life of clergy "especially in the earlier years of their service," though the conference conceded the need for changes that would relax the expectation of university educations for all clergy and would modify the forms of training for people of color. But training for ministry was understood to be limited to present and future clergy, in contrast to the 1998 Lambeth Conference that seemed to envy the new Charismatic and independent churches for the ways they would "train up and deploy every member of the congregation."[15] The bishops' focus was not on forming clergy, but the whole *laos*.

Specialized and Non-stipendiary Ministries

For all their prayers for excellence in the clergy, bishops at the 1930 Conference faced the reality that congregations were substantially neglected. Not enough priests were being ordained to keep up with the growing population of Anglican churches around the world and the growing popularity of eucharistic worship; as a result, "hundreds of thousands" of their people were cut off from the ministry of word and sacrament. Imaginative new strategies for solving the shortage were proposed, including ordaining part-time ministers with additional employment outside of the church structure. Such strategies for a broader range of ministries tended to encourage a broader range of ministers as well. This opening of orders to new kinds of models and new groups of people quickly forced a reexamination of three long-standing principles of Anglican orders. The most basic of these, which was the principle that might be said to have precipitated the clergy shortage and the strategies required to deal with it, held that priests were essential to celebrate the Eucharist. The second, "Priesthood demands the whole of life," established that ecclesiastical service must be *full-time* service. The third was the principle that Anglican priesthood

---

[15] *Lambeth 1930* (#63, 64), 59; 172; *1998* (section IV report), 241.

ministerial   pastoral   in nature   not just for
                                                         mass

was ministerial and pastoral in nature. Since the days of the Reformation "Mass priests," whose sole ministerial duty was sacramental, had no place in the Anglican imagination, and bishops at the 1930 Conference resisted anything that would significantly depart from the parochial model, which embodied the fundamental concept of a pastoral ministry. Because of the latter two principles, they could not bring themselves to commend outright the ordination of those who, having established themselves in secular occupations, would then come into the priesthood as a second career, continuing to earn their living outside of the church while helping out sacramentally on the side. But, because of the first principle—that priests are the ministers of word and sacrament—and given the pressing need for priests, they did move in the very direction they were loath to take, seeing no "insuperable objection" to the practice so long as it was authorized by the province "where need is great."[16]

After 1930, subsequent Lambeth conferences moved beyond sheer necessity toward increasingly positive motivations for alternative forms of ordained ministry. Lambeth 1958 recognized the potential usefulness of ministries offered by second-career priests for missionary work or specialized tasks but only as a supplement for "fully-trained and full-time priesthood." Ten years later, bishops were more affirmative, commending the variety of services the ordained could offer—some in parochial ministry, some in scholarship or teaching, some in community life, some in ministry in professional, business, or industrial settings. But while the second principle of full-time service was being relaxed and redefined, the third principle remained in full force: "Whatever the circumstances priesthood always involves pastoral responsibility within a particular community." The bishops' reminder presumed an important corollary: that Anglican priesthood must have some connection with a local church community, however that community was defined. The 1988 Conference decided that necessity had bred a definite good, so it welcomed and encouraged what it called "self-supporting ministry" as one component in a "massive expansion of all forms of both lay and ordained ministry" to address the

---

[16] *Lambeth 1930* (Res. #65), 175–176; 60.

"need of the world for the Gospel."[17] Anglican leaders had come to imagine more forms of ministry than parish priesthood alone.

Bishops and Deacons

During the postwar period, bishops spent more of their time discussing the episcopate. Lambeth 1958 summarized a common view of bishops consistent with the ecclesiology of the Body: "The bishop, as God's agent in the local Church, and also as that Church's representative," was from ancient days the one who, always within context of Eucharist with the faithful assembled, prayed the Spirit to come upon a candidate for any order. The 1978 meeting devoted still more thought to the role of the bishop: "All authority comes from God and that which is given to the Church involves all the people of God in responsibility and obedience."

> The bishop derives his authority from the Church, which is the Body of Christ. Christ is the head of the body, the faithful are the members. The bishop receives his authority from both Head and members, and neither without the other. This authority is not to be exercised apart from the Church, that is, without collegial consultation at proper times with brother bishops, and without ensuring that it has the support and consent of the rest of the Church as far as possible.... The bishop does not receive his authority by any succession independent of the Church.[18]

A 1988 report observed that, given the interdependence between Christ and church, orders and members, a collaborative ministry among laity, deacons, priests (and with other denominations) is crucial. The 1998 Lambeth Conference observed that the bishop, having received an apostolic authority, remains a "servant (deacon)" and "elder (presbyter)."

The same quandary about the diaconate that Henson had cited remained: the order was considered, even in prayer book language, as "inferior," barely more than a steppingstone along the

---

[17] *Lambeth 1958* (Res. #82), 1.49; cf. 2.107–110 (note the implication that only "full-time" clergy are "fully-trained"); *1968*, 100–104; *1988* (section I report, ¶124–125), 56–57.

[18] *Lambeth 1958*, 2.89, in which small revisions in ordination rites were made to clarify this point; *Lambeth 1978*, 76.

path to priesthood. Changing times and ministries made the place of the diaconate even more questionable. A committee of the 1958 Lambeth Conference, for example, noted that the tendency to use lay readers and catechists to assist in worship and teaching, commendable in itself, encroached on the role of deacons.[19]

Then the Lambeth meeting of 1968, one of the most open to emerging concepts of ministry, seriously reconsidered the role of laity and, in so doing, that of deacons. In one sweeping resolution, the conference redefined the deacons' order as one combining service with liturgical functions. It envisioned a diaconate that would include those in secular positions, in full-time church work, or in preparation for priesthood. The resolution urged eliminating any language about the order's "inferiority," and drew attention to the element of *diakonia* inherent in the ministries of bishops and priests.

The bishops also opened the order to women. On a split vote, it encouraged provinces to adjust their canons in order to recognize women who had been set apart for the specific work of deaconesses to be acknowledged as deacons, thus incorporating them into the ranks of clergy. It also recommended that the diaconate be open to men and women alike. But by 1988, two problems intertwined to create a double quandary over the concept of diaconate. On the one hand, most deacons were still transitional, ordained to continue on to the priesthood. Preparing for the diaconate, therefore, was functionally equivalent to preparing for priesthood. But training a group of ordinands for priesthood when their call was to the diaconate alone inevitably distorted the whole idea. On the other hand, some provinces had agreed to ordain women as deacons but not as priests. So a second, substantially larger group of ordinands, all women, was being trained as priests but restricted to being deacons. Again, this distorted the theology of the diaconate. Little wonder that the bishops were unhappy: "It is difficult to see a permanent diaconate with an entirely distinctive diaconal ministry coming into existence in such circumstances."[20] Progress would follow, but only as women were ordained to the priesthood

---

[19] *Lambeth 1958*, 2.106.

[20] *Lambeth 1968* (Res. #32), 38–39; *Lambeth 1988* (section I report, ¶122–3), 56.

[21] *Lambeth 1998* (section II report), 127 (cf. 181), 176.

and alternative forms of ministry—including an intentional, vocational diaconate—could be explored.

Among the Lambeth bishops, however, the idea grew that *diakonia* cannot be confined to one order, and in 1968 they said as much. Lambeth 1998 advocated that episcopal and diocesan structures reorient themselves to take "the form of a servant." The bishop is a servant, or deacon, who "models the service of Christ to the Church and the world,"[21] and stories were told about Anglicans around the globe doing just that. Not only were concepts of diaconate expanding, but concepts of *diakonia* and service as well.

The Laity

What, then, is to be the role of laity? Lambeth 1930 conceded that a bishop could authorize lay readers to administer the chalice where there was "pressing need." Lambeth 1958 was far more positive, with a committee encouraging alterations in the prayer book to make liturgy more accessible to and participatory for laity. For lay readers, catechists, and subdeacons, the committee report advised making training more available. Forthrightly associating baptism with ministry, the bishops argued:

> There is...a need for a better theology of the laity, together with an increasing realization of what is meant by Christian vocation throughout the rank and file of the Church's membership. In a real sense the laity—that is the *laos*, the People of God—are the Church.... By laity, we mean all those who are seeking to fulfil the membership of the Church which is theirs by baptism.... Ministry and laity are one.... The mission of the whole Church is to be the Body of Christ, and, through all its members, to show forth Christ to the world.

In that effort all clergy and laity share, according to the gifts each has been granted. As Liddon had suggested decades before, this was a truth that was capable of revolutionizing the church. Baptism, so the bishops resolved, means that laity are to share in the ministries and responsibilities of the church.[22]

---

[21] *Lambeth 1998* (section II report), 127 (cf. 181), 176.

[22] *Lambeth 1930* (Res. #65), 60; *Lambeth 1958*, 2.81, 2.99, 2.110, 112–113 (cf. Res. #94, 1.52).

Amid the tensions of 1968, the bishops gave lay concerns pride of place in ministerial matters: "The ministry, the service, of the Church to the world is and must be discharged mainly by the laity." Beyond church, their role "demands witness to the Christian gospel through word and deed" in a world that, at that moment, seemed to approach chaos:

> In the home, at work, in industrial disputes, in the exercise of economic power whether as employers or employed, in the bitterly divisive issues of race, it is for the laity to bring to bear a Christian influence towards social justice, compassion, and peace.

For that, they would need the renewing and strengthening grace of worship, word, and sacrament that was the clergy's task to provide. Laity also should take full part in matters of oversight—"no major issue in the life of the Church should be decided without the full participation of the laity in discussion and decision." The conference followed its own advice, if only by permitting a layperson to join a bishop and a priest in representing each province to the Anglican Consultative Council it created. The layperson, the Conference concluded, "represents the reconciling Christ, the listening Christ, the caring Christ, to those with whom and for whom he works."[23]

But something deeper was at work: Successive Lambeth conferences were redefining the term "laity" to encompass the entire people of God—the *laos* of the church, to use the Greek term meaning "people." So in 1958, the bishops defined the laity as the *laos*, the People of God, as the church. In 1968 they utilized the concept to refine the place of priests within the entire *laos*, as we shall shortly see. In 1978 they reiterated the point made in 1958 that "Christian ministry is committed to the whole people of God" and then added, as if old ideas were dying hard, "and not, as is often believed, to the ordained ministry alone." Declaring that "both mission and maintenance of the Church in the future depend upon a radical commitment to the central role of the laity," the bishops who gathered in 1988 meant by the term "laity"

---

[23] *Lambeth 1968* (Message), 24; (Res. #25–27) 37–38; (Res. #69) 49; 97, 95 (cf. entire report, 94–100).

every baptized member of the church—men and women, young and old, ordained and lay, all within the "priesthood of all believers."[24] Nearly a hundred years after Moberly, decades after the theological synthesis jelled, the point about who constitutes the church and its fundamental ministry was beginning, however fitfully, to sink in.

Whereas Moberly looked upon the unity and ministry of the Body from the perspective of priesthood, Lambeth Conferences regarded the church and its work from the perspective of a re-energized understanding of baptism. The old lay-vs.-ordained distinctions were dissolving, a 1988 section report observed, largely as a result of the church's rediscovery of the power and extent of baptism. The World Council of Churches' document, *Baptism, Eucharist, and Ministry* (1982), was an immediate influence, one that led the bishops to declare in 1988, "Baptism becomes significant...only when we become conscious of being a part of the saving life and work of Jesus Christ, our Lord," and with this gift of new life comes "the implied gift of authority for ministry." In 1998 the bishops asserted, "Baptism into the death and resurrection of Christ is the foundation of all Christian ministry." The church is most faithful to its calling when all of its members recognize their vocation as disciples of Christ and that they "received their vocation in baptism, whatever form of ministry they might exercise."[25]

So bishops were answering with new vigor the question of who ministers in the church, and their response was, "All baptized Christians." Traditional priestly tasks of blessing, absolving, and sacrificing may be led by the ordained, but "the ministry of the laity must also, but *in its own way*, be to bless in God's name, to absolve in God's name, and to celebrate the sacrifice of the Lord Jesus." At the same time, the bishops were sowing some confusion, too. What was meant by "laity"? It could mean the whole

---

[24] *Lambeth 1958*, 2.99; *Lambeth 1968*, 99–100; (Res. #41) 40; *Lambeth 1978* (section report), 82. "All baptized members of the Body are called to share in its priestly function, the offering of life as a living sacrifice, acceptable to God, through Jesus Christ" *(Lambeth 1958*, 2.99); *Lambeth 1988* (section report), 49–52; cf. *Lambeth 1998* (section III report), 192–194. Just two pages after asserting this definition, however, the report reverts to earlier meanings: "It is a particular test of *ordained ministers* to lead and to enable the *laity* in ministry within the Church and to the world" (51, emph. added).

[25] *Lambeth 1988* (section report), 51; cf. *1998* (section III report), 192–194 (q. BEM); *Lambeth 1998* (section III report,) 192.

people of God—what in 1958 and 1968 was called *laos*—or it could designate, as in 1988, "those called 'laity,'" that is, those who are not ordained. What is the primary locus of ministry for those not ordained? The answer in 1988 was, "The characteristic arena of such ministry is the world which the Church exists to save."[26] In 1998, "By their Baptism, all the members of the *laos* as Body of Christ commit themselves to its ministry in the world." Their ministry may take place in family, village, neighborhood, school, workplace, volunteer service, and government. Lest anyone infer that *laos* excluded clergy, the report denied that laypeople "are in the world and ordained ministers are not." At the same time, the bishops cited the danger of confining "lay ministry" to the church itself and so run "the risk of ignoring much of the ministry to which Christians are called."[27]

Finally, how clergy and laity were to work with each other was a persistent quandary for the bishops. At the 1930 conference, they conceded something that had been painfully obvious since World War I: "that there is some truth in the impression that the clergy are often out of touch with the life and thought of the laity." Their solution? That a candidate "gain some experience of the life and work of the world at home or abroad before Ordination."[28]

Both naive and anemic, their solution also lacked a compelling vision of a church that embraced clergy and laity in mutual effort. Bishops four decades later seemed at long last to fathom these ecclesiological trends. Lambeth 1968 drew out the ramifications of the image of the Body of Christ that incorporates laypeople and clergy alike, with a place and purpose for each.

> This understanding of the ministry of the whole people of God (the laos) means that the special function of the priest is all the more emphasized. He is the representative of the whole Church, ordained by the bishop to preside at the Eucharist and to pronounce in the name of

[26] *Lambeth 1988* (section report), 49–52, emph. in orig.; cf. *1998* (section III report), 192–194.

[27] *Lambeth 1988* (section III report), 193–194.

[28] *Lambeth 1930*, 170.

the Church the reconciling and renewing forgiveness of God. Because of his theological insight he has a special task in building up the laity for their task of relating the gospel to the world. He has to stand for God to the people of God who are going out to serve God and find God in the world. A clearer understanding of the ministry of the laity demands a corresponding clarity about the special ministry of the priest and bishop.

Bishops applied this view to themselves as well; they, too, were of the people. Rather than lording over the church like ecclesiastical princes, "as leaders and representatives of a servant Church, [they] should radically examine the honours paid to them" in liturgy, titles, address, and lifestyles. In 1998 the bishops reiterated this understanding:

> Among the baptised the three-fold ministry of deacon, presbyter and bishop orders the ministering community of God's people. The ordained ministry is never separate from or independent of that community. Indeed the ordained ministry receives its authority from Christ by the Holy Spirit within the whole Body.[29]

A century after Moberly, Lambeth articulated his vision anew. Successive conferences had adopted the ecclesiological precepts of the Body of Christ image, together with the implications of active roles for each ordained order and for laypeople as well. The bishops broadened the scope of involvement for each category. But, by the turn of the millennium, they had not fully resolved the dilemma that Moberly had faced: Precisely how, in the Body of Christ, do its members function at once differently and together?

ECCLESIOLOGY THROUGHOUT THE ANGLICAN COMMUNION

The next step in incorporating the ecclesiological vision into Anglican life was to institute it within the constitutions, canons, and official teachings of dioceses and provinces. The concept of the church as Christ's Body, ministering his reconciliation and service to the world, has frequently been folded into declarations of polity or belief. The catechism of New Zealand's prayer book describes

---

[29] *Lambeth 1968*, 99–100; (Res. #41) 40; *Lambeth 1998* (section III report), 201.

the church "as the body of which Christ is the head, and all baptised persons are members." The Episcopal Church teaches that the church's mission "is to restore all people to unity with God and each other in Christ," but the New Zealand catechism aims still higher, declaring that the purpose of ministry "is to continue Jesus' servant ministry in the world by witnessing to God's reconciling love, *to bring in* the Kingdom of God, to build up the body of Christ, and to glorify God's holy name."[30]

The Kenyan constitution, however, is the most audacious of all, stating, "The church is the body of Christ upon earth, and to it has been committed the task of continuing and completing all that Jesus began both to do and to teach." So ambitious a purpose would truly require the participation of all. Therefore the constitution also insists,

> No one order and no one office in the Church can claim exclusive possession of any one of these ministries or of all. Every Christian, by his/her baptism, is a member of the body; to each one, therefore, has been committed in his due order and proportion, a share of responsibility for the life of the Church and for all its ministries.[31]

With equal care, the Province of Central Africa includes everyone, ordained and lay, male and female: "The laity, by virtue of their Baptism and Confirmation, share with the clergy in responsibility for the proclamation of the Gospel and for the pastoral care of the people of God."[32]

This principle of shared ministry opens a diversity of functions to the non-ordained. By it, Central Africa apportions certain duties—preaching, distributing communion, conducting the daily office or burial order—to laypersons, and, "when there is no duly licensed person available, any member of the laity, being a communicant, may perform" these functions. Such latitude is unusual.

---

[30] The Church of the Province of New Zealand, *A New Zealand Prayer Book: He Karakia Mihinare o Aotearoa* (Auckland: Collins, 1989) [*NZ Prayer Book*], 931–932, emph. added; US BCP, 855.

[31] Church of the Province of Kenya, *Constitution* (Nairobi: 1992), Art. V, sec. 1, 4; V.2, 4.

[32] Church in the Province of Central Africa, *Constitution and Canons* (n.p.: 1996), Canon 18.2; cf. sec. 1, which applies the canon to women as well as men.

More conservative is the Diocese of Sydney, Australia, which retains greater control by the archbishop and clergy. Laity may lead Morning or Evening Prayer, baptize if no minister of the church is available, lead the burial office or the churching of women, and even preach. Only when the cleric in charge has requested their aid, and when they have received proper training and preparations, may they be authorized as lay readers and wear the blue scarf that the diocese bestows in token of their office.[33] Somewhere in between is the Diocese of Johannesburg, which reports that lay ministers provide for more and more home visiting, sick communions, funerals, counseling, preparation for baptism, and marriage and preaching,

> all of which used to be the sole preserve of the clergy. For many years [lay ministers] have been assisting the clergy in the sanctuary; saying prayers, administering the chalice and reading the lessons. Many of these duties are now regularly shared with other members of the congregation and they are, in turn, sharing in the responsibility for planning and arranging the services.

The priestly incumbent and parish council are called on to facilitate and support these endeavors. "While these trends are regarded by some as revolutionary, others see them as the Church going back to its roots as described in the New Testament where ministry appears to have been shared among all baptized members of the Church according to their individual talents."[34]

Duties such as these establish what the Kenyan constitution refers to as the "dignity of a lay person":

> They cannot walk worthily in their high calling, unless they realize that they too are sharers in the heavenly high priesthood of Christ, and that this sharing must find expression in holiness, in witness, and in loving service of others.[35]

---

[33] Anglican Church of Australia, Diocese of Sydney, *The 7th Handbook* (Sydney: 1994), 264–265. Deaconesses, who presumably have experience, are excepted from these restrictions.

[34] Church of the Province of Southern Africa, Diocese of Johannesburg, *Parish Guide* (Johannesburg: 1997), E-18.

[35] Kenya, *Constitution* (V.7), 8–9 (cf. Liddon *Sermons*, 199–200; *Lambeth 1988*, 44–45).

All God's people share in the work in the world: provinces and dioceses affirm the theory. But when the same provinces and dioceses spell out the sorts of work that laypeople do, they identify tasks and roles inside the church structure, not in the world beyond. They seem to prove the danger of which Lambeth 1998 warned, of defining the work of laypeople as occurring within the church and not where everyone claims it should be, in the world at large.[36]

The Ordination and Deployment of Clergy

The Kenyan constitution also indicates a place and role for clergy in terms that assert apostolicity without being dogmatic about it. "From the Apostles' times," it states, "it has been found *convenient and profitable* that a special responsibility for ministry of one form or another should be committed to persons chosen and appointed for the fulfillment of these respective tasks." The three orders grew out of practical need.[37] Kenya's description of these orders indicates the degree to which ideals expressed by theologians and Lambeth Conferences were permeating the global Communion. Among priestly responsibilities listed in Kenya's constitution, for instance, is "to preside over his parishioners assembled in Council, and at all times to be ready to listen to what they have to say." While most deacons anticipate ordination to the priesthood, "there will always be a place in the Church for those whose vocation it is to remain as deacons." Bishops, however, retain enormous power, called "rulership," as their right.[38] For priests to listen to the laity, however, implies a relationship of mutuality that many in the Communion also tried to express, but not without difficulty. A major statement by an English panel concedes that defining the proper relationship between the ministry of the whole *laos* and the ordained has been hard:

> There have been constant tendencies for the tasks of one to subsume those of the other, so that in theory it is treated as "the" ministry, whereas the two are actually

---

[36] *Lambeth 1998* (section III report), 193–194. The Diocese of Sydney exemplifies the syndrome, defining as "Lay Ministries" those rites and duties that laity may be permitted to lead (Sydney, *Handbook*, 264).

[37] Kenya, *Constitution* (V.3a), 4, emph. added.

[38] Kenya, *Constitution* (V.5.viii, 6),7–8 [§6 is misnumbered as §7; spelling corrected].

interdependent, the health of each depending on that of
the other. Both together do what neither can do alone.[39]

Theologians may say that Christ and the church ordain clergy,
but canons and laws specify how to do it. Norman Doe, a Welsh
canonist, explored the governance of each province, extra-provin-
cial diocese, and united church affiliated with the Anglican Communion. His survey found that becoming a deacon or priest follows a fairly consistent pattern. Most parallel England's requirement
that no person shall be deemed a lawful deacon or priest "except
he be called, tried, examined and admitted thereunto according to
the Ordinal" or other rite. Education and training are generally
required, though exact standards vary widely. Baptism and confirmation, which signify the candidate's participation in his or her
sponsoring community, are universally required. Every Anglican
province prescribes a minimum age for ordinations, usually twenty-
three for the diaconate and twenty-four for the priesthood, though
a few allow the archbishop or primate to grant exceptions. The
bishop uniformly makes the final determination of suitability,
especially with regard to assessments that have a subjective aspect
or that have differing standards from place to place: the candidates' spiritual and moral qualities as well as their physical and
mental condition.[40]

Various levels of the church hierarchy participate in the ordination process. It often starts with a conversation between the person
and his or her priest, who then reports to the diocesan bishop or
a designate. Then a diocesan or provincial group seeks to discern
the candidate's vocation, reporting back to the bishop, who may
then accept or reject the recommendation. Presuming the candidate passes whatever examination is required by the bishop, the
candidate submits assorted documents and testimonials. Some
churches require a public announcement, parallel to the banns of
marriage, in a congregation where the candidate is known, but
very few churches make the consent of the people as a precondition
for ordination. No part of the Communion has developed as elaborate

---

[39] Q. in Greenwood, *Transforming Priesthood*, 49; see 56–72 for summary and
evaluation re "consensus" of this ACCM paper.

[40] Doe, *Canon Law*, 129–131.

a procedure as the Episcopal Church, where the route toward ordination takes an aspiring ordinand through parish committees, commissions on ministry with their various subgroups, and standing committees, all giving permission at each and every stage. Somewhere along the way, psychological and physical exams are administered and, toward the very end, the notorious General Ordination Exam tests each candidate over several days. It is a route so tortuous that cynics renamed the "discernment process" the "discouragement process."[41] An American bishop at the 1998 Lambeth Conference compared notes with a Sudanese counterpart, who said his diocese's ordination process consisted of his saying the words, "Kneel down." As Doe's work on canon law attests, no system is quite that simple, but the American bishop was envious nonetheless.

Ordained in and by the Body of Christ—and Christ acting through his Body—clergy are then deployed by the Body for ministry. The bishop's role is central to the process, but, as Doe points out, Anglican canon law characteristically incorporates "the participation of the laity, or their representatives, in the process of appointment." Specifics diverge among provinces and dioceses, as does the degree to which this lay role operates, but appointment to a ministry is usually followed by approval of the bishop in some form or another.[42]

These principles apply most clearly in the vast majority of appointments, which are to parish churches. Indeed, appointing a clergy person may rank as the peak moment in the relationship between a bishop and local congregation. The nature of that involvement varies widely. On one extreme is the Episcopal Church, which allows substantial local latitude for the choice of a rector. National canons require a parish simply to send notification of its candidate to the bishop, who then has time—no more than thirty days—to "communicate" with the parish vestry and to

---

[41] Doe, *Canon Law*, 133–136. On ECUSA, see *Constitution and Canons* (New York: Church Publishing, 2000), III.4–12 (pp. 64–83). Shortly before this book went to press, the Episcopal Church's 2003 General Convention revised its canons regarding the ordination process in an attempt to clarify and simplify it.

[42] Doe, *Canon Law*, 137.

ensure that the person is duly qualified.[43] On the other end is the
Diocese of Mundri/Lui in the Sudan, which declares, "The
appointment of the Clergymen to their Cures is the sole responsibility of the Diocesan Bishop," though he must consult with any
assisting bishop, archdeacons, and archdeaconry church council
concerned.[44] Although most dioceses and provinces allow for some
measure of consultation, the degree of involvement by laity, in particular laity from the congregation, differs substantially. In Akure,
Nigeria, a diocesan appointments board that is responsible for
governing who goes where is composed of the bishop and most of
the major officers of the diocese (suffragan bishop, chancellor,
cathedral provost, archdeacons) plus two lay members of synod.[45]
The bishop of the Australian Diocese of Canberra and Goulburn
convenes a Clergy Appointment Board of eight members, including
three members from the parish concerned. The selection is made
by a majority that must include at least two of the three parochial
laity.[46] In Canada, the Diocese of Athabasca has its bishop consult
with the parish council or vestry, while Caledonia consults a panel
that includes the bishop or an archdeacon representative, churchwardens, lay delegates to synod, and licensed lay readers (an
unusual exercise in governance by liturgical leaders). This committee generates three names, and the bishop, if he or she
approves, invites them in order of preference to accept the cure.[47]
Similarly, in Ireland, a diocesan Committee of Patronage consists
of the bishop or a commissary plus "diocesan nominators" (four
clergy, one layperson elected by diocesan synod, and four "parish

---

[43] ECUSA, *Constitution and Canons* (2000), Canon III.17 (p. 90). However, letters
dimissory and/or a license to officiate are also required; cf. III.16 (pp. 88–89).
Diocesan procedures may be much more extensive and include the bishop in the
process more fully than the canons imply.

[44] The Province of the Episcopal Church of the Sudan, Diocese of Mundri/Lui,
The Constitution of the Diocese of Mundri/Lui (Khartoum: ECS/New Day,
1997), 50.

[45] Church of Nigeria, Diocese of Akure, *Constitution* (Ajure, Nigeria: Hope
Printer, 1989) (VII), 26.

[46] Anglican Church of Australia, Diocese of Canberra and Goulburn, *Administration of Parishes and Special Districts Ordinance 1975* (Canberra, NSW:
1996), 12–13, 17–18.

[47] Anglican Church of Canada, Diocese of Athabasca, *Handbook* (Alberta:
1994), Canon 4; Anglican Church of Canada, Diocese of Caledonia, *Constitution, Canons, Policy & Procedures Manual* (British Columbia: 1994), C–17.

nominators"); a candidate will be elected by at least six votes.[48] Before the priest enters into the position, the bishop must give final approval. That consent symbolizes an episcopal authority over clergy that is sometimes considerable. In the Diocese of Belize, for example,

> every member of the clergy serving in the Diocese shall be licensed personally to the Bishop who may appoint him to any Parish or Mission within the Diocese and may from time to time vary the Parish or Mission to which the member of the clergy has been appointed.

The power of the episcopate may be great, but it is subject to limitation. Belize's canon expresses both the authority and its limits:

> Every member of the clergy serving in the Diocese shall be liable to be transferred from one Parish or Mission to another Parish or Mission within the Diocese subject always to the power of the Bishop, after consultation with the Commission on Ministry and the Church Committee of the cure concerned.

The power of bishops often extends well beyond appointing clergy. In his capacity as a guardian of the faith, the Bishop of Mount Kenya Central may veto any proposal by the diocesan synod or standing committee if it is "unca[no]nical, unconstitutional, or contrary to the law and custom of the Church." The Archbishop of Sydney also holds this unusual right. More common is the power to authorize laity for various offices. Licensing lay liturgical ministers is a widespread prerogative of the episcopate, as we saw with Sydney and the Sudan. However, the power to select lay officers differs from place to place. In dioceses like Akure in Nigeria and Huron in Canada, the priest may choose one church-warden and the parish elects the other, but in Mundri/Lui the pastor and bishop each selects one.[49]

---

[48] Church of Ireland, General Synod, *The Constitution of the Church of Ireland* (Dublin: 1988), ch. 4, p. 32.

[49] Church in the Province of the West Indies, Diocese of Belize, *The Constitution and Regulations of the Church in the Diocese of Belize* (Belize City: 1995) (Reg. 12.2–3), 30; Church of the Province of Kenya, Diocese of Mount Kenya Central, *Constitution* (1990), 18; Akure, *Constitution* (x.5), 29; Anglican Church of Canada, Diocese of Huron, *Constitution and Canons* (Ontario: 1990), 18–20; Mundri/Lui, *Constitution*, 50.

By whatever means they are chosen, wardens are generally considered, as in England, both representatives of the laity and officers of the bishop ("ordinary"); the archdeacon officially installs them as such on the bishop's behalf. The American church is exceptional in that its canons make no comparable provision for wardens. More typical is Mauritius, which defines wardens as representatives of the laity, who stand alongside the parish priest, all reporting to the bishop:

> The Churchwardens when admitted are officers of the Ordinary. They shall discharge such duties as are assigned to them and shall be foremost in representing the Laity and in co-operating with the Incumbent; they shall use their best endeavours by example and precept to encourage the parishioners in the practice of true religion and to promote unity and peace among them.[50]

In sum, canonical provisions around the Anglican Communion perform a delicate balancing act between the authority of the clergy, notably the bishop, and the role of the laity in church governance, a hallmark of the Anglican system.

Fewer generalizations are possible regarding other forms of ministry. Most deacons are made priests after a transitional year, so canons on ordination of priests are more relevant. A few churches employ permanent deacons, including Korea, Puerto Rico, the Episcopal Church, and the churches of North India and South India. The West Indies church has ruled that an order of deacons "shall be maintained within the Church of the Province...as a distinct order of ministry...symbolic of the servant element." Although the order of deaconesses has largely disappeared, provisions remain for them in some areas. In Canada they are still set apart by the bishop for pastoral care and liturgical assistance, especially in working with women, young people, and children, teaching, visiting, and other ministries.[51]

---

[50] Church of the Province of the Indian Ocean, Diocese of Mauritius, *Constitution* (Mauritius: 1983), 26; cf. Doe, *Canon Law*, 180.

[51] Q. in Doe, *Canon Law*, 145; Anglican Church of Canada, General Synod, *Handbook of the General Synod of the Anglican Church of Canada,* 11th ed. (Toronto: 1996).

Canons have hardly addressed the relatively new phenomena of non-stipendiary and self-supporting ministries. The appointment of these clergy is usually regulated by the institutions they serve rather than by the church itself. Usually the bishop must approve their non-parochial service; once given episcopal blessing, they essentially act on behalf of the diocese rather than the parish and therefore do not need the additional consent of local parochial clergy.[52] The constitution of West Africa provides for the diocesan bishop, with advice "from an appropriate organization in his Diocese," to prescribe "how persons, who will retain secular occupations, may be ordained to the Diaconate or the Priesthood with the qualifications that will be required." Kenya distinguishes between the "itinerant" ministry of the bishop and that of the priest who is usually assigned a local ministry like a parish but adds that "it may take the special form of a hospital, school or other special community," or teaching. The handbook to the Diocese of Johannesburg notes:

> Many people who give their life to the Lord are never paid by the Church so that self-supporting priests and deacons are becoming increasingly common. Indeed in our Diocese the number of self-supporting clergy exceeds the number of stipendiary clergy and the gap seems to be widening.[53]

As ministries diverging from the familiar model of parochial priesthood develop around the Communion, canonical provisions that permit and regulate them are also likely to increase.

In conclusion, results are mixed as to how little or much the ideals of the ministerial and representative have woven their way into the ecclesiology of the Anglican Communion as expressed in its documents, legalities, and procedures. In some areas the laity have substantial say; in others, no one from the congregation has any place at the table in determining the appointment of pastors. Some dioceses and provinces allow their bishops considerable

---

[52] Doe, *Canon Law*, 142.

[53] Church of the Province of West Africa, *Constitution and Canons* (Accra, Ghana: 1990) (XII.1), 54; Kenya, *Constitution* (V.5), 6–7, spelling corrected; Johannesburg, *Parish Guide*, E-18. Note the equation of "giving [one's] life to the Lord" and service to the church.

power; others limit the prerogatives of the episcopate. Still, the vision of the Body of Christ remains the compelling ecclesiological motif of the Communion, constantly reminding all the elements of the church of their interrelationship. This vision finds expression in Lambeth statements, provincial canons, and statements of bishops around the world. In 1984 the Bishop of Ecuador articulated a Latin American perspective that is broadly shared:

> Today the Church finds itself in a real "Revolution of Ministry." Each Christian is part of the total ministry of the Church, with functions that have their base in God's call, the gifts received, and the recognition of the Church. It claims a return to the original situation of the primitive Church, defining the diaconate in general terms as a source of service in the area of practical ministry and the presbyterate as a source of service in the area of the ministry of the Word and Sacraments.[54]

While some provinces and dioceses embody this sense of ministry more fully than others, the Anglican Communion as a whole commits itself to sharing the work of the whole church, the Body of Christ.

THE BODY AND ITS MINISTRY IN LITURGICAL LIFE

Prelates may meet all they wish, conferences say what they might, canons enshrine what practices they will, and still nothing communicates so effectively with the people of God as what they see, hear, and experience Sunday upon Sunday. Through the architecture of their church buildings and the words and acts of their liturgy, the ideas articulated by theologians and bishops make their home in the lives and minds of this priesthood of all believers.

REENVISIONING CHURCH SPACES

From its earliest days, the architecture of the church expressed the church's view of itself. Doctrine influenced that self-understanding, but so did politics. After Constantine bestowed official recognition on the church in 313, the liturgy was embellished as

---

[54] Adrián D. Cáceres, "The Anglican Communion in Latin America," in *Crossroads Are for Meeting: Essays on the Mission and Common Life of the Church in a Global Society*, ed. Philip Turner and Frank Sugeno (Sewanee, TN: SPCK/USA, 1986), 278.

never before, as befitted the established religion of a great empire. Christian structures also needed ornamentation appropriate to their new-found status within the general community. Temple-like sacred zones were consecrated as Christian churches, and, as hierarchy developed, the ancient *cancelli* where pagan priests officiated became the balustraded "chancel" of the Middle Ages where presbyters celebrated.[55]

If the events of 313 marked a sudden, defining moment of transition for the church, then 1945 and the publication of Dom Gregory Dix's *Shape of the Liturgy* was the culmination and perhaps the codification of another liturgical transition that had long been underway. Weighty in heft and impact alike, this book focused public attention on the Liturgical Movement and excited the interest of architects as well as those who commissioned them. Dix's work

> provided the theological basis for a new conception of Christian society...a new order, a new pattern of community, no longer fragmented or compartmentalised into sacred and secular, but in which religion and life, dogma and mysticism, liturgy and daily living, are once again integrated within the eucharistic fellowship of redeemed humanity.

His writing directly or indirectly prompted liturgical experiments around the entire Anglican Communion, resulting in different ways of worship that affected the layout and design of worship spaces.[56] One principle is clear, argued architectural writer Peter Smith. Since buildings reflect both the individual and corporate sense of self, then "the character of Christian buildings will be determined by the self-image of the laos." He summarized the era's themes in this way:

> In the Church the Incarnation continues; Christians are commissioned to continue the many-sided work which Christ began under the guidance of the impetus of the Spirit.... At last the idea of the entire laos as having a priestly role to play in society is catching on. The

---

[55] Peter F. Smith, *Third Millennium Churches* (London: Galliard, 1972), 42.

[56] Peter Hammond, *Liturgy and Architecture* (London: Barrie and Rockliff, 1960), 101–102.

> Church is beginning to be an active agent of God in the
> world rather than a passive spectator to the good works
> of the few. If it is the Body of Christ, all the limbs must
> work, and work cohesively.

Lambeth 1988, too, saw a link between physical structures and the mission of the church: the former must serve the latter and not vice versa.[57]

Architects were thereby enlisted as evangelists, commissioned to articulate the nature of the church as the Body of Christ so that, at the Ministry of the Word, the configuration of space and furniture might provide what one observer calls a "real rapport between the priest and his assistants and the congregation." The designer also has to demonstrate the new priority of baptism alongside the Eucharist, though how precisely to accomplish that balance was (and is) a matter of debate.[58]

England led the way in constructing architectural expressions of the new theories. The chapel at Queen's College, Birmingham, is an early example. Begun in 1938 but not completed until 1947, the chapel has an unusual layout that reflects the school principal's wish to "declericalise" the liturgy against the "all-devouring presbyter" and accentuate the communal nature of eucharistic action. Among parish churches, St. Paul's, Bow Common, in London (1956–60), was one of the first to adapt the ideas. Its square plan with pews set on three sides fosters an immediate relationship of the congregation with the altar and the clergy who stand there. High and lifted up those clergy were not, but intimately close to the people about them. St. Philip and St. James, Hodge Hill, in Birmingham (1963–68) was also built on contemporary architectural and theological lines; it combines worship space with community

---

[57] Smith, *Third Millennium Churches*, 56; 94. Cf. Ronald C. D. Jasper, *The Renewal of Worship: Essays by Members of the Joint Liturgical Group* (London: OUP, 1965), 6–12; *Lambeth 1988* (section report), 53–54.

[58] New Churches Research Group, *Church Buildings: A Guide to Planning and Design* (London: Architectural Press, 1967), 442, 453, 501–502. Options in putting baptism and Eucharist on an equal plane of importance include constructing a separate baptistery; or placing a font to the side of the nave, or near the main entrance, or in front of the altar; making it moveable; or even sunken below the floor level. Although this research group advised arranging spaces to bring clergy and people together, it seemed to contradict the spirit it professed by suggesting that the priest, who should be seen to preside over the whole assembly, do so from a "cathedra" or "bishop's throne."

areas, as does St. Margaret's, Thornbury, in Bradford Diocese after it was rebuilt in 1998.[59]

From old England to New England, the summertime Chapel of St. James the Fisherman in Wellfleet, Massachusetts, was built in 1957 as an American testament to new liturgical ideas. The brainchild of several prominent clergy who summered on Cape Cod, the chapel combines a wooden simplicity reminiscent of the oldest New England meetinghouses with modern styling and current thinking on liturgy and ecclesiology. Designed for eucharistic worship, it emphasizes the corporate act of God's people. Daylight streams into the chapel's interior from a square oculus directly above the altar, which is prominently positioned in the very center of the chapel. Near the main door stands a large shell-shaped font; the seashell is a symbol of the patronal saint and a reminder of the sea nearby, while the font at the entrance to the building symbolizes that baptism is the sacramental entrance into the life of the church. The congregation sits in pews on all four sides around the altar. As the lessons of the Ministry of the Word are read from places around the small chapel, the celebrant remains among the worshipers, stepping from their midst to preside at the table for Eucharist.[60]

Renovating older church buildings no longer meant just restoring them to earlier glory but also might entail updating and remodeling them in keeping with current ecclesiological thought, while striving for simplicity, directness, relevance, adaptability, and flexibility. Gothic-style interiors were clearly at odds with modern understandings of biblical and liturgical scholarship. An altar distant from the congregation, a baptismal font out of view, or any arrangement that turned the congregation into spectators

---

[59] Hammond, *Liturgy and Architecture*, 102; Edwin Heathcote and Iona Spens, *Church Builders* (London: Academy Editions, 1997), 68; Reinhold Gieselmann, *Contemporary Church Architecture* (London: Thames and Hudson, 1972), 48.

[60] Cf. Robert Mutrux, *Great New England Churches* (Chester, CT: Globe Pequot), 1982), 75–77. Cf. also St. Paul's Cathedral, Burlington, VT (completed 1973), 95–97, which embodies a traditional form though in very modern styling and materials; St. Mark's, New Canaan, CT (1962), 206–209, which adapts Gothic principles to modern style and liturgy; and St. Matthew's Episcopal/Wilton Presbyterian Church, Wilton, CT (1971), 235–237, an ecumenical venture where each congregation has its own liturgical space, which in the Episcopal instance is the most "in the round" of these three examples.

made alterations all but essential. St. Mary's wooden construction in Jacksonville, Florida, is a Carpenter Gothic case in point. Its rejuvenation aimed at flexibility. New seating of interlocking single chairs instead of pews, no fixed pulpit, no communion rail, a portable altar, and moveable panels of nylon allow the limited space to be defined in different ways to suit diverse needs.[61]

Proponents saw the architectural changes as a solution to the growing separation between liturgical design and theology. One English priest predicted that unless the two were reconciled, we would be left with "a church fit only for the heritage trail."[62] Peter Hammond writes, "The problem is primarily a pastoral and a missionary one."[63] If left to the theologians and parish clergy, then the main portion of the Body of Christ, the laity, will be excluded from decisions central to the worship of the whole people of God. Theirs is the priesthood, too. As the structure in which the priesthood offered the sacrifices of praise and thanksgiving was changing, the role of the ordained priest, the presbyter, was shifting as well.

RE-ENVISIONING THE PRAYER BOOK template

For three hundred years, England's 1662 Book of Common Prayer had provided the template for Anglican liturgies. By the mid-twentieth century, however, the Anglican Communion was global, the Eucharist was frequent, baptism was prominent, and the laity were active, so the prayer book was ripe for review. By the late 1950s the first postwar revisions to the prayer books of a few provinces had begun to appear. The Lambeth Conference of 1958 welcomed revisions as a chance to consolidate the results of modern biblical and liturgical studies and, thereby, effect a "recovery of the worship of the Primitive Church."[64]

---

[61] Hammond, *Liturgy and Architecture*, 137; Editors of *Architectural Record*, *Religious Buildings: An Architectural Record Book* (New York: McGraw-Hill, 1979), xi, 72–73.

[62] Richard Giles, *Re-pitching the Tent: Re-ordering the Church Building for Worship and Mission in the New Millennium* (Norwich: Canterbury, 1997), 79, 7. N.b. his historical discussion, pp. 9–52.

[63] Hammond, *Liturgy and Architecture*, 153.

[64] *Lambeth 1958* (#73–74), 1.47.

Of particular concern to the bishops was the Ordinal, those rites pertaining to ordination that, strictly speaking, are not a part of the prayer book but are bound together in the same volume. It had long been conceded that Cranmer's liturgical genius seemed to have flagged by the time he attended to these rites, and times had changed—calling the diaconate an "inferior office," for example, would no longer do. Cranmer's central prayer for the consecration of priests featured the pastoral and teaching roles to the neglect of the sacramental (an overreaction, no doubt, to then-current Roman Catholic overemphasis) but never made reference to New Testament terminology of "presbyters"/"elders" that had become characteristic of Anglican thinking.[65] The climactic moment in ordinations was more injunction than prayer, in which absolution held greater prominence than baptism or Eucharist.[66]

That very year the Church of South India provided an example of what the bishops had in mind. As a union of Anglicans with those of several other denominations, the CSI had to find liturgical expressions that both reflected, and were acceptable to, the diverse traditions that formed it. So impressive were its new ordination rites that English Methodists and Anglicans immediately borrowed these ideas as they developed a proposal for a reunion scheme for themselves. Although the scheme failed, the proposed rites, along with the CSI ordinal, influenced the new American prayer book,[67] which in turn has been consulted for subsequent revisions around the Communion.

---

[65] Cf. The Episcopal Church, Standing Liturgical Commission, *The Ordination of Bishops, Priests, and Deacons: Prayer Book Studies 20* (New York: Church Hymnal Corp., n.d. [c. 1971]), 18.

[66] "RECEIVE the Holy Ghost for the Office and Work of a Priest in the Church of God, now committed unto thee by the Imposition of our hands. Whose sins thou dost forgive, they are forgiven; and whose sins thou dost retain, they are retained. And be thou a faithful Dispenser of the Word of God, and of his holy Sacraments; In the Name of the Father, and of the Son, and of the Holy Ghost. Amen."

[67] *Lambeth 1958*, 2.89; re Vatican II, cf. *Lambeth 1988*, 66; Colin Buchanan, ed., *Modern Anglican Ordination Rites* (Bramcote, Notts: Grove Books, 1987), 9–10. He cites the post-Vatican II Roman Catholic rites as an indirect influence (10). On South India's influence, which included a good synopsis of the theological synthesis on church and orders, cf. Byron David Stuhlman, *Occasions of Grace: An Historical and Theological Study of the Pastoral Offices and Episcopal Services in the Book of Common Prayer* (New York: Church Hymnal, 1995), 277, and Jasper and Bradshaw, *Companion to the Alternative Service Book*, 433–434.

As a result, modern Anglican ordination rites since 1958 have shown a remarkable consistency. Ordination is placed within a eucharistic context. The litany and sermon form part of the Ministry of the Word, followed by the ordination itself, and then the sharing of the peace.[68] Within this structure, ecclesiological concepts and notions of ministry found new expression. And so, almost exactly three hundred years after the inception of its 1662 Prayer Book, the English Church was borrowing, rather than initiating, Anglican worship prototypes.

THE BOOK OF COMMON PRAYER (THE EPISCOPAL CHURCH, 1979)   ECUSA

Episcopalians were among the first officially to revise their prayer book and Ordinal, and the outcome greatly influenced every Anglican prayer book revision thereafter.[69] The revision articulated through liturgy many of the points being developed and ratified throughout the Anglican Communion. What was intended for this book? How were its principles embodied?

The Standing Liturgical Commission (SLC) wanted to model its revision along current ecclesiological lines. Above all, this was to be the *church*'s book, "church" meaning God's corporate people as a baptismal and eucharistic community whose worship is grounded in the Paschal Mystery of the death and resurrection of Jesus. Baptism and Eucharist, the two dominical sacraments at the heart of the church, give it shape, order, and definition by allowing the church to become "a sacramental sign of the presence and ministry of Jesus Christ in the world."[70] Its primary ministry is to live out the baptismal life, bearing witness to Christ, using the

---

[68] Buchanan, *Modern Anglican Ordination Rites*, 11. The presentation of the candidate may occur at a different point from the main portion of the ordination, as in the US BCP.

[69] Paul F. Bradshaw, "The Shape of the Ordination Liturgy," *A Prayer Book for the 21st Century*, ed. Ruth A. Meyers (New York: Church Hymnal, 1996), 146. The Canadian and Japanese revisions derive directly from ECUSA (Buchanan, *Modern Anglican Ordination Rites*, 12). The US BCP was not the first revision, however. It relied to some extent on the work of the Church of South India; and Melanesia was undergoing a similar process at the same time.

[70] Leonel L. Mitchell, *Praying Shapes Believing: A Theological Commentary on the Book of Common Prayer* (Minneapolis: Winston Press, 1985), 295.

diversity of gifts. Fundamental ministry, then, finds its expression in the liturgy for baptism.[71] Ordained ministry arises within that context. Ordination rites occur consistently within the Eucharist, for

> ordained ministry is set firmly within [the] Church, in service to the Church, not separated from it or set over against it so that ordained ministers function apart from the body of the faithful as "freelance shamans." It is only within the Body of Christ that ordained Christian ministry has any meaning.[72]

In introducing the trial-rite Ordinal in the so-called Green Book, the commission wrote, "The priesthood of Jesus Christ and the derivative priesthood of his baptized people do not eliminate the need for special priestly offices in the Christian community." In ordination, some are entrusted with unique burdens and privileges, but they emphatically do not replace other Christians:

> The Christian clergyman is not being assigned to witness to the Gospel, to care for the poor, or to pray, so that other members of the Church can be dispensed from these activities. Rather, the pastor is to help his people in the fulfillment of what is their vocation as well as his. Seen in this light, the mission of the ordained minister is related organically to the mission of all the baptized. [73]

This new American revision would emphasize the ministry of all God's people, with baptism—not confirmation or ordination—as the essential rite of entry.

Another characteristic emphasis concerned the episcopate. "To indicate the centrality of the episcopate," the SLC decided to depart from earlier prayer book custom and place the rite for ordaining a bishop first, before those for priests and deacons, theoretically to avoid "the misleading impression that the three orders are simply three steps in an ascending scale of promotions." The commission's study document envisions the bishop as supported by

---

[71] See esp. the section, "The Baptismal Covenant," of creed, promises, and prayers (US BCP, 304–307).

[72] Mitchell, *Praying Shapes Believing*, 296.

[73] *Prayer Book Studies 20*, 7–8.

deacons

two sorts of helpers: assistants, or deacons, who as subordinates help to carry out his decisions; and associates or priests, who join him in making decisions and in implementing some of his tasks. (Note that this model does not allow for a lay role.) Deacons were seen as a discrete order, an order not of apprenticeship but of service, that could be either part-time or full-time. As if anticipating fears that deacons, thus defined, would infringe upon lay forms of service, the SLC emphasized that the deacon was not "the only person called to serve, but rather that his formally designated and ordained service is to provide leadership and focus for the entire Church as a serving people."[74]

With these ideas, the new iterations of *The Book of Common Prayer* began to appear: "The Liturgy of the Lord's Supper" (1966), the *Services for Trial Use* (1971, the Green Book, so-called because of its olive binding), the *Authorized Services* (1973, nick-named the "Zebra Book" for the stripes on its cover), the blue Draft Proposed BCP (1976), and then the "proposed" book of 1976, which was ratified, unaltered, in 1979. In one decade, the Episcopal Church transformed itself liturgically. Eucharist became common as "the principal act of Christian worship on the Lord's Day and other major Feasts,"[75] but at the expense of the service of Morning Prayer beloved of many. Christian community was suddenly the hallmark of liturgical practice, with members literally forced off their knees and out of the pews to exchange the peace with each other and to approach the altar for communion nearly every week. The people were to be active participants in liturgy and in mission; the deacon proclaimed as much at the end of the service, sending them out "to love and serve the Lord." Even the deacon was a new kind of cleric for most people, one who had no intention of being anything other than a deacon. Efforts to promote the inclusion of the laity took strength from words of liturgy and the teaching of the catechism. As Leonel Mitchell wrote at the time, "It is the insistence of the catechism 'that ministers are lay persons as well as clergy' which has sparked the emphasis on total ministry."[76] The new book urged that baptisms occur at public

---

[74] *Prayer Book Studies* 20, 7–8, 9, 32.

[75] US BCP, "Concerning the Service of the Church," 13.

[76] Leonel Mitchell, "Introduction: A Pastorally Sensitive Plan" in Meyers, *Prayer Book for the 21st Century*, x.

services so that the full community can participate. After the candidates profess their faith, the rest of the congregation joins them by reaffirming their own baptismal covenant; after the baptism, they welcome the newly baptized into the fellowship of the church. None of these features had been the case with the 1928 Prayer Book or its predecessors. *The Book of Common Prayer* (1979) introduced new services for ancient days (especially during Holy Week, culminating with the Easter Vigil), all striving to deepen the congregation's participation in the Paschal Mystery.

It also exhorted congregations to celebrate the Eucharist at their principal service on Sundays. To fulfill that injunction, priests suddenly needed helpers to perform the tasks that the ceremonies of the Eucharist required. And so for reasons both practical and theological, "laypersons" were added to the prayer book list of those who might assist the principal celebrant. A rubric established that laity "should normally be assigned the reading of the Lessons which precede the Gospel," and may lead the Prayers of the People (as deacons also may do). An additional provision allowed for duly licensed laity to distribute communion, "in the absence of sufficient" clergy.[77]

Other clergy, in addition to the priest presiding at the celebration, were assigned tasks as well. The revised book gave deacons a larger role—reading the gospel, leading intercessions, serving at the table, ministering the sacrament, dismissing the people. In the absence of a priest, deacons could also distribute communion to a congregation from the reserved sacrament (itself a novelty for most congregations), and for a deacon or layperson to take it to the sick.[78] If more than one priest were around, one would celebrate and others join in, standing at the altar and sharing in distributing the sacrament. As the SLC intended, the bishop held pride of place, given his prerogative to preside and preach, and to bestow the absolution and blessing. He was "expected" to officiate and preach at baptism, but in his absence the priest could use chrism the bishop had consecrated.[79]

---

[77] US BCP, "Concerning the Celebration," 322; 408.

[78] US BCP, "Additional Directions," 407–409.

[79] US BCP, 322, 332, 339, 360, 366; 298.

role of clergy and the centrality of the bishop on the one side and the place of the corporate priesthood of the Body on the other. In addition, the number of pages devoted to Holy Orders still far exceeds those dedicated to baptism.[87] The problem worsens with the SLC's explanations of what laity do. *Prayer Book Studies* notes that "lay persons have performed some tasks associated with the ordained ministry. This is to be expected, because all Christians are called to serve God in ways not unrelated to the special vocations of Bishops, Priests, and Deacons."[88] When circumstances cause these tasks of the ordained to be *replicated* by laity, the very focus of ministry becomes muddled. For example, assisting clergy are assigned roles subordinate to the celebrant but still innate to their sacramental order. However, the practice of authorizing laity to administer the eucharistic chalice in local parishes, as an expedient when other clergy are not available, has become almost standard even when other clerics are there, thereby confusing sacramental roles and circumventing canonical provisions. I will later suggest that another interpretation of the SLC's approach to lay and clerical roles might be possible and helpful.[89] The danger, however, is a variant of the one cited by the 1998 Lambeth Conference of lay ministry's becoming too focused within the church; here, the risk is of an incipient clericalism in which "lay ministry" means "clergy ministry" without the collar.

The issue of "lay" and "clerical" ministry raises a further question: *Who* are the "ministers"? The prayer book is inconsistent. References such as "bishops and other ministers" in Rite I can be explained away as a bow to traditional language. Yet if "the ministers of the Church are lay persons, bishops, priests, and deacons," why does the newly written Form V of the Prayers of the People intercede "for all bishops and other ministers, and for

---

[87] This point is firmly made by my friend and neighbor, Andrew McThenia; another is Richard G. Leggett, "'Gentle as a Dove, Living, Burning as Fire': Images and Language in the 1979 Ordinal" in Meyers, *Prayer Book for the 21st Century*, 169–170.

[88] *Prayer Book Studies 20*, 16.

[89] US BCP, 322; cf. ECUSA, *Constitution and Canons* (2000), III.3.5(a) (p. 63): "A Lay Eucharistic Minister is a person licensed to this extraordinary ministry...*in the absence of* a sufficient number of Priests or Deacons assisting the celebrant" (emph. added).

all the holy people of God" as if all the holy people do not share in the ministry?[90]

Perhaps the differentiation is inherent in the very concept of setting someone apart for ministry with such powerful rites and symbols. Whenever the church empowers one person for ministry by using a hymn to the Holy Spirit, prayer, laying on of hands, and fine vestments, as it does for ordination, that person is set apart. If and when that ordained person is called to lead a parish, *The Book of Common Prayer* so concentrates on the individual being instituted that the congregation is left largely to watch and wonder what place they *really* have in the new ministry being celebrated.[91]

Along with the question of "Who ministers" is "Who calls?" What authority calls and ordains a person to an order of ministry? The rites waffle between God and human agents as the source of vocation. The Examination sections in each ordination service indicate the inconsistency. For a bishop, the authority is essentially divine:

> My *brother*, the people have chosen you and have affirmed their trust in you by acclaiming your election.... Are you persuaded that God has called you to the office of bishop?

For a priest, the call comes from both God and church:

> Now you are called to work as a pastor, priest, and teacher, together with your bishop and fellow presbyters, and to take your share in the councils of the Church.... Do you believe that you are truly called by God and his Church to this priesthood?

So too for a deacon:

> God now calls you to a special ministry of servanthood directly under your bishop.... Do you believe that you are truly called by God and his Church to the life and work of a deacon?[92]

---

[90] Cp. US BCP 555 and 390, 392.

[91] US BCP, 559–564; cf. Steve Kelsey, "Celebrating the Ministry of All the Baptized at the Welcoming of New Leaders into the Continuing Life and Ministry of Congregations" in Meyers, *Prayer Book for the 21st Century*, 179–204. (The rite can be adapted for other forms of ministry.)

[92] US BCP, 517, 531, 543, ital. in orig.

Who then is the true ordainer? Judging from our ecclesiological survey, Anglicans stoutly answer, "God," but only when God is operating through the whole church, not just through a bishop and other ministers. However, the formula, "make N. a bishop/priest/deacon in your Church," spoken by the ordaining bishop, leaves the impression that God acts through the bishop but not necessarily through the whole church. The petition to "fill *him* with grace and power" implies that the moment of ordination is immediately transformative rather than a slow process over time that would more fully include the church.[93]

Finally, what is an "order," how many are there, and who constitutes them? The prayer book preface that seeks to uphold the participation of all also intimates that laity compose an order, alongside bishops, priests, and deacons, all of whom fulfill "the functions proper to their respective orders." Because the catechism later states that the "ministers of the Church are lay persons, bishops, priests, and deacons," the implication deepens that laity form an order of ministry. Not only does this position seem to be nearly unique in Anglican understanding, but also it creates practical tensions, as we shall see.[94]

Rightly welcomed for all its contributions, one of which was articulating a far more contemporary theology of ministry, the prayer book still encounters the same old difficulties of distinguishing, balancing, and uniting the ministries of some within the ministry of all. Nevertheless, *The Book of Common Prayer* was the first major revision in Anglicanism to adopt the ecclesiology of the late-nineteenth and early-twentieth centuries. The American book provided an influential model for Anglicans elsewhere as the process of liturgical revision spread around the Communion. But the influence has been symbiotic, because the prayer book revisions subsequently produced in the other provinces already have rebounded to enrich American liturgy and may continue to offer insights for the future of the Episcopal Church.

---

[93] US BCP, 521, 533, 545; cf. Bradshaw, "Shape," 153. Any problem is lessened by the participation of other presbyters in the laying on of hands for a priest, and of at least three bishops in consecrating to the episcopate; but this collegiality cannot be recognized in this way for deacons.

[94] US BCP, 13, 855; cf. chapter 9, below. A section report in 1968 was the first to imply, at Lambeth, that laity constituted an order of ministry: see *Lambeth 1968*, 100.

THE ALTERNATIVE SERVICE BOOK 1980 (CHURCH OF ENGLAND)

While Episcopalians were revising their liturgy, so were the English and for the same reasons. Whereas the former *replaced* their *Book of Common Prayer* (1928), the latter dared not submit alterations to the 1662 Prayer Book to Parliament, as required, and risk governmental rejections similar to those of 1927–28. They decided instead to supplement the 1662 version, which required no governmental approval, in a book carefully named *The Alternative Service Book 1980: Services authorized for use in the Church of England in conjunction with The Book of Common Prayer*. The date in the title hinted that this was but the latest example of an ongoing process (and, in fact, the *ASB* was largely replaced in the year 2000 with another, entitled *Common Worship*, as we shall see).

In contrast to the American ordination rites, *The Alternative Service Book* withholds anything specifically pertaining to ordination until after the Ministry of the Word. At that point the bishop/archbishop summarizes the nature of the order—for example, the servanthood of diaconate at the ordination of a deacon. The ordination prayer likewise focuses upon the specific order,[95] though the prayers for bishop and priest begin with identical language that is reminiscent perhaps of medieval days when bishop and priest were nearly indistinguishable in theology. This common language encapsulates a theology of the church:

> We praise and glorify you, almighty Father, because you have formed throughout the world a holy people for your own possession, a royal priesthood, a universal Church.

> We praise and glorify you because you have given us your only Son Jesus Christ to be the Apostle and High Priest of our faith, and the Shepherd of our souls.

---

[95] E.g., for deacon: "We praise and glorify you, most merciful Father, because in your great love of mankind you sent your only Son Jesus Christ to take the form of a servant; he came to serve and not to be served; and taught us that he who would be great among us must be the servant of all; he humbled himself for our sake, and in obedience accepted death, even death on a cross; therefore you highly exalted him and gave him the name which is above every name" (*ASB*, 348).

> We praise and glorify you that by his death he has overcome death; and that, having ascended into heaven, he has given his gifts abundantly to your people, making some, apostles; some, prophets; some, pastors and teachers; to equip them for the work of ministry and to build up his body.
>
> And now we give you thanks that you have called this/these your servant/s, whom we consecrate in your name, to share this ministry entrusted to your Church.

Then as hands are laid upon the head of the candidate(s),

> Send down the Holy Spirit upon your servant N for the office and work of a deacon/priest/bishop in your Church.[96]

The prayer then concludes in a manner appropriate to each order.

In these few words, the rite manages to convey several themes that we have been pursuing: (1) the holy people formed by God to be a royal priesthood and universal church; (2) the unique high priesthood of Jesus; (3) the diversity of gifts that he gave (though the list sounds more official than functional) for the purpose of ministry; (4) the calling of individuals for service, *but* in the context of the ministry of the entire church.

The Alternative Service Book introduces—or rather, recalls—ancient language. The title of its Ordinal, "The Ordination of Priests (also called Presbyters)," deliberately includes both terms.[97] Direct participation in the rite is limited to a few individuals, however. Candidates for diaconate and priesthood are presented by the "archdeacon or other person appointed" (who also cites the place where the persons will serve, a small reminder that ordination is tied to direct local ministry). At the ordination of bishops, the fact that two bishops present the candidate for consecration implies the involvement of the broader church and hints at the universal scope of the episcopal office. Other clergy and laity, however, lack

---

[96] *ASB*, 362, 393–4; for deacon, cf. 348–349. The *ASB* anticipates multiple candidates for diaconate and priesthood but a single individual for episcopate.

[97] The Church of South India used only the term "presbyter" in titling the ordination rite for the order. In both, the *ASB* implied "no doctrinal significance in the use of either term" (Jasper and Bradshaw, *Companion to the ASB*, 435).

any visible role in offering the person for episcopal ordination with one significant exception: the reading of the "Royal Mandate"[98] follows immediately upon the presentation, recalling that the choice of English bishops is ultimately a matter for a few select laity, namely the monarch on recommendation of the prime minister, who receives the advice of a commission that includes laypersons along with clergy. Still, the absence of non-mitered presenters is all the odder because, otherwise, the theme of a corporate nature to the church runs throughout *The Alternative Service Book*. After a baptism, for example, the congregation—as the rubric says, "representing the whole Church"—responds,

> We welcome you into the Lord's Family.
> We are members together of the body of Christ;
> we are children of the same heavenly Father;
> we are inheritors together of the kingdom of God.
> We welcome you.[99]

In those services, familial themes predominate. This imagery recurs at Eucharist during the president's call to the peace:

> We are the Body of Christ.
> In the one Spirit we were all baptized into one body.
> Let us then pursue all that makes for peace
> and builds up our common life.[100]

The Alternative Service Book quickly joined the Episcopal Church's *Book of Common Prayer* as a model for revisions in other parts of the Communion. For all its reliance on the 1662 prayer book, the *ASB* showed that, like its American cousin, it is a product of its time and of the theology that had come to prevail in the late twentieth century.

SCOTLAND AND WALES

Scotland and Wales each revised their ordination rites in ways that largely followed the new English pattern. The *Scottish Ordinal 1984* includes a reference to Jesus' washing his disciples' feet

---

[98] *ASB*, 370–371, 387.

[99] *ASB*, 248.

[100] *ASB*, 128 (second form).

in its prayer for the deacon and parallels *The Alternative Service Book*'s prayer for priests in enumerating those offices whose purpose is "to equip all for the work of ministry and to build up his body, the Church." The rite uses the term "presbyter" rather than "priest." A rubric allows the ordinary to anoint the new presbyter or bishop, a ceremony rarely found in Anglican rites. The prayer over the bishop-elect refers to "Christ the one High Priest." With a touch of Presbyterianism, the primus prays,

> In the fulness of time
> you founded your Church
> by the word of your grace,
> choosing in Christ, before the world was made,
> those whose lives would proclaim your glory.

In the process, the prayer answers the question, lest anyone doubt, "who is behind the church?" At the Eucharist, the new bishop presides, "his presbyters with him."[101]

Wales published a new series of services in Welsh and English. Deciding in the English text to retain the "thou" form of address to the Almighty, it follows the structure and thought of *The Alternative Service Book*. Like the Scottish rite, it mentions the forgiveness of sins as a priestly function ("If you forgive the sins of any...") yet does so not at the more accustomed point of the laying on of hands but instead at the *porrectio instrumentorum*, the conveyance of the Bible.

THE BOOK OF ALTERNATIVE SERVICES (ANGLICAN CHURCH OF CANADA, 1985)

Like the English, the Canadians issued an alternative book rather than a new prayer book, but their version closely follows the American revision, with some intriguing differences. In language, the Canadians are even more inclusive, listing personal pronouns in italics as *he/she* and *him/her*. Canadian prayers of consecration more closely resemble *The Alternative Service Book*, but the "examinations" use the American version. The prayer for a bishop concludes with the petition that, "as a ruler over your household and an ambassador for Christ, he may stand before you

---

[101] Buchanan, *Modern Anglican Ordination Rites*, 16–20.

blameless." The phrase echoes the Welsh prayer book and also the "princely spirit" phrase in the American rite.[102]

The baptismal rite follows the American revision almost word for word. What differences do occur tend to accentuate, even more than the American rite, the corporate nature of the sacrament. Canada's preface cites early Christian practices, revealing that initiation into the church "was a vital concern of the whole Christian community" not just of the individuals and their families. "Preparation for baptism was a responsibility shared among various members of the community, both ordained and lay." The celebrant gives thanks for the gifts that allow the baptized to "serve [God] as a royal priesthood," then asks the Spirit's anointing for the candidate's "new birth in the family of [God's] Church." The Canadian liturgy shows its debt to Anglican ecclesiology of previous years and also to the ecumenical discussions that led to the World Council of Churches' document *Baptism, Eucharist and Ministry*.[103]

THE CHURCH OF THE PROVINCE OF MELANESIA

Melanesia is one of the few less-developed Anglican provinces to revise its Ordinal and was one of the first provinces of the Communion to do so. In 1974 it published a booklet of rites based upon the English Anglican-Methodist proposal. The bishop's prayer over those to be ordained priests incorporates, to a high degree, the principles of a representative ministry within the priesthood of all. In a section that anticipates *The Alternative Service Book*, the bishop prepares for the laying on of hands:

> Pour forth your grace upon this your servant O Lord, that in this royal priesthood of your People he may faithfully fulfil this his priestly ministry.... Make him worthy to offer with all your People spiritual sacrifices acceptable in your sight, and to minister the Sacraments of your New Covenant. Give him a spirit of wisdom and discipline, that he may show himself wise in counsel. Make him to be an able and profitable fellow-worker

---

[102] Buchanan, *Modern Anglican Ordination Rites*, 23–26. The *porrectio*—giving of Bible and staff to the new bishop—also follows the Welsh precedent; the new priest receives a chalice and paten along with Bible. The Anglican Church of Canada, *The Book of Alternative Services for the Anglican Church of Canada* (Toronto: Anglican Book Centre, 1985), 639, 649.

[103] Canada, *Alternative Services*, 146, 157.

with his brothers in the Ministry and with your chief
pastors, the Bishops....

Then the bishop gives the new priest a Bible, and then a paten and
chalice.[104]

A NEW ZEALAND PRAYER BOOK (1989)

One of the most acclaimed prayer book revisions appeared in
1989 in New Zealand. It contains many of the themes we have
been tracing, not the least of which is its exemplary inclusiveness.
A New Zealand Prayer Book/He Karakia Mihinare o Aotearoa is
bilingual, encompassing in its worship both of the major language
groups of the country, English and Maori.

Providing for "an ordained ministry, to serve the local congregation in the name of Christ and the universal Church," the Ordinal's
preface states, "is one of the responsibilities of the apostolic
Church." Ordination rites must derive from a common understanding of ministry, which originates at the font. Consequently
each rite acknowledges "that all Christians have a ministry by
virtue of their baptism, and that some members of the baptised
community are also called and empowered to fulfil an ordained
ministry, and to enable the total mission of the Church." In contrast with the Episcopal Church's theoretical centrality of episcopate,
the New Zealand church holds each of the three orders as "equally important" even as they differ "in the tasks they do on behalf
of the whole Church." For the ordinands to pursue those tasks,
the people offer their assent as "an integral part of the service."
The ordinands also need "the enabling power of the Holy Spirit to
provide the appropriate gifts of ministry"; and that, the liturgy
directs, shall be the topic of the sermon. (It is alone among the
revised books to specify homiletical subject matter at ordinations.)

These services, allowing for an appropriate definition of
the role of each order in ordained ministry, affirm the
understanding of the Church that all ministry has its

---

[104] This *porrectio instrumentorum* is unusual in Anglican ordinations in presenting a paten and chalice as well as a Bible to new priests. But in number of pre-
sentations, Micronesia's liturgy for episcopal consecrations has the most, with
the new bishop receiving holy oil (being anointed with it himself), a pectoral
cross, ring, miter, staff, and Bible, each with a statement of presentation comparable to the US BCP's "celebration of a new ministry" (Buchanan, *Modern Anglican Ordination Rites*, 50–53; cf. US BCP, 561–562).

source in Christ's ministry, and is part of the response to the command of Christ to the Church to fulfil its apostolic mission.[105]

The officiating bishop recites a prologue to an examination that is identical for each order, varying only with the name of the order itself:

E te whanau a te Karaiti / People of God,
we have come to ordain a *deacon / deacons*
in Christ's holy Church.
Christ is head of the Church;
he alone is the source of all Christian ministry.
Through the ages it is Christ
who has called men and women to serve.

By the Holy Spirit all who believe and are baptised
receive a ministry to proclaim Jesus as Saviour and Lord,
and to love and serve the people with whom they live
    and work.
In Christ they are to bring redemption,
to reconcile and to make whole.
They are to be salt for the earth; they are to be light to
    the world.

After his resurrection and ascension
Christ gave gifts abundantly to the Church.
Some he made apostles, some prophets, some evangelists,
some pastors and teachers; to equip God's people
for their work of ministry and to build up the body of Christ.

We stand within a tradition
in which there are deacons, priests and bishops.
They are called and empowered to fulfil an ordained
    ministry
and to enable the whole mission of the Church.
Our authority is in Scripture
and in the Church's continuing practice through the ages.[106]

The statement proclaims the understanding of church, ministry, and orders now typical of Anglican revised prayer books: (1) the headship of Christ as the source of all ministry, the one who calls

---

[105] *NZ Prayer Book*, 887.

[106] *NZ Prayer Book*, 890 (|| 901, 908).

to service; (2) the sharing by all the baptized in a ministry of reconciliation in Jesus, by word and deed; (3) the initiative of Christ in sending gifts to enable ministry and build up the body (although New Zealand's listing of the kinds of people who receive these gifts—apostles, prophets, pastors and the like—seems to earmark them primarily for offices; *The Alternative Service Book* leaves a similar impression); (4) a threefold ministry of bishops, priests, and deacons called and empowered to enable the entire mission of the church, following the authority of both Scripture and tradition.

A communal emphasis infuses the bishop's consecrating prayer at priestly ordinations. Priests are thus "called to build up Christ's congregation, to strengthen the baptised, and to lead them as witnesses to Christ in the world." The prayer outlines priestly duties, especially a pastorate of sharing joys and sorrows, encouraging the faithful, recalling those who fall away, aiding the sick, proclaiming the Word, administering the sacraments, and taking "part in Christ's prophetic work."[107] The language at the laying-on of hands is especially colorful, with the people responding (as they also do for deacons and bishops):

> God of grace, through your Holy Spirit,
> gentle as a dove, living, burning as fire,
> empower your servant N
> for the office and work of a priest in the Church.
>
> May every grace of ministry rest on *these your servants*.
> Keep *them* strong and faithful,
> steadfast in Jesus Christ, our Saviour.
> **Amen!**
> **May *they* herald the joy of your kingdom,**
> **bring freedom rather than bondage,**
> **serve rather than be served;**
> **through the sacraments *they minister***
> **let your grace abound.**[108]

The candidate then receives a Bible.

---

[107] NZ *Prayer Book*, 901 (see the appendix to chapter 7 for an examination of this and other revisions' terms).

[108] NZ *Prayer Book*, 908.

A Prayer Book for Australia (1995)

In 1977 Australia's General Synod authorized revisions to a prayer book based upon the English version of 1662, and the result was published a year later as *An Australian Prayer Book*. Conservative in approach, it updated the seventeenth-century book and added more options. The bishop who wrote its preface predicted a useful life of ten to fifteen years, but it lasted for eighteen. In 1995, appreciating the need for still greater diversity in style, inclusive language, and greater simplicity in rubrics and presentation, the church published *A Prayer Book for Australia*.[109]

The Ordinal's preface states what it calls "liturgical principles" that guide its practice: (1) "The distinctiveness of each Order is clearly expressed, each being understood in the context of the ministry of the whole people of God, in the light of the unique ministry of Christ"; (2) language is contemporary while seeking to reflect the ideas of the 1662 Ordinal, "as well as relating to the roles of clergy in the contemporary Church"; (3) the liturgy should incorporate scholarly conclusions about ancient ordination prayers, bringing together the elements of the *berakah* ("blessing") prayer including laying on of hands and invocation of the Spirit, followed by the *porrectio*, public recognition, and authorizing of the ministry of each candidate; (4) the term "presbyter" appears in the title of the rite, following the example of Richard Hooker, the Scottish rite, *The Alternative Service Book*, and Roman Catholic and Orthodox usage; and (5) the Australian book continues the "distinctive feature," in episcopal ordinations, of reading oaths and declarations. Vowing allegiance to the monarch (as in the English rite) or attesting belief in the Scriptures (as in the United States) serves to place the new bishop within the community of faith, in the present and throughout history.[110]

---

[109] The Anglican Church of Australia, *A Prayer Book for Australia* (Alexandria, NSW: Broughton Books, 1995), vii–viii.

[110] *A Prayer Book for Australia*, 781. In the *ASB*, only a candidate for the episcopate is asked to state formally a belief in the faith revealed in the Scriptures, set forth in the creeds, and borne witness by the Church of England; all ordinands are asked to respond to questions attesting to the same points (*ASB*, 388–389, 373). In the US, all ordinands sign a declaration, but the subsequent questions are less direct regarding belief (US BCP 513, 526, 538; 518, 532, 543–544). New Zealand omits the formal declaration for any order.

The Ordinal makes note of the spiritual continuity of ordained work even as the sociological context has changed greatly over three centuries:

> Others now share the responsibility of ministry within the life of the parish, and this is encouraged and recognised in these ordination services. The special responsibility of the priest remains, but room is made for others to exercise their gifts of ministry as well.

Recognizing that some seek the diaconate but not the priesthood, the service is intended for all deacons regardless of whether some subsequently become priests. Presenters for each order may include "lay people as well as senior clergy."[111]

How have these ideas been expressed, and to what degree does the Australian Ordinal fit into the pattern of twentieth-century Anglican ecclesiology? The liturgy attempts to treat each order individually, reflecting the particular character of all three. Some elements are common to all. Each rite follows the same structure, for instance, while within that framework, the exhortation and prayers reflect the distinctive role that each has to play within the Body of Christ.

Laity take a role within the liturgy. For example, a layperson joins an archdeacon in presenting candidates for diaconate and priesthood. At episcopal ordinations, "two bishops, with representatives of the diocese and province (priests, deacons, and laypersons)" make the presentation. Just before the laying on of hands (for episcopate, before the examination), the officiant asks the congregation for its acceptance and support ("We accept *them* gladly!").[112]

Like *The Alternative Service Book*, the Australian prayer book uses the term "presbyter" in the title of the ordination for priesthood. It similarly places the presbyterate within the work of Jesus as High Priest. The bishop reminds priestly candidates, "In baptism we are called to be a royal priesthood.... Now you are responding to the call of God and of the Church to live and work

---

[111] *A Prayer Book for Australia*, 780.

[112] *A Prayer Book for Australia*, 787, 795, cp. 801; 800. Including a deacon in presenting a candidate is unusual.

as a priest, a pastor and teacher, for God's glory and the strengthening of God's people."[113] The connection among the candidate's priesthood, the royal priesthood, and Jesus' High Priesthood, however, remains unclear.

Use of the Body of Christ image for the church permeates this book. At each ordination, the bishop or archbishop introduces the peace, as at all celebrations of the Eucharist, with "We are the body of Christ," the congregation responding, "His Spirit is with us." At baptism the congregation welcomes the new Christian "as a member with us of the body of Christ."[114] How this "body" actually serves is only vaguely defined; after confirmation, for instance, the bishop issues a challenge that seems weak because of its generality:

> All who have been baptised and confirmed are called to study the Bible, to take part in the life of the Church, to share in the Holy Communion, and to pray faithfully and regularly. We are called to share with others, by word and example, the love of Christ and his gospel of reconciliation and hope. We are called to love our neighbours as ourselves, to honour all people and to pray and work for peace and justice. I invite all of you to commit yourselves anew to this calling.[115]

The meaning of the presbyterate, then, is clear, but the "royal priesthood" of all the baptized much less so. In this the Australian prayer book is not unique. The revision does, however, aim to foster the participation of all elements of the church in the worship and life of the Christian community.

PRAYER BOOK REVISION IN THE NEW CENTURY

By the close of the twentieth century, Anglican prayer book revisions showed certain similarities. In the first place, all claim to uphold an ecclesiology based on the whole people of God as the Body of Christ, suggesting that in ordination God acts in and

---

[113] *A Prayer Book for Australia*, 796, 793.

[114] *A Prayer Book for Australia*, 787, 797, 807, cp. 92, 127; 79 (lowercase in orig.).

[115] *A Prayer Book for Australia*, 93.

through the church. Second, ministry is shared by the whole Body. Third, the entire church participates in ordaining to a particular ministry.

Do the rites succeed in meeting these claims? Not entirely. God often seems to operate independently of the church and not through it, as the first premise asserts. Contrary to the third supposition, the liturgical sense of the whole church's being represented in the act of ordination is sometimes contravened by rubrics that limit who actively participates. But beyond the provisions that a rite may or may not make for the involvement of others is the reality that bishops hold exclusive rights to ordain, no matter how many presenters stand with a candidate or how many presbyters lay their hands with the bishop upon a priestly ordinand. Without question, purple predominates.

Two ecclesiological difficulties consequently arise from the predominance of bishops. First, there is the concept of the bishop as representative figure in the capacity of "ordinary." As the one who ordains, does she or he serve as a channel for God's grace or as a delegate of the church? Contemporary Anglican ecclesiology responds, "Both"; the bishop, like any ordained person, simultaneously represents Christ and the church. The revisions do not make that point clear. Second, there is the bishop's role within the Christian household. Several rites refer to the bishop's "rule" and "princely spirit," language that contradicts the collegial spirit expressed in some of the same rites. Ironically, such language of lordship tends to appear in provinces with well-established histories of hemming in episcopal authority.[116] In other provinces, especially younger ones that have tended not to revise their rites, the bishop functions at levels of power that approach the monarchical.

The bishop's place in the church is one concern within the broader question of how much the revisions reflect the participation of the entire church in ordination, ministry, and worship. A second concern is the choice of scriptural lections appointed for ordinations. As Leggett charges in his discussion of the Episcopal

---

[116] I.e., England (*ASB*, cf. Buchanan, *Modern Anglican Ordination Rites*, 17), Scotland (19) and Wales (22); Canada (26), and ECUSA (BCP re "princely Spirit," 521).

Church's lectionary (although his observations apply to other prayer books as well), the biblical readings tend to feature submissive roles for women and children; they also tend to exaggerate the purpose and role of orders within the church.[117] Still another question is the inclusiveness of the language of the rites: few equal the New Zealand rites, which strive consistently to be gender-inclusive as well as to incorporate the two vernacular languages of its country. The underlying question, of course, is how fully all share in ordinations given the bishop's inevitable primacy. Too often, rites say one thing but actually convey another. As I noted earlier, inconsistencies remain, sometimes within a single rite in some prayer books, with one section saying one thing and another nearly the opposite.

But, the process of revision continues. "No prayer book is the final word in worship," notes the preface to the latest Australian edition. As needs and perspectives change and grow, so must the church's worship; for that very reason, the obsolescence of some revisions, including Australia's and England's, was deliberately planned. "The fundamentals remain the same: the expression of those fundamentals must change from generation to generation."[118] Experiences of the past quarter century will undoubtedly help to produce even more effective rites that convey an understanding of orders, even as that understanding continues to develop.

Common Worship

In England, the process of revision has reached another stage already. In the year 2000, *Common Worship* began to appear in parish churches, a book containing rites for the most frequently used services but not ordination. To what degree does it continue the theological trend we have been following? *Common Worship* heightens the measure of baptismal commitment in several ways. Unlike *The Alternative Service Book*, it directs questions to the parents/godparents or sponsors. It adds a rubric permitting a large

---

[117] E.g., 1 Tim. 3:1–7, an option for the ordination of a bishop, is based on a household code that gives a dominant place to husband/father. Leggett also cautions on messianic or monarchical implications in readings given as options for the ordination of bishops (e.g., Is. 61:1–8, 42.1–9, Ps. 99) or of the prophetic for presbyters (Is. 6:1–8), etc. Leggett, "'Gentle as a Dove,'" 165–166.

[118] *A Prayer Book for Australia*, viii.

candle to be lit, thereby accentuating what is to follow. In the portion of the service called "the decision," *The Alternative Service Book* asks only three questions of the candidate (one affirmation, two renunciations), whereas *Common Worship* asks six (three affirmations, three renunciations), in a manner resembling the American and Canadian prayer books.[119] To a greater degree than either *The Alternative Service Book* or the Episcopal Church's *Book of Common Prayer*, *Common Worship* underscores the community's role in nurturing candidates who are children by saying, "*they* will need the help and encouragement of the Christian community.... As part of the Church of Christ, we all have a duty to support *them* by prayer, example, and teaching." Together, the congregation offers prayers as a "royal priesthood" and gives this welcome:

> There is one Lord, one faith, one baptism:
> N and N, by one Spirit we are all baptized into one body.
> All: **We welcome you into the fellowship of faith;**
> **we are children of the same heavenly Father;**
> **we welcome you.**[120]

"Missionary" or "service" aspects of baptism, however, although cited in the questions of the Baptismal Covenant, go otherwise unmentioned.

In eucharistic rites, *Common Worship* moves ahead of other revisions in at once affirming traditional liturgical roles customarily assigned to laity or clergy while at the same time inviting greater participation in those roles. In so doing, it emphasizes liturgical functions over the status of those who fulfill them. For laity in general, *Common Worship* expects wide involvement, expressive of the praise and thanksgiving that the whole church offers. In the words of its "general notes,"

> Holy Communion is celebrated by the whole people of
> God gathered for worship. The ministry of the members
> of the congregation is expressed through their active

---

[119] Cp. the Church of England, *Common Worship* (London: Church House, 2000) [*CW*], 353, 359 with *ASB*, 230, and US *BCP*, 304–305, which, except for a rephrased final question, is virtually identical in thought and language. The questions/commissioning in *CW* follow the act of baptism rather than preceding it as in the American rite.

[120] *CW*, 358, cf. 345; 360–361. Ital. and boldface in orig.

> participation together in the words and actions of the
> service, but also by some of them reading the Scripture
> passages, leading the prayers of intercession, and, if
> authorized, assisting with the distribution of communion.

Those same general notes list the functions a deacon traditionally exercises: reading the gospel, inviting the confession, preparing the table, and so forth. They go on to say, "The deacon's liturgical ministry provides an appropriate model for the ministry of an assisting priest, a Reader, or another episcopally authorized minister in a leadership ministry that complements that of the president." That is, non-deacons may fill those diaconal roles. In a similar way, the "ministry of the president" is a unifying one. It is assigned, of course, to a priest, but after establishing his or her presidency by greeting the people, the priest may delegate aspects of the first portion of the rite (Gathering and Liturgy of the Word) to a "deacon, Reader, or other authorized lay person." In the absence of the priest, one of those three may lead the entire Gathering and Liturgy of the Word—even those elements reserved to the priest. Canons also provide for laity to function as lay eucharistic ministers and, with appropriate permissions, to preach. In sum, *Common Worship* anticipates a eucharistic liturgy in which all play a part, emphasizing roles rather than offices, functions rather than orders, within appropriate limits as authorized by canon or rubric, and all with the priest as a source and symbol of unity.[121]

Reallocating liturgical responsibilities on the basis of function rather than office or order has the advantage of inviting greater participation, but also risks confusing the congregation as to who is supposed to be doing what. The presiding priest imposes some order on the rite, and—especially in parishes where the same priest presides week after week—provides consistency. But even greater confusion may result from the language of *Common Worship*, which uses the term "ministry" almost interchangeably for a deacon, an assisting priest, or a lay reader. "Minister" usually means

---

[121] Lay eucharistic ministers must be licensed; and canon dictates that the sermon "shall be preached by a duly authorized minister, deaconess, Reader or lay worker or, at the invitation of the minister having the cure of souls and with the permission of the bishop, another person" (*CW*, 158–159).

one who is ordained, but not always.[122] The familiar words of the "prayer for the whole state" adroitly ask in one form for grace "to all bishops, priests and deacons" (instead of "bishops and other ministers"), but in the next form prays, "Enlighten N our bishop and all your ministers." Another form avoids the problem altogether:

> For N our bishop,
> for the leaders of our sister Churches, and for all clergy
>   and people,
> let us pray to the Lord.[123]

There is no mistaking, however, who is meant by the people of God. The image of baptism into the Body is reiterated in nearly every version of the Eucharist, sometimes with a missionary twist:

> Faithful God,
> in baptism you have adopted us as your children,
> made us members of the body of Christ
> and chosen us as inheritors of your kingdom:
> we thank you that in this Eucharist
> you renew your promises within us,
> empower us by your Spirit to witness and to serve,
> and send us out as disciples of your Son.[124]

All in all, *Common Worship* advances the early twentieth-century theological trends that the American prayer book began to articulate in the 1970s. It emphasizes anew the unifying purpose of presbyteral priesthood, while at the same time revitalizing possibilities for fuller, even clearer participation of all in the liturgical life of the priestly people of God.

By now the vision of the church as the Body of Christ has gained a broad acceptance. For conferences, canons, and prayer books to incorporate the ideas of the corporate priesthood and

---

[122] *CW*, 158–159.

[123] *CW*, 158–159; 183, 227; 283, 284, 286.

[124] *CW*, 297 (#2); cp. US BCP, 367–368. *Common Worship* retains the call to the peace from the *ASB* (128 and elsewhere): "We are the body of Christ. / In the one Spirit we were all baptized into one body. / Let us then pursue all that makes for peace / and builds up our common life." (*CW*, 290 [#2]).

representative ministry (as many have) indicates the degree to which concepts developed largely within one party of the Church of England gained Communion-wide adoption. The theology of liberal Catholics like Gore and Moberly moderated the extreme Anglo-Catholicism of Carter or Baverstock, while centrist leaders like Temple made the vision acceptable to a larger audience. Elements of contradiction still remain, nonetheless, and old understandings persist. Sometimes they are embedded in the very canons and revisions that were designed to move beyond them, while disputes continue over the ways that people represent Christ and the church. The process of receiving the vision, in the "gradual and dynamic process" that the Lambeth bishops described in 1988, continues.[125]

---

[125] *Lambeth 1988* (section II report, ¶147), 117.

V
New Directions in Ministry

In the first half of the twentieth century, an incarnational vision of church and ministry coalesced, while in the second half that vision became reality in the liturgies, the canons, and even the architecture of the Anglican Communion. As it did so, however, the vision was both criticized and altered, in part because of the changing circumstances that dramatically affected how Anglicans would understand their Communion, their ministry, and their priests.

As the Anglican Communion changed, so did the practice of priesthood. Technological advances alone altered how the church did its business, especially in the developed world, as telephones, automobiles, photocopiers, and computers all became necessities of clerical life. But more significant trends were also afoot, and one was ecumenism. Though what William Temple called "the great new fact of our era" did not succeed in uniting denominations, advances were made and agreements were reached on vital matters like baptism, Eucharist, and ministry. Ecumenism remained much on the leadership's mind and, increasingly, in the churchgoer's practice, as doors opened to greater interdenominational understanding.

A further significant trend was a shift in the Anglican Communion's center of gravity. By the 1950s, as scholar Adrian Hastings remarked, "America was now the self-chosen standard bearer of civilization, capitalism and Christianity, as Britain had been in the nineteenth century."[1] The passing of this standard became more pronounced in the decades that followed, given a decline in English religious life as "believing" became divorced from "belonging."[2] By century's end, furthermore, attention shifted to the new and fast-growing provinces in Asia and Africa. In 1985 Archbishop of Canterbury Robert Runcie politely reminded Episcopalians that most Anglicans used English as their second language and that there were "more black members than white."[3] By Lambeth 1998, these newer provinces were insisting on being heard. According to Ian Douglas, a scholar of the Anglican Communion, that conference

> signaled a turning point for Anglicanism. In debates over international debt and/or human sexuality, it became abundantly clear that the churches in the Southern Hemisphere would not stand idly by while their sisters and brothers in the U.S. and England set the agenda.... For the first time ever, the Anglican Communion had to face head-on the radical multi-cultural reality of our post-colonial, post-modern Christian community.[4]

Furthermore, these recently evangelized churches were becoming the most energetic evangelists even outside their own homelands: Latin Americans doing mission work in Europe and Africans aiding in efforts in America.[5]

For the entire Anglican Communion, therefore, finding an adequate supply of trained Anglican clergy was a chronic problem. Ever since the 1908 Lambeth Conference, bishops had bewailed a

---

[1] Hastings, *History*, 459.

[2] Cf. Grace Davie, *Religion in Britain Since 1945: Believing Without Belonging* (Oxford: Blackwell, 1994), 18–27, which observes that lower levels of "belonging" characterize religion and other aspects of life as well.

[3] Philip Jenkins, *The Next Christendom* (Oxford: Oxford University Press, 2002), 2; Runcie q. from an address to General Convention, in Ian Douglas, *Fling Out the Banner!: The National Church Ideal and the Foreign Mission of the Episcopal Church* (New York: Church Hymnal, 1996), 8.

[4] Ian Douglas, "Authority After Colonialism: Power, Privilege and Primacy in the Anglican Communion," *The Witness*, vol. 83, no. 3 (March 2000), 11. See also "The Exigency of Times and Occasions: Power and Identity in the Anglican Communion," in Ian T. Douglas and Kwok Pui-lan, eds., *Beyond Colonial Anglicanism: The Anglican Communion in the 21st Century* (New York: Church Publishing, 2001), 24–26. Cf. Greenwood, *Transforming*, 61, who cites critiques of a British- and Empire-oriented ecclesiology.

[5] Richard Kew, *Brave New Church: What the Future Holds* (Harrisburg, PA: Morehouse, 2001), 11.

lack of personnel both in England and overseas.[6] The reasons varied from global North to global South. In burgeoning provinces such as Sudan and Uganda, the challenge was one of growth, with legions of new Christians outstripping the capacity to call, train, and ordain clergy. In the United States and the United Kingdom, the problem was a decline in numbers of clergy and parishioners alike. Although the Episcopal Church's leadership thought it faced a "glut" of clergy in the 1980s, some warned that age and retirement would soon remove far more from the vocational pipeline than were entering it.[7] In England, ordination numbers peaked in the 1960s and started declining to the point where ordinations could not keep up with clergy retirements, although in the 1990s things began looking up again.[8] One major reason why: In 1992 the Church of England's General Synod voted to join the United States, Canada, Hong Kong, and New Zealand in ordaining women to the presbyterate. With these decisions, the masculine image of priestliness began to yield to a more inclusive understanding.

The struggle to include women fully in the church's life had made halting progress since New Zealand allowed women on vestries as early as 1922. Bishop R. O. Hall of Hong Kong ordained Deaconess Florence Li Tim Oi to the priesthood in 1944 as a wartime exigency to provide pastoral care and sacramental ministry in Macao. By 1948 China proposed experimenting with ordaining a deaconess as a priest, although that year's Lambeth Conference rejected the idea out of hand. Thirty long years later, the 1978 Conference allowed each province to decide the issue on its own. One of its committees ventured "that only as women are fully accepted as members of the Body of Christ in its mission and ministry can it be said that the Body is moving toward completeness."[9]

---

[6] F. R. Barry, *Vocation and Ministry* (Welwyn: James Nisbet & Co., 1958), xii, 8.

[7] In 1974, 19.4% of the 8,532 active clergy were below the age of 35, and 22.5% above 55; by 2000, only 3.9% could be called "young" and 39.8% had reached 55—and from a smaller pool of 7,721, a decrease of 9.5% ("Looking at the Age Gap: Now and Then," *Congregations* 27:2 [March/April 2001], 9).

[8] Church of England. "Petertide sees a further rise in ordinations—26/06/1999" <http://www.cofe.anglican.org/cgi-bin/news/item_frame.pl?id=41> (April 26, 2001).

[9] *Lambeth 1948* (Res. #113, 115), 52; *Lambeth 1978* (Res. #21–22), 45–47; (section report) 81. David M. Paton, *R.O.: The Life and Times of Bishop Ronald Hall of Hong Kong* (Hong Kong: Diocese of Hong Kong and Macao, 1983), 125–148.

As that committee's statement implies, the question of women's ordination to the priesthood inspired a new consideration of priesthood and orders generally. For instance, in England, a ministry council report entitled *Gender and Ministry* (1962) perceived the real issue to be not the relative status of men and women but "the nature of the ministry." In what sense, asked the report, did the priest's calling to be "in Christ"' differ from the lay Christian's? What was meant by "indelible seal," given that other vocations also required a lifelong commitment? And why was the ministry of Holy Orders singled out from the church's many ministries? More Christians, the report surmised, would be encouraged to consider non-clerical service "if the too-prevalent attitude towards the clergy as the recipients of some semi-magical status could be clearly and forcibly disclaimed, discouraged and discarded."[10]

Why was it so hard to understand and honor the nature and role of laity? If deliberating whether women could be priests reanimated conversation about the priesthood, the debate also added fuel to the continuing drive for larger roles for laity. Who were these "laity," anyway? Were they the *whole* people of God, as the Greek etymology suggested (*laos* = "people"), or did the connotation of "laity" simply as "non-clergy" prevail? Both issues—lay involvement in the life of the church and the ordination of women—emanated from the larger question of how the whole people of God were to share in the priesthood of the Body generally, and in the representative priesthood of presbyterate specifically.[11]

Along with women in priesthood and laity taking on functions previously reserved for the clergy, new forms of ordained service continued to appear. One form was the diaconate as a distinctive, lifelong vocation, as chapter 8 will discuss. New varieties of priestly ministries also emerged: some were focused on secular businesses and industries; some were directed at the parish but supported by

---

[10] Q. in Jacqueline Field-Bibb, *Women Towards Priesthood: Ministerial Politics and Feminist Praxis* (Cambridge: Cambridge University Press, 1991), 85–86.

[11] It may be significant in this regard that Anglican religious orders, ever since their regeneration, have drawn more women than men. By 1940 they outnumbered males by more than nine to one: about 1,400 to 150. Since then, numbers (if not the ratio) have increased on both sides. See Francis Penhale, *The Anglican Church Today: Catholics in Crisis* (London: Mowbray, 1986), 86.

non-church sources; a third limited the priest's ministry to a particular location. Chapter 10 will explore these growing phenomena. But, as a result, old stereotypes were dissolving. No longer was the Anglican clergyperson necessarily male, a priest, or in full-time parochial ministry. Nor, for that matter, did the priest in full-time parish ministry command unquestioned authority in the church and automatic respect from the public.

New models for ministry appeared as well, especially in America during the postwar period. One took its inspiration from the corporate world. The Episcopal Church elected Henry Knox Sherrill to become its first full-time Presiding Bishop in 1947, and he compared his duties to those of the head of a multinational corporation.[12] Another model was the "therapeutic." Developments in mental health during the 1950s and 1960s began to be appropriated into pastoral care as a course called Clinical Pastoral Education (CPE), which became a standard rite of passage for seminarians, who would spend a summer functioning as a chaplain in a hospital, mental institution, or prison. At the same time, parish clergy rated pastoral counseling as their top priority. Then in the late 1960s, as social issues clamored for attention, some clergy favored a more "prophetic" model, which led them to preach God's justice in sermons, develop new programs for the needy, and join protest movements. These various patterns influenced how clergy perceived themselves, how they went about their work, and indeed how they understood the nature of that work. All these patterns had their critics, as we shall see, and to some extent, at least in the American church, all are still with us.

Not only were models of ministry shifting, so was basic theological thinking. In 1955 people in the pews might have heard of the significant names in theology: Barth, Bonhoeffer, Brunner, Bultmann, Niebuhr, Tillich. A decade later, however, what captured public attention was the theological query that *TIME* magazine splayed across newsstands in 1966, just in time for Easter: "Is God Dead?" At the same time, movements of spiritual renewal

[12] Cf. Douglas, *Fling Out the Banner!*, 226–228; The Episcopal Church Foundation, *The Zacchaeus Project: Discerning Episcopal Identity at the Dawn of the New Millennium* (n.p.: 1999), 50.

began to spring up, and soon Charismatic Christians, with their emphasis on the gifts of the Holy Spirit, were influencing mainline denominations in many a country, even receiving commendations from Archbishop Michael Ramsey and—later and more cautiously—from the 1978 Lambeth Conference.[13] Allied to these renewal movements was Cursillo, adapted for Anglicans from a Roman Catholic movement that focused on a three-day "little course"—hence the Spanish word *cursillo*—that combined theological talks, group-process exercises, and spiritual disciplines. Cursillo coincided with, and may have contributed to, a revitalization of Bible reading, prayer groups, lay ministries, and healing ministries.[14] At about the same time, two authors won acclaim for their writings on the spiritual life: Henri Nouwen, whose *Wounded Healer* was the first of an outpouring of books that went on until his death, and the English Anglican Kenneth Leech, whose 1977 book *Soul Friend* introduced a new generation to spiritual direction. Aided by this spiritual renewal, Evangelical Anglicanism staged a comeback in the 1980s and influenced the 1988 Lambeth Conference's call for an official Decade of Evangelism in the 1990s. This effort yielded mixed results, but one of its fruits was the highly successful Alpha program, a ten-week introduction to the Christian faith that began at Holy Trinity Church, Brompton, in London.[15]

These were but some of the influences upon the church at large in the late twentieth century. Directly or indirectly, they influenced clergy and laity, the understanding of ministry, and indeed the understanding of the church itself. For all the changes, however, there was continuity as well. Forms of parochial service bore a fundamental similarity to what prevailed a hundred years before;

---

[13] A. Michael Ramsey, *Holy Spirit: A Biblical Study* (Cambridge, MA: Cowley, 1992); *Lambeth 1978* (Res. 7), 39; cf. section report, 72–74. Cf. Harvey Cox, *Fire from Heaven: The Rise of Pentecostal Spirituality and the Reshaping of Religion in the Twenty-first Century* (Reading, MA: Addison-Wesley, 1995), ch. 2.

[14] Cf. Melinsky, *Shape*, 250 on "spirituality" in ministerial training. It is noteworthy that the essay in *To Be a Priest* (1975) describing professional functions or roles lists "counseling" but other than a vague mention of "reconciler" makes no reference to anything related to spiritual direction; see 114.

[15] Alpha North America <http://www.alphana.org>, The Official Website from the Headquarters of Alpha <http://www.alpha.org.uk/> (April 27, 2001).

the wholesale transformation between 1800 and 1900 was not repeated a century later. *What* clergy did was not all that different—even though how they did it, what models inspired them, and who worked with them showed considerable variation.[16] Sermons continued to be delivered, the Eucharist celebrated, shut-ins visited, the poor remembered, the young taught, and the community served. As Australians observed in their newest prayer book, "While the spiritual role of ordained ministers remains much as it was in the seventeenth century, the sociological contexts in which they work have undergone significant changes."[17] Their observation is not entirely true, for the theological context changed as well. But basic functions endured, as did the priesthood, and as did the vision of the Body of Christ.

"To Be a Priest"

In the late 1960s and into the 1970s, against the backdrop of the Vietnam War, protests on campus, Black Power movements, urban riots, and Watergate, American Episcopalians debated how to revise *The Book of Common Prayer* and whether to ordain women. As soon as John Maury Allin was elected Presiding Bishop in 1973, he set out to resolve what he called, with a knack for the understated, a "problem" that was dividing the denomination: the ordination of women. Allin therefore requested brief essays from authors who represented the church's diversity and *To Be a Priest* was the result, a veritable mosaic of the church's viewpoints on what its editors carefully termed "the ministerial priesthood and the episcopate."[18] Of the book's opening two essays, one is by

---

[16] Cf. George Guiver et al., *The Fire and the Clay: The Priest in Today's Church* (London: SPCK, 1999), 43–44, 65; and William Countryman: "A Protestant preacher of the nineteenth century, who was expected to spend many hours in preparing sermons, might be quite astonished to find how little time many of his twentieth-century successors spend in their studies" *(Border, 122)*.

[17] *A Prayer Book for Australia*, 780.

[18] Robert Terwilliger and Urban T. Holmes III, eds., *To Be a Priest: Perspectives on Vocation and Ordination* (New York: Seabury, 1975), vii–ix. They took pains to distinguish "ministry" from "priesthood": see x. That Allin believed that essays and education would bring reconciliation may be another sign of his times. Arguably, it succeeded.

Robert E. Terwilliger, known as a leading Anglo-Catholic, and the other is by C. FitzSimons Allison, equally known for his Low Church polity.

Terwilliger based his theology of priesthood upon the sole priesthood of Christ, which is at once the "termination, but also the fulfillment of the priesthood of the Old Covenant." Jesus' obedience, living, dying, and rising all "make him our priest, that is, they unite mankind to God in him." Then this "priesthood of Christ is sent forth into the world." Choosing and commissioning the apostles are parts of the gospel, argued Terwilliger with a nod to Michael Ramsey. Through apostles, the church comes into being; apostles are *in* the church but also *to* the church, which, as the Body of Christ, constitutes a priesthood of all believers.[19] In a process that he calls "various but not chaotic"—a process parallel to the slow but consistent development of Scripture and creed—a canon of ministry emerged in a manner "best understood as works of the Spirit which came through the works of men." Eventually bishops appeared, whose presiding role represented the local Christian community but united it with all others, and presbyters, who "represented not just the local congregation but the apostolic universality of the high priesthood of Christ creating the Church eucharistic." The bishop's ordination bestows Christ's commission and folds the ordinand into Christ's priesthood—all a gift of the Holy Spirit so that "the priesthood of Christ can be actively present in him and through him, that by his ministry men may be reconciled to God."[20]

In tracing the presbyteral connection to Christ and the apostles, Terwilliger understates the church's role. Not so FitzSimons Allison. His first step for understanding Christian ministry is "that a vocation to ministry must be twofold: it must be an inner call to the individual and it must be validated by the corporate body.... Neither one, without the other, is sufficient." His second step is to wonder why there is a ministry at all. For Allison, function and purpose relate the presbyter/priest to the sacrifice of Christ, in three ways:

---

[19] Terwilliger, "What Is a Priest? One Anglican View," in *To Be a Priest*, 3–4, 5–6.

[20] Terwilliger, "What Is a Priest? One Anglican View," in *To Be a Priest*, 6, 8, 10.

as he *"represents* that event as elder of the folk,*"* as a preacher of the Good News, and as the one who presides at the eucharistic celebration that unites the priestly body with its Lord.[21]

Terwilliger stresses the priestly relationship with Christ, while Allison centers on the priest as representative of the church. Neither excludes the other; indeed, each holds elements of the other's view. They conclude differently on women's ordination, a disagreement that may obscure their harmony on ordained ministry. Each upholds a theology of ministry that is in some way apostolic; neither claims a clear dominical institution of a priesthood; and neither holds a strictly sacerdotal idea. Both stand within the Anglican consensus of the earlier part of the century. Together they convey the two-pronged point that revisers of *The Book of Common Prayer* were at that time writing into the catechism: that the ministry of the lay person/bishop/priest/deacon "is to represent Christ [Terwilliger] and his Church [Allison]."[22]

To Be a Priest marked the entrance of Americans into serious discussion of priesthood and orders in Anglicanism. It was only the beginning.

URBAN T. HOLMES AND REVITALIZED SPIRITUALITY

Urban T. Holmes, who died in 1981, was a theologian, prolific writer, and seminary dean who found that his era's social and ecclesiological upheavals caused "paralysis" in parishes and an identity crisis among clergy. A clear concept of what it means to be ordained, he argued, no longer existed.[23] There were two reasons for this, the first being the postwar "therapeutic" movement in pastoral care, which adapted insights gleaned from the relatively new sciences of psychology and psychiatry. The second was the imperative of the 1960s to be a prophet proclaiming God's word in the face of social injustice. Holmes's *The Future Shape of Ministry* (1971) endeavors to reclaim a spiritual basis for parishes and clergy alike. As orders evolved over the centuries, from the early

---

[21] FitzSimons Allison, "What Is a Priest? Another Anglican View," in *To Be a Priest*, 11–13 (ital. in orig.).

[22] US BCP, 855–856.

[23] Urban T. Holmes III, *The Future Shape of Ministry* (New York: Seabury, 1971), 126, 140.

church until today, Holmes notes, models, movements, and theories of ministry all had legitimacy in their day. From an emphasis on the sacramental person during its first five centuries, the church moved to that of the sacramental rite in the Middle Ages and thence to the sacramental Word of the Reformation and beyond. There were reasons in each era that the church emphasized what it did. With that background, Holmes turns next to the uncertainties and problems of role and function that parish and priest both face at the close of a turbulent decade. Given the ambiguity of their role, a lack of integrated education, a moribund spirituality, and a suspicion that they were not doing what they were ordained to do, Holmes sees the clergy as enmeshed in conflicting priorities.[24]

Pastoral care was the dominant purpose and duty for clergy. Clinical Pastoral Education programs became crucial courses for budding parish clergy, which helped to hone pastoral skills and promote self-awareness under trained supervision. They also provided training for seminarians to deal with crises of life and death, all vital tools for parochial ministry. In so doing, though, CPE reinforced the image of the priest as caregiver, which in Holmes's opinion not only exalts one role out of many but also reveals a faulty anthropology in not grasping "the social dimension of human personality." He accused CPE of being "persistently anti-intellectual," poorly equipped theologically, unjustifiable on theological grounds, and downright secular.[25]

The overall emphasis on the pastoral, furthermore, sets up an inevitable conflict with the other priority, which was the prophetic and its strong focus on political, economic, and social issues. As a college chaplain in the "therapeutic" mode, Holmes founded a pastoral counseling service for students, only to be told at a gathering of chaplains that his main role on campus should be that of "change agent."[26] But for Holmes, changing the world provided

---

[24] Holmes, *Future Shape*, 9–91. His approach, however, risked making ecclesiological conviction a product of its own day and, thus, able to be discarded in a later one: Cf. Leander S. Harding, "What Have We Been Telling Ourselves About the Priesthood?" *Sewanee Theological Review* 43, no. 2 (Easter 2000), 150. Holmes, *Future Shape*, 140–141, 159.

[25] Holmes, *Future Shape*, 173, 176–178.

[26] Holmes, *Future Shape*, 143. At that time the jibe was circulating about the "Episcopal college chaplain doll": "Wind him up and he takes a Stand."

just as deficient a model for priesthood as the therapeutic approach of Clinical Pastoral Education. The biblical purpose of prophecy, he noted, quoting St. Paul, is to build up the Christian community, not the world at large. Evangelism remains the central task for the church in the world.[27]

In a subsequent book, *The Priest in Community,* Holmes risked a substantial departure from the models of the postwar period. He claims to propose a theology of Christian ministry that moves away from "a purely clinical understanding...to a symbolic and conceptual understanding of the relation between God and man" that is based in the life of the church as "a community for theological reflection." Within that community, the priest is a "liminal" or "threshold" figure who symbolizes God.

> Some people would deny that in the priest we "see" God, but I think we do. When a parishioner comes to talk with his priest he perceives this as a conversation with God through the priest.... This unconscious association is very much at the root of asking a priest to pray for you, when logic would say you could do it just as well for yourself.[28]

Whether or not he realized the extent of what he was doing, Holmes called the priesthood away from the predominating functional models to an ontological understanding of the priestly role. The corporate understanding sees the priest as the head of an institution. In the therapeutic model, CPE trains the pastor in what to *do*, while, as a "prophet," what matters is what the priest says and does. Despite the general consensus at the time, ordination is not, strictly speaking, required for either pastoral ministries or prophetic action. Ordination, however, stands at the heart of what Holmes imagined. For him the priest is set apart; ordination does not make the priest into someone different. The priest is first of all a person of God, within the community of the faithful.

---

[27] Holmes, *Future Shape,* 173, 176–178, 143, 191–192.

[28] Urban T. Holmes III, *The Priest in Community: Exploring the Roots of Ministry* (New York: Seabury, 1978), 7, 34, 86.

The Rise of Mutual and Total Ministry

If the 1960s caused some to wonder whether the congregation could survive, the 1970s gave an answer: Yes, but only under shared leadership. In lieu of an institution dominated by clergy, the 1970s envisioned an organism that involved all people, the *laos*. Two main concepts were brought forward to show how to unite clergy and laity in their efforts. One was the idea of "mutual ministry," formulated most notably by the seminary dean James Fenhagen. The other, "total ministry," was a method developed in the Diocese of Nevada to address immediate difficulties within the diocese, but after that it was adapted more broadly.

The dean first of Hartford Seminary Foundation and then of General Theological Seminary, James Fenhagen saw the congregation as "of crucial importance to modern life" in sustaining the inner resources for "facing a profound crisis of faith." It can reaffirm the Christian gospel's conviction "that the hope of the world lies not in man's technological genius but in the creative energy of God." Addressing questions of meaning, value, compassion, and faith is itself a ministry that is by nature "mutual" in the ultimate sense, for it shares with God a divine work. "We are participating," Fenhagen wrote in *Mutual Ministry,* "in what is fundamental to the redemptive activity of God."[29] He was distressed by the chronic lack of mutuality between the clergy and the laity that his research revealed, including a sense of isolation of laity from the clergy. Equally troubling, he found, was a sense of the marginalization of the church itself as an institution in a society that considers religion a "personal matter." How clergy and laity perceive each other and how they sometimes forge unspoken and unhealthy bargains in relation to each other are additional issues of concern. For instance, laity might look upon clergy as paragons of faith, while clergy might enjoy their place upon a pedestal.[30] At the same time, Fenhagen also found numerous instances of effective working relationships between clergy and laity, characterized by a common sense of pilgrimage that united them and freed the clergy from

---

[29] James C. Fenhagen, *Mutual Ministry: New Vitality for the Local Church* (New York: Seabury Press, 1977), 6–7, 63.

[30] Fenhagen, *Mutual Ministry,* 23–26.

having to know all the answers. Systems of accountability that allow for mutual feedback and opportunities for learning by one from the other all contribute to a positive sense of mutuality. So do carefully designed programs of lay theological education, undergirded by the recognition that "most of the crucial issues of mission are those which confront laity in the context of their daily lives," and they have the "credibility and opportunity" to minister in ways that most clergy do not.

Urging shared authority, mutual ministry, and interdependence, Fenhagen advocated that the minister move away from the center of attention and activity into a position of enabling others to use and share their gifts; better that the ordained enable others to minister than that the clergy do it themselves. Mutual ministry requires that laypeople be recruited for appropriate tasks, then trained and supported. For ministry to be genuinely mutual, moreover, the enabler must also be enabled, such that fostering interdependence among both clergy and laity becomes the task of the congregation as well as of the ordained person.[31]

The role of the local church, then, was a vitally important one for Fenhagen. The congregation is what sustains ministry, especially mutual ministry. The congregation does not give authority to minister; that comes, basically, from Christ.

> When laity claim they cannot exercise ministry in the Church because they lack authority, my immediate initial response is, "Who says?" The authority is there. It has been given in baptism. No one can take it away; no structure, no institution, no church, no clergy can take away that which is fundamental to who we are in Christ.

The church does, however, validate and regulate that authority according to what seems to be needed. Furthermore, it sustains ministry through its communal life of the Spirit. Prayer and ministry, worship and education stand at the heart of the Christian community, and these nurture and support vocations of service.[32]

---

[31] Fenhagen, *Mutual Ministry*, 111–124.

[32] Fenhagen, *More Than Wanderers: Spiritual Disciplines for Christian Ministry* (New York: Seabury, 1978), 14–15, 85. On pp. 85–100 he offers pragmatic suggestions for fulfilling this purpose.

Stewart Zabriskie and Wesley Frensdorff, two successive bishops of Nevada in the 1970s, 1980s, and 1990s, used this same theoretical foundation to champion what they called "total ministry." With limited funds, vast distances, and sparse populations, the Diocese of Nevada had little choice but to do things differently. These two bishops encouraged a style of ministry that relied not on clergy so much as on communities to respond to needs and opportunities that each locale might discern. At the heart of "total ministry" was the conviction that all Christians hold a vocation by their baptism to "become part of the community's ministry." Within the Body of Christ—note Zabriskie's basic image of the church—"there is one ministry of the one body, which is Christ's ministry as exercised through that body." As a result, parishes engage in varieties of ministries, calling forth the services of their people and the gifts they bring, no gift being more important than another.[33] Some can be readers or teachers; others can lead outreach efforts. "The priest becomes the maintenance person, the temple person," writes Zabriskie, by which he means the one who "gathers the community for its sacramental life, for the feeding and energizing that is central to the ministering community." The deacon is the mission person, encouraging and helping to train the community for its service in corporate vocation.[34] (Nevada borrowed heavily from the example of Alaska, including its extensive use of the Episcopal Church's "Canon 9" provisions, which allowed for a priest or deacon to be ordained from a given congregation to serve that community.)

Total ministry has brought new energy and a desire to participate to small churches in remote areas, and these churches' communities have benefitted from their service. But as one critic, Leander Harding, observes of Fenhagen's work, the model of the church as servant predominates—and servanthood on the local scale, with little reference to a body greater than the diocese.[35] Zabriskie's

[33] Stewart C. Zabriskie, *Total Ministry: Reclaiming the Ministry of All God's People* (Bethesda, MD: Alban Institute, 1995), x, 5–7. In this regard, see chapters 8–10 on deacons, laity, and non-traditional ministries. The Nevada model borrowed upon the work in Alaska of its bishop, William Gordon (1948–74).

[34] Zabriskie, *Total Ministry*, 48; see ECUSA, *Constitution and Canons* (2000), Title III, Canon 9 (p. 76–78).

[35] Harding, "What Have We Been Telling Ourselves?" 161.

work illustrates the same problem. Nearly every example of a thriving congregation cites good works of community service to human social need, but service is not the only definition of a prospering congregation. Evangelism, for one, receives hardly a mention. Yet as Harding recalls, evangelism is what so excited Michael Ramsey and his vision of the catholic church.[36] To truncate that wide vision, even for something so vital as service to the world, diminishes a mission of the church that is always broader than any of its features.

THEORIES IN PRACTICE, PROBLEMS IN PRAXIS

To Be a Priest introduced Americans into discussions of orders and ministry that the British had been pursuing for decades. It, and the works that followed, brought a distinctively American accent to the conversation. Where the British spoke to similar concerns, they did so more abstractly than the direct Americans—who also had specific crises in mind. *To Be a Priest*, the work of Holmes and Fenhagen, and the concept of total ministry all were vividly conscious of the paroxysms of the 1960s and 1970s that called into serious question the older ways of "doing church."

Though torn by the tumults of the era, the Episcopal Church had always been less afflicted by party spirit than the Church of England, at least with regard to churchmanship. The spectrum defined by Terwilliger and Allison is not nearly as wide as the one between Baverstock, the Anglo-Catholic, and Thomas, the Evangelical, and no one could accuse Holmes or Fenhagen of being partisan the way critics did of Moberly.[37] On the contrary, Episcopalians have often been able to pull together a consensus within their church. Its catechetical definition of ministry as representing Christ *and* the church, for instance, is itself a synthesizing statement.

Additionally, this pragmatic mentality engendered a host of practical approaches, including the managerial and therapeutic

---

[36] Zabriskie, *Total Ministry*, e.g., 29, 44–47, 58, 59–61, cp. 55–56; cf. Ramsey, GCC, 68–69.

[37] Without discounting serious theological division, N. T. Wright suggests that party spirit in the church may reflect divisions within British society at large, along with class, region, education and accent (*New Tasks for a Renewed Church* [London: Hodder & Stoughton, 1992], 10).

models, and the idea of total ministry. These directly concerned the day-by-day functioning of congregations. And, though these concepts were not exported as quickly as Hollywood movies or McDonald's franchises, coming as they did at a time of American cultural ascendency, they did spread around the Anglican Communion. Total ministry, for example, received acclaim from as far away as New Zealand and Australia.[38]

Not always were these approaches well-considered, however. Their proponents tended to grasp them with great enthusiasm and attempt to make these the norm without always taking the time to analyze them first or asking if they were suitable for every situation.

The therapeutic model offers a case in point. When World War II ended, a good number of veterans, hardened by battle and often wounded in soul, decided to go to seminary and be ordained. As part of their training they entered Clinical Pastoral Education programs in hospitals or mental institutions, which, using the tools and insights of psychology, intensified their self-awareness in the process of elevating their pastoral skills. Leaving seminary, these veterans-turned-clergy entered suburban America, the vast new world characterized by geographic mobility and rootlessness, the world of the "organization man," the "suburban wasteland," and the "lonely crowd." If nothing else, suburbia was a fertile place for CPE-trained clergy to apply their skills.[39] Churches thrived as places of healing and of pastoral care, while pastoral counseling soared to the top of priorities for clergy. Every priest was expected, at least to some degree, to be a pastor. So CPE became a standard requirement for clerical training; even a 1958 Lambeth Conference committee commended to the whole Communion "a greater emphasis upon pastoral theology as a scientific study" and noted its contributions to the Episcopal Church.[40]

Much good resulted from this pastoral emphasis. Churches in the United States prospered as never before, a testimony at least in part to the fact that many people found their needs being met.

---

[38] Zabriskie, *Total Ministry*, xiv; Eleanor Johnson and John Clark, eds., *Anglicans in Mission: A Transforming Journey* (London: SPCK, 2000), 18.

[39] Sydney E. Ahlstrom, *A Religious History of the American People* (New Haven and London: Yale University Press, 1972), 951, 956.

[40] Holmes, *Future Shape*, 140–141; *Lambeth 1958*, 2.104.

CPE training came in handy especially for clergy assisting those who faced times of severe loss. The entire focus upon pastoral ministry gave a renewed impetus and a contemporary dimension to the historic Anglican tradition of the parson's care of souls.

At the same time, these results skewed the self-perceptions of clergy and laity alike. For one thing, not all clerical positions required pastoral gifts, though their training presumed they did. For another, not all clergy possessed those gifts, but given the American church's assumption that clerical ministry was pastoral ministry, they were expected to have them. As for ordinary churchgoers, few if any had the credentials of CPE or seminary, so—the assumption went—how could *they* have a pastoral ministry? That was reserved for the professional caste, the clergy. In other words, training, gifts, ordination, and position were all identified as one.

For these reasons and others, Urban Holmes was one of the first to call the theological and practical foundations of the therapeutic model into question, later to be joined by John Snow, who taught pastoral theology at Episcopal Divinity School. Like Holmes, Snow concluded that a generation or two of American clergy who were fascinated by the insights of their clinical-pastoral training ended up biblically shallow and theologically superficial. As he wrote in his book on the ministry, *The Impossible Vocation*, such clergy equate pastoral theology with counseling:

> It was with a poorly assimilated mixture of theology and psychotherapeutic theory that many of us had our formation in seminary during the fifties and early sixties. We were far more inclined to use therapeutic theory than theology as a basis for judgment and decision where we saw any conflict between the two.[41]

Furthermore, when the psychological tools of the therapeutic approach were applied to other aspects of parish life—fund-raising, teacher recruitment, conflict resolution, problem-solving—then the insights of pastoral care could fuel manipulative behavior. In "CPE parishes,"[42] as they were sometimes caricatured,

---

[41] John Snow, *The Impossible Vocation: Ministry in the Mean Time* (Cambridge, MA: Cowley, 1988), 12–13.

[42] Interview with the Rev. John Martiner, Brewster, MA, July 25, 2000.

where the priest began to be perceived, and in some
cases perceived himself, as a counselor for troubled people, the personality of the priest suddenly became more
important to the church than his calling. The traditional doctrine of priesthood, the doctrine of the priest as
mediator between the congregation and God, was lost
when the priest as "caring person" seemed to take on
the very role of God.[43]

Hugh Melinsky, who studied the English version of the "CPE
parish," concluded that the therapeutic model could distort clergy-lay relationships. "The pastoral model does tend to emphasise
people as weak and dependent. It is true that one part of the shepherd's task is caring for the lost and damaged, but the more important one is leading the flock to good pasturage, because without
that they will die."[44] In other words, the pastoral model was effective in caring for the flock, but not necessarily in leading it.

Then suddenly, leading the flock to some very different places
was all the vogue. Models changed, without any warning to priest
or people, when the assumptions of the 1950s were swallowed in
the social crises of the 1960s. Urban Holmes' experience as a college
chaplain, expected at one moment to be a caregiver and at the next
to be a prophet, found parallels in parish life. The pastor who had
soothed discord and comforted the troubled was taking stands on
emotionally laden and divisive topics like civil rights and the Vietnam
War. Parishioners might even see their parson on the front page of
the newspaper, being arrested at a sit-in. Some were thrilled and
some appalled, but many were confused.

If that were not enough, at this very moment of changing roles
and expectations for the clergy, a passion for liturgical change
erupted throughout most of the church. Replacing the old prayer
book with a new one and, in many places, even rearranging the
church's furniture and moving the altar all affected the image of
the priest—often contradictorily. Having the priest celebrate the

---

[43] Snow, *Impossible Vocation*, 17–18. Snow is not concerned here, as we have
been, with defining the "traditional doctrine of priesthood" nor with the precise
terminology of "mediator" but with a shift of connotation by priest and people
alike.

[44] Melinsky, *Shape*, 147.

Eucharist while facing the people and contemporizing the language of liturgy diminished the distance between priest and people.[45] Making a celebration of the Eucharist the norm rather than Morning Prayer, along with the use of formal eucharistic vestments, stressed the priestliness of the officiant. Reconfiguring the chancel to provide for a free-standing altar, as John Snow observes, literally turned the priest around; instead of facing the east wall, the celebrant confronted the congregation "eyeball to eyeball" and often on the same level.

> Yet at the same time, paradoxically, it placed the priest in *loco parentis*. In the previous form of the rite, the priest faced in the same direction as the congregation and yet was removed from them, as leader and pioneer. Thus the priest represented the congregation before God.... When, instead, the minister faces the people, he or she becomes both parent and partner, indeed, almost parent and adversary in a culture that is as competitive and free of rules as ours.

The very attempts to reduce hierarchy and separation seemed to create new forms of the old monsters. While the priest was being proclaimed as "representative," whom did the priest represent, God or people, when the congregation was arranged in a circle around the altar? The priest, Snow concludes, "has to a degree lost the theological significance, the sacramental power, to move the transferential consciousness of the congregation beyond the priest leading worship, to God, the center of worship."[46]

Would the "management model" provide a better alternative? Developed on American soil amid a business-dominated postwar culture, the corporate model also found its way abroad. Senior English clergy pursued courses in business strategy, organizational culture, and how to "devise change strategies and generate strategic options" to help them better lead the church. Not everyone was impressed: "McDonaldisation of the Church," sniffed one

---

[45] For instance, the Latin *Dominus vobiscum/Et cum spiritu tuo* that led to the "The Lord be with you/And with thy spirit," in modern liturgies became, "The Lord be with you/And also with you," or as an alternative in England, "The Lord is here/His Spirit is with us" (cf. US BCP 361; ASB 139 || CW 201).

[46] Snow, *Impossible Vocation*, 126–127.

professor.[47] Episcopalians had already found that the priest as administrator only further muddied the waters: Was the priest an employer? Were laity employees? "Moses was a great pastor because he knew where he was going and managed, with difficulty, to take his flock with him," Melinsky wrote but admitted, "few of them would have regarded him as a kindly pastor."[48] Though Episcopal Church canons require standard business methods for church accounting procedures, a church is not a company:

> Employees are not members of the firm; they agree to work for x hours at £y an hour, and if their work is unsatisfactory they can, under certain conditions, be dismissed. It is far otherwise with the church and its members. Here the laity are as much members as the clergy.[49]

Models, in short, have their drawbacks. Each of these three models—the pastoral, the prophetic, and the managerial—took one element of clergy responsibility, defined it in a particular way, and magnified it out of proportion to other aspects that constitute the whole of a balanced clerical life. Thus conflicts in expectations were inevitable for clergy and congregations alike. The therapeutic model pictured the priest as the tenderhearted caregiver and healer, but that was incompatible with the prophet for social justice or the efficient administrator of the local ecclesiastical franchise. So while the church in every age needs to minister to its people pastorally, manage its ecclesiastical institutions effectively, and pursue God's justice in the world faithfully, the goals themselves, and how those aims are fulfilled, warrant constant scrutiny.

ROLAND ALLEN AND RADICAL MISSION

In Roland Allen proponents of total ministry found a patron saint. A priest of the Church of England, his on-the-job experience

---

[47] Quoted in Furlong, C of E, 219.

[48] Snow, Impossible Vocation, 18–19; Melinsky, Shape, 147, drawing on work of J. R. Mathers. An army psychiatrist in WWII, Mathers was commissioned with finding why the rate of sickness varied from unit to unit. He discovered that sickness went down as morale went up; and morale depended on soldiers' being given clear aims of what they were expected to do and clear instructions on how to do it. He concluded that health depended more on the commanding officer than the medical officer—and was dismissed, though his work has been substantially confirmed.

[49] Melinsky, Shape, 162

as a missionary totaled merely a few years in China, but it was enough to convince him of how the church should pursue its mission. His writings, although published starting in 1912, did not seize the church's imagination until the 1960s; in that sense, this early-twentieth-century writer was more of a late-century figure.[50]

Allen's vision was fired by the ways in which the New Testament church exploded in size. He was also infuriated by the ineffectiveness of the church of his day in spreading the gospel in non-Western lands. He implied this contrast in the title of his first book, *Missionary Methods: St. Paul's or Ours?* "Our" methods, he alleged, are impractical and theologically inappropriate. As Allen described it, the turn-of-the-century process of starting a mission involved several English missionaries, including a priest or maybe even a bishop, who would collect vestments and vessels, journey forth to an Asian city or African village, buy land, build buildings, educate a few local leaders, and only *then* begin to evangelize. The method relied on human resources and funds coming largely from "home," and were scant to begin with. The product, furthermore, was a replica of an English parish in an Asian or African setting, dependent upon English donations, and identified in the native population's mind with the English benefactors.[51]

The methods Allen attributed to Paul were, by contrast, simple, personal, direct, and effective. In Paul's day, one person told another of Jesus, and Christianity raced across the world. Every Christian had on hand the needed tools to relate the good news of Christ: the story of Jesus, a rudimentary faith, a nascent creed, basic leadership, and the sacraments of life. These same tools, Allen asserted, are still available twenty centuries later. With these tools, together, of course, with the Spirit, a Christian community

---

[50] Gerald Charles Davis, ed., *Setting Free the Ministry of the People of God* (Cincinnati, OH: Forward Movement, 1984), 14; Michael Hollis, "A Doctrine of the Church," *International Review of Mission*, 39 (1950), 461–462. A good synopsis of Allen's teaching can be found in Alastair Redfern, *Ministry and Priesthood* (London: Darton, Longman & Todd, 1999), 85–93.

[51] Allen, letter to the Bishop of Central Tanganyika, April 12, 1920, in David Paton, ed., *Reform of the Ministry: A Study in the Work of Roland Allen* (London: Lutterworth, 1968), 105; *The Spontaneous Expansion of the Church* (1927; reprint, Grand Rapids, MI: Eerdmans, 1984), 22–24; *Missionary Methods: St. Paul's or Ours?* (2nd ed., 1927; reprinted Grand Rapids, MI: Eerdmans, 1962), 52–56, 71.

is truly the *church*, and can grow through the personal gifts that the Spirit grants to people, without regard to their order.[52]

In that light, buildings, foreign leadership, diocesan infrastructures, and other elements of standard missionary strategy are unnecessary, even counterproductive. Instead, Allen wanted to rely primarily on self-governing, self-supporting, and self-propagating churches.[53] He envisioned congregations linked with the wider Body (episcopate providing an important connection) but free to develop their own evangelistic mission in their own areas under leadership called forth from within their own ranks. These congregations would decide whom to admit as members and whom to recommend as leaders. The *community* would perceive the call, not outsiders or single individuals; nowhere in the Bible does so vital a decision rest with a single person. Therefore Allen proposed that "every little group of communicants" decide who will serve best, from among its own number, and submit that person to the bishop for affirmation as a leader (clergy or lay). Episcopal involvement is a crucial means of affirming the local church's connection to the church at large, so that both locally and in broader spheres such as the diocese, "the call of God is established through His church."[54]

Insofar as developing leadership is concerned, the church of Allen's day contrasted almost totally with his vision. In practice, recruitment for ordination depended upon young men who offered themselves for a vocation, with the church then deciding whether or not to accept. Allen would turn that around so that the community perceived a person's vocation first and only then proposed it to the

---

[52] Allen, *Spontaneous Expansion*, 26–30; Paton, *Reform*, 26.

[53] The idea had been earlier expressed by Henry Venn (1796–1873), the longtime leader of the Church Missionary Society. See Stephen Neill, *A History of Christian Missions* (New York: Penguin Books, 1964), 260. Allen applied the idea in new ways, particularly with regard to *local* churches. He disagreed strenuously with Bishop Alfred Tucker of Uganda, for instance, who also employed the "Three Self" principle but in provincial terms, that is, aiming at an independent *national* church as opposed to independent congregations. For Allen, this smacked of more Western denominationalism, and led toward "expelling" missionaries rather than "coming away" from them. See Paton, *Reform*, 35 (on Venn, see 82).

[54] Allen, *Missionary Methods*, 100, *The Compulsion of the Spirit*, ed. David Paton and Charles Long (Grand Rapids, MI: Eerdmans, 1983), 96–97.

individual: "Were the call of the church put first, the internal vocation could respond to that." In practice, the church then sent the prospective priest to school, where the emphasis would be almost wholly intellectual—poor training, Allen protested, for missionary work. The process also nearly guaranteed that the candidates would be uniformly young; and while the young should not necessarily be excluded, older people, with the experience of longer years of faithful life, got left out. On all three points, the church of 1920 differed from the church of the first century:

> The training on which the apostolic writer lays the greatest stress is the training which God alone can give, the training of life and experience; the training on which we lay the greatest stress is the training that we can give, the training of the school or the college. The training on which we lay stress is the training which is suited to the young; but God does not call only the young to be his ministers. Men are not only converted to Christ in youth: they are converted often late in life and, in the apostolic conception, they are generally called to the ministry of the church after years of experience.[55]

Though Allen's assumptions were "pre-critical" insofar as the biblical scholarship of his day was concerned, his principles were forward-looking enough for a later generation contemplating his writings to see, not obsolete period pieces, but theories that highlighted the church's purpose as the Body of Christ. Though writing in the 1920s, when the British Empire was still largely intact, his ideas challenged the ecclesiastical counterpart of colonialism by questioning the then-current missionary strategy that ensured Western domination in the new mission fields. His alternative gave authority, instead, to the local, indigenous Christian populations, a concept that appealed to post-colonialism. It may be no coincidence that Allen's writings started gaining widespread notice in 1956, the very decade when Britain was granting independence to its colonies. His ideas also appealed to an Anglican mindset, just at the point that the Communion was grasping the implications of the ecclesiological vision of the Body of Christ. Allen's ideas,

---

[55] Allen, *Compulsion*, 98.

which had seemed initially so radical, operate within the emergent Anglican theory of ministry. He provided a framework in which laity could take an even greater role, deacons and priests could be called forth and trained more directly for mission, and thus tapping gifts from among their own people, congregations would pursue the proclamation of the gospel. But he relied on bishops, he assumed a priesthood in fundamentally familiar ways, and he emphasized an integral role for laity, all within a basic ecclesiological perspective that Temple or Ramsey could understand. For all his pushing of the boundaries of the Anglican consensus, Allen remained very much within it. In the end, his was a church-based model that relied on the image of the Body of Christ; he dared to apply that image to every local community of Christians, whether in England, Canada, China, or Nigeria.[56]

RE-IMAGING ECCLESIOLOGY: A. T. AND R. P. C. HANSON

Any idea that ministry exists apart from the church was anathema, not only to Roland Allen but to two Irishmen, Anthony and Richard Hanson. Individually and then together, as they probed the nature of the church and its ministry, these brothers were among the first to move away from the "body" imagery that dominated mid-century ecclesiology. In *The Pioneer Ministry,* published in 1961, A. T. Hanson draws on a theme from St. Paul, arguing that "ministry is responsible to Christ, though its task is to serve the Church." The ministerial task is "not to undertake some specialist activity from which the rest of the faithful are excluded, but to pioneer in doing that which the whole Church must do." The phrase "pioneer ministry" comes from a description of Christ's work given in Hebrews 12:2.

> The ministers are servants for Christ's sake; they accept the same lowly service which Christ came to do. They preach Christ because in him God has revealed his glory, a glory that can be known by all Christians. And the aim

---

[56] Cf. Michael Ranken: "Ministry in Secular Employment and the Church's Mission," in Church of England, ACCM, "Ordained Ministry in Secular Employment: Reflections on the History and Theology" [Occasional paper No. 31, February 1989], 10.

of their ministry is, not only that all men should see his
glory in Christ, but that all who see it should themselves
show it forth.[57]

In the mid-nineteenth century Anglican theology had largely
shifted its focus to the Incarnation, from Christ's atonement and
passion to Christ's birth. A. T. Hanson wanted to revive the earlier
focus. Given "the objective fact of Christ's death," he wrote, ministry is founded on that redeeming act, as is the church's task "of
mutual caring and redemption which its very being involves."
Ministry becomes then a work of reconciliation, derived from the
reconciling act of God in Christ on Calvary. It is apostolic, in that
God through Christ establishes a faithful "remnant" (parallel to
the Old Testament faithful few who await the Messiah) of apostles
who "are the Church, the nucleus of the Church in that area."[58]
Apostles in turn share this ministry with the church through the
institution of *diakonos*. Embracing more than the work of deacons
alone, the term *diakonos* refers to ministry and service in which
the "apostolic task...passes over into the hands of the Church,
what we today would call the laity." *Diakonos* means *every* Christian,
too: "[D]iakonia is very much the work of the whole body, and
not of the ordained ministry only, and the individual Christian
must play his part in the work of the whole body."[59] Fearing that
the ideas of more "catholic" theologians like Moberly promoted a
ministry that theoretically could function without any church at
all,[60] Hanson strives to root the ministry within the life of the community. But in the end, he sounds much like Moberly:

> The ministry must not be represented as doing anything
> that the Church cannot, or should not, do. If we think
> of any of the distinctive functions of the ministry, we
> must say that the ministry only carries them out as the
> representative of the Church.... It is not the priest who

---

[57] A. T. Hanson, *The Pioneer Ministry* (London: SCM, 1961), 59, 62, 72, 75.

[58] A. T. Hanson, *Pioneer Ministry*, 80, 84, 87.

[59] A. T. Hanson, *Pioneer Ministry*, 98–100, 105.

[60] A. T. Hanson, *Pioneer Ministry*, 88, quoting Quick's observations on the
absurdities that can arise when a formal ministry exists independently of the
Body.

celebrates the Eucharist, but the priest and the local church, and the local church celebrates through him.[61]

Eighteen years later, Richard Hanson published *Christian Priesthood Examined*. There he objects to the notion that any official ministry "in our modern sense" (note the qualifier) existed in apostolic days.[62] The idea that officers were appointed to posts and were in time succeeded by others, Hanson states, is neither historical nor scriptural. Instead, he believes that Jesus in Matthew 28:18–20 and John 20 conferred his blessing and commission not upon "the church's ministers but upon the church." Leaders and presbyters there were, but nothing was universal or essential about their office. Richard Hanson ends by denying both the "catholic" concept of a divinely appointed apostolic ministry and the more "protestant" concept of a scripturally authorized one.[63]

Since the priesthood that had developed over two millennia is collective, then each Christian shares in this priesthood of all believers without being "an official minister." Yet the church may also delegate authority, all the while knowing that this authority "rests upon the priesthood of Christ expressed in and through the priestly authority of the church."[64] Christ *did* found the church, Richard Hanson maintains, while the ministry came later as situations evolved, needs changed, and as eucharistic understanding developed. Official ministry, now that we have it, is an inescapable part of tradition and not without its advantages.[65]

By defining genuine ministry as much more than ritual, he reiterated the idea of ministerial priesthood, with all ministerial authority based within the church. Richard Hanson uses the example of an insane French Roman Catholic priest who entered a confectioner's shop, made the sign of the cross, and uttered the

---

[61] A. T. Hanson, *Pioneer Ministry*, 155–156.

[62] R. P. C. Hanson, *Christian Priesthood Examined* (Guildford and London: Lutterworth Press, 1979), 9; cf. 12, 17, 89.

[63] R. Hanson, *Priesthood*, 8–9, 11, 10; 17–18; note the similarity with Streeter's observation (cf. chapter 3, above).

[64] R. Hanson, *Priesthood*, 26–27.

[65] R. Hanson, *Priesthood*, 44–52 (∥ Urban T. Holmes, in "A Response to *The Diaconate Today*," in John H. Morgan, *The Diaconate Today: A Study of Clergy Attitudes in the Episcopal Church* [n.p.: 1979], appendix), 94.

words *Hoc est corpus meum*. Upon hearing of it, the Archbishop of Paris is said to have bought up and reverently consumed every baked morsel in the shop. An Anglican priest might be crazy enough to try something similar, but he could not consecrate a bakery unless the whole church intended it, because priests are not free agents but representatives.[66] To a greater degree than his brother, then, R. P. C. Hanson continued the ecclesiological trends of his century. The church is "like one body with many limbs," and the priest, as celebrant, transcends a cultic function to serve as

> the concentration of the priesthood of Christ's people who leads them into their priesthood, not fulfilling it instead of them, as their substitute, but as their representative and spokesman and leader. And he has, by ordination, the authority of the church, the authority of Christ acting and ordaining in the church, not only to represent them to God but also to speak to them on God's behalf, in God's name.[67]

By 1987 the Hanson brothers published *The Identity of the Church*, where they concur that no church may claim to be apostolic in the sense of a single continuous chain of individuals or to be purely scriptural in its modern iteration. "The only body that goes uninterruptedly back to the apostles is the whole body of Christians." For them, church means the "totality of the denominations." In biblical terms, "the church *is* the people of God and that it is called to be the body of Christ." Yet they caution against saying too much: For all that scholarship reveals of history, it is Scripture that fundamentally reveals Christ's priesthood and the derived priesthood of the church. Moreover, the church may be Christ's body, but it is not Christ.[68]

Nor are clergy the church. Ministry is not *essential* to the existence of the church, the authors explain, but one cannot expect the church to continue without it. "The emergence of an official ministry very early in the second century was a development manifestly

---

[66] R. Hanson, *Priesthood*, 84–85, 96.

[67] R. Hanson, *Priesthood*, 109, 102–103.

[68] A. T. Hanson and R. P. C. Hanson, *The Identity of the Church: A Guide to Recognizing the Contemporary Church* (London: SMC, 1987), 111, 43; 106, 40.

blessed and guided by the Holy Spirit." No one sat around in the upper room inventing a church replete with ministerial succession, but the "very concept of a New Testament implies a church."[69] A relationship with Christ is at once highly personal and inherently corporate.

It is communal, too, in a vitally important way. Instead of Anthony's earlier metaphor of the faithful remnant, here the Hansons come together to envision a "pilgrim people of God," open to the future and always journeying forward, constantly remembering the church's pilgrim nature. Previous authors we have examined generally gazed back upon the roots of church and ministry; the Hanson brothers look instead toward the church's ultimate consummation. Toward this great end, history provides a sense of the grounding of the church in human experience: "The church in any age is made up of actual historical men and women, and it is in them primarily that the continuity of the church consists." It is not, then, the continuity of ministry that matters but "the continuity of the people of God," which fundamentally arises from "the members of the church themselves."[70] Anthony's initial concept of Christ as the foundation of ministry and ministry as the foundation of the church is replaced by Richard's pattern, whereby Christ is the foundation of the church and the church itself is the cornerstone of ministry.

Several idiosyncrasies hamper their work. Each occasionally appears not to have understood those with whom he disagrees (Anthony with Temple, Richard with Gore) so that they see differences rather than similarities. Richard responds to stereotypes of priestly ideas, particularly on the "catholic" side, that are not held by other serious authors; as the Hansons observe, it takes time for theological ideas to filter to the pew—and it also may take time for theological ideas to make their way to the one at the altar. Still, their balance of scholarship and Scripture, along with the reiteration of the nature of the Body of Christ and the implications they draw, are all in line with the Anglican consensus. Their reservations about apostolicity can help us to reconsider what "apostolic" can mean, while their emphasis on the breadth and scope of the

---

[69] A. and R. Hanson, *Identity*, 60, 126, 80.

[70] A. and R. Hanson, *Identity*, 41–42.

Body of Christ can help us to understand the church, its ministry, and its priesthood in their eschatological dimension.

THE MOVEMENT OF THE SPIRIT

Not surprisingly, the spiritual revival in Anglicanism took many forms as it came to influence how people looked at the church and its ministry. The East African revival began in the 1930s and continues to this day, contributing both to the astronomical growth in the Anglican provinces of that region and also to their strongly Evangelical temperament.[71] Later the Charismatic movement, with its emphasis on the work of the Holy Spirit, became more prominent in the Western churches, making this revival something of a Communion-wide phenomenon. Robert Terwilliger, for instance, drew out the theological significance of the Spirit for the Body:

> In these days of new awareness of the Spirit it is urgent for Christians to repossess their sense of the work of the Spirit in the whole life of the body of Christ. The Church is that community which exists by the continual invocation of the Holy Spirit. Its life is not its own. It has its existence and its identity only because of the perpetual coming of the Spirit.[72]

This new awareness of the Spirit inspired practical implications as well. For example, the Charismatic Movement gave a substantial boost to lay ministry because it stressed that the gifts (or "charisms") of the Holy Spirit, along with many works of the church that reflect these gifts, are not restricted to clergy. Laity, therefore, could discover what gifts they had and then put them to use. At the same time, the role of clergy was reaffirmed, in that orders and sacrament are among the means whereby the Spirit bestows gifts. "Ordination is also a charism, a sacramental

---

[71] Cf. Allen Anderson, "African Anglicans and/or Pentecostals: Why So Many African Anglicans Become Pentecostals or Combine their Anglicanism with Pentecostalism," in Andrew Wingate et al., *Anglicanism: A Global Communion* (New York: Church Publishing, 1998), 34–40.

[72] Terwilliger, "What Is a Priest? One Anglican View," in *To Be a Priest*, 7.

charism," Terwilliger wrote, given as the church invokes the Holy Spirit to bestow, through the bishop, a holy order.[73]

Not only can heightened awareness of the Spirit deepen our appreciation of the nature of ordination, it can also help to underscore the nature of priesthood as a representative of both God and church. Urban Holmes found in what he called "the neo-Pentecostal movement" a reminder that the presbyter is one whose life has been seized by the Holy Spirit to become a divine agent. "If the priest is an 'angel,' a messenger, it is as one from God"—not just from the church. Theologian Hugh Melinsky also observed that because the Spirit is both transcendent and imminent, coming from God and bestowed upon Christians in baptism, "ministerial authority is both from above and from within; not from God without the Church, nor from the Church without God, but from God within the Church." In that light, the Spirit can be trusted to lead the church into new developments (might Melinsky have the ordination of women in mind?) and to revivify old ones (such as the priesthood?), submitting all to the testing of Scripture, especially the Incarnation. In that light, too, clergy spirituality takes on renewed importance, in a form that "is both personal and corporate...real to each person but also nourished and developed by a long and rich tradition which needs to be familiar both to the clergy and to those to whom they minister." As one further implication, Melinsky encourages a more complete application of the Trinity to the ministerial life of the whole church.[74] Indeed, the renewed appreciation of the Spirit heightened the church's awareness of both the spiritual and the trinitarian foundations of its corporate life—and that of the priesthood.

REVIVING TRINITY, DEEPENING COMMUNITY

On May 1, 2001, the entire Anglican Communion prayed for the Diocese of El Camino Real in California. Through the Anglican Cycle of Prayer, which in the course of a year offers petitions for each diocese and province, the diocese requested intercessions "for a faithful, progressive and open church and a diverse community

---

[73] Terwilliger, "What Is a Priest? One Anglican View," in *To Be a Priest*, 7.

[74] Holmes, *Priest in Community*, 154; Melinsky, *Shape*, 267–268, cf. xiii.

in the pattern of the Holy Trinity."[75] The Trinity was fast becoming the new image for expressing the nature of Christian community, reflecting the unity and diversity of Father/Creator, Son/Redeemer, Spirit/Sanctifier. "The eternal, mutual self-giving and receiving of love of the three persons of the Trinity is the source of identity and unity of the Anglican Communion and of all Christian Communions," explained one theologian-bishop, Mark Dyer. "It is a source of our fellowship with God and one another."[76]

As the twentieth century waned, the incarnationalist ecclesiology came under fire. The 1968 Lambeth Conference, reacting to what it called the "Debate about God" (which included allegations that God was dead, at least in terms of traditional understandings), along with the myriad social crises of that year, feared that phrasing God's connection to the world in incarnational terms alone missed the transcendent quality of the Divine. "Properly interpreted, the doctrine of the Trinity addresses itself precisely to the false division between experience of God as transcendent and experience of God as immanent." As well, debates over the ordination of women in the Church of England showed that basing ecclesiology on the person of Christ could be distorted by focusing on Jesus' manhood in order to exclude women from the ministry.[77]

Robin Greenwood cited other problems. Incarnationalist theology could never clarify the roles of clergy and laity as Christly representatives. A "monist" attitude toward God, a doctrine of apostolic succession, and clergy handbooks that considered orders to be a priest's personal possession, all bred an individualism among Christians in general and clergy in particular. Incarnationalist theologians failed to balance the church's "internal and external relationships," so busy were they in trying "to validate Church of England ecclesiology historically through the ministerial priesthood" rather than pursuing a wider interest in the world. The

---

[75] Anglican Consultative Council, *Anglican Cycle of Prayer* (Cincinnati, OH: Forward Movement, 2000/1), 47.

[76] In introducing the *Virginia Report* on Anglican interrelationships to the Anglican Consultative Council. James Rosenthal, ed., *The Communion We Share: The Official Report of the 11th Meeting of the Anglican Consultative Council, Scotland, 1999* (Harrisburg, PA: Morehouse, 2000), 183.

[77] *Lambeth 1968* (committee report), 70; Melinsky, *Shape*, xiii.

incarnationalist emphasis "was on God's lordship and transcendence...rather than on his present personal interaction, and relatedness." The resulting understanding of God led to "belief in a highly authoritarian changeless institution which, assured of its own rightness, aspired to reflecting the divine transcendence." Instead, more recent theology—trinitarian theology—has spoken "of a God who engages vulnerably with the world." An imperfect church shares in broken human society because of a God who creates, redeems, and has entered into history, interacting in the present while leading into the future. And "all ministry belongs essentially to Christ and is never the possession of any human being."[78]

So revivifying the concept of Trinity, many believed, could bring people together. The diversity and unity inherent in the doctrine of three-in-one provide a model for Anglican relationships worldwide, declared the *Virginia Report* to Lambeth 1998.[79] Trinitarians visualized a church caught up and participating in the pattern of God as Trinity, which thereby "replicates" divine relationships in the church. Greenwood summarizes three main points to this conception:

> First, God's being is most accurately understood by Christians as Trinity: a communion of Father, Son and Holy Spirit. Second, it is essential to God's purpose for the universe that all relationships should be understood as echoing the trinitarian pattern. Third, the Church, having a particular task to prepare the way for godly relationships in society and creation, must allow its ministerial arrangements to echo the trinitarian relationships of loving communion.[80]

Thus trinitarian ecclesiology offers "a radically different basis for understanding the Church" from that of Anglicanism earlier in the century. Through it, the church is seen as more than the Body of Christ: "The Church is born, not just in relation to the Son of God, but to the entire Trinity." Its nature is one of "a differentiated

---

[78] Greenwood, *Transforming Priesthood*, 29, 60–64.

[79] *Lambeth 1998*, 24–30, 50–51.

[80] Greenwood, *Transforming Priesthood*, 87. Cp. the four points he derives from four theologians (Leonardo Boff, Colin Gunton, Jürgen Moltmann, and John Zizioulas), 69–70.

unity, simultaneously one and many"; and this nature in turn promotes, in theory, distinctiveness, freedom, and appreciation of persons not as individuals alone but in relationship with each other. This ecclesiology helps the church become that sign and foretaste "of God's final ordering of all things in Christ," in a life "totally bound up with that of the whole creation which is its context."[81]

> As part of that trinitarian community, clergy and laity can discover, affirm and grow into a deeper corporateness and can become clearer and more confident about their distinctive contributions.... This interlinking of the ministry of lay and ordained can be rooted in an understanding of how relationships can realise, in the life of the Church, a participation in the life of the Trinity.[82]

While relationships based on the Trinity can breed ambiguity by overemphasizing its mystery, they can also promote diversity, pluralism, balance, and mutuality—all virtues lauded in the 1960s.[83] As for the ordained, their responsibility

> is to be a means for the Church as an institution to sustain its living tradition, its responsibility to Christ; and so ordination is a sacrament of (and thus a means of sustaining) the catholicity of the Church.... The ordained are not the sole means of achieving this, but they have this particular responsibility of holding up to the Church its true nature and calling.[84]

Much of this may sound like a familiar song that, because it is played on unaccustomed instruments, seems new and different.

---

[81] Greenwood, *Transforming Priesthood,* 81–82, 86, 112, 92, cf. 94–108.

[82] The Church of England's Advisory Board of Ministry, *Ordination and the Church's Ministry: An Interim Evaluation of College and Course Responses to ACCM Paper No. 22* (London: ABM, 1991), 20, 21; cf. Greenwood, *Transforming Priesthood,* 118.

[83] *Ordination and the Church's Ministry,* 23–26. "Mutual Responsibility and Interdependence" was one such statement, proposing new interrelationships between Anglican provinces, utilizing the Trinity to express the theme of diversity within unity. Cf. Fairweather, *Anglican Congress 1963,* 117–122; Douglas, *Fling Out the Banner!,* 247–254.

[84] *Ordination and the Church's Ministry,* 34.

But the idea of Trinity is far from new, even in its ecclesiological application earlier in the century. Michael Ramsey employs it even while cautioning against its use. His biblical study of the Spirit discourages depending on simple trinitarian formulas, like those of Matthew 28:19 or 2 Corinthians 13:13, and relies instead on the more theological approach taken by Moberly in *Atonement and Personality* (1901). Ramsey suggests that "the invisible God is made known in the visible mission of the Christ and in the response of the Spirit to him from within human lives." He underscores the eschatological, too, tying the two doctrinal concerns together:

> The issue...is not one of terminology, or of persons of the triune God. It is the issue of the relation between the action of God in the ecclesia as the eschatological community upon which the New Testament doctrine of the Spirit is concentrated, and the action of God in the created world near and far.

Gore used to say, Ramsey recalls, that in reciting "I believe in the Holy Catholic Church" from the Creed, what he meant was, "I believe in the Holy Spirit revivifying the Church." In all ages, in every denomination, the Spirit refreshes the church. "It is to minds and hearts and wills which are ever open, ever receptive, that the Spirit speaks while they on their part test what is of the Spirit by the test of witness to the crucified and risen Jesus."[85]

So at least to some degree, trinitarian ecclesiology is anticipated by the incarnationalists. Both models, furthermore, sought to address some of the same problems, like the abiding quandary of how laity and clergy relate together within the church.[86] The trinitarian approach is not necessarily more successful. For example, it is sometimes employed to counteract the dominance by one group over another (usually clergy over laity): as the divine persons are co-equal and unified in heaven, so may we be on earth. Yet the gendered language of "Father, Son, and Spirit" can inherently distort both the doctrine itself and the human relationships it is meant to improve, especially if taken to justify human hierarchies, which

---

[85] Ramsey, *Holy Spirit*, 121, 123–124; 127–128.

[86] Cf. Moberly on the Trinity, *MP*, 2.

ordination has been known to do. Shrouded in mystery as it is, moreover, the Trinity takes considerable explanation in a way that the Incarnation does not because every person has a body—a ready-made metaphor. In other words, switching doctrinal motifs provides no guarantee against distortion. A renewed understanding of Trinity might not turn matters around. Still, it could help, and many have found it useful.[87]

THE REVIVAL OF EVANGELICALISM

During the same period that saw a rekindling of the Spirit and a reapplication of the Trinity to the nature and work of the church, Evangelical Christianity began to thrive anew in large part thanks to the preaching of John Stott in the 1950s. Evangelicals rediscovered their role within the Church of England and throughout the Anglican Communion with a theology and fervor they had not known for nearly a century. By 1988 they had come into their own: the Lambeth Conference declared the 1990s as a "Decade of Evangelism."[88]

But theirs was a new Evangelicalism, without the former defensiveness and its scriptural and theological rigidity. Modern Evangelicals embraced theologies of atonement, redemption, and mission with a new doctrinal breadth. They also incorporated some of the more recently developed emphases of the incarnationalist school, such as the importance of sacrament and the place of

---

[87] Greenwood, *Transforming Priesthood*, 110–140. Others using the Trinity as an ecclesiological basis are Elaine Bardwell ("The Pastoral Role of the Deacon") and Andrew Burnham ("The Liturgical Ministry of a Deacon"), both in Christine Hall, ed., *The Deacon's Ministry* (Leominster: Gracewing, 1992), 46–49, 68; Ian Douglas, "Baptized into Mission: Ministry and Holy Orders Reconsidered," *Sewanee Theological Review* 40, no. 4 (1997), 433. Cf. *Lambeth 1988*, 130–131; *Lambeth 1998*, 27–29; Anglican Consultative Council, *Being Anglican in the Third Millennium: The Official Report of the 10th Meeting of the Anglican Consultative Council* (Harrisburg, PA: Morehouse Publishing, 1996), 154. See also the report of the 5th International Liturgical Consultation, 1985, 298–301, the English House of Bishops Theological Group in a report on eucharistic presidency ([Church of England, General Synod], *Eucharistic Presidency* [London: Church House Publishing, 1997], x, 13 [¶2.2], 36 [¶4.8], 40 [¶4.18] etc.); Standing Commission on Ministry Development, "Toward a Theology of Ministry" (May 2000), 15; "House of Bishops Pastoral Study on Priesthood: The Priest in the Gathered Community" (2000), 11.

[88] *Lambeth 1988*, Res. 43 (cf. 44), 231.

ministerial orders. As the Catholics moved closer to the center of the theological spectrum in the first part of the century,[89] so did English Evangelicals in the century's latter half, if works by Alister McGrath, Tim Bradshaw, N. T. Wright, and Gordon Kuhrt are any indication.

All four scholars accepted the by-then common understanding of the church as the totality of God's people. Tim Bradshaw, for example, defines the church as "the whole body of Christians who are joined to Christ in the bond of the Holy Spirit."[90] They all express that overarching theme using different motifs; whereas Anthony Hanson had employed the idea of the remnant, Bradshaw proposes the equally biblical idea of covenant, while Wright speaks of "God's rescue operation" devolving upon "Israel's representative," Jesus, who reconstitutes humanity in himself.[91] They all follow the Hansons in their understanding of ministry while still valuing tradition, apostolicity, and scholarly work on the Bible and church.[92] To some degree they all hint at the eschatological with a vision of the pilgrim people of God extending into glory. Wright discerns in the simple act of prayer, for instance, "one more sign of inaugurated eschatology, of the beginning of the End in Jesus Christ and his people."[93]

None of these authors equates Christ and church as one and the same, or the church and the ministry. On the contrary, Gordon Kuhrt asserts (sounding vaguely like Terwilliger, with whom he has little else in common) that "the primary New Testament teaching about priesthood is about either Jesus Christ himself or about the whole Church of Jesus—and *not* about the clergy or ordained

---

[89] *Lambeth 1988*, Res. #43 (p. 231); Welsby, *History*, 212–215.

[90] Tim Bradshaw, *The Olive Branch: An Evangelical Anglican Doctrine of the Church* (Carlisle: Paternoster, 1992), 141; cf. N. T. Wright, *Evangelical Anglican Identity: The Connection Between Bible, Gospel & Church* (Oxford: Latimer House, 1980), 27.

[91] Bradshaw, *Olive Branch*, 129–37; Wright, *Evangelical Identity*, 15.

[92] Cp. A. and R. Hanson, *Identity*, 43, 111; cf. Wright, *Evangelical Identity*, 25–27.

[93] A. and R. Hanson, *Identity*, 41; Wright, *Evangelical Identity*, 18, cf. 28–29.

leaders."[94] Ordained ministry serves the necessary purpose of promoting and guaranteeing apostolic fellowship, which links the church with the past while, in the present, continues the apostolic work of reexpressing and living out the gospel. In ordination, the church "formally authorizes the minister to fulfil this office because she is convinced that this person is called by God to do so and has the necessary qualities."[95] Call and gifts are recognized by the church through its commissioning and authorizing by the bishop as the church's appointed agent. For Wright, promoting unity ranks among the most important attributes of ministry: A presiding minister "is the one in whose *office* the church can see the mark of visible unity with other contemporary congregations and with the great church."[96]

Unlike the old-style Evangelicals, these newer Evangelicals have adopted a more inclusive tone as well. In a remark typical of their openness to the Anglican spectrum, Wright proposes "a Catholic Protestantism (or vice versa)," even to the point of commending vestments and the clerical "dog collar," using the Reformers as his authority. Alister McGrath envisions incorporating the key strengths of the three wings of the Church of England in an evangelistic strategy: the apologetic of the mainline element, which attempts to explain Christianity meaningfully to the world; the Evangelical emphasis on evangelism; and the long Catholic tradition of spirituality.[97] Bradshaw admires what he calls "Anglo-Catholic ecclesiology," whose "aesthetically pleasing and philosophically coherent" vision summons the church to its purpose of bearing "the marks of the crucified Lord in sacrificial love to the world." But he doubts whether the New Testament warrants a sacramental church with priestly ministry and, more, how the

---

[94] Gordon Kuhrt, *An Introduction to Christian Ministry* (London: Church House, 2000), 9; cf. Terwilliger, "What Is a Priest? One Anglican View," in *To Be a Priest*, 3–4.

[95] Bradshaw, *Olive Branch*, 154–157, 159, 161. He regrettably equates "ministry" with "presbyterate."

[96] A. and R. Hanson, *Identity*, 41; Wright, *Evangelical Identity*, 15–18, 28–29. This latter point is why Wright opposes lay Eucharistic presidency.

[97] Wright, *Evangelical Identity*, 22, 33; Alister E. McGrath, *The Renewal of Anglicanism* (Harrisburg, PA: Morehouse Publishing, 1993), 57–60.

church's self-offering on the altar relates to the once-for-all offering of Christ, arguing that "the church is not so much a form of Christ as the people of Christ, in covenant with him."[98] He also spots, as earlier Evangelicals did not, the dangers of individualism within Evangelicalism, which affects the balance between the leadership of clergy and the ministry of every member. A "team idea" would help, he suggests, as would a sacramental notion of corporate community in Christ.[99]

Of the four, Gordon Kuhrt, Archbishop George Carey's director of ministry, comes closest to pursuing an older Evangelical line. In an introduction to vocation and ministry, he conveys emphases not heard with such strength since Griffith Thomas. Reciting familiar themes—the centrality of Christ, the involvement of the *whole* people of God and its priesthood, a diaconal understanding of ministry[100]—Kuhrt is notable for his reliance on Scripture for his primary evidence and structure. From that basis, he concludes that the roles of preaching and teaching are primary functions of the church's leadership, with setting a moral example and providing pastoral care less important.[101] Sacramental aspects of ministerial leadership receive much scantier attention from Kuhrt than from Wright or Bradshaw.

The bold entry of Evangelicals into ecclesiology bears witness to their eagerness to extend their principles to every aspect of the church's life, including matters like ministry and orders that their earlier representatives ignored. They also manifest the degree to which nineteenth-century partisanship eased as the twentieth century

---

[98] Bradshaw, *Olive Branch*, 77–78, 138. I have difficulty seeing Bradshaw's distinction, given McGrath's lauding of Anglican Catholic spirituality, its inherent sacramental conviction, what we have read that emphasizes the church as a people of God inspired by the Spirit, and Bradshaw's own oft-acknowledged debt to Ramsey.

[99] Bradshaw, *Olive Branch*, 198–199.

[100] Kuhrt, *Introduction*, 9–10.

[101] Kuhrt, *Introduction*, 31–40, with barely a page each for example/pastoral care, the remainder for preaching/teaching. Kuhrt diverges from other accepted understandings, as in his calling bishops "senior presbyters" (p. 52), thus implying they are not a distinct order—ironically enough, a position more in line with Roman Catholic teaching, which makes little theological distinction between bishops and priests.

progressed. The Anglo-Catholic Michael Ramsey earlier had shown an appreciation for the doctrine of the atonement, so prized by Evangelicals. Now, Evangelicals have come to value such Catholic treasures as spirituality, sacrament, incarnation—and Michael Ramsey. They demonstrate the degree to which once-divided theological parties have drawn much closer to each other on an understanding of church and ministry.

THE "PERSON" AND THE PRIESTHOOD: TWO NEW VIEWS

Radically different are two recent works that explore "personhood" and its implications for vocation and ministry. The first, from the United States, essentially departs from the theological consensus of the earlier part of the century, while the second, from England, largely affirms it.

In his book *The Language of Ordination*, William Countryman, a professor of New Testament, takes characteristic ideas of the Anglican consensus and extends them ecumenically. In 1999 he brought out *Living on the Border of the Holy: Renewing the Priesthood of All*, and there Countryman drastically redefines priesthood. "By 'priest,'" he writes, "I mean any person who lives in the dangerous, exhilarating, life-giving borderlands of human existence, where the everyday experience of life opens up to reveal glimpses of the HOLY—and not only lives there but comes to the aid of others who are living there." Such a person "introduces us to *arcana*—hidden things, secrets," from constructing a budget to roasting a turkey or luring a mate. His argument can be summarized from a few paragraphs deep in his book:

> The fundamental priesthood of Christians is no more and no less than the true life of humanity in the presence of GOD, illuminated by the priesthood of Christ. Whenever someone is living attentively in the borderlands where we meet the HOLY and is ministering and being ministered to there, that person is a priest....
>
> This priesthood, fundamental and Christian, can exist without benefit of clergy or even, when necessary, without benefit of membership in the community of the church. Still, as human beings, we have an ongoing need for religion with its sacramental priests, and these priests have a significant effect on the priesthood of the whole people.... Their proper function is to model sacramentally—

and so to foster and facilitate—the life of the whole
priestly community.

> They can do this only if they find their place *in* and *for*
> the larger priestly community; they cannot do it by casting
> themselves in a role over against the rest of humanity.[102]

Like so many before him, Countryman seeks to unite clergy
and laity in common life, allowing a distinctive but not divisive
role for the ordained. Like some but not others, he considers clergy
of the *bene esse* but not *esse* of the church. But he is unique, as far
as I can tell, in equating the Christian priesthood with what he
frequently calls "the priesthood of humanity."[103] His radical redefinition emphatically places the ordained within the context of the whole
people; but it is not necessarily the people of God as Anglican theologians generally understood the term. This is not simply the "priesthood of all believers"; it is the priesthood of *all*, or as N. T. Wright
says in another context, "the priesthood of no believers at all."[104]

Still, the issues Countryman raises are those Anglicanism has
sought for generations to address and to fit into an ongoing pattern. How does one relate a "sacramental priesthood" to the
priesthood of the whole? The problem is not new; neither is Countryman's answer:

> The sacramental priest is not particularly different from
> other Christians; she or he should not be seen as distin-
> guished primarily by magical power or greater knowl-
> edge or holiness or by the imagery of parent or executive or
> sales representative, but by her or his sacramental roles.[105]

---

[102] Countryman, *Border*, 137, emph. and small caps in orig. Countryman's thesis on general priesthood intriguingly resembles the thought of Florence Nightingale. In addition to her more famous pursuits, she also contemplated theology
and believed that "[a]ll knowledge and science being holy, the profession of any
science made the priest." Cf. Val Webb, *Florence Nightingale: The Making of a
Radical Theologian* (St. Louis, MO: Chalice Press, 2002), 225–228 (q. on 226).

[103] In my opinion, there the confusions begin. If what makes a priest is a search
for the holy or an encounter with the numinous, would a Muslim, Buddhist, or
inquiring atheist be part of this priesthood of humanity?—or the *Christian* priesthood? Does birth confer priesthood, or the search, or a spiritual experience?

[104] Wright, *Evangelical Identity*, 31.

[105] Countryman, *Border*, 133, 129.

That statement seems to define ordained priesthood as cultic practice—a functional perspective. But when he envisions "an ordained ministry that can readily be seen and understood as a sacrament of the ministry of the whole church and, ultimately, of all humanity," he implies an ontological essence and a larger purpose that moves the ordained away from the altar or font and into the mainstream of life—much as Robert Moberly had hoped a century before.

If he sounds like Moberly on the subject of a representative ministry, he does not on the topic of sacrament. "It is of the nature of a sacrament that it should afford a relatively localized and tangible sign of a relatively diffused and pervasive grace." Baptism concretely expresses God's choice of the person being baptized, "a choice that antedates the baptism, pervades one's life, and cannot be fixed to a single time or place." Eucharistic bread signifies the divine care that sustains life well beyond the brief moment of receiving it. Similarly, the ordained few serve in the iconic role, "diffused throughout the people of GOD," as "sacramental images of the more fundamental priesthood all share with Christ." Countryman is reminiscent of Lightfoot when he states, "We can meet the HIDDEN HOLY without these rites. The rite is rather a showing forth of this experience, a concrete, sacramental re-presentation of it, reminding us and reaffirming for us how GOD meets us in the border country." But that statement seems to contradict the second clause of the catechism's definition of sacraments as "outward and visible signs of an inward and spiritual grace, given by Christ as *sure and certain means by which we receive that grace.*"[106] Sacraments effect more than they evince. If so, Countryman stands diametrically opposite from Roland Allen, who resigned his cure because he believed baptism should be administered only to those manifesting faith.[107]

Countryman's approach makes concepts of community difficult, although he does hold out a place for it: "Ordained ministry

---

[106] Countryman, *Border*, 94–95, 103; Catechism, US BCP (1979), 857, emph. added.

[107] Cf. Redfern, *Ministry and Priesthood*, 85–86. Contrast words of George Guiver: "[N]ot only does it illustrate—something happens in it which happens in no other pourings of water. God does something to us through the water. It is the same with the Eucharist and with the other sacraments" (*Fire and Clay*, 30).

exists, in part, as a way of articulating the life of the community."
What constitutes community, however, in this individualistic
approach? "Our priesthood is a fulfillment of the potential that
resides in the humanity of each of us. It is the experience of communion both with the deepest REALITY and with one another."[108]
But social does not invariably mean communal. His concept of
priesthood is based upon the individual, in vague association with
Jesus (who "illuminates" it) but in no sense *deriving* from either
Christ or the church. Neither a "Body of Christ" metaphor nor a
trinitarian one has any real place here. Defining "church" cannot
really be done; and he does not. Though he says that the entire
church must be involved in reforming a basic understanding of the
ordained priest, one wonders exactly how, and whom he has in
mind.

Perhaps Countryman's most important point is his insistence
on the encounter with the living God. Meeting Jesus, finding the
Holy Spirit, whatever the language might be, all describe that
"experience of communion both with the deepest REALITY and
with one another." Whether or not one agrees that this experience
constitutes a "priesthood," the point remains that it abides at the
heart of human life, giving rise to growth and insight of amazing
diversity and potential.

In a collection of essays called *The Fire and the Clay*, a group
associated with the theological college run by the Community of
the Resurrection in Mirfield, England, explores priesthood from
the angle of personhood: "Who is the real me?" This question, the
writers suggest, will lead someone first to faith and then to vocation. For these essayists, the question of personhood is a central
one in ministry: "What it is to be a person receives a new shape
and definition." The Mirfield approach resembles Countryman's
in its focus upon the individual but develops the point in more traditional ways. Answering that question, "Who is the real me?"
occurs in relationship with Jesus and his community. Jesus, at once
wholly human and the image of the invisible God, makes evident
the gift of God that can be granted to all. "Baptism into Christ is

---

[108] Countryman, *Border*, 132, 20, 135; cf. 143: "Vocation is never a purely individual matter, for priesthood always implies that our lives are interconnected and
interdependent. Every priest is part of a community of priests."

the acknowledgement of our need which brings us into life in the Church where we receive the gifts of the Spirit. We are drawn into fellowship with one another and find ourselves at home within a greater fellowship, *koinonia*—the Trinity." It is a fellowship of dependence on each other and on God, for "that is what it means to be a creature." From all this emerges ministry:

> Through commitment to Christ in baptism and to one another in the communion of faith, acceptance of our need of God may become the receiving of the gift which transforms dependence into the way of life.... We, who have some awareness of the gift we receive through our baptism into Christ, are to help bring others to know what it is to become "real", to help them grow into true personhood.[109]

The sharp-eyed reader will have spotted their allusion to the Trinity; reference to the "Body" metaphor is also not far away.[110] The writers avoid dogmatic assertions about precisely how the human structures of this Body evolved. They also take a gingerly view of ministry so that it incorporates the ecumenical many rather than the denominational few. Since priesthood is shaped and formed by the whole life of the priestly people, "it is neither possible nor desirable therefore to iron out, or put in parentheses, different ministerial structures with their different 'memories', without distorting the gift God has given." The principle applies also in relationship to the laity. As for the ordained priest, "The heart of the priest's ministry is the making visible of the gift of personhood which is Christ's alone." Not for nothing is the presbyter

---

[109] Guiver et al., *Fire and Clay*, 11, 13, 14–15. It should be noted that this book and Countryman's were published in the same year (1999) and show no knowledge of each other.

[110] "In the mercy of God, the Church exists as the body of Christ. It is the company of those who have recognized the fullness of being in Jesus Christ and seek to follow him. In the generosity of God, this gathering of human persons is no mere society, but a real representation of the life of Christ" (Guiver et al., *Fire and Clay*, 16; cf. 20). See also p. 91: "This 'identity-in-relationship' is in fact a reflection of the very nature of God, the God who is Trinity, for God is relationship and communication within himself. Each person of the Trinity exists, if you like, for the sake of the others, and each gains identity within the context of each other."

called "parson," "the *persona* who represents Christ to his people."[111]

The Mirfield writers reiterate a more catholic understanding. Like Countryman, they claim that baptism, for instance, effects *something*, but rather than simply manifesting an identity that is already present, baptism brings about a powerful change: "By the water in baptism something is effected which no other water can do; the bread in the Eucharist unites us with God in such a way that it is totally different from the ordinary bread it was until a few minutes ago." In contrast with Countryman's somewhat vague conception of sacrament, the Mirfield view is one of explicit relationship with Christ. Sacraments "are directly connected with the birth, life, death and resurrection of Jesus." They are a consequence of Incarnation.

> Christ has taken all that is good in what it is to be human and brought it together in a new synthesis with the divine. All those who are taken up into the sacrament of Christ's body the Church are affected by this, and its typically human structures have this added dimension. A bishop, a priest, a deacon, a reader, a server, a musician, a flower arranger, fulfill roles which can be paralleled in ordinary human society but (whether good examples of it or not) they act out in their roles the mystery of the incarnation; they make present the sacrament of the Church.

These essays make a claim similar to—though more precise than—Countryman's. "Ordained priesthood, like any other particular way of being a baptized Christian, exists in dependence on Christ and in and for the sake of the whole body."[112]

With *The Fire and the Clay*, we come full circle. Our study of a century of theology closes with a reassertion of a catholic position with which it began—and also the same perplexity: How does the individual, clergy or lay, relate to the corporate body? On that, we have surely seen a range of responses. Anglo-Catholic clergy were accused of individualistic excess. Roland Allen depreciated the individual call in favor of a corporate one. Both Hansons tried

---

[111] Guiver et al., *Fire and Clay*, 20–25, 27, 17.

[112] Guiver et al., *Fire and Clay*, 30–32, 33, 51.

to balance the corporate concern with the individual. Greenwood feared that the "monism" of incarnational theology bred individualism in some Anglo-Catholic clergy, and Bradshaw bemoaned the ways Evangelicalism fostered it. Countryman seems to revel in individualism, basing his "priesthood of all" upon a highly personal and personalized discernment, howevermuch aided by others. Snow and McGrath see potential strengths in having a multiplicity or "pluralism" of voices, attitudes, and local theologies, points of colorful light on a larger spectrum.[113] The doctrine of the Trinity was proffered as a means to explicate, from profoundest theology, a concept of diversity and unity; but then, the image of the Body of Christ had been used precisely for the same purpose.

Interestingly, in 1999 appeared a reaffirmation of the "Body of Christ." A mission commission reported that year to the Anglican Consultative Council its conviction, in the words of missionary and bishop John V. Taylor, that "only by being Christ himself can the Christian community remain the source of that living water which is also the wine of life." The report added:

> When we use the Pauline image of "the body of Christ" we may be referring to the incarnate Christ, to the eucharistic body or to the mystical body, the Church. The three are, of course, intimately connected. The Church is the sacrament of the gospel. The Church is the mission of God because it is the expression and instrument of the Sent One.[114]

The contrast is intriguing between this and the *Virginia Report* to the Lambeth Conference just one year earlier. The *Virginia Report* was produced by a theological commission, and it utilized a doctrinal metaphor. The mission commission reverted to a biblical image, which itself was the veritable motto of MRI, the one pan-Anglican missionary effort there has ever been. One is theological in derivation, the other scriptural: full circle indeed.

On that basis, we may turn to a new explication of old puzzlements of priests and laity, church and orders in a new millennium.

---

[113] Cp. Snow, *Impossible Vocation*, 158, with McGrath, *Renewal*, 124.

[114] Johnson and Clark, eds., *Anglicans In Mission*, 17.

P   A   R   T   T   W   O

VI
Reenvisioning the Church and Its Ministry

At the start of this new century and millennium, familiar questions have presented themselves again. What is a priest? What is the nature of orders? Even more essential, what is the nature of the church, and according to whom? Perceptions of priesthood are shaped by conceptions of the church. The ministry of the ordained arises out of the church, not the other way around.

Because denominations vary as to how they understand the church, they also differ in the role and place they give to their ordained. William Countryman makes this observation in contrasting Roman Catholic and Anglican bishops in the United States. In *The Language of Ordination*, he points out that the Roman Catholic bishop is appointed by Rome from a small group of nominees proposed by other American prelates, while the Episcopal bishop is elected by one diocese and confirmed by other dioceses. The Episcopal bishop shares in formulating official teaching, while the Roman Catholic is more of a spokesman for what the Vatican decrees. We might extend Countryman's observation to other denominations: The Methodist bishop has few sacramental duties but enormous weight in the appointment of clergy, while the situation is just the opposite for the Episcopalian. With Lutherans, a bishop is bishop only so long as he or she holds that office; with Anglicans, once a bishop, always a bishop. Not only does the specific life of each communion vary in its use of the ordained and the functions it ascribes to them, as Countryman rightly concludes, the life of the denomination shapes the very nature of the ordained—who they are as well as what they do. Understanding Anglican priesthood, no less than episcopate, depends upon understanding the church as Anglicans perceive it.[1]

Part One of this book looked back upon the Anglican reappraisal of the church at the turn of the twentieth century, when the biblical image of the Body of Christ became the dominant means of explaining the nature of the church. As Paul describes in 1 Corinthians 12, all Christians share the life of Jesus Christ as "members" of his Body. Those in Holy Orders are no more and no less part of this Body than the laity. The ordained do hold certain roles and functions within the church but only in relationship with the Christian community as a whole. Ultimately the entire people of God, made one with Christ and each other by the Spirit through baptism, together serve as the "royal priesthood" that 1 Peter 2:9 cites, with that priesthood derived from the priesthood of Christ himself. To use an image that was increasingly employed at the close of the twentieth century, the church resembles the Trinity—for all its diversity, an abiding unity prevails that joins the people of God together through Christ with the Godhead, all by the power of the Spirit.

Far from holding a unique perspective, Anglicans share much with Christians of other denominations. Furthermore, to place too strong an emphasis on an "Anglican perspective" may be misleading, not because there is no Anglican view but because there are so many. Controversies at Lambeth 1998 and since concerning the Bible, human sexuality, and the authority of the community over against the independence of provinces and dioceses: all involve differing visions of what the church should be, how it should be organized, and how it can be held together. Cultural and ecclesial differences undermine any attempt to define what a worldwide Anglican Communion believes.

These realities have led some to doubt that any distinctively Anglican doctrine can exist on any topic at all—either because what Anglicans hold is so broadly shared by those of other

---

[1] L. William Countryman, *The Language of Ordination: Ministry in an Ecumenical Context* (Philadelphia: Trinity Press International, 1992), 3.

communions or because Anglicans can find so little in common among themselves. In *Unashamed Anglicanism,* theologian Stephen Sykes affirms that there are tenets that Anglicans hold as uniquely their own,[2] and I believe that my earlier chapters uphold his contention. Anglicans *do* have a point of view even though they are not unanimous in their perspective. But I have tried to show a general understanding that has and is still being articulated in canons and prayer books, by bishops in their conferences, and by theologians in their writings.

On this basis, Part Two looks not ahead so much as around. It strives to articulate an understanding of priesthood and orders that prevails in the Anglican Communion at this moment in time—an understanding that arises directly out of an Anglican understanding of the church with the following six hallmarks. First, this Anglican understanding of the church must be biblically based, and second, it must arise from within the historical continuity of the people of God, implying both a respect for tradition and for the scholarship that has explored it. Third, it must be able, to the greatest degree possible, to be embraced by the Anglican Communion as a whole. Fourth, this understanding must embrace and arise from the *laos,* the *whole* people of God. Fifth, it must be flexible enough to be applied in distinctive ways. Sixth and last, it must be ecumenically sensitive while reflecting its Anglican origins and bias. It must recognize the place of Anglicanism within a much broader perspective, borrowing from and contributing toward the understanding of other Christians. In other words, Anglican ecclesiology has value, but it is not the only valid ecclesiology. How can we say that? Because the Bible tells us so.

BIBLICAL IMAGES OF THE CHURCH AS COMMUNITY

Various biblical images have been used by Anglican writers to describe the church, with "Body of Christ," "olive branch," "remnant," and "royal priesthood" being only a few. In his 1960 study of New Testament imagery, Paul Minear identified ninety-two other possibilities, while thirty years later Keith A. Russell examined

---

[2] Stephen Sykes, *Unashamed Anglicanism* (Nashville: Abingdon Press, 1975), ch. 6, 101–121; cf. also McGrath, *Renewal,* 65.

discrete bodies of New Testament literature—the synoptic gospels, Paul's letters, 1 Peter, Revelation—for the vision each held of the church. In Russell's opinion, Mark saw an "alternative community"; Matthew, "households of justice"; and Luke, "signs of the kingdom." In his epistles Paul described "communities of reconciliation," while Peter wrote of "homes for the homeless." John the Divine wrote to "communities of resistance."[3] Since all these images describe the same phenomenon, what shall we make of their variety? One way is to see within them the rich and varied texture of what they all seek to describe. Having deduced several points of interrelationship, Minear recommends both a "synoptic" way of thinking, which embraces all the images as part of a single continuum, and a "reciprocal" mode, which sees the images as "almost yet not quite interchangeable."[4] Minear's synoptic approach places images like "Body of Christ" and "royal priesthood" alongside each other as mutually complementary, while the "reciprocal" explores the connections that one has with the other—how, for instance, the "Body" may be "priestly."

For all their diversity, these metaphors and explanations all concern Christ, and almost all describe community. Each image relates somehow to God, often specifically to Jesus, and thus to the connection between the Godhead and the human that is possible through Christ. With this "vertical" relationship—between God and human beings—comes the "horizontal," the relationship between human beings themselves, which, in Christ, is communal in nature. Every image that Russell delineates implies community. While Minear's list is not altogether communal, by my count nearly ninety percent could be considered corporate rather than individualistic in nature. They concern a *people*. Like tesserae in a mosaic, they fashion a biblical picture of a community that is at once a fellowship with God and a community of mortals.

---

[3] Paul Minear, *Images of the Church in the New Testament* (Philadelphia: Westminster Press, 1960), 268–269; Keith A. Russell, *In Search of the Church: New Testament Images for Tomorrow's Congregations* (Bethesda, MD: Alban Institute, 1994), *passim*.

[4] Minear, *Images*, 221. A third way, "retroactive or depth thinking," contemplates what was in the mind of the author and is of less relevance to us here.

Minear's synoptic and reciprocal approach holds two implications for understanding the church. First, even though the Bible describes the same phenomenon in many different ways, no one image is allowed to stand alone. Instead, each contributes toward a lush but balanced complexity in which no image predominates but all work together to enrich our understanding of the whole. Second, Minear's two ways of thinking about biblical imagery can help us to contemplate the theologies of the church, which themselves so often arise out of biblical or credal images. No one theology need necessarily exclude another, but various perspectives may exist, as do the images, in a healthy balance, one amplifying or correcting another.

Minear's dual approach may be useful not only in comprehending the differences among ecumenical forms of expression, but also in making the pluralistic perspectives within Anglicanism an asset as well, especially on matters of orders and ministries. One image need not fit all; one metaphor may balance and enhance another. So it may be with two of the most prominent ecclesiological images of the twentieth century, the Body of Christ and the Trinity.

THE BODY OF CHRIST AND THE TRINITY

By the start of the twentieth century, the image of the Body of Christ took on new prominence and luster, thanks in part to theologian Robert Campbell Moberly. As I tried to show in chapters 3 and 4, this ancient image reappeared in the theology and liturgies of the Anglican Communion. By the century's end, the doctrine of the Trinity had come into vogue for explaining interrelationships within the Christian community. Credally based and serving as a model for communal relationships marked by diversity within a prevailing unity, the image of Trinity has woven its way into both the theological reports and the prayers of Anglicanism. Together these images of Body and Trinity form the central motifs of current Anglican ecclesiology, and they are far from incompatible ideas. Because the two images are so traditional and so well-known, Minear's synoptic notion can allow a widespread acceptance of each of them, without having to make a choice that pits one against the other. More importantly, they seek to uphold the same ideal of unity and diversity as an attribute of God and therefore of God's people.

It is important to remember that these are both metaphors; and metaphors derive more from the world of poetry than of science or law. A bard may sing, "My love is like a red, red rose," trying to express an essence of meaning that transcends precise or technical language. Taking a metaphor too literally, for instance, can make the image grotesque; overinflating it can defeat its very purpose. To describe God as Trinity ascribes qualities to a deity who in the end stands above all names and beyond all human attributes. To refer to the church as the Body of Christ is to try to take hold of an entity that, if it is of God, will always exceed our grasp. Nevertheless, each way of speaking lets us transcend the immediate realities of an all-too-human institution and realize that vastly greater forces are at work. As James Barnett wrote in his book on the diaconate, the

> Church's organic nature and unity are but the reflection of God. God is within himself a community of persons who are united with one another in perfect harmony and oneness, yet each person of the Trinity possesses individually personality and function. God has called and constituted the Church to be such a community of persons in the world, realizing the oneness of humanity and expressing the perfect harmony of life together as each member grows into his or her own fullness.[5]

In other words, how we relate to one another can be a manifestation on earth of the very nature of God. Both metaphors, Trinity and Body, affirm this understanding.

The very mystery of the Trinity provides two vitally important advantages in explaining the nature of the church. First, its inexpressibility may challenge the words of preachers and the understanding of congregations, but at the same time serve as

> a constant warning against over-simple theologies, blasphemous in their attempts to pin down the Being of God. Religion is destroyed without mystery—indeed paradox.... We worship a mysterious, not an anthropomorphic God.[6]

---

[5] Barnett, *Diaconate*, 6.

[6] Frances Young, "A Cloud of Witnesses," in John Hick, ed., *The Myth of God Incarnate* (Philadelphia: Westminster Press, 1977), 42.

Simplistic definitions of the church cannot suffice in describing an entity that shares the mystery of God. Even more important, the Trinity expresses a sense of the human union with a God who is both exalted over all creation and as intimate as Jesus, a union ultimately cosmic in scope. In the words of the epistle to the Colossians, Christ

> is the head of the body, the church; he is the beginning, the firstborn from the dead, so that he might come to have first place in everything. For in him all the fullness of God was pleased to dwell, and through him God was pleased to reconcile to himself all things, whether on earth or in heaven, by making peace through the blood of his cross. (1:18–20)

Because of that union, even in something as simple as prayer, notes James Fenhagen, "we participate in the creative energy of God by which all life is connected and sustained."[7]

The letter to the Colossians refers to the Body of Christ, the other great theme that Anglicans have come to prize. Recent scholarship of the New Testament and classical literature, especially in studies by Dale Martin and Allen Rhea Hunt, revive and expand the meaning of the Pauline image in ways that may be exceptionally important for our study. Ancient writers from Plato onward, according to Martin, generally related the human body to the universe at large. They made no hard distinction between "inner" and "outer" body (a point Moberly reiterated). The correlation between the human body and the universe worked as well when it came to the body politic. "The microcosm of the body was used to explain how unity can exist in diversity within the macrocosm of society," Martin writes. This analogy could justify a social hierarchy to instill concord within a household or a city-state. In one schema, the father was likened to the head, and the slave to a foot. In another, the right hand represented male members and the left hand, females; in a third, daughters were eyes and slaves were again destined to be feet. What applied to the family applied no less to the *polis*.[8]

---

[7] Fenhagen, *More than Wanderers*, 33.

[8] Dale B. Martin, *The Corinthian Body* (New Haven and London: Yale University Press, 1995), 16–18; 92–93, 31.

Paul seems to accept this way of thinking, except on one point: He rejects the hierarchical. If anything, he reverses it, observing in 1 Corinthians 12:22–23 that "those members of the body that seem to be less honorable we clothe with greater respect." Martin understands Paul to use the image, complete with this inversion, to promote unity and harmony based upon the common Christian experience of Christ.

> The higher elements of the body are called upon to yield to the lower elements. The spirit is to yield to the mind, the head to the genitals, the Strong to the Weak; and the higher-status Christians to those of lower status. In all cases, what Paul says of the human body, he expects to be applied in the church, the body of Christ, "in order that there be no schism in the body."[9]

Additionally, Paul assumes that "individual bodies have reality only insofar as they are identified with some greater cosmic reality." Individually or corporately, the Christian body "has no meaning apart from its participation in the body of Christ."[10]

Paul may have been influenced by *another* "body" in working through his theology, for colorful Jewish speculations on a "body of Adam" were circulating in his day. The scholar W. D. Davies detected a first-century rabbinic notion of the incorporation of all humanity into the "body of Adam." Israel was Adam's head while Babylon made up the trunk. Other nations represented the body's

---

[9] Martin, *Corinthian Body*, 103, cf. 1 Cor. 12:25 and 1:10. Martin contends that the Corinthian church was torn between one group exerting its status over another, the "strong" versus the "weak," Paul siding with the latter. Cf. David L. Bartlett, *Ministry in the New Testament* (Minneapolis: Fortress, 1993), 53: "What is stressed [in Paul's understanding of gifts] is the interdependence of all Christian people."

[10] Martin, *Corinthian Body*, 131. That, Martin says, together with the identity of inward and outward, leads Paul to fret mightily over inward pollution caused by misuse of food or sex: cf. 168ff, 174ff. Eduard Schweizer comments with regard to the Colossians passage that the concept of universe as divine body is frequently found, with Zeus, the heavens, the spirit, or the Logos at the "head." However, in Pauline usage, Christ never appears as head; in 1 Cor. 12:21, the head is but one of many members. The emphasis in Colossians, then, rather than the organic connection, is on Christ as the preeminent Lord of the entire cosmic order. (Eduard Schweizer, *The Letter to the Colossians*, trans. Andrew Chester [Minneapolis: Augsburg, 1982], 58, 72; cf. Schweizer, σῶμα, *TDNT*, VII, 1037, 1054).

limbs, and Akra di Agma, wherever that was, embodied his private parts. Beneath this polemical notion lay an understanding on which Paul could build a concept of the Body of the "new Adam" as Christians united with one another and with Christ, manifesting the redemption that brought them together in anticipation of that day when God's purpose for all nations would be fulfilled. Whereas the "Body of the First Adam" is animated by natural life, the "Body of the Second Adam" lives by the Spirit. One enters it by putting off the old and putting on the new, thereby advancing the very purpose of God, which is "to gather together in one all things in Christ."[11] Yet, it could never be completely shaken in this mortal life. With these observations in mind, Martin writes,

> insofar as human bodies are subject to death at all, it is due to their incorporation in the body of Adam (1 Cor. 15:21–22). The body of Adam is the location of death, and it is human participation in that body, even after baptism, that makes possible a Christian's experience of death at all. Christians, although incorporated into the body of Christ through baptism, are still burdened, at least until the resurrection or transformation of their bodies in the eschaton, by their participation in the body of Adam.

Human beings continue to share this existence because they participate in Adam's body; as his body is earthy, so are those of Christians (15:47–48), even as they have been redeemed to be part of the Body of Christ.[12]

In this light, Holy Orders within the Body of Christ take on a significance for the "body of Adam," that is, humanity. The late Charles Price perceived a relevance for orders beyond the church. As each ministerial order symbolizes Christ, in each way Christ "is

---

[11] W. D. Davies, *Paul and Rabbinic Judaism: Some Rabbinic Elements in Pauline Theology* (London: SPCK, 1958), 54–57; Eph. 1:10. Cf. John Halliburton, "The Laity in the Ministry of the Church," in Christine Hall and Robert Hannaford, eds., *Order and Ministry* (Leominster: Gracewing, 1996), 107. Davies notes that the OT uses the name "Adam" generically for humankind and though the rabbis did not do so in the same way, Adam remains the typical representative of humanity. He suggests that the term "Christ" may stand for the new humanity, i.e. Christians (57, n. 4).

[12] Martin, *Corinthian Body*, 132.

a symbolic representative of Adam, of humankind." Like a good deacon, Adam was set in the garden to till and keep it. Like a priest, Adam stood between God and the creatures of God; and like a bishop, he had oversight over it. So each element is "expressive of what it means to be human in the world which God created.... When the Church is truly the Church, women and men in Holy Orders are representative persons, standing for and implementing the true spirit of humanity in the world, and enabling the whole Church to engage in that ministry to the world."[13] Holy Orders matter greatly for the church, but they also matter for everyone else.

Within the Body of Christ, the Spirit guarantees that inspiration comes to all, not just to a privileged few. For Paul, God reveals his wisdom (*sophia*) through the Spirit. If divine wisdom defines the community, it should function as a source of unity among Christians rather than as a source of factionalism. The Corinthians, however, in their quarrels with each other, mimic the world and its rulers rather than emulate Christ. They ignore the Spirit that unites all believers into one body. Their divisiveness belies who they are and, because outward reveals inward, gives further cause for Paul's frantic concern.[14] When the Corinthians argue over *who* receives these gifts, they put the focus on the recipient rather than the giver and forget that it is God who bestows charisms in the first place. Since God composes the body and distributes gifts, no one has any right to complain or to boast. On the contrary, God intends the gifts to foster unity. Those who receive these gifts, moreover, can use them properly and validly only in and for the Christian community.[15] Paul's understanding of charisms and inspiration, in Hunt's summary, contrasts again with secular society.

---

[13] Charles P. Price, "The Threefold Cord: A Case for Cumulative Ordination," *The Orders of Ministry: Reflections on Direct Ordination, 1996*, ed. Edwin F. Hallenbeck (Providence, RI: North American Association for the Diaconate, 1996), 24–25.

[14] Allen Rhea Hunt, *The Inspired Body: Paul, the Corinthians, and Divine Inspiration* (Macon, GA: Mercer University Press, 1996), 71, 87, 77; 86.

[15] Hunt, *Inspired Body*, 111, 116, 119–20. Hunt suggests (111) that what makes the Body inspired, and perhaps what makes the Body, is the Spirit coming to Christians who then come together—an assumption that I believe warrants further scrutiny.

When charisms come at all, some classical writers believed, they come to a select few, and then only partially and for the benefit of a small elite. For Paul, on the other hand, in granting charisms to mortals, the Spirit blesses the whole Body and all who are part of it, for the benefit of everyone. If Hunt's theory is correct, the image of the Body, far from promoting hierarchy, expresses the opposite: a unity forged by Christ and blessed by the Spirit who bestows gifts upon each member, for the benefit of all. By God's grace, then, each member, and each gift, merit mutual respect.

Together, these metaphors of Trinity and Body reveal something that a local congregation can easily miss amid concerns for a leaking roof, straining budget, or pressing pastoral crisis. As James Barnett writes:

> To think of the Church throughout the world as it exists today as the universal Church is great, but there is a sense in which it is even greater to think of the Church in any parish as being the universal Church, as being the Body of Christ with all of its power and gifts and life![16]

As one of the countless spheres in which Christ is at work, the church provides a connection so intimate that it becomes part of his Body and, more, part of the Trinity. The images lend the most exalted purpose to the humblest circumstances. What Christians do and are fits into a pattern that encompasses the entire cosmos. The Eucharist brings a vision of this grand pattern before the worshiping congregation week by week as the congregation joins "with angels and archangels and all the company of heaven."

Critics of Anglican theology charge that Anglican ecclesiology comes too close to equating the church with God's kingdom, whereas Christ's work so vastly surpasses the church that the human mind can hardly comprehend it. The kingdom radically transcends church and every other earthly institution; it allows us to anticipate the final reign of God in the last days. We cannot bring it in, for Christ has already inaugurated it, nor can we complete it. All we can do is participate in it, even now. For the church remains very much a part of that work. It is a witness, in its word

---

[16] Barnett, *Diaconate*, 7.

and in its deed. It is a sign, by its worship and in its life. And it is, corporately, priestly.

Indeed, this is where the priestliness of the church itself becomes so important. The church is priest to creation—proclaiming Christ, ministering Christ, and deriving all that it does from the Christ who gave himself to and for the world. Its mission and ministry is to mediate between God and humanity, announcing its Lord to the world in word and deed, and bringing the world before its Lord in prayer, worship, and service, knowing that it is not so much the church that acts but Christ acting through the church in the power of the Spirit. As the Welsh catechism states, "The mission of the Church is to be the instrument of God in restoring all people to unity with God and each other in Christ."[17] Other Anglican provinces make similar statements. Of course this is not a task for any one group within the church, but the essential purpose for the entire church. It relies on all its components, on each level of its life, all inspired and empowered by the Spirit. In this sense, the church itself is priest to the world.

ORGANIZING THE COMMUNITY ON EARTH

The church, then, is a human institution that is always more than human. As the Body of Christ, the community of the faithful in the Triune God, the church has been granted a transcendent quality unlike that of any other entity on earth. Yet it exists *on earth,* which explains—though does not justify—many of its problems. So it faces the necessities of earthly life, such as organization and leadership. The need for these was evident even before the day of Pentecost, when frightened disciples overseeing the tiny band of Jesus' followers chose Matthias to join them, and Luke perceived the Holy Spirit to be at work in their choice (Acts 1:15–26). How the church expresses itself in human terms by what it teaches, how it worships, and how it lives are themselves evangelical statements of its mission. It portrays its Lord. If Jesus is able to take bread and wine and make them become for us his body and blood, then

---

[17] [The Church in Wales,] *The Book of Common Prayer for Use in The Church in Wales* (Penarth: Church in Wales Publications, 1984), II, 691; cf. chapter 4, above.

he may take human lives and institutions, make them holy, and work through them. So while the organization of the church is an earthly necessity, it may also be a means whereby Jesus can act and reveal divine grace.

How that organization and leadership came to be is a matter of contention, as we have seen in earlier chapters. At this moment the consensus appears to be that we can find nearly anything we seek in the church's ancient governance and organization.[18] Churches in different times and places developed varying structures, as scholar David L. Bartlett concluded. He approached the New Testament much as Keith Russell did and examined the various constellations of literature: Paul's undisputed letters, each gospel, the Acts of the Apostles, and the pastoral epistles. As Bartlett wrote in *Ministry in the New Testament*, each faced different issues at various points and produced diverse results. The gospel and letters of John seem to be radically egalitarian, acutely conscious of the Spirit, and committed to service. Luke-Acts, by contrast, points to the discipleship of all and the leadership of some, in a manner more patriarchal than hierarchical, as if to imply a familial quality to the Christian community. So the possibility exists that, in the earliest decades of the church, bishops and deacons oversaw Greek-speaking congregations, whereas in Jerusalem "presbyters" or "elders" took charge. "Different churches apparently have different structures," he concludes, while a threefold ministerial order did not emerge until around 110 CE.[19]

A structured ministry, as in the church's creeds and liturgy, only developed over time. What seems so familiar to Christians today existed on the day of Pentecost, if it existed at all, only in embryonic form. Belief in Jesus comprised a nascent creed; his followers gathered in an upper room in some form of community and worship. The apostles and possibly some others exercised some manner of leadership, judging from the selection of Matthias to replace Judas and from Peter's role in explaining the experience of Pentecost (Acts 1–2). Peter referred that day to what came to be

---

[18] Streeter, *Primitive Church*, ix, 261 (see chapter 3, above).

[19] Bartlett, *Ministry in the NT*, 39. He refers to Pauline communities but in the course of the book extends his point to others. See also Jill Pinnock, "The History of the Diaconate," in Hall, *Deacon's Ministry*, 11.

known as the Old Testament, or Hebrew Bible, but those books had not been authoritatively determined by Jews, much less Christians, to constitute a "canon" of Scripture. So while the Spirit may have given the apostolic band the power to speak in tongues of all nations, a threefold order of ministry, a New Testament with twenty-seven books, a defined creed, and a weekly liturgy were not among the gifts bestowed that day. Nonetheless, the rudiments of all of these elements of the church's life were present from its beginning.

A "CANONIST" APPROACH TO HOLY ORDERS

During its first centuries, the church met in council to decide which books would constitute its Scripture. The process of determining what we now know as a Bible of sixty-six books (not including the Apocrypha) is termed the development of the "canon," from the Latin word for "rule" or "authority."[20] The church also developed a rule of worship that led to the "canon" of the Eucharist. In the same period, fundamental convictions were hammered out and enshrined in the several creeds of the church, the Nicene being the best known. In each case, the Christian community reached conclusions about which books to read as Scripture, which credal affirmations to hold as dogma, and which sacraments to use in worship. In each case, the process of deciding and refining occurred, sometimes painfully, over centuries. It was a process undertaken by the community of the faithful, the church.

A "canon" of ministry also emerged over the early centuries. We have traced the developing perception that, while the earliest church may have had no "ordination" as we know it, and no "offices" in our modern sense (to use Richard Hanson's phrase), three forms of leadership emerged, however unclearly: overseers or bishops, *episkopoi*; elders or priests, *presbuteroi*; and servants or deacons, *diakonoi*. This concept of the emergence of a canon seems well-recognized in other spheres. Few dispute the canon of Scripture. Creeds are used, even with ecumenically agreed-upon

---

[20] The process may well have entailed the editing of individual books as well as their interpretation: see Brevard S. Childs, *The New Testament as Canon: An Introduction* (Philadelphia: Fortress Press, 1984), 3–53, and his *Biblical Theology of the Old and New Testaments* (Minneapolis: Fortress Press, 1993), 70–79. Cf. J. N. D. Kelly, *Early Christian Creeds*, 3rd ed. (London: Longman, 1972).

language. Likewise with sacraments: some traditions doubt them altogether and many define them differently from others, but in the end, baptism and Eucharist are generally accepted.[21]

Of the four, ministry has been the most consistently controversial. Ecumenical dialogues, like those between Lutherans and Anglicans at the end of the twentieth century, have not disputed much over creed or sacraments and certainly not over the canon of Scripture. Ministry, however, notably the historic episcopate, has generated much heat. The "canonist" approach, along with recent scholarship, may open the way for further ecumenical rapprochement. It can also help Anglicans to consider the basis of their orders of bishop, priest and deacon, but to do so with deeper humility. This approach presumes that we cannot find one singular form of ministry that was universally accepted in the life of the early church, for Elizabethan divines like Whitgift and Hooker taught that no specific form of polity is mandated by Scripture.[22] Nor can we recapture or replicate the past and presume it to be "correct"; we cannot be what Michael Ramsey called "archeological." Therefore we cannot deny the ministry or derivation of the orders of ministry found in other denominations solely on the basis of the Bible or ancient church practice. All traditions and theories of ministry may be subject to scrutiny but usually not on biblical grounds alone.

Alongside these negatives, a "canonist" approach leads to several more positive convictions. First, Christ is the source, head, and Lord of a church that was, is, and shall continue to be inspired by the Spirit. The church is at once the Body of Christ and the community of the Triune God. Second, the church represents and re-presents the living Christ to the world. Its very life as a community of faith is one means whereby it makes its proclamation: As Jesus was both medium and message of the triune God, so the church is both medium and message of Jesus. As Ramsey posited, it is "evangelical."

---

[21] E.g., World Council of Churches, Faith and Order Commission, *Baptism, Eucharist and Ministry* (Geneva: WCC, 1982) [*BEM*], 2–17.

[22] Melinsky, *Shape*, 93. John Whitgift was an Archbishop of Canterbury under Elizabeth I, and Richard Hooker a leading Anglican apologist who wrote *The Laws of Ecclesiastical Polity* (1594–97).

Third, any formal ministry represents both Christ and the church. Ministry can never stand apart from its Lord, who provides its power, authority, and inspiration. Nor can it be separated from its community through which (at least in part) its Lord continues to act. On the contrary, ministry in the name of Jesus goes from strength to strength as it ever more fully represents Christ and even more fully represents the church.

From these initial statements about the nature of ministry, we need to go even further and say that the threefold ministry is a *biblical* ministry. For all its hidden beginnings, the ministry of deacons, presbyters, and bishops is scriptural. It is also *traditional,* grounded in the church's historical experience. Ministry also must have four *marks,* or characteristics: it must be baptismal, rooted in discipleship; diaconal, marked by servanthood; sacrificial, or eucharistic; and apostolic. The organization of the church itself yields four characteristic ways in which the church pursues the mission that Christ bestows and inspires: in its community of discipleship, of servanthood, of sacrifice, and of apostolic witness and order.

A COMMUNITY OF DISCIPLES

Baptismal liturgies vary in precise wording, but all ask the same basic questions of those being initiated into the Christian faith and life:

Question   Do you turn to Jesus Christ and accept him as your Savior?

Answer   I do.

Question   Do you put your whole trust in his grace and love?

Answer   I do.

Question   Do you promise to follow and obey him as your Lord?

Answer   I do.[23]

With those promises, and the water and grace of sacrament, the person becomes a disciple of Christ. From the 1549 Prayer Book

---

[23] US BCP, 302 (||Canada, *Alternative Services*, 159).

until now, Anglicanism has accepted the concept that baptism means discipleship. The one who is baptized pledges, in the words of 1549, "to folowe the example of oure saviour Christe, and to be made lyke unto him." Bartlett argues that while "apostles" in Luke-Acts were the circle of twelve who accompanied Jesus, bore witness to him, and then died without successors in an office, the "disciples are the whole community of believers" who provide for a "continuity in the community of faith." The term does not refer solely to the twelve, for Luke describes as "disciples" a great number of people who surrounded Jesus, as well as those in Antioch who were first called "Christians."[24] Hence to commit oneself to Christ in baptism is to commit oneself to following Jesus as a disciple and the church as a corporate disciple of its Lord. From this, all other ministry derives. In the Scottish Episcopal Church the bishop reminds every ordinand, "In baptism every disciple is called to make Jesus known as Saviour and Lord and to share his work in renewing the world."[25]

Revisions of *The Book of Common Prayer* throughout the Anglican Communion have placed a fresh emphasis on the baptismal covenant, and with it, the concept of "baptismal ministry." Its basic pledge is the renunciation of evil and the commitment to Jesus as Savior. The American and Canadian rites develop the theme in asking candidates to continue in the apostles' teaching and fellowship, to resist evil, to proclaim the good news of Christ, to seek and serve Christ in all persons, and to strive for justice and peace. All these spell out implications of the basic commitment each candidate makes to Jesus.[26] This list of commitments spells

---

[24] Bartlett, *Ministry in the NT*, 135, where he cites a long list of examples; Acts 11:26.

[25] Episcopal Church in Scotland, *Scottish Ordinal 1984* (Edinburgh: General Synod of the Scottish Episcopal Church), 1984, 2, 9, 16.

[26] US BCP, 302–305; Canada, *Alternative Services*, 154, 159. No other Anglican initiatory rites go so far in detailing baptismal responsibilities: see England's *ASB* (223–260), BCP for Wales (652–669, 704–708), Australia (51–62), and Ireland's *Alternative Prayer Book 1984* (755–761). NZ asks candidates for confirmation—not baptism—for a more specific commitment to Christian service along lines similar to ECUSA and Canada (383–395, see esp. 390–391). Admittedly, the *ASB* and Irish rites presume the candidates will be children. From this limited survey, it would appear that the emphasis on baptismal *ministry*, expressed and pledged in the context of the rite itself, is not (yet?) matched beyond North America.

out more fully the injunction made in the Australian prayer book, "Live as a disciple of Christ."[27]

With this baptismal pledge of discipleship, all ministry begins, because baptism is where all Christian life starts. By it, Christ constitutes the *laos*, the people of God. However, at this point we must make two crucial distinctions. The first is between the whole people of God—the *laos*, a Greek word for "people," and the term that derives from it, "laity" (hence layman, laywoman) who are the approximately ninety-nine percent of Christians not in Holy Orders. Every Christian is part of the *laos*, but not all Christians are "laity."[28]

The second distinction is between "discipleship"—the act of following Jesus—and "ministry," the more specific forms of service a disciple may pursue as a result of following Jesus and sharing in the community of faith. Robert Hannaford explains in brief a contentious point we will explore later; he writes, "Discipleship is what the individual owes as a duty towards God, whatever his or her specific order or calling, while ministry is an act performed at the instigation of the Church."[29] We must go one step further to affirm that ministry belongs to the entire church, and by entering into the church through baptism, a person will participate in the general ministry of the faithful. Bishop, priest, deacon, and laity all share in the life and work of discipleship, for all are called to follow Jesus and have pledged to do just that. The aim, then, is to become *like* Jesus, in thought, word, and deed.

There are as many ways to follow Jesus as there are Christians, but discipleship will always include a life of service, sacrifice, and witness. Whether ordained or not, each person joins in the ministry of the entire people of God. Likewise, every ordained person shares in the general discipleship. As Helen Oppenheimer asserts,

---

[27] *A Prayer Book for Australia*, 60.

[28] Cf. General Synod, *Eucharistic Presidency*, 1–2: "It is often pointed out that this use of the word 'lay' obscures the fact that the whole Church is the laity and thus encourages 'clericalisation' within the Church.... However, for the sake of clarity, unless otherwise stated, we shall understand *'laity' as referring to those baptised members of the Church who are not ordained to the threefold ministry of bishop, priest or deacon* and the '*clergy*' as referring to those who are so ordained."

[29] Robert Hannaford, "Foundations for an Ecclesiology of Ministry," in Hall and Hannaford, *Order and Ministry,* 43. See chapter 9, below.

"Whatever it means to affirm the priesthood of all believers, it would be well to affirm also the laity of all priests."[30]

A COMMUNITY OF SERVICE

"Love one another as I have loved you," Jesus told his disciples; and he demonstrated what he meant by washing their feet (John 13:1–11). With that example, Jesus introduces the role, place, and function of servanthood into the nature of the church. Thus in the American and Canadian baptismal rites, the candidate promises "to seek and serve Christ in all persons," loving one's neighbor as oneself. The entire congregation affirms that pledge, betokening the corporate nature of the commitment: As the whole church is baptismal in its discipleship, so it is diaconal in nature, meaning that it is grounded in service to its Lord, praying for God's grace for all God's people. One element of discipleship is *diakonia*, service. The commitment of *diakonia* is a commitment to Christ, indeed a call from Christ to serve not only those within the community of the church but also to those who are beyond it.[31]

Each baptized person shares in the corporate responsibility of service. According to the liturgical scholar Louis Weil, "The call to servanthood begins at baptism, and it is the shared vocation of every Christian to live out that servanthood in ways appropriate to our individual lives."[32] Those ways are as numerous as individual Christians and the spheres in which they work, play, and live. Servanthood can be expressed in business and politics, health care and the arts, in family life, clubs, and church, from a shop or schoolroom to the highest reaches of diplomacy among nations— in other words, in every aspect of human endeavor where Christians may be found. Ideally, exercising *diakonia* can alter the nature of Christian involvement in those endeavors, because

---

[30] Cf. Raymond Brown, *Priest and Bishop: Biblical Reflections* (London: Geoffrey Chapman, 1970), 16; Helen Oppenheimer, "Ministry and Priesthood," in Eric James, *Stewards of the Mysteries of God* (London: Darton, Longman & Todd, 1979), 11. She does not make the distinction between *laos* and "laity."

[31] See John E. Booty, *The Servant Church: Diaconal Ministry and the Episcopal Church* (Wilton, CT: Morehouse Publishing, 1982), 40–51, 58.

[32] Louis Weil, "Should the Episcopal Church Permit Direct Ordination?" in Hallenbeck, ed., *Orders of Ministry*, 62–63.

instead of striving to wield power, it seeks rather to serve. As Bishop Bennett Sims reflected on the servant nature of leadership:

> Our drive and our ability tend to seduce us into thinking of ourselves as defined by the job we do: I am the father (commander) of this family; I am the president (in control) of this company; I am the rector (ruler) of this parish; I am the professor (biggest brain) in this classroom. The servant leader, by contrast, thinks: I am the fellow-human whose *responsibility* it is to love and guide this family, to serve and lead this parish, to point the direction for this company, to stimulate the learning process in this classroom.[33]

The *laos*, in short, is diaconal. So the laity share in diaconal service, as do all orders of ordained service. The most obvious servant ministry is the diaconate itself, which takes its name from the term and has always been understood as a servant order—although precisely how it has functioned as servant has varied over time, as we shall see in a later chapter.

Presbyters have the chief responsibility for the sacramental life of the church, particularly the Eucharist. Presiding over the celebration, itself a dramatic form of service, recalls and re-presents the supremely sacrificial act of Jesus in his self-offering on Calvary. As Paul reminds us, Jesus is the ultimate servant; being found in the form of a slave, he humbled himself, "and became obedient to the point of death—even death on a cross" (Phil. 2:6–8). In the Eucharist, Christians make the only offering they truly can—themselves, their souls and bodies—and in this, they are led by the priest in the most public of ways. Presbyters have other functions, exercised in different ways, but as John Booty notes, these have a common focus:

> Most are responsible for administering parish churches, some work in institutions serving the community, others are worker-priests. Furthermore, their specific styles of ministry may differ, depending on personal abilities and on the cultures in which they live and work. Whatever

---

[33] Bennett J. Sims, *Servanthood: Leadership for the Third Millennium* (Cambridge, MA: Cowley, 1997), 19, emph. in orig. For an extended discussion of the larger point, see 113–177.

> the circumstances as priests they are signs or symbols pointing to the Servant Christ, our great High Priest, and enablers of the priesthood of all believers, which is to say enablers to sacrificial service.[34]

Anglican tradition shares with others the practice of not ordaining priests unless they are first ordained deacons. The point is not only that presbyters are deacons, but that the presbyterate is also diaconal.

Bishops, too, perform diaconal service. In the service of consecration in the American prayer book, they are asked, "Will you be merciful to all, show compassion to the poor and strangers, and defend those who have no helper?" Furthermore, encouraging and enabling others to fulfill their servanthood is another diaconal role required of bishops: "As a chief priest and pastor, will you encourage and support all baptized people in their gifts and ministries?"[35] A liturgical manifestation of the bishop's servant role might be to wash the feet of the people on Maundy Thursday evening, recalling Jesus' demonstration of humble service. A practical manifestation might be to initiate a program of support for children in the region covered by the diocese or to take public stands of advocacy and witness.

A SACRIFICING, PREACHING, RECONCILING CHURCH

Each baptized person also shares in the corporate responsibility of praise, proclamation, reconciliation, and sacrificial offering to God. The catechism of older American prayer books would ask, "What is my bounden duty?" and follow it with the answer, "My bounden duty is to follow Christ, to worship God every Sunday in his Church, and to work and pray and give for the spread of his kingdom."[36] Today baptismal candidates are asked, "Will you

---

[34] Booty, *Servant Church*, 64.

[35] US BCP, 518, ‖ Wales, 715; NZ, 918; Aus. 804; *ASB*, 389 in which the bishop is asked to hold "special concern for the outcast and needy." None outside of ECUSA and Canada (*Alternative Services*, 637) are asked to *support* such efforts, though it is often implied as with the *ASB*'s expectation that the bishop "promote mission" (388); New Zealand wishes for the new bishop to "give encouragement."

[36] US BCP (1928), 291; cp. 1662 BCP: "My duty towards God, is to believe in him, to fear him, and to love him with all my heart, with all my mind, with all my soul, and with all my strength; to worship him, to give him thanks, to put my whole trust in him, to call upon him, to honour his holy Name and his Word, and to serve him truly all the days of my life."

continue in the apostles' teaching and fellowship, in the breaking of bread, and in the prayers?" while in the Eucharist, the priest prays on behalf of all, "And here we offer and present unto thee, O Lord, our selves, our souls and bodies, to be a reasonable, holy, and living sacrifice unto thee."[37] The people are offering, through and in Christ, a "sacrifice of praise and thanksgiving."[38] Worship has always been seen as a primary responsibility of Christians, but never exclusively through liturgy. Rather, it is *all* of one's life, and the community's life, offered to God for whatever divine purposes may await. Within the setting of ritual, the community brings before God the prayers and praises of all its people and through them the needs and concerns of all the world. Diaconal service puts these prayers and praises into action, even as the service takes on the quality of worship as a sacrificial act presented to God.

The Christian community thus functions in a sacrificial and priestly mode. Individuals, ordained or not, may assume sacrificial roles inside and outside the church, again in ways as diverse as the number of Christians and all their concerns, ranging from the mundane to the breathtakingly dramatic. Some may be directly addressed to God or God's work through the church: the baptized person who devotes his or her life to God in monasticism or in preparing the altar for worship on a Saturday morning. Other sacrificial acts are done for fellow human beings: giving blood or donating a kidney; caring for a sick child or parent; volunteering one's time for a community project; or devoting a lifetime to find a cure for disease. In ways great or small, each may share in what truly is a sacrificial "royal priesthood." As a Church of England report states,

---

[37] US BCP, 304 (‖Canada, *Alternative Services*, 159); US BCP (1979), 336 [‖ 342], (1928, 81); cf. US BCP, 369: "Unite us to your Son in his sacrifice, that we may be acceptable through him...." (‖ Canada, *Alternative Services*, 199).

[38] US BCP (1979), 335, 342, 363, 369; cf. 375, "a living sacrifice in Christ, to the praise of your Name." (‖ Wales, 14; Ireland, 55; Aus., 132; NZ, 423, Canada, *Alternative Services*, 195, 210, 242 [repr. from 1962 BCP]; cp. *ASB*, 132, 134, 192, 194; CW, 187, 190, 193.

> Christians stand where only the greatest and most high-
> ly privileged of Old Testament characters stood. They
> hear the direct call to faith as Abraham did; they see
> God in Christ face to face as Moses did; they enter the
> holy of holies and know the divine Name, as did Aaron
> and his successors as high priest. This is priestly privi-
> lege, now to be taken up by all Christians on behalf of
> the world.[39]

Presbyters lead the way in this ministry. As those who routinely preside at the Eucharist, they are largely defined by this cultic role. The priestly role is not limited to their service as cultic
leaders, however, for the Anglican pastoral tradition has always
cherished priests' moving beyond the altar to care for their people,
wherever they may be. Nor is pastoral care limited to priests.
Although they are granted the responsibility to express and convey God's forgiveness, so each Christian is expected to "forgive
those who sin against us." Laypeople as well, in the words of the
American catechism, are "to carry on Christ's work of reconciliation in the world." The bishop entrusts preaching primarily to
presbyters, but "the Word is given within the exchanges of all
Christians who seek to interpret life in terms of the Gospel and to
stand for their faith."[40]

Within the liturgy deacons take on specific functions, including
reading the gospel, leading the Prayers of the People, and assisting
at the eucharistic sacrifice. Sacrifice is inherent in their servanthood. Most are non-stipendiary, but their personal commitment
may involve far more sacrifice of time, effort, and even pride as
they work with the marginalized and poor. Surrounded by the suc-
cess-oriented, materialistic preoccupations of Western nations,
theirs is a sacrifice akin to Christ's. Deacons, by their lives, work, and
word, are called to proclaim the gospel.

Bishops have long been understood as the chief priests, preachers,
and teachers of the diocese. As priests they also share in the sacrificial role of the Eucharist, for "the priestly responsibility of a

---

[39] *Ordained Ministry Today,* 18.

[40] US BCP, 855 (the prayer book allows deacons and laity to declare God's forgiveness in a non-sacramental use of the rite of reconciliation [452]); *Ordained
Ministry Today,* 34.

bishop is expressed in the role of chief priest in the diocesan community, usually functioning as presider and preacher in all eucharists in which he or she is present."[41] Beyond the eucharistic, their role as leaders of their people and as proclaimers of the Word has in the past led bishops to be singled out for persecution, even costing their very lives. Many are those whom the church has commemorated as "bishop and martyr." Their innate position, too, as unifying symbols for the diocese, and between the diocese and the entire church, is itself a reconciling one.

AN APOSTOLIC CHURCH OF WITNESS

Finally, every Christian shares in the corporate responsibility of apostolic witness and oversight. Candidates for baptism are asked, "Will you proclaim by word and example the Good News of God in Christ?" The question implies an apostolic role for every baptismal candidate who answers, "I will, with God's help."[42] That part of the "bounden duty" that pledges "to work and pray and give for the spread of [Christ's] kingdom" gives it another expression. So, too, in the Episcopal Church, does the fact that every member also belongs to the Domestic and Foreign Missionary Society, theoretically sharing in the church's apostolic mission worldwide. As N. T. Wright, now bishop in Lightfoot's old see of Durham, declares, "We ourselves are summoned to be God's agents in bringing this earth-shattering message to the world—and to the church!—that so desperately needs it."[43]

Witness is one aspect of the apostolic purpose, and oversight is another. Although the link between the first apostles and bishops has long been debated, the book of Acts indicates that the earliest church was overseen by apostles. They chose Matthias to share in their witness but also in their decision-making. When the need arose for helpers, they designated seven. A council of apostles decided on what to prescribe in admitting Gentiles to the faith, and whom to send to evangelize them (Acts 1:15–26; 6:1–6;

---

[41] Standing Commission on Ministry Development [SCMD], "Toward a Theology of Ministry," 27; cf. US BCP, 322.

[42] US BCP, 305, ‖ Canada, *Alternative Services,* 159.

[43] Wright, *New Tasks,* 169.

15:1–29). In these ways theirs was a ministry of oversight, or in Greek, *episkope*. From that term comes the English "episcopal," and obviously, bishops are the most vivid examples of *episkope* in the church. As the leaders of their dioceses, they oversee the work of the church in their area and share with other bishops (and, to greater or lesser degrees, with other clergy and laypeople) in governance of the church at large.

Bishops cannot be alone in that role. The entire *laos* joins in the task. People exercise their *episkope* in typically diverse ways. For example, a parent oversees a family and a supervisor oversees employees. Officials of government have responsibilities of oversight in society. People in the church share in councils and committees on congregational, diocesan, national, and communion-wide levels, where bishops, priests, deacons, and laity are all represented.[44] Presbyters often function as advisors and counselors to the bishop, specifically sharing in *episkope*. Deacons often oversee programs in the local church, including educational offerings, intercessory prayer, and ministry to the sick as chaplains in hospitals. As with discipleship, servanthood, and sacrifice, there are as many opportunities for oversight as there are Christians.

THE MULTI-LAYERED MINISTRIES OF ALL THE BAPTIZED

Every Christian, then, has the functions of oversight, leadership, and witness, though not all the *laos* are bishops. They are responsible for service, sacrifice, and worship, even if not all are deacons or priests. The characteristic tasks of the church are those in which everyone may participate in the ordinary course of their lives as Christians, even though some of these are associated with one of the ordained ministries. In fact, each role is something the Christian faith encourages in order to fulfill its mission; and as that happens, boundaries between the roles begin to vanish. A parent, for example, will function in many different ways—tending a child's injured knee or bruised pride, fixing a meal or teaching a child how to cook, mending clothes, driving a child to a piano lesson after overseeing practice sessions. Being a doctor, psychiatrist,

---

[44] Cf. Doe, *Canon Law*, 44–45.

chef, teacher, chauffeur, and drill-master is all part of an average parent's job. Similarly, one can be diaconal, priestly, and episcopal without being ordained, simply because one is baptized. These are all opportunities for the whole people of God.

So the first conclusion is that everyone can, should, and realistically does participate in each of these areas of Christian responsibility. The second is that no role is exclusive. Every person's role in the life of the church, whether baptized person, deacon, priest, or bishop, is informed and enhanced by sharing in every category of Christian ministry. All ministry subsists within each ministerial task; one is inseparable from the other. Trinitarian doctrine offers a parallel: as Creator, Redeemer, and Sanctifier are distinct yet one, so ministry is distinct yet one, shared by each person.[45]

If each person is at once a manifestation and a microcosm of the whole, then the idea of a "representative" ministry takes on new shades of meaning. Each Christian embodies the entire range of ministry—discipleship, service, sacrifice, and witness. The individual reflects and represents the whole, not simply in functional ways, but in the very truth of being part of this greater Body, one with Christ and with all who are part of his Body. Each shares in all.[46]

Although these three areas correspond roughly to diaconate, presbyterate, and episcopate, the match is not identical. Deacons may be leaders in *diakonia*, presbyters in the church's priestly ministry, and bishops in *episkope*, but their roles are more nuanced than those categories imply. Human classifications can never tell the whole story. These labels are also essentially adjectives, not nouns, describing ministries rather than specific offices or orders. It is to the nature of Holy Orders that we now turn.

---

[45] Here is an example of the importance of Minear's "synoptic" approach. Of the two predominant images, the Trinity is more useful regarding the multiplicity of roles. To take the Body image, if a member is like an "arm," it cannot function as an eye. The Body motif serves more effectively to stress the interdependence of members.

[46] There is some New Testament evidence for precisely this phenomenon. Bartlett sees a division of labor between the diaconal seven in Acts 6, and the apostolic twelve. In his view, Luke seems to understand "the primary, though not exclusive, function of the seven to have to do with charitable administration; the primary, if not exclusive, function of the twelve is to preach the word. In the appointment of elders in Acts 20,...the two functions are combined, in Paul and presumably in the elders as well" (Bartlett, *Ministry in the NT*, 127).

HOLY ORDERS AND THE PEOPLE OF GOD

By now it should be clear that everyone shares in the entire ministry of the faithful. Each person, whether layperson, deacon, priest, or bishop, participates in the diaconal, sacrificial, and apostolic work of the whole church. Laypeople share in priesthood; priests, bishops, and deacons are part of the *laos*. No order is inherently superior or inferior to another. Because the church exists in human history, however, it inevitably appoints some to lead it. One mode of recognizing this leadership is ordination, by which the church sets apart certain persons for particular roles, functions, and offices within the Body. Other roles, functions, and offices do not involve ordination. Certain laypeople may be selected as eucharistic ministers, parish wardens, or organizers of efforts to improve latrines or literacy. A deacon may be appointed by the bishop as archdeacon to oversee the deacons of the diocese. A priest can be made rural dean, canon of a cathedral, or rector of a parish; a bishop might be chosen to become primate. These leadership positions may require some certification or authorization, but no orders are bestowed on a person beyond what has already been received.

The church claims in each case that the Holy Spirit is involved. Congregations ask that vestry members be elected "prayerfully," and they, like others entering into "lay ministries," may do so with a service of commissioning that includes prayer. Bishops, patrons, or congregations select parochial clergy in a process that typically involves asking divine guidance, and the cleric may enter into new duties with a special service of institution.[47] None of these rites of authorization, however, compares in magnitude with ordination.

Is ordination an act of Christ or of the church? After generations of a debate that is likely to continue, the consensus (as we saw in Part One) is "both." They cannot be separated, if Christ is Lord of the church. After all, the church is intimately involved in every step of the process of figuring out whom Christ may call to

[47] E.g., US BCP, "For the Election of a Bishop or Other Minister," 818, "Celebration of a New Ministry," 559–565, and the "Form of Commitment to Christian Service," 420–421; also the "Commissioning for Lay Ministries in the Church," ECUSA, *The Book of Occasional Services* (New York: Church Hymnal, 1994), 179–195.

special service. Where does the potential candidate come from, if not from the *laos*? Baptism, together with confirmation, is a prerequisite for ordination in every Anglican province.[48] Moreover, who decides who is to be ordained, if not the church? Procedures may vary, with the bishop figuring largely, but the choice is made within the community. Finally, who ordains, if not the bishop, who does so as the ministerial representative of the church? Others assist and participate, and some provinces make explicit the involvement of the whole people.[49]

Ordination involves the particular as well: a particular locale where ministry will be carried out. English ordinands serve their "title" in a specific ecclesial setting, and bishops are consecrated to serve in a given diocese.[50] At the same time, by invoking God, Anglicans clearly perceive ordination to be an act of the divine. The Spirit is *bestowed*. Ordination is the act of Christ, through the operation of the Spirit, mediated by the church through the person of the bishop.

As a result, Anglican ecclesiologists developed two primary ways of speaking of the ordained. First, Holy Orders are *ministerial*. The word "ministry" has two implications of note, and the first is that it means "service." The minister is a servant. Furthermore, this service is on behalf of another—the one who employs the servant, the one who is the beneficiary of the service, or both. To take an example from Great Britain: the prime minister is the chief servant of the sovereign. Before moving into 10 Downing Street, the newly elected prime minister kisses the sovereign's hands as a sign of fealty in the process of becoming chief servant to the nation over which she reigns and her primary representative to the world beyond. Yet at the same time the prime minister was chosen by the majority party of the House of Commons, which is composed of members elected by their constituencies. Chosen through an electoral process, ratified by the crown, the prime minister thus becomes a servant of both nation and monarch. Christian ministry has a

---

[48] Doe, *Canon Law*, 130.

[49] New Zealand makes the people's assent "an integral part of the service," and the Church of North India's constitution declares, "the authority of the whole church is represented in ordination" (Doe, *Canon Law*, 137 fn. 46).

[50] Doe, *Canon Law*, 135.

similarly complex origin and purpose. It finds its origin in Christ, its power in the Spirit, its ultimate responsibility to the Almighty through its Lord, and its meaning in service to the Lord alike of church and creation.

Second, Holy Orders are *representative*. They represent their twofold origin: Christ and the church. They have no meaning apart from either. Their authority derives from Christ and the church, and the ordained always have a responsibility to each. Anglicanism has never entrusted "freelance" ministry with the authority of the faithful community: independent service may be valuable, even inspired by the Spirit, but it does not represent the church.[51] At issue is not the importance of the church to retain institutional hegemony so much as the corporate manifestation of the Body of Christ. Ministry represents Christ; it also represents the people of Christ.

Several words have been proposed to express this representative quality. "The ordained...may be described as 'signs,'" writes H. J. M. Turner. The "diaconate, because of our Lord's words, is a 'sign' which declares to the Church and to the world the true nature of every Christian ministry." The episcopate, too, "is intended primarily to be a 'sign': the bishop signifies the unity of the diocese with the catholic church throughout the centuries and throughout the world, while within his diocese the bishop is meant to be personally the focus of unity." Finally, with presbyterate, "one cannot so easily speak of a single 'sign'." Not only are priestly roles diffuse, they have moved beyond their original function as part of a council of elders. Nonetheless, they too serve as "signs" of a wider church.[52] Stephen M. Kelsey agrees: "A sign is that which points to a reality beyond itself, participating to some extent in that reality, but not exhausting that reality." As the wedding ring in marriage signifies love within one relationship, so we can "speak of ordination as a gift to the church so that the church can be a gift to the world."[53]

---

[51] Cf. Article XXIII, Articles of Religion. The early church faced the quandary with wandering prophets, and the *Didache* laid down some tests as to a prophet's legitimacy.

[52] H. J. M. Turner, "Ordination and Vocation," in Hall and Hannaford, *Order and Ministry*, 129–130.

[53] Stephen M. Kelsey, "Celebrating Baptismal Ministry at the Welcoming of New Ministers," in Myers, ed., *Baptism and Ministry*, 26.

An icon is an image born of the Orthodox tradition. As pictorial representations of a saint or of some aspect of divinity, such as the Trinity, icons attempt not to portray a figure but to draw the viewer *through* the image to contemplate a greater reality, a virtual window opening into the mysterious realms of eternity. The computer age uses the term to describe a small graphic image symbolizing a particular program; click on the icon and the program mysteriously opens. As a metaphor for ministry, the ordained are like icons— less important in themselves than that onto which they open. As icons they represent and reveal Christ and his church in specific ways, as, for example, diaconal service or priestly sacrifice, which are far vaster in scope than whatever a particular deacon or priest may do.

"Symbol" is a more general term that seeks to convey the same meaning. Clergy are outward signs of a deeper, less visible reality. A bishop's presence in a congregation symbolizes the entire church of Christ and the congregation's link with it.

> In the person of the ordained, as the symbolic person, the *laos* can see an image of the ministry of Christ, can heighten their awareness of God's presence, can sense the immanence of that power which is God.... The sacramental person as symbol points to and participates in a reality greater than the person or his or her office, allowing one who apprehends the symbolic function also to participate in that greater reality.[54]

"Symbol" may be vague; more specific is the idea of "focus." To focus is to move from diffusion to precision, from vagueness to clarity, as a camera lens can bring an object into clarity. We speak of focusing our attention, of bringing things "into focus." The action involves both the viewer and the viewed. A priest draws together a congregation at worship and brings focus to what is going on: the gathered people's prayers and praises as the Body of Christ, and the eucharistic presence of Christ in his Body (both bread and people). As William Countryman writes, "We should expect to find ordained ministry pointing to the reality of the

---

[54] Joe Morris Doss, "The Unified Symbol of Ministry: Sacramental Orders," *Anglican Theological Review* 71, no. 1 (January 1980), 30–31.

church's ministry—not offering a full and exhaustive embodiment of it, but focusing it in such a way as to draw attention to the holiness and divine power of all gospel ministry."[55]

For many churchgoers the term "sacramental" holds a high level of familiarity and understanding. As an adjective, it places us in the realm of sacrament without miring us in debates over whether ordination is a "sacrament," as a noun might do. The basic definition of sacraments as "outward and visible signs of inward and spiritual grace, given by Christ as a sure and certain means by which we receive that grace,"[56] clearly grounds our understanding in the life of Christ as well as in the church, which William Temple often called the sacrament of Christ.[57] From that point of view, the ordained become outward and visible signs of the spiritual realities of Christ and his church.

Another sacramental reality pertains to the ordained. Ordination resembles baptism and marriage in denoting a *state* of grace as opposed to an *event* of grace. Baptism creates a new life of relationship with God and the community of faith. Holy matrimony creates a new union of two people within the baptized community. Ordination authorizes certain people within the community to live and work and act in particular ways, but what matters is not simply what they do (the functional question) but how they live and what they are (the ontological question). In fact the vocation of marriage has been used as an analogy to the vocation of ordination. Like priesthood, marriage signifies a union of people that is intended to represent the spiritual union between Christ and his church. Marriage brings

> new obligations, new responsibilities. In fulfilling these [we sow] the nature of marriage. Yet marriage is more than just...doing all the right things. We know what the signs and acts of love are but by themselves they are not love. Yet love is empty without them. They disclose love.

---

[55] Countryman, *Language*, 45. See also the English bishops in *Eucharistic Presidency*, 28 (¶3.22); [Church of England,] General Synod, *The Liturgical Ministry of Deacons: A Discussion Document* (n.d. [c. 1999]), 1.

[56] US BCP, 857 (‖ Catechisms in Australia, 815; New Zealand, 932; Wales, 696).

[57] E.g., "The Church," in *Foundations*, 342–343, 347; CV, 234.

This writer concludes that "priesthood is disclosed through these characteristic acts which belong to the ministry of Christ, and to the equipping of all God's people for that ministry."[58]

Anglican liturgical scholar Boone Porter studied ancient ordination prayers, and he noticed that such prayers tend to designate what is being prayed for without exactly defining it. "They scrupulously avoid any suggestion that we, in the course of our pilgrimage, can comprehend exactly what episcopate, presbyterate, or diaconate is," Porter wrote. "These orders are gifts from God, and like his other supernatural gifts they transcend earthly understanding."[59] God's gifts being what they are, human beings will never be able to understand them completely. Our knowledge will remain imperfect, which is another cause for humility on the subject of orders as on all else. We can make only tentative efforts to define them. More important, of course, is to practice the ministry that Christ gave to his church.

Mystery can produce confusion. How even now we try to grasp the doctrine of Trinity illustrates that. But mystery can also inspire wide variety, and yield a powerful vibrancy, which opens interpretations and practices reflecting the communities that develop them. Orders have always been something of a mystery; but that very mystery may allow the people of God to make of them what they will—or, to put the matter more theologically and hopefully, for Christ to make of them what he wills.

FINDING A NEW ETHOS

In the church of the nineteenth and early twentieth centuries, people went to Morning Prayer on Sunday. They sat, sang, listened, and knelt as the rector led the prayers, read the lessons, and gave the sermon. A few from the congregation would pass the plate and fix up the altar afterwards. On the whole, both laity and clergy knew their place and stayed there. Almost all deacons were transitional—new, usually young, soon to become priests at a time when to be a priest meant to serve a parish church. A few of the

---

[58] Raynes, *Called By God*, 7; *Ordained Ministry Today*, 28.

[59] Q. in Stuhlman, *Occasions of Grace*, 240.

ordained would help the bishop, and some would teach or act as chaplains, but most by far worked in congregations. All the while, the bishop presided from the top. Such was a common picture of the church.

Organizationally the church was like a pyramid, with laity at the bottom. Between the laity and the clergy was a bar dividing the two sorts of Christians. Above the bar, clergy were arrayed in the three orders with deacons, priests, and then bishops. An ambitious cleric, having arisen from the laity, would progress upward until reaching the episcopate. (See Figure 1.)

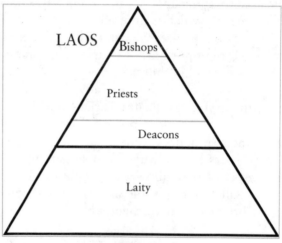

Figure 1

Two nineteenth-century trends continued into the twentieth and altered the hierarchical picture. One trend sought to reinvigorate the laity. In Part One I wrote of a few foresighted Anglicans who wrote and preached a different ecclesiology that placed the *laos* on a more equal footing with clergy. Throughout the twentieth century, that theology took hold, especially in the Episcopal Church. The American Standing Liturgical Commission, for example, tried to eliminate the pyramidal schema—with its "career ladder" implications—by placing the ordination of a bishop as first of the rites in the Ordinal. The prayer book also referred to the laity as an "order," while stressing in its catechism that "lay persons" are ministers of the church alongside bishops, priests, and deacons.[60]

The other nineteenth-century trend tried to professionalize the clergy as "specialists." Seminary training, Clinical Pastoral Education, ordination, vestments, the clerical collar, and an income that, though low by comparison with other professionals, might exceed that of their middle-class parishioners, all set clergy apart. Such a degree of separation was nothing new; for well into the nineteenth century the parson might be one of the very few educated people in the parish. In that century, however, the priest came to be seen as one distinctly set apart for holy work as a "religious specialist."[61]

A third trend has recently become more prominent, namely, the emergence of the diaconate as a distinct, lifelong order of min-

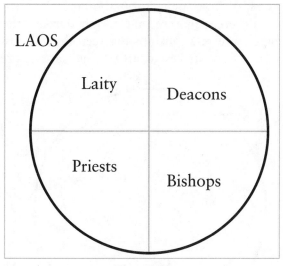

Figure 2

istry. A servant order, discrete from that of laity and priests, it is dependent upon the episcopate. Figure 2 depicts these three trends as an ecclesiastical pie in which each "order" constitutes an equal slice, although each has different functions. This "pie chart" trend

---

[60] US BCP, 13, 855.

[61] Cf. Russell, *Clerical Profession, passim.*, and chapter 1, above.

may have contributed to some of the questions the church now faces: Should the church ordain clergy directly to the order to which they seem to be called, either deacon or priest? Should laypeople preside at the Eucharist? Should clergy be considered professionals at all, given the expense of paying a professional salary? What are clergy needed for these days, anyway, when the laity do so much? Does a parish church even need a priest? Moreover, it has become clear that this picture does not fit in any event, as hard-and-fast divisions of labor disappear. Laity take on more tasks traditionally associated with the clergy—teaching, visiting, administering, even preaching. And some clergy move beyond the parish into the realms more associated with the laity—in specialized ministries such as therapeutic counseling, or as "worker priests" or non-stipendiary clerics earning their livings as teachers, shopkeepers, bankers, doctors, or factory laborers.

I suggest a different picture that may better suit the growing understanding of interrelationships between the various elements of the *laos*. This view strives to affirm the participation of the

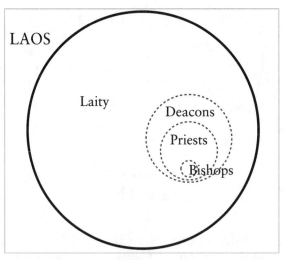

Figure 3

entire people of God in the life of the church—a "priesthood of all believers" that extends into every aspect of ministry as well, as this chapter has suggested. All share various roles and duties at least to some degree. Because hard divisions between elements of the church do not capture the reality of ministry shared among those of different orders, the picture should use dotted lines rather than solid ones. Within the *laos*, some are specialists, designated to signify or fulfill particular functions. These are deacons, priests, and bishops. They take on specific ministries of service and proclamation, worship and teaching and pastoral care, and oversight. Yet these relate to each other, and to the whole *laos*, as parts of the same entity: they are one Body—interdependent, diverse, yet unified within the community of faith. Consequently, all are essential. The ministry of one cannot be divorced from that of any other, without making itself incomplete. On the contrary, whatever one order specializes in doing, all share to some extent. And this sharing extends to clergy and laity alike: The purpose and role of Holy Orders is never confined to the Holy Ordered alone. Rather, even as certain specific roles are designated for some, the general roles of the church's ministry are those in which all may freely participate: each in service, in sacrifice, reconciliation, and proclamation, and in oversight, and all in discipleship.

The next chapters will explore the ramifications of this model.

VII
The Presbyter As Elder

In the previous chapter we explored questions about the nature of orders, how they interrelate, and how the church shapes our theology of ordination. We turn now to an Anglican concept of priesthood itself.

MANY CULTURES, ONE ORDER?

Immediately, though, we confront a problem: Of all orders, the nature of priesthood has always been difficult to generalize, across history or across cultures. For well over a century, the contrast has been noted between the concept of *presbuteros* or "elder" and the more sacerdotal understanding rooted in the Latin *sacerdos*—and along with that distinction, the differing styles of some clergy as "parson" and others as primarily sacramentalist. Nowadays, as the world and the church grow increasingly diverse, it is equally difficult to generalize across cultures, perhaps most of all about priests. Bishops' roles are fairly standard; deacons, outside the Episcopal Church in the United States, are primarily priests-in-waiting. But to the question of what is a priest, any number of responses are likely, depending upon who is asking the question and where it is being asked, whether in the United States, Nigeria, or Australia. Is it possible to speak of ordained priesthood in ways that reflect the distinctive qualities of a pluralistic Anglican Communion while still maintaining certain principles that make sense to all?

Finding ways to maintain and even define unity in the midst of diversity has challenged Anglicanism from the start, not least in issues of ministry. So, as the next chapters shall explore, leaders in the West Indies and the United States called for a distinctive diaconate in the 1870s. By the 1920s, Australians inspired by missiologist Roland Allen were pushing for a non-stipendiary, or "voluntary," clergy. Lambeth Conferences initially scuttled all these ideas, largely out of cultural concepts long established in England of what clergy should be and do. In our own era, heated disputes take place as to whether homosexual persons may be ordained, with many churches in the United States favoring the idea and many in the Two-Thirds World no less adamantly denying it.

While the idea of ministerial representation cannot settle issues like these, it can offer a framework in which a particular province or culture may influence what it wants in its own clergy. To be a "representative" roots an ordained person within a community of faith that will inevitably reflect its own cultural distinctiveness. More basically, baptism grounds a person in a particular community and, hence, in a local culture. It establishes the context in which Christian life will take place and, therefore, the Christian ministry that the community pursues through its laity and clergy alike.[1] Its work, and its workers, will manifest the context from which each springs. The priesthood of a presbyter in Zimbabwe will differ in many respects from those of a presbyter in Hong Kong, Scotland, or Florida. At the same time, the ordained are charged with representing the far broader entities of Christ and his church at large. The loyalty of the ordained person—indeed, of the *laos* as a whole—can never be solely devoted to that immediate community (parish church, diocese, province) but must also embrace the wider realities that he or she represents. The priest and priesthood of Zimbabwe, Hong Kong, Scotland, and Florida will therefore have more similarities than differences. Thus the conditions for both unity and diversity are theoretically present in ways that can allow, and even prize, the cultural distinctiveness of each member of the Anglican Communion while binding them into a broadly defined whole.

A theory of ministerial representation, then, allows for Communion-wide generalizations while also permitting them to be

---

[1] Cf. Fredrica Harris Thompsett, "The Primacy of Baptism: A Reaffirmation of Authority in the Church," in Douglas, ed., *Beyond Colonial Anglicanism*, 259.

locally applied. We may speak, therefore, of an understanding of presbyterate that transcends the local church even as it is specifically lived out on the local level. But the principle of "provisionality" applies here, in that what we now understand may not be what future Anglicans understand. There may be bishops, priests, deacons, and laity, but the forms in which Christians shall live out those categories may differ in decades ahead as they do now around the globe. Still, if they genuinely spring from the Scriptures and are as grounded in the life of the faithful community as they seem to be, they shall endure.

WHAT IS A PRIEST?

A sociologist of religion might define a priest as an intermediary set apart by a recognized induction into an office to function on behalf of others.[2] To say, "The priest is the one who presides at the Eucharist" would be common where weekly celebrations of Holy Communion are the norm, and it is a definition that finds its heritage in the sacramental emphasis of *sacerdos*. In regions such as Africa, the word "pastor" is commonly used to describe the parish priest. Many in Britain might say, "The priest is the vicar," referring to the local parish parson; or across the Atlantic, "The priest is a rector," which is the American equivalent.

These answers all define priesthood by function, by what the presbyter actually does. Accordingly, the Episcopal Church's catechism largely defines the order in a functional way: a priest is "to represent Christ and his Church, particularly as pastor to the people; to share with the bishop in the overseeing of the Church; to proclaim the Gospel; to administer the sacraments; and to bless and declare pardon in the name of God."[3] The idea of a representative and ministerial person summarizes the Anglican understanding that evolved in the late nineteenth and into the twentieth centuries. But the catechetical definition indicates what the priest *does* more than what the priest *is*. Recognizing that the two—doing and being, function and ontology—exist in an interdependent dynamic,

---

[2] Oxtoby, et al., "Priesthood," in *Encyclopedia of Religion*, XI, 529.

[3] US BCP, 856.

such that what we do shapes what we are and vice versa, we must step back to clarify some assumptions.

So what *is* a priest? Given the confusions mentioned in the very beginning of this book, the question is neither pointless to ask nor simple to answer. In *Priesthood Here and Now,* John Inge observes, "A functional definition of priesthood runs the risk of becoming too narrow: continually asking questions about what distinctive tasks the priest has to perform tends to produce very short and perhaps not terribly useful lists which cannot define my priesthood. Ontological definitions, on the other hand, tend to be too vague to be useful."[4] Yet some response is crucial if Anglicanism is to understand the place and purpose of the largest segment of its ordained ministry. If Anglican churches are to relate to other communions in matters of orders, and especially if they are to pursue their mission as the people of God, then they need to discern whether their theology of orders will fit into a system of mission appropriate to Anglicanism.

We might begin with some basics.

THE PRIEST IS A PERSON

This first point is so self-evident that we are in danger of missing its significance. Priesthood is never some abstract concept but takes root in the lives of human beings. This personal quality reflects two closely tied realities: first, the incarnational way in which God acts and second, the relational way in which Christ works. God came to earth as a human being. Jesus summoned human beings to be his followers. Individuals are baptized into a community of people, and some of them are ordained.

Priesthood, then, is not merely a theoretical concept; it is a highly personal one. So, too, with all orders. Recent archbishops of Canterbury, for example, have gone to great lengths to personalize their office so that it be seen not as a pinnacle of the hierarchy but as a position filled by a human being. To that end, these archbishops have traveled widely and frequently throughout the Anglican

---

[4] John Inge, "Best Powers of Mind and Spirit," in *Priesthood Here and Now: Reflections on the ASB Ordinal by Priests Serving in the Diocese of Newcastle,* ed. Michael Bowering (n.p.: Diocese of Newcastle, 1994), 149.

Communion. Similarly, the positive examples offered by individual ordained women can frequently transform opposition to women priests to acceptance and support. A layperson might say, "I'm not too sure about women's ordination, but I do like Nancy"—and suddenly the entire concept becomes acceptable. The point remains that priesthood is the ordination *of people*.

THE PRIEST IS BAPTIZED

He or she is a Christian, "buried with Christ in his death...shar[ing] in his resurrection...reborn by the Holy Spirit."[5] Any ordained person comes from among the baptized *laos* of the church. Canons of every province require full Christian initiation as a prerequisite,[6] as if to affirm that the person to be ordained comes out of the baptismal community of faith. As the liturgical scholar Aidan Kavanagh states, Christians "do not ordain to priesthood; they baptize to it."[7]

The priest, therefore, shares with all the people of God those characteristics and responsibilities of the baptismal community. Above all, the individual priest is a disciple of Jesus. The priest joins in the diaconal, apostolic work of worship, witness, and service. This link with both Christ *and* the church can never be forgotten.

THE PRIEST IS PART OF THE EUCHARISTIC COMMUNITY

Perhaps priesthood is most evident in the liturgical context, as the priest presides over the celebration of the Eucharist. However, the role of presidency does not in any sense remove the priest from the community. Rather, priesthood is lived out within the context of that community, which is at once eucharistic and baptismal, local and global, gathered in the earthly moment yet existing from Pentecost until the ultimate millennium. Eucharistic presidency may constitute the clearest, but by no means the only, sign of the presbyter's priesthood in intimate relationship with the community.

---

[5] US BCP, 306, and Canada, *Alternative Services*, 158.

[6] Doe, *Canon Law*, 130.

[7] Q. in Thompsett, "Primacy of Baptism," in Douglas, ed., *Beyond Colonial Anglicanism*, 259.

THE PRIEST REPRESENTS CHRIST

All Christians do. No more and no less than any other Christian, priests as part of the Body of Christ become a living example of the Lord. But they do take on a special role most conspicuouly at the Eucharist when they function *in persona Christi*, speaking and acting for Christ. The priest is the one who speaks the words "This is my body," "This is my blood." The priest and the ordained priesthood, like the general priesthood of the entire Christian community, all draw their purpose and meaning from the high priesthood of Christ himself. The moment the presbyter repeats the words of Jesus from the Last Supper is the moment at which this connection with Christ's high priesthood may be most evident.

THE PRIEST REPRESENTS THE CHURCH

Again, all Christians do. Because the priest is baptized into the Body of Christ, she or he remains intimately and inescapably part of the Christian community. Baptism is one reason we can claim that priesthood is never distinct from the community of the faithful as a whole. At the Eucharist, the priest also speaks on behalf of the community in offering its prayers and praises, its "sacrifice of praise and thanksgiving" to God. In that sense the priest functions *in persona ecclesiae*.

THE PRIEST IS MINISTERIAL

Because they are ordained, priests are appointed to a particular role and function within the Body. They are to represent and serve Christ and the church both in terms of *doing* and of *being*. The presbyter not only *acts* in a priestly way but *is* priestly. Moreover, the priest is also deacon. The significance of this will wait until the next chapter; but we must always remember that the priest comes out of the servant order of the church.[8]

THE PRIEST AS PRESBYTER

Priests have yet one more characteristic: they are "presbyters." The old Greek word meaning "elder," which stands etymologically behind the noun "priest," returns with renewed significance in ascertaining the nature of the order in the present day.

---

[8] In the next chapter we will also consider changes that would alter this concept by ordaining priests directly from the laity and not first as deacons.

Shortly after I began this study of priesthood, my son and I went to Uganda for a clergy conference and were relaxing in the home of the Rev. Mabel Katahweire. Mabel and her husband Ernest had been friends of mine for nearly two decades. Mabel was at that time the education officer for the Church of Uganda and the sponsor of our trip. She was one of the first women of her province to be ordained priest; she and Ernest were both canons of their home diocese's cathedral. Some friends of hers, a young Roman Catholic couple, came to their apartment for a visit. Midway through, the husband addressed our hostess as "Mother Mabel," turning to explain to me, "She is not my *real* mother; she is my *spiritual* mother." He added that in Uganda one has many "mothers" and "fathers"; as part of the extended family, uncles and aunts serve in a parental role and are treated as such. In Uganda and other African countries such as Zimbabwe, the title is applied out of respect for one old enough to be a parent. Immediately a Greek word sprang to my mind: πρεσβύτρος, or *presbuteros*, translated "presbyter," meaning "elder." I remembered how often I have been called "Father." In some areas, including the United States, the title of "Father," and more recently of "Mother" for women priests, is growing.

Though the use of parental terminology may not be as universal among Anglicans as it is among Roman Catholics, the concept of presbyter/elder extends far back in history and remains widespread in various cultures. The ancient Greek term described someone who was senior in age and wisdom, one to whom honor was due. He might have headed a Spartan college or served on a board, or held administrative or judicial functions as a member of an executive committee or some sort of corporation.[9]

In the New Testament books, the word appears in two senses. One describes Jewish leaders whose role is not clear but who, as colleagues of chief priests, oppose Jesus.[10] In its Christian form, *presbuteros* (or its plural, *presbuteroi*) appears in two places. One is the book of Acts, where the "elders" seem to be leaders of the Christian communities. They receive aid for their people during

---

[9] Gerhard Kittel, ed., *Theological Dictionary of the New Testament,* ed. and trans. Geoffrey W. Bromiley (Grand Rapids, MI: Eerdmans, c. 1964–c. 1976), VI, 653 (cf. 651–683).

[10] E.g., Mt. 21:23; 26:3, 47, 57; 27:1, 3, 12, 20. Mk. 8:31; 11:27. Lk. 7:3; 9:22; 22:52, 66.

periods of famine (11:30). As Paul and Barnabas created churches in Asia Minor and Antioch, they would appoint "elders...in each church, [and] with prayer and fasting they entrusted them to the Lord in whom they had come to believe" (Acts 14:23). When the elders from the church in Ephesus confered with Paul in Acts 20:17, they functioned like the elders within a family, with a responsibility to be good teachers and shepherds, following an Old Testament tradition that Jesus also exemplified.[11] Along with serving as teachers, exemplars, and overseers, or shepherds, the elders shared decision-making with apostles like Paul and Barnabas in guiding the nascent church. For example, when the question arose of whether Gentiles must be circumcised, "[t]he apostles and the elders met together to consider this matter" (Acts 15:6).[12]

The other set of instances occurs in the pastoral epistles, the Johannine letters, James, and 1 Peter. These references indicate that elders, who were themselves appointed, also set apart other elders (1 Tim. 4:14; Titus 1:5). They taught and preached (1 Tim. 5:17), anointed the sick (James 5:14), and exercised a "rule" and authority (1 Tim. 5:17; 1 Pet. 5:5). They were also subject to scrutiny (1 Tim. 5:19), as many an ordained person has been since. Any relationship of these "elders" with bishops or apostles remains unclear; the author of 1 Peter claimed to be "an elder myself and a witness of the sufferings of Christ" (5:1), which sounds very much like the description of an apostle (Acts 1:22). Titus is alluded to as a "bishop" (1:7). The reference to Timothy's receiving gifts through "the laying on of hands by the council of elders" or presbytery (4:14) recalls for us the contemporary custom of bishops' coming together in order to lay hands upon a new member of the episcopate. But evoking that scene points out the danger of reading a later understanding back into earlier texts, or—given their diversity—presuming a unanimity of practice that was not necessarily true. Whether these biblical sources are themselves later writings also looking backwards is a matter of scholarly debate.[13]

---

[11] Cf. Bartlett, *Ministry in the NT*, 147.

[12] Cf. 15:2, 22–23; 16:4.

[13] Cf. Luke Timothy Johnson, *The Writings of the New Testament: An Interpretation*, rev. ed. (Minneapolis: Fortress, 1999), re Acts, 245; re the pastorals, 423, cf. 424–431 for a discussion of factors involved; re 1 Peter and James, cf. 455, though, he argues, they should not be dismissed or ignored on either account.

The letters of John, by contrast, evoke a sense of family. Here the titles of leaders and images of the church are personal and familial. Lacking an emphasis on a preeminent apostle or on apostleship as an office, the "elder" is more like a brother or father. The writer refers to his readers as "children." Christians are described in sibling relationship, as in 1 John 4:21: "Those who love God must love their brothers and sisters also." Any authority stems from a community modeled on family, where members are equal and leadership is informal, and the authority is the Holy Spirit.[14]

So while the New Testament cannot be said to reveal a "doctrine of the priesthood," nonetheless it hints at what at least some leaders in Christian communities were doing in early, if not the earliest, days. They would teach. They would preach. They would visit and anoint the sick. They would appoint others to positions of leadership, as they themselves were appointed and commissioned through prayer and laying on of hands. They would have some measure of respect and authority within their communities, sharing in councils and meetings pertaining to issues before the church. These were the sorts of roles that "elders" would play. Moreover, they are a corporate group, almost invariably referred to in the plural.[15]

What is absent from this list may be the most familiar role to contemporary Anglicans: presiding at the Eucharist. Its absence from these texts does not mean we can assume that presbyters did not preside, any more than we can assume that eucharistic celebrations were not held because they are not mentioned. But for all the roles that scholars have discovered for presbyters, liturgical leadership is apparently not foremost among them. In fact, these elders may have had relatively little to do, liturgically speaking, beyond appearing with the bishop. Only later as dioceses grew and congregations increased in size and number did presbyteral liturgical leadership appear.

---

[14] Bartlett, *Ministry in the NT*, 108–11.

[15] Of 33 NT references to Christian elders, only four are singular in usage, with three of them being a personal statement by the author (1 Pet. 5:1, 2 Jn. 1:1, 3 Jn. 1:1).

That moment of growth and change was also about the time
that the "presbyter" (*presbuteros*) became more commonly called
a "priest" (*hiereus*), with its implication of being an intermediary
between God and humankind.[16] It was a subtle but important
shift. Jewish priests presided over sacrifices; so did pagans. For
Christians to have a "priesthood" in the sense of *hierateuma*
implied, that they performed sacrifices, too, that the Eucharist was
itself a sacrifice. But until the time of Tertullian, Hippolytus, and
Cyprian in the third century, a different concept prevailed.[17] The
role of the priest was more like that of an elder, meaning an
authority in the community who taught and led by example, not
one who sacrificed. And this concept of elder may help to identify
the nature of the presbyter for our present and future.

THE PRESBYTER AS AN ELDER

Nearly every book on the priesthood written by an Anglican
cites the etymology of "priest" as deriving from the Greek for
"elder."[18] The notion of what constitutes an "elder," however,
remains fluid, especially as societies vary. In Uganda, one is considered an "elder" on the day one is married, regardless of age,
while in the United States, a person may vote at the age of eighteen but not drink alcoholic beverages legally until twenty-one.
Australian aboriginal cultures provide a striking example of how
being an "elder" does not necessarily correspond with age. "Men
of ritual importance" figure large within a community—people
with considerable religious experience and knowledge as well as
influence. Usually middle-aged, they draw esteem more for their
connection with spiritual dimensions than for the number of their
gray hairs. As bearers of communal tradition, they direct the ceremonies of the community, which are performed by others in a

---

[16] Paul Bradshaw, *Liturgical Presidency in the Early Church* (Bramcote, Notts.:
Grove Books, 1983), 21–22. But presbyters may have presided over ordinations
of bishops for their communities: 22–23.

[17] Cf. Barnett, *Diaconate*, 101; Cyprian was first to use the priestly term *hiereus*
to describe Christian presbyters, and the word "priest" also emanates from the
Latin, *sacerdos*, which stresses priestly and cultic functions.

[18] Among many examples, see John Macquarrie, *A Guide to the Sacraments*
(New York: Continuum, 1997), 168; R. Hanson, *Priesthood*, 79; Oxtoby, et al.,
"Priesthood," in *Encyclopedia of Religion*, 529.

cooperative enterprise.[19]

Christian practices sometimes reflect these sociological phenomena. In the Shona culture of Zimbabwe, in central Africa, for instance, relational terms of "father/brother, mother/sister" refer respectfully to those who are old enough to be one's parent or, if less so, an older sibling. There is one exception. Regarding clergy (who at the time of writing are all male), one term only—"father"—applies to the priest, regardless of age. Priesthood implies a headship of the churchly household, which is parallel to that of the blood family. It signifies respect for and the authority of the "most important person in the family," to quote a Shona priest.[20]

I am not advocating the use of parental terminology over any other, nor do I encourage the authoritarian attitudes that often accompany such language. However, I would suggest that the concept of "elder" holds several important implications for the presbyterate, the first being that it *roots the elder and leader within the community.* An elder is "older." Older than whom? An "elder" thus necessarily presumes a community in which the authority of an elder may be exercised among those who are younger. Second, the term is *relational,* for the title of elder has no meaning or purpose apart from others. Third, the question of chronological age is somewhat incidental because the church commissions the individual to be its, and Christ's, representative. While there is some correlation between age and office, ecclesiological and sociological evidence gives priority to the "office" of elder rather than age. Not all "elders" are old, but not all the elderly are "elders." Finally, an elder represents something beyond him- or herself. The elder embodies the tradition of the community, even personifying the community itself, while serving as a veritable incarnation of wisdom.

Though evidence is scanty about practices in the early church, a few indications suggest that age had something to do with office.

---

[19] Ronald M. Berndt, "Australian Religions: An Overview," in *Encyclopedia of Religion*, Mircea Eliade, ed. (New York: Macmillan, 1987), I, 533; cf. Berndt, "Law and Order in Aboriginal Australia," in *Aboriginal Man in Australia*, ed. Ronald M. Berndt and Catherine H. Berndt (Sydney: Angus and Robertson, 1965) [167–206], 174. I am indebted to Sarah Ogilvie, graduate student at Oxford, for bringing to my attention this feature of her native land.

[20] Interview with the Rev. Gift Makwasha, Cambridge, MA, March 8, 2001.

Pope Siricius (384–399) ordered that there would be no deacons ordained under the age of thirty, no presbyters under forty, and no bishops under the venerable age of fifty. A council at Hippo in 393 allowed for deacons to be ordained at twenty-five. In the West, a deacon commonly became a presbyter/elder at the age of thirty, though the tradition of senior career deacons shows that reaching a certain age did not necessarily mean becoming a priest.[21] Some centuries later, a canon from Anglo-Saxon England declared that the "presbyter is the mass-priest, or old 'wita'; not that every one is old, but that he is old in wisdom"—the "wita" being a sage or philosopher, or a member of a governing council. [22]

So while the number of years did not necessarily correlate with the role of "elder," in earlier centuries someone ordained in his mid-twenties might well be considered fully mature, if not "elderly." In Reformation days, a deacon ordained at the prayer book minimum age of twenty-three and presbyter at twenty-four was entering orders at about the same age that men got married That age was also toward the end of the average person's span of life. A child born in England in 1640 had an expectancy of only thirty-two years. A "youth culture" flourished until around 1750, with almost half the population being below the age of twenty.[23] Clergy were old, by comparison.

Of course, life expectancies have lengthened all around the world. In the United States, life expectancies hovered around thirty-eight for children born in 1850 and somewhere only in the forties around 1900.[24] At the turn of that century, only eight percent of the English population lived beyond sixty, while in 2000 the rate

---

[21] Church of England, *Deacons in the Ministry of the Church* (London: Church House, c. 1988), 11 (¶14).

[22] Canons of Elfric, q. in Daniel Rock, *The Church of Our Fathers* (London: John Hodges, 1903), III, 140–142; J. R. Clark Hall, *A Concise Anglo Saxon Dictionary* (4th ed., Toronto: University of Toronto Press, 1984), s.v. "wita," 413.

[23] Lawrence Stone, *The Family, Sex and Marriage in England 1500–1800* (New York: Harper & Row, 1977), 46, 48, 50, 68, 72; cf. 1662 BCP, 554. Life expectancy, of course, was lowered with the high infant mortality rate; but the decade of the 1920s claimed substantial numbers as well (Stone, 70).

[24] "Life Expectancy by Age, 1850–1998" <http://www.infoplease.com/ipa/A0005140.html> (April 9, 2001). Precise figures are not available here, as they are broken down into two categories ("white males/females") for 1850 and four for 1900–02 ("white/all other males/females").

was twenty percent.[25] American expectancies for men now approach seventy years, and for women, seventy-six (about five years fewer for each than in England!).[26]

Those in North America and Europe who anticipate life to last well into their seventies might think it strange to call a quarter-century-old priest an "elder," but that is not quite as true everywhere. Life expectancies in South Africa and Uganda, according to a 1998 study, average almost fifty-four for men and fifty-eight for women; in Brazil, fifty-nine for men and seventy for women.[27] An ordinand of twenty-four would be relatively older in these less-developed cultures than those in ones where lifespans are longer.

But as the average span of years has increased, so too has the average age of ordination—in the Church of England to the mid-thirties, in ECUSA to the mid-forties.[28] So few are being ordained at younger ages that, in 2000, only four percent of Episcopal clergy were below the age of thirty-six, compared with forty percent who are fifty-five or older.[29]

"Elder," however, entails more than numbers of years. In the late nineteenth century, the story goes, a *grande dame* of the parish approached the newly ordained young curate as he was vesting and asked why she, at her age, should listen to him. What did he have to say? "Madam," he replied, "when I put on this stole, I am

---

[25] Andrew Blaikie, "Ageing: Old visions, new times?" *The Lancet*, 354, suppl. 4 (Dec. 18, 1999) <http://proquest.umi.com/pqdweb?TS=98684...1&Dtp=00000007412342&Mtd=1&Fmt=4>(April 9, 2001), 2.

[26] "Life Expectancy at Birth for Selected Countries, 1950–1998" <http://webcenter.netscape.infoplease.com/ipa/A0774532.html> (April 10, 2001).

[27] "Life Expectancy at Birth for Selected Countries, 1950–1998."

[28] Cedric Pulford, "English ordination figures surge higher," *World* (September 1999) <http://www.anglicanjournal.com/1225/07/world02.html> (June 3, 2003); "Concerns of Ordained Ministry Highlighted in Recent Statistics," *The Living Church*, 211, no. 26 (Dec. 24, 1995), 6.

[29] By contrast, in 1974, 19% of Episcopal clergy were under 36, and 22% were 55 or older. Also by contrast with another profession, over the same period, the percentage of younger attorneys remained nearly constant at about a quarter of the total. "Looking at the Age Gap: Now and Then," *Congregations*, 27, no. 2 (March/April 2001), 9; Hillary Wical, "Clergy by the Numbers," *Congregations*, 27, no. 2 (March/April 2001), 6. In 1995 the average age of clergy registered with the Episcopal Church Deployment Office was 51 ("Concerns of Ordained Ministry," 6).

two thousand years old."[30] Brash though 1.
reminds us that the presbyter bears the traditiо
The priest represents Christ but also the church, ·
sand-year-old human institution with all of its teachings ᴀ
joys and woes. He or she is the servant of Jesus and tⱨℇ ɒoɒy, as
elder, presbyter, and priest.

How, then, does this elder/presbyter/priest function? How is the nature of the office revealed in practice, which then helps to define its nature further? As an English report on the ministry states, "What a priest does, discloses what priesthood is."[31]

THE PRIEST AS MINISTERIAL ELDER

In Part One we discussed how Moberly and other theologians of the time drew out the ministerial nature of priesthood. In the previous chapter, I also suggested that there are two important aspects to the concept of ministry: first, a sense of service and servanthood; and second, an exercise of servanthood that primarily benefits or serves another. Considering the words that Anglican rites ascribe to the order may give a sense of how the priest/presbyter/elder functions in this ministerial capacity.[32] We should remember that these characteristics may not be unique to the order. Nor does priesthood necessarily supplant what others do but instead may reflect the activity of the whole Body. The priest is both a functionary with specific tasks and also something of an ambassador, who by his or her presence represents others.

In catechisms and ordination rites, a variety of pictures appears, some consistently and frequently. They fall into several categories which give a sense of what the Anglican priorities are.

Leading worship is perhaps the priest's clearest duty. Ordained to a "sacred priesthood," which suggests a distinction from the

---

[30] Q. by Hardy, "Priestly Ministries," 155. The story continues that he later became a bishop of Michigan. Re-told slightly differently by Margaret K. Schwarzer, "Youth's Authority: A Spiritual Revolution," in Nathan Humphrey, ed., *Gathering the NeXt Generation: Essays on the Formation and Ministry of GenX Priests* (Harrisburg, PA: Morehouse, 2000), 52.

[31] *Ordained Ministry Today*, 27.

[32] See the listing of terms in the appendix to this chapter. For sake of ease I will not footnote the terms but refer the reader instead to this appendix.

general priesthood of all, the presbyter is a minister of sacraments of the New Covenant. Somewhat surprisingly, the American rite does not refer to the priest's "presiding" at the Eucharist as the Church of England's *Alternative Service Book* does, choosing instead to have the priest "share" in its celebration. Perhaps to answer Roman Catholic objections, both the English and Canadian prayer books refer to the "spiritual sacrifices" that the priest offers.[33] Several also note priestly leadership in prayer and intercession.

As the priest is minister of the sacraments, so she or he is minister of the Word. In each rite the new priest receives a Bible in token of the special responsibility to proclaim, preach, and teach. New Zealand instructs the newly ordained to "take part in prophetic work." England calls them "messengers," as does Australia, and asks them to "teach and encourage by word and example."

The next major category is that of pastoral care. This terminology of shepherding suggests the care and concern that the priest offers the people he or she is called to serve, as several rites mention. It will be characterized by love, care, encouragement, service. Like the shepherd of Jesus' parable who seeks after the lost, the priest will seek those who fall away, according to the *New Zealand Prayer Book*, and has a special ministry to tend and heal the sick. *The Alternative Service Book* lists a series of terms that describe the priest's caring leadership of the faithful: "admonish," "feed," "provide for," "search," "guide," and "build up."

To "admonish" and "call to repentance" also has as corollary the ability to declare forgiveness and blessing. Each rite specifies these as special responsibilities for the priest, though only England and Canada go so far as to say that priests should "absolve" and "bless." Others have them "declare forgiveness" and "pronounce God's blessing."

Many Anglican rites include language that emphasizes the presbyter's role in the oversight of the church but none so strongly as in the United States and Canada. They mention the priest "sharing in the councils" (as does Australia) as "wise councilor[s]," who work faithfully with others in the life of the church. With regard

---

[33] E.g., in *Apostolicae Curae* (cf. R. William Franklin, ed., *Anglican Orders: Essays on the Centenary of Apostolicae Curae, 1896–1996* [Harrisburg, PA: Morehouse, 1996]); see chapter 11, below.

human beings and deity. It summarizes one—if not *the* central—attribute of priestly nature.

> Holiness is a religious rather than an ethical quality. It denotes a sense of being set apart, yet without any of the unctuous piety of the "holier than thou" variety. Without ceasing in anyway [sic] to be entirely human, the priest is called to be a man of God. His life, his words and actions, should make it easier for others to be aware of the presence of God. Any sense of separatedness is not a denial of closeness to his fellow men, for the Holy God to whom he is called to be close chose to reveal his concern for men through the Incarnation.[36]

This seventh point is the truly dangerous one, because, as Martineau implies, it would seem to set the presbyter above the laity or even the whole *laos* in a superior relationship with God, which revives the risk of clericalism. This risk intensifies to the degree that the priest does act *in persona Christi*, perhaps most clearly in blessing and absolution. Although the danger will always be present, two antidotes may also be inherent in the priestly role. First, the priest also functions *in persona ecclesiae*, that is, functioning for the church as well as for Christ, in a dynamic balance. The second antidote lies in the ministerial quality of this order (amplified, I will propose in the next chapter, by its grounding in the servanthood of diaconate), all of which finds its inspiration in the person of the One who causes all ministry to be. Hugh Wybrew, vicar of St. Mary Magdalen in Oxford, writes that

> Jesus shows us that the heart of priesthood is the offering of self to God. The offering is made through obedience to God's will, an obedience motivated by love. It is inseparable from self-giving love for others, and is made in and through every aspect of ordinary daily living. The Christian called in ordination to priestly ministry receives a vocation to nothing less than a share in the self-offering of Jesus Christ himself. [37]

---

[36] Martineau, *Office and Work of a Priest*, 142–143.

[37] Hugh Wybrew, *Called to be Priests* (Oxford: SLG Press, 1989), 4.

Priests are by no means the only ones who offer this self-sacrifice. Indeed, inherent in priesthood is the purpose of revealing the priesthood, and thus the self-sacrifice, of all God's people. The representative quality of priesthood helps to make that evident.

THE PRIEST AS REPRESENTATIVE ELDER

If all Christians represent Christ and his church, how the presbyter does so is not unique so much as distinctive. Reviewing the categories we just identified may show why. In each case, the "elder" represents *both* Christ and the church and becomes "exemplary" in a way that may transcend what the revisers of ordinals may have had in mind.

1. The priest is *a person of the sacrament,* while the sacrament as an outward and visible sign conveys and reveals an inward and spiritual grace. The ultimate sacrament is Jesus. "He is the reflection of God's glory and the exact imprint of God's very being," according to the Letter to the Hebrews (1:3). The prologue to John's gospel states, "No one has ever seen God. It is God the only Son, who is close to the Father's heart, who has made him known" (1:18). Because the church is Christ's Body, it too holds a sacramental character. It outwardly reveals the inward presence of the incarnate, risen, and ascended Lord. For this reason, Temple linked the Incarnation as "the perfect sacrament intensively" with the church, that "Spirit-bearing Body" that is "the direct outcome of the divine act of the Incarnation and the continuance of its principle."[38] As Christ is sacrament, so is his church. As a representative of both, the priest becomes not only the primary officer presiding over sacramental rites but more basically a reflection and manifestation of Christ and church. The priest is "sacramental" both in function and in being.

2. The priest is *a person of the Word.* Jesus is *the* Word, the "Logos" of John's prologue who "became flesh and lived among us" (1:14). Preaching and teaching are central duties of the priest, following Jesus' example, and also following the church whose responsibility it is to proclaim and explain the Christian faith. The

---

[38] Temple, *CV* [234–235] 167–168.

apostolic commission handed to the disciples (Mt. 28:18–20) devolves upon a church founded upon their doctrine and teaching. The elder as the preacher and teacher serves as an outward representation, as well as functionary, of that ministry. As if in witness to this reality, Christians in the Sudan consider the preacher a representative of Christ to such an extent that they hear Jesus speaking through the preacher, so that to make noise while listening is to interrupt Jesus himself.[39]

3. The priest is *a person of care.* "I am the good shepherd," Jesus says in the gospel of John, and Luke's gospel is filled with parables that Jesus tells of shepherds, parables that we finally see pertain to himself. He stands as the eternal model of pastoral care and concern, exemplary for the church as his Body, and for all of his disciples.

4. The priest is *a person rooted in community.* The very nature of God, as trinitarian theologians observe, is community. God's nature therefore provides the ultimate model for the Christian community. The priest, like any ordained person, arises from a local Christian community, is ordained by the Christian community in the larger community of the diocese by a bishop who represents the universal Christian community, and returns to a local Christian community to serve. There the priest calls the community together in worship and fellowship, all in the presence of Christ.

5. The priest is *an example to others.* Jesus, of course, is the paramount example. Christian spirituality looks constantly to him, whether it be the fourteenth-century book *Imitation of Christ* or the contemporary question, "What Would Jesus Do?" The church, too, strives to be exemplary. What that means in practice has been different in different eras and cultures. Bishop Martineau links the exemplary nature of priesthood to that of the church as a whole and all its people:

> The life and words and work of a priest need to form a unity, from which it follows that his life must communicate Christ as his words and work do. The priest is

---

[39] Interview in Roanoke, Virginia, Feb. 24, 2001 with Lomole James Simeon, chancellor of the Diocese of Khartoum. Evidently the principle applies whether the preacher is lay or ordained.

called to represent the Church to itself, and to be a spokesman of the Church of [sic] the world. His life is seen by the world, and judgement of his life is judgement of the Church. Therefore as the Church is called to be holy, so the priest is called to holiness; so also is every churchman.[40]

6. As *a person of blessing and of reconciliation,* the priest clearly represents Jesus. "Once he came in blessing, all our sins redressing," goes an Advent hymn. With that Christly purpose constantly in mind, the very mission of the church, as the catechism of the Episcopal Church states, is "to restore all people to unity with God and each other in Christ."[41] The priest plays a specially ordained part in that work.

7. Finally, a priest is *a person of God,* representing the high priesthood of Christ and the priestliness of the church. As I remarked earlier, this is the most dangerous of this series of statements, for it is open to too many misinterpretations. Hebrews 10:10 points to the high-priesthood of Christ, uniquely and solely offering himself, "once for all," which is a vitally important passage for Anglican understandings of Christ's priesthood and its distinction from—and connection with—that of the church. The royal priesthood may stretch beyond the church, but it also includes it, and the presbyter offers a glimpse into the even greater priesthood of Christ. As elder, the priest can never forget the source of any priesthood, which is *from* Christ, *through* the church, and based upon discipleship and service to him. Hugh Wybrew summarizes the thought:

> On the one hand the priest is ordained to be a sacrament of Jesus Christ who chooses particular members of his priestly body to make his own priestly ministry present and effective to the Christian community. The ordained priest speaks and acts in the name of Jesus Christ in relation to the Church, and his ministry is intended to enable the whole Christian community to become the royal priesthood it is called to be.... On the other hand,

---

[40] Martineau, *Office and Work of a Priest,* 142.

[41] ECUSA, *The Hymnal 1982* (New York: Church Hymnal, 1982), #53; US BCP, 855.

and at the same time, the priest is representative of the Christian community, and speaks and acts in its name. Through baptism he is a member of the laos..., the People of God, and though ordained remains a "lay-man" in the proper sense of the word: a member of the laos of God.[42]

In parlance at least as old as the thirteenth century, the presbyteral elder was called the "parson." The word derives ultimately from the Latin *persona* (in itself interesting for its parallel use to describe the trinitarian *personae* of Father, Son, and Spirit) that bequeathed the English word "person." The priest personified Christ but also the parish. He embodied Christ and also the whole congregation—indeed, the whole church—in visiting the sick or in presiding over sacraments. He would express in word and deed what the entire parish might wish, such as its sense of blessing upon a couple uniting as husband and wife, or its welcome back into the fullness of the baptismal community of one who had gone astray.

A parish I served early in my ministry was near a submarine base. Invited occasionally to some military event, I would glimpse that highly structured and hierarchical world at work. The commanding officer of a ship would represent that naval unit in an almost personal way. When he was about to board or leave the submarine, a bo'sun's pipe would sound as a disembodied voice would announce through the ship, "*Will Rogers* arriving" or "*Louisville* departing." When it came time for that captain to rotate off, a change-of-command ceremony before the entire crew—and plenty of guests like me—would indicate that the new man was in charge, and whatever feelings they had for the retiring commander, their loyalty now belonged to the new captain.

There the military analogy ends. No clergy person has the authority or command that a naval officer possesses, and woe to

---

[42] Wybrew, *Called to be Priests*, 5. However, Eric James claims, "I searched in vain for a single sermon that says that one of the main tasks of those ordained is to help those *not* ordained to be ministers of Christ and stewards of the mysteries of God." He continues, "If this is what people have been taught for a century and more, small wonder that the clergy do not find it easy to adjust to a wider conception; that ordinary men and women feel left out; and that the world of work and politics and science, for instance, is spoken of so often as outside the realm of the 'mysteries of God'" (James, *Stewards of the Mysteries of God*, 2).

anyone who thinks he or she might. While some provinces give more power to clergy than others, Anglican tradition diffuses it and incorporates others, including laity, into the decision-making responsibilities. But there are points of similarity. A bishop in England adopts the name of his diocese, often in Latinized abbreviation; Bishop Rowan Williams has become "Rowan Cantaur" as the Archbishop of Canterbury, personifying the diocese in a person (and vice versa). The "parson" is called upon to speak on behalf of the congregation at a public event. Many a rector or vicar has experienced the ire of a parishioner who was visited by a subordinate or a layperson and not the "chief"; whether justified or not, the reaction attests to the identification of priest with parish. This attitude reflects a relationship that develops over time, especially as the priest exercises those traits of which bishops speak at ordinations, of loving and caring for the people in a pastoral and spiritual work, in a sense of servanthood, and in a genuine sharing in the Christian life and witness.

So priestly ministry, like any ministry, is both ministerial and representative, established and grounded in the relationship with Christ and his Body. As Doss writes, "No action of ministry...is ever a solitary function or taken in isolation from the community."[43] Presbyterate finds its meaning within the people of God, the "royal priesthood."

But why is *this* ministry appropriate to a presbyter, an "elder"?

THE PRIEST WHO LEADS

What ordination rites articulate, along with most of the vast sweep of theological thinking, is an understanding of the presbyter as a leader in the Christian community, but one of a particular kind. The various jobs a priest is expected to undertake—as president of the eucharistic assembly; as pastor; as preacher, teacher, and guide; as leader of the community, broadly construed; as the conveyor of blessing and reconciliation—all place the presbyter in a position of seniority with regard to the church both locally and more broadly. As leader of ritual, the priest calls the community

---

[43] Doss, "Unified Symbol," 30.

together and presides over its worship like a mother calling the family to supper. As preacher, the presbyter expounds the divine Word, which, together with the cultic role, has overtones of the shamanism that theologian Urban Holmes thought marked the priesthood.[44] As teacher, the elder takes a lead in communicating the truths of the doctrine and heritage of the faith and, in so doing, becomes a bearer of the tradition. The priest takes the role of a "professor" in an educational sense but also as one who *professes* and thus teaches by the act of professing. In the care that the elder offers, the priest assumes almost the role of a doctor or healer; in fact, a benefice or rectorship is still sometimes called a "cure of souls." Each of these is a position of leadership and seniority, the position of an elder.

This seniority is not defined by years but by identification: The community of the faithful *identifies* this person as one who will fill this role for it. So seniority is a derived attribute, authorized by the church at large through ordination and appointment or license by the bishop, and by the congregation in its invitation to the priest to come (in those provinces where this is normative) or by its acceptance of the person, or both. Liturgically, this is symbolized by the institution or induction of the new priest, whatever the rite may be called. Its function is not unlike that of the military change-of-command, establishing the credentials and spiritual authority of the ministerial person while allowing the congregation to claim this priest as its own.

The elder, then, is one to whom the congregation particularly turns. He or she bears an authority that is granted from without but authenticated from within. Training, experience, gifts, charisms, and the personality that the priest brings join with the acclamation that the people offer. But in the end, the presbyterate—the role of elder—is effective to the degree that it finds its meaning in the relationship among the people of Christ, blessed by the Holy Spirit.

What image may we use? The Eucharist may provide one, as the elder calls the community together as if for a corporate meal. Though the elder convenes the assembly, the ultimate host is Jesus. Around the table, concerns are shared with him and with each

---

[44] Holmes, *Priest in Community*, 78–82.

other as the elder articulates what is perceived to be the concerns of this unseen yet ever-present host and makes sure that Scripture is read and homiletically interpreted. In that context, the elder may have things to share as if from Christ, or may take special care to bring issues to the table of all the people. The priest's is a voice from God, but also the voice of the voiceless: all are heard, knowing that it may be through *them* that God may speak. Although the corporate body may determine what to do, the priest enables, facilitates, and guides the decision-making.

Yet speaking as this kind of representative demands distance from the local community. That Jesus was received as a prophet everywhere except in his own hometown of Nazareth points to a reality of human life. Many clergy have experiences of a guest preacher's being heard more clearly than the familiar pastoral voice that has been trying to convey the same points and sometimes even better. For the one who speaks the Word of God and who voices what the voiceless cannot, some distance is required in order to reflect objectively on the Word and on the community, an intimate relationship with those who may not be heard, and a connection with the wider community of the faithful. If the community (on whatever level) needs a reminder of its true and eschatological character because it has drifted away, then the priest faces a tough task. Success will rely on the innate connections with the larger community and the God who stands within, but also above, it.[45]

In Anglican understanding, the parish church is not the only level of community. Each local church belongs to a diocese, a provincial church, the Anglican Communion, and ultimately to the universal church throughout the world and throughout history. Anyone who is aware of these connections can find solace, strength, and inspiration in that larger community. The priest also *reveals* that wider community, even as the richness of the Body of Christ becomes more evident. Bishop Thomas Ray noted the contribution of the diaconate along this line and extended it to priests, who

---

[45] Advisory Council for the Church's Ministry, *Call to Order: Vocation and Ministry in the Church of England* (London: ACCM, [1989?]), 33-34; cf. Anglican-Roman Catholic International Commission, *Agreed Statements on Eucharistic Doctrine and Ministry and Ordination with Elucidations* (Cincinnati, OH: Forward Movement Publications, 1980), 21-22 (sec. 13).

reveal to us the depth of the mystery of the meaning of baptism. Rooted in our sacramental theology, priests remind us that we are a community of reconciliation, a community of sisters and brothers committed to breaking down the artificial barriers that separate and segregate and isolate and dehumanize.... Priests help us see hurt and isolation and segregation and say, "I am sorry, forgive me." Sacramentally the priest now explodes our awareness and understanding of priestly ministry into a daily ministry that touches our lives at all times and in all places.[46]

Presbyters, then, are elders of a community that is nothing less than the Body of Christ on earth, priestly representatives of Christ the high priest, within the priesthood of all his people. As elders of a community, though, they necessarily work and live with others. Their presbyterate involves them with the bishops who oversee their work. Their presbyterate also involves them directly with deacons, laypeople, and other priests with whom they work; so an understanding of presbyterate, then, has to consider the working relationships with these others. To those relationships we now turn, for presbyterate is by nature collegial.

APPENDICES

A. SOME PRACTICAL QUESTIONS

If the ideas I have expressed about the nature of priests, presbyters, and elders have any merit, a wide array of questions about the nature of priesthood arises. What those questions may be and how they can be addressed will depend upon who is asking them and in what context. Let me simply suggest some possibilities:

1. How does the presbyter function both as a ministerial and a representative person?

2. What implications does this hold for initial training, for continuing education, and for opportunities for rest, reflection and "reconnecting"?

---

[46] Thomas K. Ray, "The Small Church: Radical Reformation and Renewal of Ministry," *Anglican Theological Review*, 78, no. 4 (Fall 1996), 623–624.

3. Hugh Wybrew comments, "If priests and deacons are called to be walking sacraments, they should be seen to be growing into the holiness of Jesus Christ into which their ministry is meant to help others to grow."[47] What is the connection between priestliness and personhood?

4. How does the elder relate to others engaged in ministry—bishop, other priests, deacons, laypeople (and to others beyond the Anglican church structure)? What is the measure of collegiality?

5. How might these concerns affect terminology, attire, pay, and lifestyle?

6. How does priesthood reveal the ministry of others?

B. The Language of Presbyterate

The words used in the ordination rites of churches in the Anglican Communion to describe what a priest does and what a priest should be give a sense of what a priest *is*. The following is a sampling of words taken from liturgies of various Anglican provinces. The categories are mine and somewhat arbitrary; and the interrelationship between these categories must be stressed. Often, what is cited mixes nouns and verbs.

Abbreviations (see bibliography for full reference)

ASB   Church of England, *The Alternate Service Book* (1980)

Aus   Anglican Church of Australia, *A Prayer Book for Australia* (1995)

Can   Anglican Church of Canada, *The Book of Alternative Services of the Anglican Church of Canada* (1985). Can, 646–647, and US, 531–532 (the examination) are word-for-word identical so Canada's parallel to those ECUSA page numbers is assumed.

SO   [General Synod, Scottish Episcopal Church] *Scottish Ordinal 1984*.

NZ   Church of the Province of New Zealand, *A New Zealand Prayer Book* (1989)

US   ECUSA, *The Book of Common Prayer* (1979)

---

[47] Wybrew, *Called to be Priests*, 11.

PASTORAL
  Minister/ministry (general): US 527, 532; Can 649 ("ministry among the people")
  Presbyter: US 531; ASB 351; SO 9, 11, 13
  Pastor: US 531, 532, 534; Aus 793; NZ 901; SO 11
  Shepherd to whom one is sent: ASB 356
  Love: US 531; Aus 793
  Serve people to whom called: US 531 (see "servant," below).
  Encourage: NZ 901
  Recall those who fall away: NZ 901
  Heal/minister to the sick: ASB 356; NZ 901
  Care for: ASB 359; Can 649; SO 9
  Admonish, feed, provide for, search, guide, build up: ASB 356–357

PRIESTLY/MINISTER OF SACRAMENT
  Sacred priesthood: US 527; Can 645
  Priest: US 531, Aus 793; SO 11
  Minister of sacraments of the New Covenant: US 532; ‖ Aus 793; SO 11
  Share in celebration of Eucharist: US 531
  Preside at the Eucharist: ASB 356; SO 10
  Offer spiritual sacrifices: ASB 363; Can 649
  Lead in prayer and worship: ASB 356; Aus 793
  Draws together in worship those [who go forth in mission]: SO 10
  Intercede: ASB 356

MINISTER OF WORD
  Minister (of) the Word of God: US 532; SO 11
  Proclaim: ASB 356, 359; Can 649; SO 10, 11
  Take part in prophetic work: NZ 901
  Preach: US 531; Aus 793
  Teacher/teach: US 531, 534; Aus 793; SO 10
  Teach and encourage by word and example: ASB 356
  Messenger(s): ASB 356; Aus 793 (see "watch over," below)
  Uphold catholic doctrine founded on the Scriptures: SO 11

OVERSIGHT
  Share in councils: US 531; Aus 793
  Wise councilor: US 534
  Watch over: Can 649

Work faithfully with others (presbyters, laity, general): Can
   649; US 532

SERVANT
   Servant/serve: ASB 356; Aus 793; US 535
   Minister: See above
   Lead as servant: Aus 793
   Example of obedience to the way of Christ: SO 12

FORGIVENESS AND BLESSING
   Absolve/declare forgiveness: ASB 356, 363; Aus 793, 796; Can
      649; NZ 901; SO 10, 13; US 531
   Bless/pronounce God's blessing: ASB 363; Can 649; US 531;
      SO 10; Aus 793, 796
   Call hearers to repentance: ASB 356

COMMUNITY LIFE
   Baptize, prepare for confirmation: ASB 356; NZ 901
   Share in administration of baptism: US 531
   Promote unity, peace, love: ASB 358 (‖ SO 13)
   Nourish Christ's people: US 531
   Strengthen [Christ's people] to glorify God: US 531
   Enabling [people] to respond to God's call: SO 9

PERSONAL QUALITIES
   Taking on trust: US 531
   Assuming responsibility: US 531
   Effective example: US 532, 535; ‖ ASB 356, 359; SO 11
      ["example of obedience"]
   Pattern life to be a wholesome example: US 532; ASB 358
   To be worthy of calling: Can 649
   Personal prayer and self-offering: US 532; SO 11
   Fashion life in accordance with gospel: US 531
   Holiness: SO 13

VIII

The Reemerging Diaconate

In one of his letters, the early bishop Ignatius of Antioch refers to the deacons as his "special favorites," worthy to be entrusted with the ministry of Jesus Christ.[1] In the late twentieth century, deacons are rapidly becoming favorites of the church.

By one definition, they had never left. With few exceptions, from the fifth century on, deacons served in the person of bishop or priest, or one who would be ordained a presbyter, most likely within a year. At least in theory, by virtue of previous ordination, the diaconate was part of the presbyteral persona even though the priest or bishop would rarely identify himself as a deacon. Diaconate was virtually covered over by subsequent ordination, disappearing from view and from consciousness. A "real" deacon the priest or bishop was not.

Then as the twentieth century waned, the idea of the diaconate as a "full and equal order" reemerged. Prompted by Lambeth resolutions, efforts were made to move the diaconate beyond functioning as a probationary period for priests. As deacons came to be ordained (especially in the United States) specifically for ministries of service, questions began to arise: What is the impact

---

[1] Ignatius of Antioch (c. 35–c. 107), *Magnesians* 6.1.

of diaconate on the idea and practice of priesthood? What is its relationship to the nature and ministry of the laity? What is a deacon's purpose in the life of the *laos*? These quandaries underscore again the need for careful understanding of the role of each category, a recognition of their interdependence, and the vital need for mutual cooperation and collegiality in pursuing the ministry of the whole church.

A BRIEF HISTORY OF DEACONS

FROM THE NEW TESTAMENT TO MOBERLY

In one vital sense, diaconate began with Jesus.[2] "I am among you as one who serves," he told his disciples (*ho diakonon*, Luke 22:27). Jesus confused them even more when, according to John, he tied a towel around his waist and washed their feet at the last supper with them before he died (13:3–11). He hinted pointedly that they should do likewise, for "whoever wishes to become great among you must be slave (*doulos*) of all" (Mark 10:44).[3]

From the time of Irenaeus, who died at the end of the second century, Acts 6:1–6 was traditionally considered the origin of the diaconate. In that passage the apostles, needing help, appointed and laid hands on seven people ostensibly to distribute necessities of life to the Christian community, because

> it is not right that we should neglect the word of God, in order to wait on tables. Therefore, friends, select from yourselves seven men of good standing, full of the Spirit and of wisdom, whom we may appoint to this task, while we, for our part, will devote ourselves to prayer and to serving the word. (Acts 6:3–4)

---

[2] Good surveys can be found in Barnett, *Diaconate*, 13–131; Edward R. Hardy, "Deacons in History and Practice," in *The Diaconate Now*, ed. Richard T. Nolan (Washington: Corpus Books, 1968), 11–35; Church of England, *Deacons in the Ministry*, 7–22; Jill Pinnock, "The History of the Diaconate," in Hall, ed., *Deacon's Ministry*, 9–24.

[3] "In the New Testament Christ himself is seen as the diakonos" (*The Ministry of Deacons*, World Council Studies No. 2 [Geneva: World Council of Churches, 1965], 33).

Whether Irenaeus was correct has been questioned.[4] Acts never records that waiting on tables is what the seven actually did. Stephen and Philip were better known for their evangelistic words than their charitable deeds, and so these two fill the image of apostle more than deacon. Nonetheless, Paul mentions some people called "deacons" alongside "bishops" (Phil. 1:1); and by Timothy's time, deacons carry certain expectations as to what their characteristics should be (1 Tim. 3:8–13).

Deacons' subsequent history, like that of all the orders, remains shrouded in some mystery. Still, by the mid-second century, deacons seem to have become well ensconced in the church's life. We have already seen that on his way to martyrdom in Rome, Ignatius called them "my special favorites" and "fellow slaves." Justin Martyr describes deacons distributing eucharistic bread and wine to those present in a congregation and taking them to the homes of those who were absent, while Hippolytus depicts them as assistants "to serve the bishop and to carry out the bishop's commands" and "to make known to the bishop such things as are needful." Presbyters, meanwhile, may have been little more than councilors.[5] Moreover, evidence from the fourth century shows women deacons possessing theological significance: as the male deacon was something of an icon of Christ, she was an icon of the Holy Spirit, with the bishop signifying God the Father. She held a special ministry to other women that was not exclusive, but understood to represent the qualities of the Spirit.[6]

From that era until the end of the sixth century, deacons thrived during what some have called "the golden age of the diaconate as a distinct order." Long associated with the bishop, deacons

---

[4] E.g., by P. Hinchcliff, "Deacon," *A New Dictionary of Liturgy and Worship*, ed. J. G. Davies (London: SCM, 1986), 208: "[T]here is no evidence at all to support the tradition that the seven...[of Acts 6] were deacons."

[5] Ignatius, *Magn.* 6, *Phila.* 6 (cf. *Trall.* 2); Justin, *Apol.* 65, 1, Hippolytus, *Apostolic Tradition* 9.2–3 (in Bart D. Ehrman, *After the New Testament: A Reader in Early Christianity* (New York: OUP, 1999), 329. Following Hippolytus would exclude deacons from governance, however, for "[h]e does not take part in the council of the clergy" (9.3). Cf. Hinchcliff, "Deacon," 8.

[6] Pinnock, "History," in Hall, ed., *Deacon's Ministry*, 14–16, from the *Didascalia Apostolorum*. John Chrysostom was convinced from 1 Tim. 3:8–13 that some deacons were women; cf. Pinnock, "History," 11.

294 Priesthood in a New Millennium

assisted him in his liturgical, administrative, and pastoral functions, often far beyond their traditional charitable role. As a result, deacons could become prominent, even powerful. One of the most influential figures of the Council of Nicaea in 325, the theologian Athanasius, attended as a deacon. Six deacons were directly elected as popes, including Gregory and Leo, each of whom came to be called "the Great." As centuries passed, while Eastern Christians continued to regard deacons highly, in the West, as dioceses were divided into parishes, the local presbyter assumed many roles of both bishop and deacon in the absence of assisting clergy. Liturgically, the presbyter celebrated and blessed, ancient prerogatives of the episcopate, while the presbyter read the gospel and prepared the table as deacons used to do, filling the job description the apostles had given the original seven. Pastorally, presbyters often offered acts of mercy, another role attributed to deacons. Yet ancient roles became confused, creating an overemphasis on presbyters in parishes.[7]

The Middle Ages saw the solidification of the tradition that presbyters first be ordained deacon, but the need for priests made permanent deacons a rarity. Given the medieval church's great emphasis on the Mass, confession, and absolution, priesthood was the paramount order of ministry and the church saw little reason not to hasten ordinands into work where they were needed. As a result, the diaconal transition between the lay state and the priesthood could last just a few weeks. Paradoxically enough, the medieval diaconate served the church by virtually disappearing: priests were what the church needed, so priests were what deacons became. A few remained in prominent positions, such as the scholarly Alcuin, educator for Charlemagne, who was probably a deacon. But if a deacon were nominated to a bishopric, he quickly became a priest in order to ascend to the cathedra.[8] Thomas à Beckett was a deacon administrator of the church and a servant of the state when Henry II chose him to be Archbishop of Canterbury, so he

---

[7] Pinnock, "History," in Hall, ed., *Deacon's Ministry*, 19–20; Hardy, "Deacons in History," in Nolan, ed., *Diaconate Now*, 15; Leonel L. Mitchell, "Direct Ordination to the Presbyterate," in Hallenbeck, ed., *Orders of Ministry*, 42; cf. Barnett, *Diaconate*, 95–105; *Deacons in the Ministry*, 10 (¶11–13).

[8] *Deacons in the Ministry*, 15 (¶24).

was ordained priest one day and bishop the next.

Continental reformers praised the diaconate but one that had service as its focus. When the dissolution of the monasteries disrupted the charitable work they had provided, Luther proposed a diaconate to fill the void, to restore the office to what he saw as its original intent, and also to free pastors to concentrate on word and sacrament. In practice, some charged with administering welfare were called "deacons," some were not. They could be simply members of elected boards of parishes, especially in places where Lutheranism was not established as a state church.[9]

Calvin redesigned the diaconate to be one of four offices of the church. He saw a close connection between worship and ethics, between duty to God and duty to neighbor; this connection was manifested by deacons who were laity, caring for the poor as an official ministry of the church. Congregationalists came to develop a liturgical function for their deacons in the distribution of the eucharistic elements, whereas in the Baptist tradition, deacons took responsibility for the congregation's welfare in various ways—visiting and taking communion to the sick, preaching and leading worship on occasion, aiding the needy, and assisting in planning worship.[10]

For all the changes wrought in ordained ministry in Reformation-era England, however, the diaconate was hardly touched. English reformers largely held onto the medieval practice but made two significant changes. One was to eliminate the "minor orders" of clergy, which had the effect of increasing the importance of the diaconate as the first step into the clerical life while also opening to laity the roles previously held by subdeacons, acolytes and

---

[9] Lake Lambert III, "Called to Serve: Diaconal Ministry in the ELCA," Division for Ministry, Evangelical Lutheran Church in America (July 2001), 1; Günther Gassmann, *Historical Dictionary of Lutheranism* (Lanham, MD: Scarecrow, 2001), s.v. "Diaconate," 90; Susan Wilds McArver, "A History of the Diaconate," in Duane H. Larson, ed., *From Word and Sacrament: Renewed Vision for Diaconal Ministry* (Chicago: Evangelical Lutheran Church in America, 1999), 71.

[10] Elsie Anne McKee, "John Calvin on the Diaconate and Liturgical Almsgiving," Ph.D. diss. (Princeton Theological Seminary, 1982), 351–352; cf. also McKee, *Diakonia in the Classical Reformed Tradition and Today* (Grand Rapids, MI: Eerdmans, 1989). Cf. Davies, ed., *New Dictionary of Liturgy and Worship*, 209.

such.[11] The other change was made by Cranmer who, in the new ordination rite, referred to the diaconate as an "inferior office" in a prayer that the candidates "may be found worthy to be called unto the higher ministries."[12]

The implication of a distinctly less important order behind bishops and priests would linger through the centuries. Necessity might cause rapid advancement through the diaconate: American candidates like Samuel Johnson or Samuel Seabury who had to cross the Atlantic for ordination would be "just" a deacon for only a week or even a few days. Some stood back from priesthood for far longer. Those who held teaching fellowships at Oxford or Cambridge at the time were required to be in orders, so some slipped in as deacons and remained as such, with little reason to become priests in an era when Holy Communion might be administered once a term. Nicholas Ferrar, who died in 1637, was rare in dedicating his life as a deacon outside of academia. As the church began to place more emphasis on its sacramental life, together with the growth of urban parishes and a new sense of professionalism, a new urgency arose for helpers and for training.[13] Yet even an Archbishop of York could break prayer book rubrics specifying that new deacons should be deacons for at least a day. About to ordain a nephew to a family living, Edward Harcourt (1757–1847) reportedly told the young man, "I think it will save both you and me some trouble if I shoot through both barrels; so I will ordain you both deacon and priest this afternoon."[14]

FIRST SIGNS OF RENEWAL

Charitable work by a dedicated few took on new life in the mid-nineteenth century. During the "Lutheran Awakening," which

---

[11] The Anglo-Saxon church, for example, listed seven hierarchical "degrees of order": doorkeeper, lector, exorcist, acolyte, subdeacon, deacon, and priest. By this reckoning, a bishop was a priest enabled to ordain, confirm, and also to consecrate churches—not a separate order. Cf. Rock, *Church of Our Fathers*, III, 140–142.

[12] 1662 BCP, 567–568; cf. George Every, "The Diaconate in the Anglican Communion," in WCC, *Ministry of Deacons*, 46.

[13] Every, "Diaconate in the Anglican Communion," in WCC, *Ministry of Deacons*, 46; *Deacons in the Ministry*, 16 (¶30).

[14] Bullock, *Training, 1800 to 1874*, 73 (cf. 1662 BCP, 568).

coincided with Romanticism and also the Oxford Movement in England, the pastor of the Lutheran-Reformed parish at Kaiserswerth organized with his wife an order of single women to offer nursing and pastoral care in a lifelong commitment. Soon deacon brotherhoods were started for men. Among Lutherans, the Swedish Church established a similar program.[15] Meanwhile, communities of sisters in the Church of England were one of the fruits of the Oxford Movement. The Community of St. Andrew (1861) specifically aimed at being diaconal. Its leader, Elizabeth Ferard, was ordained as a deaconess a year later by Bishop Tait of London. The order of deaconesses grew, usually understood as an order of laity, and was recognized by the 1897 Lambeth Conference (though not until 1923 by the Convocation of Canterbury and 1925 by that of York).[16] Until R. O. Hall in Hong Kong raised the point in the 1940s and James Pike presented his California deaconesses a stole in the 1960s, no one thought of them as equivalents to deacons at all.[17]

The idea of a diaconate that was more than transitional and also involved more than social work was taking shape among Anglicans. Just three years before the Germans organized their sisterhood, Thomas Arnold, the energetic headmaster of Rugby School, proposed an "inferior" order of ministers who would form a corps equivalent to non-commissioned officers in the military. Coming from poorer classes of English society, they would bring working people and their perspective into the church's administration. In 1841 he advanced a more refined idea of a non-stipendiary diaconate that would alleviate the shortage of clergy in urban areas, bridge the division between laity and clergy, broaden

---

[15] Gassmann, *Historical Dictionary of Lutheranism*, s.v. "Lutheran Awakening," 32; Mildred Winter, "Deaconess," in *The Encyclopedia of the Lutheran Church*, ed. Julius Bodensieck (Minneapolis: Augsburg, 1965), 660–661; Pinnock, "History," in Hall, ed., *Deacon's Ministry*, 23; *Deacons in the Ministry*, 30–33 (¶77–88, 90). Florence Nightingale's visits to Kaiserswerth helped shape her healthcare innovations. The community considered her to be a deaconess, like themselves. C.f. Webb, *s*, 79, 84–86, 127.

[16] Pinnock, "History," in Hall, ed., *Deacon's Ministry*, 21; *Deacons in the Ministry*, 18–19 (¶35–41).

[17] Cf. Emily C. Hewitt and Suzanne R. Hiatt, *Women Priests: Yes or No?* (New York: Seabury Press, 1973), 11. Deaconesses were said to be "ordained" and sometimes were understood to be part of the "third order of ministry," until as late as the 1940s.

the spectrum of classes participating in the church's life, develop a shared ministry within teams, bring religious concerns into business and workplace—and all at lowered cost. Much of his reasoning found its way into rationales for both the diaconate and non-stipendiary ministry.[18]

Some Anglicans beyond England grasped the new diaconal vision and sought to implement it. In 1853, Episcopalians proposed that deacons comprise an evangelistic order and wrote the proposal into canon in 1871. Though the experiment lasted only until 1904, it produced the Native American, David Pendleton Oaker-hater, as a missionary to the Cheyenne.[19] Meanwhile, bishops from the West Indies forwarded the idea to the 1878 Lambeth Conference, which paid little heed, though English churchmen and Parliament itself took measures in the 1880s to approve a permanent, non-stipendiary diaconate. Only a few deacons were ordained.[20]

The idea reemerged in the 1920s. Hensley Henson saw the diaconate, however "inferior," as securing for its recipients the full commission of Christian ministry. He noted the "settled practice" of treating it as "no more than a brief apprenticeship to the priesthood" but claimed that it marks a "decisive step out of the secular into the ecclesiastical life." He recommended a longer period of at least three years so it "could be made into a real apprenticeship to the priesthood."[21] Roland Allen, typically ahead of his time, imagined it as vastly more than an apprenticeship for some other order. He corresponded with Bishop George Azariah of Assam about establishing a diaconate in India that was permanent and oriented toward service.[22] Swedish Lutheran bishops, meanwhile, had done just that, ordaining deacons to ministries of pastoral care though they were not considered "clergy" and took no liturgical role. When Gabriel Hebert visited Sweden in 1928, he found much to

---

[18] Patrick H. Vaughan, *Non-Stipendiary Ministry in the Church of England: A History of the Development of an Idea* (San Francisco: Mellen Research University Press, 1990), 26–31.

[19] *Lesser Feasts and Fasts* (New York: Church Publishing, 2000), 348.

[20] Hardy, "Deacons in History," in Nolan, ed., *Diaconate Now,* 34; Hall, ed., *Deacon's Ministry,* xiii; *Deacons in the Ministry,* 1; Vaughan, *Non-Stipendiary Ministry,* 42–54.

[21] Henson, *Ad Clerum,* 127, 43.

[22] Letter to Allen, June 18, 1925, in Paton, *Reform,* 123.

commend these deacons despite their liturgical absence at the Lord's table.[23]

Still, as the mid-twentieth century passed, Francis J. Hall's description remained the norm: "In a vast majority of cases, the ministry of deacons is in practice temporary only, and preparatory for ordination to the priesthood."[24] At Episcopal seminaries, Urban Holmes trenchantly remarked in 1979, "Frankly, we train priests, not deacons. Reflection upon the diaconate is, to my best knowledge, incidental."[25]

Serious efforts to restore it arose in mid- to late century in the United States and Britain, although perhaps to fend off other developments some found to be less desirable. For Episcopalians, the need was for help in parishes, but they were reluctant to involve laity. Beginning in 1952, however, the Episcopal Church authorized ordaining deacons as voluntary pastoral and liturgical assistants. They would retain secular employment and foreswear "advancement" to the priesthood, though given the large number who became priests, critics carped that the only mark of its permanence was its impermanence. Many deacons, nonetheless, were esteemed for their faithfulness.[26] Three times, lay deputies to General Convention approved of deacons—even as they rejected proposals to follow England in allowing laity to administer the chalice. In England, meanwhile, the diaconate provided a way to avoid ordaining women. Its 1968 report entitled *Women in Ministry* was in effect a review of diaconal ministry, while the legislation establishing a distinctive diaconate was entitled, "Deacons (Ordination of Women) Measure 1987." Pursue it they did: in 1992, of 1,568

---

[23] Christopher Irvine, *Worship, Church and Society* (Norwich [UK]: Canterbury Press, 1993), 29–30. Including deacons liturgically subsequently became an important issue for the "high church" party in Sweden.

[24] Francis J. Hall, *The Sacraments* (1921; reprint, Pelham Manor, NY: American Church Union, 1969), 270.

[25] Holmes, "A Response to *The Diaconate Today*," in Morgan, *Diaconate Today*, 131.

[26] *Deacons in the Ministry*, 39 (¶110); Hardy, "Deacons in History," in Nolan, ed., *Diaconate Now*, 34. Some provinces in Asia and Africa attempted a "permanent diaconate" as a means of upgrading catechists and evangelists, sometimes with similar results: cf. Every, in WCC, *Ministry of Deacons*, 49. When I arrived in my most recent parish, in Virginia, the memory was still cherished of a professor who exercised a primarily liturgical diaconate for about twenty years.

deacons, 1,194 were women.[27] Yet even the very thought that women could be deacons without becoming priests in itself revised thinking about diaconate: if it could be permanent for some—namely women—it could be permanent for others. Moving in a very different direction, a working party in England recommended in 1974 that General Synod abolish the order altogether. The synod did not but instead "took note" of another report setting forth three options: having all candidates for priesthood pass through it; omitting it; or enlarging it to a distinctive and permanent order. The latter eventually was the route taken.[28]

The Scottish Episcopal Church approved a permanent diaconate in 1965. Its prayer book revisions in 1929 and 1984 alike described for them a role that was practical as well as liturgical. Few men stepped forward, however, and of those who did, many became priests. Its deaconesses by 1988 had been ordained deacons.

In 1970 the Episcopal Church ended its earlier experiment and took a new route, one aimed at service beyond the parish. That year's General Convention repealed its canons on permanent deacons and declared all its deaconesses to be deacons. The process of prayer book revision, which led to the 1979 *Book of Common Prayer,* made liturgical room for deacons in various ways. Meanwhile, a group dedicated to training deaconesses reorganized to become the National Center for the Diaconate, which in 1986 reconstituted itself again under the name of the North American Association for the Diaconate (NAAD) to include Canadians. NAAD has provided publications and counsel on organizing diocesan diaconal programs, training candidates, clarifying roles, and helping deacons, priests, bishops, and laity to work effectively together within the life of the church. As of 2000, some 2,200 deacons serve the Episcopal Church in approximately seventy diocesan programs; about one hundred serve the Anglican Church of Canada in several dioceses. "It would seem," English commentators noted,

> that the "vocational" diaconate in America has developed a leadership for service and thereby has both alerted the Church to its responsibility to society and also enabled new ministries of outreach by laity as well as deacons.

---

[27] Hardy, "Deacons in History," in Nolan, ed., *Diaconate Now,* 35; *Deacons in the Ministry,* 1; Hall, ed., *Deacon's Ministry,* 5.

[28] *Deacons in the Ministry,* 1.

> There is increasing emphasis on deacons identifying needs
> and responding with appropriate ministries.[29]

Other provinces with a distinctive diaconate include Korea, the churches of North India and South India, and the West Indies, which insists that an order of deacons "shall be maintained within the Church of the Province...as a distinct order of ministry...symbolic of the servant element."[30]

Whether at the end of the day a revivified diaconate is a worthy development remains a matter of dispute. In his 1992 study of ministry, M. A. H. Melinsky has his doubts. He sees the same three options that General Synod considered in 1974: consolidating diaconate into a "permanent" or "distinctive" order, abolishing it, or continuing it as an apprenticeship for priesthood. What to call a distinctive deaconate is part of the problem: all orders, including diaconate, remain "permanent" and to use the term "distinctive" assigns to one order a quality that should characterize all. Furthermore, Melinsky adds, is all commendable service in the church included in an order of deacons? Where would the limits be? And why should some be ordained for their service, if all Christians are called to be lights in the world and salt of the earth? Abolishing the diaconate had been proposed in 1974 on the basis that deacons are not essential to the church in exercising its principal functions, but questions remained. Would Anglicans dare to eliminate one of the historic three orders? And how would this go down in ecumenical discussions? But Melinsky points out that the Lambeth Quadrilateral does not include a threefold order among its essentials: bishops, yes; deacons and priests, not necessarily. He concludes that the diaconal apprenticeship has "more to be said for [it] than is often supposed....This is a task of complex and subtle difficulty, not to be learned simply by books or lectures or even by group dynamics, but most effectively by personal discipleship"—a different form of training than seminaries traditionally provide.[31]

---

[29] *Deacons in the Ministry*, 39–43 (¶113–126); NAAD, "History of NAAD and the North American Diaconate" (http://www.diakonoi.org/naadhist.htm) (13 April 2001).

[30] Q. in Doe, *Canon Law*, 145.

[31] Melinsky, *Shape*, 135–137.

As Melinsky was writing, however, new perspectives were also emerging on *diakonia* and diaconate that might make some combination of his first option (a distinctive order) and his third option (an apprenticeship for priesthood) viable and even desireable.

UNDERSTANDING DIAKONIA

In these decades of renewing the diaconate, theologians have articulated several different points of view. Some, like James Barnett in his pathbreaking study, take the "organic" approach inherent in the image of the Body of Christ. Subsequent writers like Elaine Bardwell, in urging the establishment of the diaconate in England, reflect the more trinitarian tenor of their times. Some, like Ormonde Plater, combine the two: "Canon law reflects a theology of the church as the body of Christ, the creation of the Father through the Son and filled with the Holy Spirit. Ordained ministry is a product of the body of Christ."[32] Without venturing an extensive doctrinal explanation, I wish to suggest several characteristics of diaconal ministry that arise from what we have eplored thus far.

THE CHURCH AS SERVANT

Diaconal ministry is, first and foremost, a ministry of the entire Body of Christ. As Jesus served, so must the church and all of its members. To be a Christian is to be a follower and servant of Jesus. No order holds exclusive possession of any ministry. On the contrary, the baptismal promise to seek and serve all people pertains to all: "The whole Church, as Christ's body, shares in his ministry of service, *diakonia*, which is focused and epitomized in the persons of those whom the church has called to the diaconate and authorized as deacons."[33]

By their presence, deacons are "outward and visible signs" of this ecclesial servanthood. Their very name derives from the Greek verb generally translated "to serve," as in Mark 10:45. But what

---

[32] Barnett, *Diaconate*, 137–139; Elaine Bardwell, "The Pastoral Role of the Deacon," in Hall, ed., *Deacon's Ministry*, 46; Ormonde Plater, ed., *Deacons in the Episcopal Church: Guidelines on their Selection, Training and Ministry* (Providence, RI: North American Association for the Diaconate [hereafter, NAAD], 1991), 6. Cf. Larson, ed., *From Word and Sacrament*, 112–120.

[33] Pinnock, "History," in Hall, ed., *Deacon's Ministry*, 9.

do they signify? Like all Christians and their orders, deacons represent Christ and the church. As a Lutheran scholar puts it, "Diaconal ministry is an embodied, not disembodied ministry," meaning that it always functions as a ministry of the entire Body no matter where it may occur.[34] Deacons illustrate the church's witness to God's kingdom through the particular mode of servanthood, which reveals a crucial truth about that kingdom. They are *ministerial*. But as Hannaford observes, this servanthood connotes an eschatological dimension:

> The diaconate is therefore a powerful sign of the relationship between the Kingdom of God and the Church. It signifies both the presence of the Kingdom in the Church's ministry and also something of the transcendent demand of the Kingdom addressed to the Church.[35]

In this light, charitable work far exceeds mere benevolence. To share the good things of this life with those who have not is a sign of the kingdom of God itself. In this regard *diakonia* is also a sign of judgment on the general neglect of those in need, a neglect that the church seeks to correct but in which it also shares.

So the representative ministry of deacons is one that strives to bring a witness not only *from* the church *to* the world, but also *to* the church *from* the world. As servants of Christ, they address the church and the world. As servants of the church, they address the church and the world. This message, I believe, underscores the importance of due authorization that comes from ordination. As one comment on the diaconate overstates, "I don't think ordination is important to the individual, but it is important to the congregation, and gives the deacon position and authority."[36]

---

[34] Richard Carlson, "Diaconal Ministry from a Pauline Perspective," in Larson, ed., *From Word and Sacrament*, 29–30. Duane Larson in his essay underscores the representative nature, derived from the representational quality Jesus himself, of diaconal ministry (ibid., 120–126).

[35] Hannaford, "Theology of the Diaconate," in Hall, ed., *Deacon's Ministry*, 38.

[36] Episcopal Church, Permanent Diaconate Evaluation Committee, *Raising Up Servant Ministry: Eight Dioceses Work Toward the Future of the Diaconate and the Enablement of Servant Ministry* (New York: 1985), 20. I would not agree that the sacramental grace is unimportant to the individual deacon! Rather, its grace matters to the person and the community alike.

WHAT KIND OF SERVICE?

But what is that position and authority to be? In 1979 the push for a renewed diaconate was underway but still so undefined that Urban Holmes wondered if "diaconate is an order of ministry in search of a reason." A 1983 survey provided statistics to bear witness to the confusion over the nature of these new deacons; and on an ecumenical level, the 1982 World Council of Churches' commentary on its document *Baptism, Eucharist, and Ministry* observed, "In many churches there is today considerable uncertainty about the need, the rationale, the status and the functions of deacons."[37]

If one problem is the nature of diaconate, a second is how deacons should relate to others in the church. What kind of relationship will diaconal ministry have with priestly ministry? Even more, will deacons diminish what the laity should be doing at the very moment when the laity are beginning to do it? As laity increased their participation and expanded their role, this question was of sufficient concern to draw the caution of the 1958 Lambeth Conference, even as it commended a "distinctive place" for the office and function of a deacon in the church's worship and witness. Lay readers and catechists, it noted, had assumed most of the traditional duties of the deacon. The result, for all its positives, created confusions of roles and would complicate any efforts to clarify them.[38]

William Countryman raises a third problem, one that concerns language. Servants, he reminds us, have largely vanished from the Western world. No longer do households employ staffs of maids or gardeners. "Since the metaphor of clergy as servants has no real foundation in our lived experience, it becomes a kind of blank check, capable of holding any content at all, while concealing the content under the apparent humility of 'service.'"[39] Again, what is a deacon? It is a question that helps to define priesthood as well as diaconate.

---

[37] Holmes, "Response," in Morgan, *Diaconate Today*, 128; Timothy Sedgwick, foreword to *Raising Up Servant Ministry*, 3–4; BEM, 27.

[38] *Lambeth 1958*, 2:106-107.

[39] Countryman, *Border*, 99.

The United States was the primary setting for a trend that redirected the understanding of *diakonia* away from pastoral assistance to human service, which of course was how the first deaconesses were understood 150 years earlier. Ormonde Plater has identified three "types" of (non-transitional) deacons on the basis of their work outside the liturgy:

1. *Carriers of the sacrament.* This was the most common function of the "perpetual deacons" of the 1952–70 era in the Episcopal Church. Deacons brought consecrated eucharistic elements to the sick and shut-in who could not attend worship.

2. *Providers of social care.* For about a decade beginning in 1971, diaconate took the form of direct ministry to those in need, usually outside of the church structure. This diaconal model stood at the opposite extreme of the earlier, sacramental mode, and it defined diaconate primarily in terms of a focal point and exemplar of servanthood.

3. *Promoters of social care.* Beginning in the mid-1980s, deacons increasingly saw themselves as leaders of service: "Deacons are to lead, support, and encourage others to serve the poor, sick, and needy in the world." Their role was discerning areas for service and inspiring others to join in ministry. Unlike the implication of an individualistic, even "freelance" ministry of the second formulation, this third model is necessarily connected with the church, arising out of "a rich understanding of baptism" in which all Christians "seek and serve Christ in all persons." This last model, Plater argues, "remains the prevalent concept of the diaconate in our time."[40]

This understanding provided a means of relating to laity and other clergy by promoting the deacon as an "enabler" of lay ministry. A study carried out in 1983 cites three ways in which enablement can occur. First, by *sacramentally representing* the servant ministry as an important part of the church's ministry and through this symbol inspiring members of the congregation to engage in servant ministry. Second, by *engaging personally* in various

---

[40] Ormonde Plater, "The Search for Diaconal Identity," *Diaconal Ministry: Past, Present and Future: Essays from the Philadelphia Symposium, 1992,* ed. Peyton G. Craighill (Providence, RI: NAAD, c. 1994), 65.

diaconal ministries in the congregation, community, and institutions, thus serving as a model for the rest of the congregation. And third, by *directly enabling* lay members by designing programs to volunteer their time caring for the sick, visiting shut-ins, and raising money to help the needy of the community. One bishop remarked at the time, "Deacons symbolize, remind, and enable the Church to be servants.... In my ideal model, the deacon is really leading and developing servant ministry rather than being a servant him or herself full-time."[41]

This entire model of ministry defines diaconate as caregiving. Indeed, a NAAD guidebook states, "The main function of deacons is to serve those in need," with need usually defined in social terms. It recommends that personal qualifications for candidates include "several years of *diakonia* particularly of works of social care."[42] But does human service—tremendously important though it be—constitute the sum total of diaconal ministry beyond the liturgy? Some observers of the diaconate raise doubts about the adequacy of confining diaconate to this arena, since the historical record hints at a longstanding diversity that extended *diakonia* well beyond the exercise of charity alone. One scholar claims, "The notion of deacon as 'servant to the suffering world' compartmentalizes too narrowly this wonderfully problematic movement of the early church."[43] Both practice and theory have moved beyond these compartments.

In practice, three kinds of deacons now function in North America, distinguished by the primary locus of their ministry. First, there are *parish deacons* based in local congregations. They function in the liturgy week by week, assisting in pastoral care of parishioners and usually serving others in a ministry of social care beyond the parish. Usually unpaid and often part-time, they are (like all deacons) under the general oversight of the bishop as exercised by the rector. This is the most common form of diaconate. Next, there are the *diocesan deacons*. Following in the long tradition of deacons aiding the bishop in overseeing the diocese, these

---

[41] *Raising Up Servant Ministry,* 23, 27.

[42] Plater, ed., *Deacons in the Episcopal Church,* 17, 7.

[43] Hall Taussig, "Diaconal Special Agents," in Craighill, ed., *Diaconal Ministry,* 22

serve in administrative positions directly under the bishop's oversight, functioning liturgically in a cathedral or in one or more parishes. Such deacons may be salaried and full-time, and from among them might an archdeacon be appointed to oversee the community of deacons. Finally, there are the *professional* or *special deacons*. Sharing many characteristics of the parish or diocesan deacons and based in a parish, these are deacons called to some other work, usually full-time and often professional. They include ministries in prisons or state institutions, hospitals or places of care. This category also includes members of religious orders.[44]

So it cannot be said that all deacons engage directly in social care. Their practical role is much broader, enlarging the scope of the kind of service that they offer. Scholarship has begun to confirm this redefinition of the theory of diaconate.

REDEFINING DIAKONIA

As Urban Holmes's desire for a more penetrating look at the diaconate was fulfilled in an outpouring of books and articles, the theology of the diaconate also received deeper and more extensive thought. The thought was largely uncritical until John Collins's work, *Diakonia*, which cast a gray cloud across the sunny ideal of diaconal social servanthood. There Collins scrutinizes the language of diaconate to discern how the words of servanthood were used in ancient Graeco-Roman, Jewish, and Christian cultures. He finds that simply equating *diakonos* with "servant" is not necessarily correct; the more appropriate etymology of "servant" is *doulos* or "slave." The *diakonos* was one whose service was as messenger or go-between. Rather than the person who performs menial labor, the deacon as an agent and attendant might be entrusted with a message from one important person to another, or to a group. The notion of deacon as specifically and solely a servant of the poor, needy, and outcast, he argues, arises more from the German Evangelicals of the 1830s than from ancient and biblical understandings. Collins concludes, startlingly, that the language of *diakonia* better fits Christian missions than Christian social service.

----

[44] Plater, ed., *Deacons in the Episcopal Church*, 3–4.

> When we ask, in the light of our study, whether such language [of caregiving] accords with early Christian idiom, we can only say in brief that it does not. Further, we need to add that early Christians would not understand why their modern counterparts have so restricted the ambit of the ancient word that it now applies only to the caring sphere of the Christian life.[45]

Collins's hypothesis finds support from many sources. To name a few, the concept of deacon as messenger coincides with the examples of Stephen and Philip who carried the apostolic message, Stephen to his death, Philip to the eunuch (Acts 7; 8:4–8, 26–40). When the Episcopal Church added Philip, to its calendar of lesser feasts, it termed him "deacon and evangelist." The early history of deacons who were entrusted with high responsibilities, moreover, sustains this theory, whether it be Cyprian, who used them as "ambassadors," or Gregory the Great (himself a deacon when elected pope), who had senior deacons to administer papal estates.[46] In the 1662 Prayer Book, the deacon is charged "to search for the sick, poor, and impotent people of the Parish" and then "to intimate" that information "unto the Curate"—the rector or vicar, i.e. a priest—for the needs to be addressed, making the deacon a middleman (who, in another implication of "inferiority," cannot function on his own).[47] American Lutherans, in their recent reconsiderations of *diakonia*, perceive it to be a lay ministry that is nonetheless "*of* Word and Sacrament because it is a ministry *from* and *by* the Word and Sacraments."[48] Along the same line of Word, the Anglican writer Elaine Bardwell sees a theological rationale

---

[45] John N. Collins, *Diakonia: Re-interpreting the Ancient Sources* (New York and Oxford: OUP, 1990), 254.

[46] *Deacons in the Ministry*, 9 (¶10), 13 (¶21).

[47] 1662 BCP, 565. Note that the deacon is not directly charged with attending to those needs. This may reflect the ministerial monopoly of the priests of that era, along perhaps with an unwillingness to entrust responsibility to one who is essentially an apprentice; but it also shows a "messenger" quality to the diaconate.

[48] Lambert, "Called to Serve," 6. In 1993 the Evangelical Lutheran Church in America (ELCA) established a roster of diaconal ministers who are distinguished from the presbyterate by their focus on word and service rather than word and sacrament; they are "consecrated" rather than "ordained" to what in 1993 was understood as a lay rather than clerical ministry. Gassmann, *Historical Dictionary of Lutheranism*, s.v. "Diaconate," 90; Larson, ed., *From Word and Sacrament*, 6, 125.

for a prophetic role for the deacon, not only in the obvious function of proclaiming the gospel in the liturgy but also in searching out "the careless and indifferent." Preparing the eucharistic table symbolizes preparing the way of the Lord, and the deacon lives this out within both the church and the world.[49] In each case, the deacon acts as intermediary.

The approach that Collins and others propose can simultaneously sharpen and broaden our understanding of *diakonia*. By contrast, if limited to the ethical domain of social service, the concept may be both too diffuse and too narrow, as if *any* social service qualifies a candidate for diaconal orders, but *only* those engaged in social service need apply. Hannaford spoke to this difficulty, along with the potential theological rootlessness that can result.

> The problem with this is that ministry is detached from its theological basis in the divine commission bestowed upon the whole Church and is attached instead to the ethical responsibilities shared by all Christians.... When diakonia is interpreted as humble service and treated as an ordinary, and indeed univocal, feature of Christian life, it becomes impossible to distinguish not only between the ordained and non-ordained ministry but also between what is and is not ministry. Ministry becomes part of the undifferentiated responsibility of all Christian individuals.[50]

If Hannaford is correct, Collins's work may also help in resolving the major issue of contention, which is the alleged conflict between the "ministry of the laity" and the "ministry of the deacon." The concept of a servant as "messenger" points a way forward. As one rooted in costly service, with Stephen the martyr in mind, the deacon brings a message. The message is, on the one hand, the gospel to the world; on the other, the deacon brings to the church a word of the world in all its needs and agonies. The deacon becomes a genuine go-between, carrying vitally important messages—one for the church and one of life-and-death significance for the world. Though the deacon may serve in some social capacity, the primary

---

[49] Bardwell, "Pastoral Role," in Hall, ed., *Deacon's Ministry*, 54–55 (q. *ASB*, 344).

[50] Robert Hannaford, "Foundations for an Ecclesiology of Ministry," in Hall and Hannaford, eds., *Order and Ministry*, 25–26.

purpose of the deacon lies beyond the service itself. It finds its liturgical focus, first, when the deacon proclaims the gospel in the Eucharist, in giving a word to the church, a word to the world; second, in leading the intercessions; and third, in sharing in the administration of communion, as if to feed both church and world on the body and blood of Jesus, the Word made flesh. In each function, the deacon *communicates*. These three areas of gospel, intercession, and table correspond with Collins's categories of messenger, agent, and attendant.[51]

Diaconate, then, may become a unique role within the church. The church specifically assigns deacons with a distinctive task through a process of calling, testing, and ultimately ordination. Their job differs from what all Christians are called to do in that these "messengers" are designated by the church as envoys both to its own and to the population at large. In one sense, all Christians share in this form of *diakonos*, be they laypersons, bishops, priests, or deacons. They join in proclaiming in word and deed the Good News of Christ as a baptismal responsibility.[52] Serving the needy whether within the church or outside of it, improving the quality of life for humanity, binding up wounds, feeding the hungry, *and* proclaiming the kingdom of God—all fulfill what Jesus asked his disciples to do. A deacon helps to reveal the nature of this double task as well as, on occasion, leading the effort. The deacon's message to the church, therefore, may differ from what others may offer. He or she speaks, in this sense, prophetically. Thus the deacon serves the assembled Body of Christ in a particular way, as a messenger by word and deed *to* the church.

IMPLICATIONS FOR THE INTERMEDIARY MINISTRY

If this understanding of the deacon as a messenger is correct, it may hold important, even exciting, ramifications for the church. One possibility is that a revived diaconate will help to sharpen the understandings of various ministries generally. The Diocese of Northern Michigan, for example, has pioneered new ways of utilizing orders in the Episcopal Church:

---

[51] Plater, "Search for Diaconal Identity," in Craighill, ed., *Diaconal Ministry*, 69.

[52] US BCP, 305; Canada, *Alternative Services*, 159.

> Congregations across the country are discovering that
> when deacons are in place in a congregation the entire
> congregation grows in its understanding about how to
> respond to the needs of the world. If the role of priest
> were clearer, less muddled by hierarchical expectations,
> the priests among us could become clearer models for
> how we can exercise priestly ministry in our daily
> lives.[53]

For deacons, a sharper and more focused role in the life of the church can better illustrate what they are specifically called to do. It does not so much replace their current efforts as clarify what those efforts are, and why they are done by a deacon. To take one example, a bishop perceives the need to develop a ministry to prisons in the diocese, one that includes evangelical outreach and social concern for inmates and their families. The bishop appoints a deacon to organize a program in one prison, recruit lay and clergy volunteers (even involving whole parishes), and communicate the results to the diocese at large with the goal of developing similar programs in other prisons. A layperson could fill these functions, but ordination gives to the deacon the particular responsibilities for this work on behalf of Christ and church. In negotiating with prison authorities, the deacon carries the special authorization of the bishop, which bestows an official legitimacy upon the deacon, and that authorization may be just as important in communicating with the diocese.

A deacon's task differs from that of the laity, not so much in its outward manifestation but in its more basic aim. As one example, for the layperson, a ministry of social caregiving arises out of the discipleship of every baptized Christian; laypeople care for others because this is what Jesus did, and this is what it means to follow him. For the deacon involved with social care, all those motives are also present, but in addition is the motive of communication. This work is at once a proclamation by the church to the world in the name of Christ and a proclamation to the church from the world in the name of Christ. Both layperson and deacon

---

[53] Carol Hosler, "Northern Michigan's Response for Direct Ordination: Baptized to Apostolic, Priestly, Diaconal Ministry," in Hallenbeck, ed., *Orders of Ministry*, 8.

serve to represent Christ and the church, but with the deacon matters are more precise. Service becomes not only an act but a veritable word—that is to say, a declaration in the form of deed. To see the deacon's role in this way can in turn assist in raising the consciousness of the entire church. As the authors of *Deacons at Your Service* write, "The renewal of the diaconate would not be a confiscation of ministry from the laity, putting it firmly in the hands of yet more clergy. It would be a means of enabling the *whole* church to respond to the urgent cry from the world for effective ministry and caring."[54]

Unlike the laity, furthermore, deacons as ordained persons are under *orders*. Organists, churchwardens, lay diocesan or parish aides, church school teachers, or committee leaders may hold responsibilities of office, but they do not make the same promises or have the same expectations as one who is in an "ordered" ministry.[55] They are not, for instance, subject to the bishop's reassigning them routinely or on the basis of need, nor do they assume the same discipline that the canons expect of the clergy. Deacons do.

If the relationship between layperson and deacon shifts, so it does among deacon, priest, and bishop. Many deacons fulfill their ministries in parish settings, placing them closer to presbyters than to bishops. In Collins's redefinition, the deacon may assist the priest not only in the service she or he renders, but also by acting as a "go-between" for the priest and the world. As the intermediary between church and world, the deacon is able to bring a different set of concerns to the discussion, offering a balance of concerns and a variety in perspective, so that the gospel can be heard from different sources. As for the bishop, the deacon can become not only the "eyes and ears" but the mouthpiece as well, speaking to the bishop, but also speaking *for* the bishop to the communities within and without the church. In the rite of consecration the bishop pledges "a special concern for the outcast and needy"[56]; the deacon helps the bishop to demonstrate just that.

Furthermore, so long as priests and bishops are first ordained as deacons, deacons may bring out the diaconal qualities of priestly

---

[54] Alison White and Di Williams, *Deacons at Your Service* (Bramcote, Notts: Grove Books, 1987), 3.

[55] Melinsky, *Shape*, 135–136.

[56] ASB, 389 (‖ US BCP, 518; NZ, 918; Aus., 804).

and episcopal ministries. We shall pursue this point in discussing proposals to eliminate the prerequisite of diaconate for priesthood.

Allowing this vision to come to life, however, may make several demands upon the church as it does its work today. An easy step is removing the requirement that deacons be licensed by the bishop to preach; if theirs is a "messenger" order, permission to preach ought to be inherent in ordination.[57] If bishops retain the right to license deacons, the license to preach should be given freely. More complex would be revising ordination rites to incorporate what may, in fact, be the long-overlooked but highly traditional emphasis of deacons as "go-betweens." How deacons are trained, too, is diverging from the training of priests; instead of the academic model of seminary or theological college experience, diaconal programs begun in various dioceses of the Episcopal Church tend to focus upon practical, hands-on preparation. Likewise, local settings are proving to be more appropriate for diaconal training "in the world" than campuses purposefully set apart for reflection. Not that theological content is ignored: for the deacon to serve as a "messenger" of the gospel and as an agent of the church, an understanding of the gospel and the church's teachings and traditions is required.

Creating an environment in which deacons may more fully function in this mediatorial ministry confronts the church with another challenge, that of trying to attain a level of partnership among all parties that can allow deacons to exercise their role. Collegiality is the key, along with the mutual trust, recognition, and appreciation that must accompany it. If deacons return to anything like their primitive role, task, and status, they may well face the resentment of others. Something very like this evidently happened in the fifth and sixth centuries; during this "golden era," deacons accumulated considerable power, whereupon bishops and priests began to diminish their role. Today, especially if deacons attain to renewed levels of responsibility, then their integrity lies in keeping central their fundamental purpose, which is that of serving

---

[57] Doe, *Canon Law*, 146. Brazil already identifies proclaiming the Word of God to be among the deacon's functions (ibid.); compare the anemic statement in ECUSA's BCP ordination rite, "You are to assist the bishop and priests in public worship and in the ministration of God's Word and Sacraments" (543).

as messenger. To that end, Philip the deacon and evangelist and Stephen the martyr make for especially poignant patron saints.

THE QUESTION OF DIRECT ORDINATION

If the diaconate is as distinctive and important as we have alleged, then why does it not stand on its own? If someone is called to the priesthood, why ordain that person first to the diaconate? Does that not condemn the diaconate to the "inferior" status that has been so rightly expunged from the language of our prayer books—especially when such a diaconate will last but a year or less as an apprenticeship to priesthood rather than in the service that *diakonia* implies?

As the the third millennium begins, no province of the Anglican Communion ordains priests who have not first been ordained deacons, nor bishops who have not been ordained priests and thereby deacons. Thus Anglican practice parallels that of Greek Orthodox and Roman Catholic churches. This sequence, by which one order follows upon another after a period of time (an "interstice"), is known as the *cursus honorum*.[58] This Latin term denotes the career ladder of Roman republic days, in which a man aspiring to high ranks of military or civil service would serve in successive offices on his way to his goal. In secular medieval Europe, the ascent was similar: the ambitious squire became a knight and kept ascending as high as possible in a hierarchy headed by king and emperor. Not surprisingly, the church borrowed from the culture. Though known by the time of Cyprian, the *cursus* took on new relevance at the time of Constantine, when rising through the church's ranks suddenly became as enticing as rising through the empire's. The aspiring young cleric, having started in "minor

---

[58] Doe, *Canon Law*, 132; J. Robert Wright, "Sequential or Cumulative Orders vs. Direct Ordination," *ATR*, 75, no. 2 (Spring 1993), 246–247; John St. H. Gibaut, *The Cursus Honorum: A Study of the Origins and Evolution of Sequential Ordination* (New York: Peter Lang, 2000), 320–323. See also Mitchell, "Direct Ordination," in Hallenbeck, ed., *Orders of Ministry*, 42; Louis Weil, "Should the Episcopal Church Permit Direct Ordination?" in Hallenbeck, ed., *Orders of Ministry*, 53–54; John St. H. Gibaut, "Sequential Ordination in Historical Perspective: A Response to J. Robert Wright," in Hallenbeck, ed., *Orders of Ministry*, 75–80.

orders" of doorkeeper, reader, and acolyte, would advance to the "major orders" of subdeacon, deacon, and priest. Though priesthood was the pinnacle of orders in late medieval theology, a fortunate few would continue to the lofty realms of bishop, metropolitan (archbishop), and, for some, pope. The progression was, among other things, a means of testing to ensure the worthiness and experience of leaders. But as Louis Weil notes from experience, "We are ordaining people and sending them into pastoral situations to which their transitional diaconate is inappropriate to the needs of the community."[59] Candidates for priesthood would solemnly assert first that they were called to the diaconate, "with fingers crossed," in order to reach the presbyteral goal.

With the return of a distinctive diaconate, the argument has been made for "direct ordination" that sometimes goes by another Latin description, *per saltum*, meaning "by a leap." Someone called to priesthood would "leap over" the step of diaconate; similarly, a bishop could be ordained directly from diaconate (or, presumably, from the laity). Only that, it is argued, can restore the diaconate as "a full and equal order." Barnett, who uses that last phrase as his subtitle, was among the first and most ardent advocates of *per saltum* ordinations. For him, the *cursus honorum* has been largely responsible for the decline of the diaconate, so the first step in genuinely restoring the "essential character of the ministry of the pre-Nicene Church is the reassertion of the principle that each order and office is a distinct and distinctive vocation to which the Holy Spirit calls the various members of the Church as he wills."[60] Abandoning the requirements of passing through successive orders or offices, it is argued, becomes a necessary part in that restorative process. Weil writes that Gregory Dix, known for his research into the ancient liturgies of the church,

> characterizes the understanding of orders in the pre-Nicene Church as organic, each ministerial function relating directly to the whole Christian society, rather than relating to other ministerial functions in some defined, sequential pattern. In this context, direct ordination

---

[59] Weil, "Should the Episcopal Church Permit Direct Ordination?" in Hallenbeck, ed., *Orders of Ministry*, 60.

[60] Barnett, *Diaconate*, 145.

occurred when a local church discerned gifts for a particular ministry in a person, then elected and ordained
that person without requiring some transitional ordinations
along the way.[61]

In other words, if someone in the early church were perceived to
have charisms for ministry, the community would ordain that person
to an order appropriate to those gifts. In current liturgical practice,
a prior order is (usually) not presumed; *The Book of Common
Prayer* requires a candidate to be presented without vestments or
insignia of a current order. Byron Stuhlman comments that "baptism
is (from a liturgical if not from a canonical standpoint) the only
prerequisite status for ordination to any order."[62]

North Americans have been among the strongest proponents
of direct ordination, though with evident endorsement from the
1958 Lambeth Conference. In 1992 the Council of Associated
Parishes called on the church

to return to the early tradition of ordaining persons
directly to the order to which they have been called. The
only sacramental prerequisite for ordaining a bishop,
priest, or deacon is baptism. All members of the church
should be eligible for ordination directly to any of the
three orders.[63]

Against that enthusiasm, J. Robert Wright of General Seminary
stood virtually alone in questioning a proposal that would essentially remove the diaconal element from the priesthood. I share his
point of view, in part because of the questionable rationale for
what amounts to a drastic change in traditional practice accepted
across Anglican and ecumenical lines and in part because the theology of orders I propose considers *diakonia* so important that it
undergirds all ministry altogether. Collins's scholarship, I believe,
makes the case for the traditional practice all the stronger.

---

[61] Weil, "Should the Episcopal Church Permit Direct Ordination?" in Hallenbeck,
ed., *Orders of Ministry*, 55.

[62] Stuhlman, *Occasions of Grace*, 282.

[63] *Lambeth 1958* (Res. #88, recommending that each province "consider whether
the office of Deacon shall be restored to its primitive place as a distinctive order
in the Church, instead of being regarded as a probationary period for the priesthood"), 1.50; 2.106–107; Associated Parishes Council, "Calling for Direct Ordination—Toronto Statement," in Hallenbeck, ed., *Orders of Ministry*, 9.

"Direct ordination" concerns only priests and bishops. All deacons are "directly" ordained. At issue is whether diaconate is an obligatory step along the path to other ordinations, hence demeaning the order to the status of a stepping stone. Although some scholars argue that direct ordination was the universal or standard practice in the early church,[64] it is impossible to generalize about what the early church did or did not do, and this chapter has explored evidence that "direct ordination" was not necessarily standard practice. Even so ardent a proponent of direct ordination as John Gibaut nonetheless confessed that "all one can say is that both direct *and* sequential ordination have ample witnesses" in history.[65]

Opponents of sequential ordination through the three orders quote F. J. Hall who observed—echoing Thomas Aquinas—that ordination to a "greater" order presumes a "lesser." *Per saltum* ordinations, they argue, would restore dignity to diaconate and integrity to all three orders. But "leaping over" one order to the next as a means of uplifting that which has been leapt over hardly exalts that which has been skipped. Moreover, given widespread understandings of the distinct functionalities of each order (e.g., deacons for service; priests for sacraments; bishops for oversight and ordination), a priest ordained *per saltum* will be assumed to have receive the servanthood of diaconate in the bargain—automatically, as it were. And a bishop directly ordained also will receive the liturgical powers of priesthood. These presumptions inescapably perpetuate a cumulative or prioritized understanding of the three orders anyway.

While both ecclesiological metaphors of Body and Trinity seem to argue for direct ordination, in chapter 6 I proposed that in fact a bishop *is* diaconal and a deacon *is* presbyteral—if only in certain aspects of their lives and ministries. More broadly, the philosophical thinking that sustains the organic image holds that the body is a microcosm of the whole. That principle ascribes both diversity and inclusion to the corporate body, which can be many things at the same time: it can be priestly *and* diaconal. So too with the individual. A person may at once be child/spouse/parent, or supervisor/peer/employee, or a myriad other roles in home, work, community, and church. The primary roles shift periodically as new

---

[64] Associated Parishes, "Toronto Statement," 9; Ormonde Plater, "Direct Ordination: The Historical Evidence," 38, Mitchell, "Direct Ordination," 41, all in Hallenbeck, ed., *Orders of Ministry*.

[65] Gibaut, "Sequential Ordination," in Hallenbeck, ed., *Orders of Ministry*, 91, emph in orig.

responsibilities arise, without necessarily obliterating what one has been before. My parents have died and so in the family context I am primarily spouse and parent, but in a spiritual and psychological sense I remain their child, and they my parents.

Proponents of direct ordination also make much of the fact that the "transitional deacon" has his or her eyes focused primarily upon priesthood, reducing diaconate to a mere "apprenticeship." In England and other provinces in the Anglican Communion, the one-year diaconate has become the standard. Within the Episcopal Church, however, canons allow a shortening of the one-year period to six months, and this is practiced perhaps more often than not for those deacons moving on to priesthood. Even so, in a parish setting, which is where most new priestly bound ordinands are placed, the apprenticeship is *also* to the diaconate if the supervising rector takes parochial work at all seriously. For diaconate is inherent in the Anglican concept of parochial priesthood. In *The Country Parson*, Simon Goodenough describes Parson Hawker of Morwenstow "striding through the driving snow on a stormy night in his wild Cornish parish to bring fuel and blankets to his isolated flock...clad in his claret-coloured coat and flying tails over a blue jersey with a red cross knitted on one side, with his brimless plum beaver pulled down over his head, fishing boots above the knee and a yellow poncho when he rode his mule."[66] Eccentricities aside, Parson Hawker forms part of the lore that constitutes the ethos of Anglican presbyterate, whose self-sacrificing service to the "flock" is diaconal in nature.

Well beyond the parson, tremendous diaconal ministry occurs within the congregational structure, whether of pastoral care, of social service, or of serving as the agents or messengers of Christ and church, as Collins's research suggests. That work may not be called "diaconal" nor would it ever be done by deacons alone even if more distinctive deacons existed. In their absence, the work devolves upon priests and laypersons. One priest writes that "much of the work of the parish priest in most congregations is diaconal, rather than priestly, in nature. Thus, I exercise the diaconate almost daily."[67] From priests and laity, as well as from

---

[66] Simon Goodenough, *The Country Parson* (Newton Abbot, London and North Pomfret, VT: David & Charles, 1983), 38.

[67] Charles B. King, Jr., "A Confusing Proposal," in Hallenbeck, ed., *Orders of Ministry*, 13.

distinctive deacons, the transitional deacon has much to learn when growing into the new role the bishop has bestowed on behalf of Christ and church. The new deacon can learn, moreover, not only from the ordained but also from laity whose discipleship leads them into servanthood or from nearby deacons who are pursuing effective ministries. Apprenticeship to priesthood is no less an apprenticeship to diaconate.

Hensley Henson's plea for a longer diaconate for those proceeding to priesthood remains a point worth pondering. Among the reasons underlying both his suggestion and the *cursus honorum* generally is the chance to examine and prepare candidates for the office to which they will be ordained. Currently in the Episcopal Church, bishops and commissions on ministry often require aspirants for Holy Orders to live for a time as laypersons in the life of the church before moving toward orders. The same principle can be applied to diaconate; ordinands could serve for at least a year as deacons before becoming priests. That would require only the institutional will to avoid making exceptions and allowing "priestings" in six months, as mine was. The main objection may be utterly pragmatic, that parishes and rectors want priests to share in providing sacramental ministry as soon as possible. With this in mind, some dioceses have begun ordaining its candidates as deacons well before they graduate from seminary, in order to produce priests more quickly. But what does this say about diaconate? The process does allow for a full experience of diaconal ministry in the final year of preparation.[68] I am not aware, however, of any programs aimed specifically at addressing the diaconal side of priestly training, and while field-work placements theoretically can be expanded, I wonder how likely that would be to give a thorough grounding in diaconate.

Finally, the history of the diaconate suggests that direct ordination was practiced at least to some extent. But what was the purpose of that? Gibaut concedes, "It would seem that in the patristic

---

[68] Cf. Benjamin A. Shambaugh, "A Call for Curacy: Following a Residency Model by Getting Congregations Involved as 'Teaching Parishes,'" in Humphrey, ed., *Gathering the NeXt Generation*, 50; and Weil, "Should the Episcopal Church Permit Direct Ordination?" in Hallenbeck, ed., *Orders of Ministry*, 60–61. Along a similar line, Leonel Mitchell suggests considering the preparatory stages of "postulancy" and "candidacy" as equivalents of "minor orders" that permit the church to examine the fitness of potential ordinands (Mitchell, "Direct Ordination," in Hallenbeck, ed., *Orders of Ministry*, 44).

period sequential ordination met a pastoral rather than a theological or sacramental concern."[69] Likewise, pastoral needs of the modern church may, in the end, take priority over historical precedents or even theological conviction left over from earlier days. However, what is considered "pastoral" in one moment in time can sometimes be merely expedient. History, theology, and, ultimately, the Spirit's guidance cannot be ignored.

At this juncture my critique turns toward the positive: that "serial" ordination serves an enormously helpful pastoral purpose precisely because of the importance of *diakonia*. Identifying the diaconal nature of parochial ministry, which includes care both to the congregation and to the wider community, can be a reason to celebrate. From my experience, too many congregations lambaste themselves for "not doing enough in the community" when in fact they are intensely active either individually or corporately. Some, of course, can indeed do more or do it differently so that their service is more genuinely diaconal. Deacons can help them to identify, classify, analyze, and improve upon what *diakonia* they are already offering.

For one of the major contributions to the diaconate as an order is its witness to the servanthood of the church. I have argued that this witness is itself a distinctive aspect of ordained diaconate, amplified when it is proclaimed within the wider gospel that is the deacon's ambassadorial role. Barnett is convinced that it "informs all orders of the primary work we are all sent to do."[70] I agree but in a somewhat different way. In a double sense, the diaconate edifies the work of the church at large and the discipleship (in this regard) that all claim to pursue. As for the ordered few, diaconate, with all its rich meaning, becomes a foundation for all ordained ministry. The Diocese of Chile tried in 1986 to remove transitional diaconate, but the move was defeated by one vote in provincial synod of the Southern Cone "largely on the grounds that bishops and priests should never lose sight of their *diaconia*."[71] Priests and bishops alike trace their ministry to this humble servanthood, and

---

[69] Gibaut, "Sequential Ordination," in Hallenbeck, ed., *Orders of Ministry*, 80.

[70] Barnett, *Diaconate*, xiii–xvi.

[71] Plater, "Historical Evidence," in Hallenbeck, ed., *Orders of Ministry*, 37 (spelling in orig.).

would do well to remember it—as would the entire church.[72]

The criticisms of current practice, however, warrant attention. Were the church to reaffirm the traditional practice of ordaining first to the diaconate and then to the priesthood, this ecclesial practice should be true to itself so that diaconate is an explicit element of the presbyteral persona. Supervising clergy can ensure that the newly ordained they oversee have an effective exposure to diaconal as well as priestly work. A training program might well include significant involvement in a diaconal project. Dioceses, likewise, can provide programs of training and mutual support that could include *all* deacons, without distinction, which would also serve to build up the collegiality so crucial to the church of the new century. Only then will deacons "know how to work as part of a team, how to work with volunteers, and how to strengthen others in their ministry in the world."[73]

Only as deacons are accorded esteem as *deacons*, however, can they be part of a team. Many a deacon, ordained specifically to that order, cites the recurring question, "So when will you become a priest?" That should become as absurd as a priest's being asked, "So when will you become a bishop?" Some day, the question will be relegated to the dustbins of obsolete concepts, along with the hierarchical sense that it perpetuates. In the Body of Christ, where each member has a role and purpose, each warrants—and should extend—respect. Then the Body can function most truly.

DIACONATE AS FOUNDATION

A dear friend of mine was proceeding toward ordination. She clearly had a call to priesthood and everyone knew it. Not only had she published several fine books on spirituality, but for some time she had also led a ministry of spiritual direction that extended even to some in monastic orders. Around six months after her diaconal ordination, I stopped by the church where she was the

---

[72] The one possible exception, in which I believe direct ordination does make more sense, is that of "local" priests whose role is specifically limited (cf. chapter 10). However, the ecumenical and inter-Anglican concerns that Wright raised are substantial enough not to proceed until much further discussion has occurred.

[73] Plater, ed., *Deacons in the Episcopal Church*, 14.

assistant and asked when the priestly step would come. Not for some months, she answered. She was in no hurry, she added, because to her surprise, she was discovering the value of diaconate.

If discipleship is the foundation of all of Christian life, diaconate is the foundation of all ministerial life, for the very nature of ministry is rooted in baptism and service. "I am among you as one who serves," Jesus told his disciples as he commended them to do likewise. As all are disciples, all have a diaconal ministry to offer. Their being and their servanthood break down barriers between church and society, between one order and another, between human and divine. As Thomas Ray writes,

> The diaconate became a fresh, clean, clear window through which we could see that ordained ordered ministry is not territorial.... The diaconate revealed to us that this order was called not to do our servant ministry for us, but to reveal to us a dimension of the depth of the meaning of baptism.... Ordination orders every deacon to remind us, to reveal to us, encourage us, affirm us in that serving ministry that is already deeply embedded in our lives, hallowing our homes, workplaces, neighborhoods, community, and church, but rarely recognized, affirmed, and respected.[74]

Deacons have, in the end, an eschatological brightness about them. They reveal what the new reality of God is about and what, in God's good time, all shall know and be. So deacons may be servants of the church, serving laypeople, priests, bishops, or world, but ultimately, their service is the perfect freedom of the kingdom that shall come.

But perfect freedom is not unduly confined. Therein lies the danger of a circumscribed diaconate, one that is so focused on an individual aspect of *diakonia* that other manifestations are not possible. To define a deacon solely, or primarily, as one directly connected with human service limits a broader range of servanthood. It is as limiting in one respect as it is in another, that of restricting the diaconate to those preparing for priesthood. As powerful and vital as caregiving must always be in the life of the Christian church and as great a contribution as many deacons can

---

[74] Ray, "Small Church," 622. (Ray was Bishop of Northern Michigan at the time.)

make in expressing a major concern of the entire Body of Christ, diaconate so conceived may become too specialized a ministry within a broader framework. Evangelism might well be considered alongside social care and, it has two patron saints among the earliest seven—Stephen and Philip—who, if they were in fact deacons, may provide an even stronger biblical warrant for the deacon as evangelist as well as servant.

Notice the vibrant diversity among presbyters. Some are parish clergy, some diocesan officials. Some serve as academicians in universities, seminaries, or other schools as teachers, headmasters, deans, or chaplains. Non-stipendiary ministries have come to flourish in new fields of endeavor, as we shall explore in a later chapter. The same can be said of bishops. Most are heads of dioceses while some are in specialized ministries of suffragan, national-church administration, or assisting parishes or dioceses as retirees. As of this writing, one American bishop is headmaster of a prestigious boarding school and another is the dean of a seminary. Their service generally surrounds duties that are appropriate to their order, but they are not strictly limited in what they may offer.

Of the three ordained orders, diaconate has shown the most flexibility in adapting to the needs of the age. The initial concern of the earliest church was proclaiming the gospel, and whether or not Stephen and Philip can be considered diaconal figures, that is certainly what they did. In subsequent centuries, bishops required help in tending to human concerns and administering the church; they evidently handed considerable responsibility for those tasks to deacons. Given the medieval emphasis upon the Mass, the church needed priests, and that is what deacons quickly became, serving in this case by virtually disappearing. With the decline of monasteries and the charity they provided, Martin Luther wanted deacons to meet the continuing demand for human care. When the Industrial Revolution produced enormous social dislocations, diaconal ministries were revived, often for and sometimes by women. In postwar America, the booming life in parish churches craved help, and diaconate was reinvented again as a parochial servanthood. In the post-1960s era of social consciousness, the role of deacon was channeled anew into social service.

Not only has diaconate been the most adaptable of the three orders, but it is also the most directly missionary. Bishops may be the chief missionaries, but they necessarily occupy themselves with the mission of their dioceses and the church at large. With many an exception, priests primarily focus upon parish communities. Deacons, however, share with laity a focus upon the world about them, in service, evangelism, and mission.

If the diaconate has any hope of becoming a "full and equal order," then it too ought to be freed from the limitations that the thinking of an era imposes. For deacons can be ecclesiologically adaptable, able to serve in ways that a constantly changing world demands. If given the license, guided by the Holy Spirit and the bishop, remaining fully engaged with the Christian community, deacons hold the possibility of once again being entrusted, as Ignatius admired in the second century, with the ministry of Jesus Christ.

IX

The Ministry of the Laity

What is the province of the laity? To hunt, to shoot, to
entertain. These matters they understand, but to meddle
with ecclesiastical matters, they have no right at all.[1]

Few Anglicans would dare utter these words that Monsignor
George Talbot wrote to his Roman Catholic Archbishop
Manning in 1857, although one Anglican came close. In 1868 the
Rev. Luke Rivington, SSC, soon to become a Roman Catholic,
described "the office of *the laity, whose high and noble preroga-*
tive it was to LISTEN and OBEY."[2] By contrast, at about the
same time, the Church of England created the office of Reader as
an opportunity for the layman to share in the church's ministry. At
least some laity would do more than listen.

A trend had begun, one that grew as the twentieth century
progressed. Increasing numbers of laity became involved as the
church in England and around the Anglican Communion
embraced the lay order in theory and in practice. At first, like
many a cherished heirloom, lay inclusion had been an idea more

---

[1] Q. by many, including Tiller, *Strategy*, 67, and Kenneth G. Grubb, *A Layman
Looks at the Church* (London: Hodder & Stoughton, 1964), 26.

[2] Reed, *Glorious Battle*, 134 (emph. in orig.).

admired than used. Then in the postwar years, it was dusted off, tried out, and found to be useful after all. In the enthusiasm for its renewed usefulness, though, how lay ministry functions within the church's ministry and work has not always been carefully considered. Tensions within the shared priesthood of the *laos*, and also for and with presbyters, have been the result.

In theory, the principle of full lay participation is as old as Anglicanism itself, and it profoundly influenced the Anglican understanding of ministry. As far as Anglican reformers were concerned, clergy are never to operate alone either in leadership or in worship. After all, monarchs nominated bishops and other key clerics, while lay patrons often appointed vicars of parish churches. Parliament must approve changes to the official *Book of Common Prayer* (as it twice refused to do in the 1920s and has not been invited to consider since). For eucharistic celebrations, at least one or two others *had* to be present: there would be no "private masses." Moreover, ending the "minor orders" shifted at least some responsibilities previously held by clerics onto the shoulders of Reformation-era laypeople. In 1840 Thomas Arnold, the famous headmaster of Rugby School, called for an even greater role for the laity, saying, "To revive Christ's church is to restore its disenfranchised members, the laity, to the discharge of their proper duties in it." George Moberly's 1868 Bampton Lectures echoed this theme, and two years before he spoke, the church had already created a veritable minor order of Readers who were all laity. Lightfoot provided a theological basis when he upheld the unity of all Christians in personal communion with God without distinction: "As individuals, all Christians are priests alike." He was so emphatic that Moberly and Gore felt he overstated his point. But Moberly *fils*, like his father, made a place for the laity at the ministerial table, and Liddon predicted that reviving the laity would revive the church. Edward King, an Anglo-Catholic teaching at Oxford prior to becoming Bishop of Lincoln, advised his clerical brethren of the late 1880s to "remove the idea that clergy are the church. Try to make the laity realize the part they have to play in the matter." Temple wrestled with whether laity could preside at some kind of Eucharist. Admittedly, all these champions of laity were themselves clerics. A joint committee of the Convocation of Canterbury that produced *The Position of the Laity in the Church* in 1902 consisted of seven bishops, three deans, four archdeacons, six other clergy, but not a single layperson.[3]

Still, the issue was not new when the prominence of the laity came into its own in the postwar period. *Lumen Gentium*, the 1964 Roman Catholic declaration of the Second Vatican Council, made headlines when it stated that laity were to be included more fully in the life of the church. With less publicity, Anglicans had already taken much the same direction at Lambeth in 1958. The assembled bishops looked at the daunting missionary task confronting the church and realized the vital role that laity must play for the church to have any hope of success. By "laity" they meant "all those who are seeking to fulfil the membership of the Church which is theirs by baptism."[4] The theme also ran through the Anglican Congress of 1963, which "realized the fundamental importance of the laity as partners with the clergy in the whole work of the Church." The Mutual Responsibility and Interdependence (MRI) document declared, "Men and women in every nation and every church are searching in an unprecedented way to find how to serve as Christians and to fulfil Christ's ministry to the world in their own lives."[5] Any number of works heralded the "liberation of the laity," and by the 1960s, they were being written by laypeople themselves.[6] "A very clear sense of lay leadership in local churches has been an important fruit of the Episcopal

---

[3] Q. in Esther de Waal, "New Style Parson: The Professionalisation of the Nineteenth-century Clergy," in James M. M. Francis and Leslie J. Francis, eds., *Tentmaking: Perspectives on Self-Supporting Ministry* (Leominster: Gracewing, 1998), 74; G. Moberly, *Administration*, xi, 194, 204, 227, 244 (see chapters 1 and 2, above). Lightfoot, *Christian Ministry*, 1, 7; Liddon, *Sermons*, 199–200; q. in Chadwick, *Spirit of the Oxford Movement*, 295; Grubb, *Layman*, 26.

[4] *Lambeth 1958*, 2.112–114. Does the phrasing imply a distinction between those baptized who "seek to fulfill" their membership from those who do not?— a live issue in established England where many are baptized but few are active.

[5] "The Congress Message" and "MRI," in Fairweather, *Anglican Congress 1963*, 265 and 120.

[6] Especially notable are Hendrik Kraemer, *A Theology of the Laity* (London: Lutterworth Press, 1958); Stephen Neill and Hans-Ruedi Weber, eds., *The Layman in Christian History: A Project of the Department on the Laity of the World Council of Churches* (Philadelphia: Westminster Press, 1963); Grubb, *Layman* (1964); Anne W. Rowthorn, *The Liberation of the Laity* (Wilton, CT: Morehouse-Barlow, 1986).

Church's shift in emphasis over the past fifty years," the Zacchaeus Project concluded in 1999.[7]

It may not be too much to say that Anglican laity are more visibly active in liturgy and in ongoing mission and ministry than ever before. Their involvement has been progressing for centuries. From the days of the Reformation, the Church of England's "governor" has been a layperson—the monarch—and Parliament has retained official say.[8] American Episcopalians wrote lay participation into their constitution in 1789 by mandating that laity are to constitute half of the House of Deputies of its General Convention. Australia established a synodical polity that involved laity and non-purpled clergy in the 1850s.[9] In 1970 the English revamped their Church Assembly, created in 1919, into a General Synod that included laity. But the tide was taking Anglicanism well beyond governance alone. A 1969 report to the Church of England delineated the trend:

> We inherit a structure of ministry, appropriate enough
> to an earlier period of church history, which consists of
> orders of clergy doing things to or for a receptive or
> passive laity.

The clergy teach	The laity learn
preach	listen
administer sacraments	receive them
exercise pastoral care	are cared for

> We are steadily moving into a situation in which we
> want to speak dynamically of diversities of lay ministry;
> a situation in which the whole church must engage itself
> afresh in mission. We want to use the phrase "lay ministry"
> not just in the old sense of an obedient laity...but in a

---

[7] Episcopal Church Foundation, *Zacchaeus Project*, 30.

[8] Parliament also retains control over certain decisions of the Church of England, such as changes to *The Book of Common Prayer;* and Parliament, other than those bishops who sit in the House of Lords, is composed of laity to the explicit exclusion of clergy. For current canons, see Doe, *Canon Law*, 45, 165–166.

[9] Cf. Bruce Kaye, "The 1850 Bishops Conference and the Strange Birth of Australian Synods" (The Sydney Smith Lecture, Melbourne, Australia), 15 November 2000 (unpubl. paper).

further sense which sees the church as no longer, even vestigially, coterminous with society, but as sent to penetrate it.[10]

Laypeople came to assume a wide range of responsibilities that had been long associated with the clergy—in part because the latter were in short supply, in part because of their eagerness to share in the ministry of the church, and in part because of the theological inclusiveness of emerging ecclesiology.

Yet the increase in lay activity has also brought confusion. Who does what in the life and ministry of the church? For laypeople to take on new roles has allowed the church in some places to endure and in others to thrive. It has also caused some clergy to question their own identity and purpose. At the same time, *lay* identity has shifted. From his English vantage point, Wesley Carr notes the dynamic:

> As the role of the clergy changes, or is believed to change, so that of the laity is bound to be affected. This change, however, is not merely one of role. It is...to do with the priest's authority. Where there is such uncertainty, parallel questioning on the part of the laity will ensue about their authority as Christians. This causes in part the current polarizing of views on what is lay ministry. At one pole the desire is expressed for a quasi-clerical role. Training then becomes the acquisition of knowledge and techniques. The other pole is the view that the laity constitute the church in the world and that lay development has little or nothing to do with their role as church members.[11]

Some have proposed that laity themselves constitute an order of ministry, while others declare that laity should have the right to preside at the Eucharist—which is precisely what the diocesan synod of Sydney, Australia, did in 1999. In that sense, the very concept of lay ministry itself has run the risk of becoming "churchified," if not "clericalized." Instead of occurring primarily in "the world"— meaning work, home, and community—it can come to mean those

---

[10] Church of England, ACCM, *Ordained Ministry Today*, 14.

[11] Wesley Carr, *The Priestlike Task: A Model for Developing and Training the Church's Ministry* (London: SPCK, 1985), 89.

services that maintain the church, such as lay eucharistic ministers, altar guild, and vestry or comparable governing bodies. Important though these functions are, they dramatically limit the concept of lay ministry.

A book on priesthood, then, must consider the laity, who share in the priesthood of the *laos* and who minister, in their way, alongside presbyters. For us the question take three forms: (1) Is there a ministry of the laity? (2) Is there a lay "order"? (3) Should laity preside at the Eucharist? How we answer these questions will influence concepts of priesthood and efforts at mission because they directly concern clergy-lay relationships, identity, and who does what in the church—and why.

THE MINISTRY OF THE LAITY

When I was a fresh young rector in the mid-1970s, a time when the ministry of the laity was all the rage, a parishioner came to me to apologize. Each Sunday she attended the early service without fail, and her husband often read a lesson. But she still felt uncomfortable. Tackling responsibilities of a full-time job, a healthy marriage, friendships, and care for her parents, she simply lacked the time or energy to do anything else for the church and therefore could not share in "lay ministry." Such was her definition.

I began to think of others in the congregation: the engineer who was on the town council, the naval officers' wives who took responsibility for supporting families of crew members on the husbands' ships, and the many who balanced family, work, community, and church. How they found time to be active in the parish beyond regular worship, I could only wonder, yet many of them gave tremendously of themselves. Nonetheless, as that parishioner showed me, some of them felt guilty about not doing more.

They need not have. Lambeth 1958 said so, as did its successors. The message from the bishops was clearly that lay ministry primarily takes place in the world of work, community, and family. "Penetrating society" with the gospel is the purpose, starting in the home. A 1958 Lambeth committee urging lay involvement stressed the importance of the Christian home as a setting of ministry. The workplace is another arena in which the laity "must bear their witness" through deed and word that convey "the hope that is in them," and by their qualities of sympathy, compassion, under-standing, and insight.[12] Nearly forty years later, the tenth Anglican Consultative Council (1996) reaffirmed that the ministry of the baptized "is the fundamental ministry of the Church," meaning, first, that the ordained serve to equip and enable ministry and thus, second, baptismal ministry "is chiefly not sanctuary or churchly ministry, but rather a matter of being a Christian parent, employee, employer, unemployed person, or a voter, etc., with integrity."[13]

So for laity to "have" a ministry has became a commonplace. To summarize the thought, the church as the Body of Christ is a holy nation and royal priesthood. It serves Christ in the world and the world in the name of Christ. Baptism incorporates each Christian into the church and into its ministry. Through baptism, each Christian shares in the church's ministry. It is a ministry, moreover, that is primarily aimed at the community around and beyond the church itself. Laity have the particular ability to bring the gospel to the world in which they spend their lives.[14]

Baptism is its origin. Among Anglican baptismal liturgies, the American and Canadian rites state most vigorously the imperative for mission in which laypeople share, especially through the five questions asked of the candidates and also of the congregation as they renew their vows. These questions concern worship, recon-ciliation, evangelistic proclamation, human service, and justice. From these, theologian Ian Douglas concludes, "Participation in God's mission...lies at the heart of the baptismal call. Baptism is thus a commission, 'co-mission,' in God's mission." The five questions identify the priorities each baptized member pledges to pursue as a member of Christ's Body, and each of these, Douglas argues, warrants "equal attention." To elevate one aspect of the covenant over the others distorts the whole, as an Evangelical might do in accentuating proclamation or a theological progressive might in highlighting justice. Furthermore, these are ministries belonging to

---

[12] *Lambeth 1958*, 2.112–114; *Lambeth 1968*, 93–98; *Lambeth 1978*, 83–84; *Lambeth 1988*, 49–53.

[13] ACC, *Being Anglican*, 152.

[14] Cf. *Lambeth 1988* (section report), 49–54.

all the baptized; those baptized members who are in orders support the *laos* in mission.[15]

Three problems arise, however. First, what are the locus and the focus of lay ministry? Second, does the fact that each Christian shares in the ministry of the church mean that each Christian has a ministry? Finally, what relationship does a specific ministry have to the work of the church as a whole?

WHAT IS THE FOCUS OF LAY MINISTRY?

In theory, theologians and bishops locate the ministry of the laity primarily in the world. In practice, lay ministry often connotes ministry *in* the church, which at its best can mean supporting a wider ministry to the world but too often overshadows ministry *beyond* the church. As early as 1963, Mark Gibbs, an ardent English advocate of the laity's role, identified a dichotomy in thinking about laity. Those laypeople he calls "Type A" tend to minister beyond the church walls "in their careers, in trade, in teaching, in local or national politics, in different voluntary (but not church) organizations such as Rotary or the Woman's Club, and above all, in their home and family life." What he calls "Type B," on the other hand, are the "good" laity,

> always around the church premises, having somehow the time for a great range of church work, and to the amazement and reluctant admiration of their fellow laymen, actually finding that their main interest in life centers on their church and its organization. They are keen lay preachers, Sunday school teachers, fund raisers, church officers, and the like. Laity type "B" are invaluable in the running of many churches.[16]

Yet these laity draw all the attention, at least liturgically. Consider, for example, the "Commissioning for Lay Ministries" in the Episcopal Church's *Book of Occasional Services.* Of sixteen categories of lay ministries, fourteen serve the internal Christian community. The prayer book itself, by contrast, makes no such limitation on

---

[15] Douglas, "Baptized into Mission," 434–437; cf. US BCP 302–305; Canada, *Alternative Services,* 154, 158–159.

[16] Mark Gibbs and T. Ralph Morton, *God's Frozen People* (Philadelphia: Westminster Press, 1964), 22.

the work of baptismal ministry, either in the baptismal covenant or the "Form of Commitment to Christian Service."[17]

As helpful as these church-centered ministries are, their prominence creates three disadvantages. For one, it "churchifies" ministry by implicitly identifying "ministry" with what occurs in and around the church or under its auspices. But the purpose and strength of lay ministry, Anglican leaders keep reminding, lies *outside* the church walls, not within them. "[T]he primary ministry of the great majority of Christians is their service of humanity in the everyday work of the world," declared the bishops at Lambeth, 1988.[18] In that spirit, some churches place signs over their exits that read, "You are now entering the mission field."

The second disadvantage is that a "church-directed" connotation of ministry inevitably clericalizes the ministry of all. Who epitomize the church's work better than the clergy? Many of the liturgical and pastoral functions—reading, administration of the Eucharist, visitation, and the like—have long been associated with a "parson." Including laity in these functions has widespread benefits, such as breaking down clerical monopolies, involving more people in the church's institutional activities, providing a sense of personal connection with the church, and expanding and improving what the church can do. But involving laity in these church-directed enterprises runs the risk of initiating a raft of what used to be called "minor orders" and perpetuating an ecclesiastical hierarchy with clergy at the top—which is the direct opposite of what many in the lay-ministry movement intend.

Defining lay ministry in clerical or "churchy" terms also risks confusing the nature of ministry and therefore of the division of labor within the Body of Christ. The best current example of this phenomenon is the suggestion that laity preside at the Eucharist, a question to which we will turn at the end of this chapter. Ruth Etchells, an English contributor to John Tiller's 1983 report, notes there that "a high proportion of those currently training for what till now has been called 'lay ministry' thought of themselves as in

---

[17] One of the exceptions is "evangelist," and the other, the generic "other lay ministries" (*The Book of Occasional Services, 1994* (New York: Church Hymnal, c. 1995), 160–176; US BCP, 304–305, 420–421).

[18] *Lambeth 1988* (section report), 44.

the future being a sort of clergy person." Tiller himself summarizes the problem: "The ministry of the whole people of God to be engaged in mission in the world is made absolutely clear. It is equally clear that the Church has often thought of lay ministry as assistance for the clergy in running the parochial organization."[19]

The third disadvantage lies in how church-centered ministry limits the vision of mission. If this kind of ministry is supposed to sustain the church, then those not engaged in church-related ministries may have little sense of ministering at all. This was my parishioner's inference; what she did on the job, in her home, or in her community did not "count" as "ministry" precisely because her efforts stood outside the ecclesiastical structure.

This last disadvantage may be the greatest of all. The primary theological and liturgical emphasis has always been on the sense of mission that laity are uniquely able to offer to the ministry of the church *beyond* the church, precisely because their jobs, activities, and families take them into the society at large. To minimize this emphasis does more than an injustice to lay ministry. It also narrows the work of evangelism and mission, cramping the church's responsibility under Christ, rather than opening the people of God to the myriad opportunities for mission and ministry that each baptized member encounters every day, wherever he or she may be. Two priests, one from England and the other from Nigeria, pose the issue, "When we confine our God to the inside of church buildings, how can we expect believers to exhibit a true Christian character in the workplace?"[20]

DOES EVERY CHRISTIAN HAVE A MINISTRY?

Anglicans have long accepted that laity participate in the church's ministry as members of the Body of Christ. But can it be said that each layperson has a ministry?

Many will answer with a strong "Yes!" For them it is a very short distance from the concept of all Christians sharing in the mission and ministry of the church to the conviction that each Christian has a particular ministry and is thus a "minister." The

---

[19] Tiller, *Strategy*, 62–63.

[20] Richard Kew and Cyril Okorocha, *Vision Bearers: Dynamic Evangelism in the 21st Century* (Harrisburg, PA: Morehouse, 1996), 68.

progression can be seen in the work of Mark Gibbs. In the 1960s Gibbs argued for a place in the church's ministry for laity in general. Nearly twenty years later, he wrote of Christians with secular responsibilities who assumed that they had particular "ministries" in the world. Similarly, in *The Liberation of the Laity*, Anne Rowthorn asserts the role of laity as "prime ministers" of the church in the world, who "have the right to expect the clergy to fulfill their main function—that of supporting the former's ministries."[21]

In the 1980s and 1990s, this idea caught on. New Zealanders enshrined the basic concept in their prayer book:

> By the Holy Spirit all who believe and are baptised receive a ministry to proclaim Jesus as Saviour and Lord, and to love and serve the people with whom they live and work.[22]

In the Episcopal Church, countless Sunday bulletins and parish newsletters list as "ministers" on their mastheads, along with the names of the clergy, "The people of Christ Church," or, more specific still, "All the baptized members of Saint Ethelwald's." The baptismal covenant as contained in the new American/Canadian rites is at the very heart of the principle. The Spirit bestowed at baptism gives the gifts to minister, and, as James Fenhagen has written, Christ gives the authority. With that philosophy in mind, a lay canon of Grace Cathedral, San Francisco, told a gathering of Episcopal lay professionals that an invitation to preach caused him to realize that he "was just as unworthy—and as worthy—as any priest to proclaim the Word, that his authority came through his baptism."[23] The laity have their gift and the clergy have theirs, all arising from one

---

[21] Gibbs and Morton, *God's Frozen People, passim.*; Mark Gibbs, *Christians with Secular Power* (Philadelphia: Fortress Press, 1981), 3, 5; Rowthorn, *Liberation*, 5, 123. The debt of this school of thought to Hendrik Kraemer must be acknowledged, who, among other points, claimed that "the specific place of the laity is at the frontiers, where the real dialogue between Church and World becomes an event," and who challenged the church to reorient itself to support the opportunity that such a dialogue provides (see *Theology of the Laity*, 172).

[22] *NZ Prayer Book*, 890 (|| 901, 908).

[23] Fenhagen, *Mutual Ministry*, 14; Ed Stannard, "Lay professionals urged to feel their authority, given in baptism," *Episcopal Life*, July 20, 2001 <http://www.ecusa.anglican.org/ens/2001-190.html> (July 21, 2001).

common source. As Brian Spinks, an English priest now teaching at Yale, explained the interrelationship:

> All Christians have a ministry, since all are made members of the royal priesthood through baptism. It is through baptism into the ecclesia that all ministry derives, since we are in Christ. Within the royal priesthood there are distinctive ministries, and in the past a number of ministries have been singled out for liturgical recognition. The distinctive ministries of bishop, presbyter and deacon cannot be entirely separated from other gifts, charisms and offices, since they all stem from baptism.[24]

Some have even called baptism "the ordination of the laity," as we shall see.

Others, though, deny that *each* Christian has a ministry. Their rationales vary. One line of thinking differs from the prevailing view on the very nature of baptism. As the English author Robert Hannaford understands the sacrament, "Baptism represents neither admission into a fixed order nor the bestowal of a generic capacity for the reception of other orders. Baptism is important for ministry because it marks an individual's incorporation into the ministerial community of the Church." He posits what Ruth Etchells calls a "communal" approach to ministry, one that reveres a role for the church as the primary instrument of Christian mission, from which the individual baptized members derive their part.[25]

Hannaford further questions whether, if everyone has a "ministry," the term loses its significance.

> If baptism, which is given to all, is treated as something akin to ordination, we are once again in danger of loading too much onto the idea of ministry.... When ministry is applied to the general Christian life of the baptised the danger is that the idea ceases to have any clear meaning.... *Baptism does not, then, so much bestow a ministerial*

---

[24] Brian Spinks, "Ordination," *Liturgy for a New Century*, ed. Michael Perham (London: SPCK/Alcuin Club, 1991), 84.

[25] Hannaford, "Ecclesiology," in Hall and Hannaford, eds., *Order and Ministry*, 42; Etchells, q. in Tiller, *Strategy*, 62.

> *calling as call someone into the ministerial community of the Church.*[26]

Another British theologian, Helen Oppenheimer, observes the difficulty that arises when the name of "ministry" can be attached to whatever a Christian may do in the name of Christ. "The notion of ministry," she writes, "tends to gobble up everything into itself so that it becomes impossible to sort out what is not ministry."[27] Her point of view is shared by Episcopal priest John D. Alexander, who writes, "Endless talk about all the baptized being ministers tends subconsciously to reinforce the insidious notion that ministry is the church's only purpose." Thus "ministry" is too narrowly construed. Such an implication, he adds, when added to a diaconal-style connotation of "ministry" as human care, reduces the church to being hardly more "than a vaguely spiritual social services agency." It also diminishes the importance of deepening the life of Christian discipleship.[28]

But can *ministry* be equated with *service,* as Alexander fears it might? John N. Collins, the Australian Roman Catholic layman who in *Diakonia* seeks to elevate yet limit the diaconate, denies that they can be. Answering the question posed in his title, *Are All Christians Ministers?*, Collins bravely questions virtually all English translations of the term "ministry" in the New Testament, starting with William Tyndale's. They misunderstand "ministry/*diakonia*" as different forms of relatively mundane "service," he argues, whereas the terms really apply to the "sacred mission" or "mandate" that derives from God. Where the *Revised Standard Version* translates 2 Corinthians 9:1 as "the offering for the saints," Collins proposes "the sacred mission to the blessed people," reflecting the church's fundamental purposes to which, he argues, Paul refers.[29]

---

[26] Hannaford, "Ecclesiology," in Hall and Hannaford, eds., *Order and Ministry*, 42–43, emph. added.

[27] Q. in Tiller, *Strategy*, 66.

[28] John D. Alexander, "Rethinking 'Ministry of All the Baptized'," *The Living Church*, vol. 226, no. 2 (Jan. 12, 2003), 23–24.

[29] John N. Collins, *Are All Christians Ministers?* (Collegeville, MN: Liturgical Press, 1992), 58.

Collins, I think, overstates the point. Still, he and others of this view take the very different perspective that ministry, in Collins's words, is "public, organized, accredited, and faith-filled," and enriches "those who established it and those to whom it was extended." A "minister," he says later, "is one appointed to a task."[30] These definitions by no means exclude the laity from ministry. Those who are properly called "ministers," though, must by this definition be publicly accredited by the church for some purpose that extends the mission that the church derives from Christ. Such a "ministry" would not automatically include everything a Christian (ordained or lay) may do; and not every Christian is a "minister."

Those of the "communal" approach caution against the enthusiasms of those who proclaim the ministry of all. They hold a place for the Christian community against what can become a rampant individualism producing ministerial chaos in the absence of any order, control, or coordination. For the church to accredit Christian service, on the other hand, applies corporate discernment to the questions of what are Christians' gifts, how they might be channeled, and how they can be supported.

However, this latter view inevitably links its concept of ministry to the institutional church. It defines "ministry" as what the church defines as ministry. But as myriad leaders—some of the stature of William Temple[31]—urged, the power of the ministry of laity lies beyond the scope of the church and in the life of the world. Furthermore, what the church formally authorizes, as we saw earlier,[32] tend to be churchly ministries that closely resemble *clerical* ministries. The potential for laity is vastly greater.

Each perspective points out the difficulty of the other. Obviously, some balance is needed that appreciates both the multitudinous gifts that God gives to the baptized and also the need to bring some coherent order, structure, meaning, and support so that they can be effectively employed. In fact, each view has been tempered.

---

[30] Collins, *Are All Christians Ministers?*, 65, 115.

[31] Cf. Temple's exhortation to Oxford undergraduates, *CN*, 95, *CFL*, 137; also, *RSJG*, 163.

[32] E.g., in *BOS*, 160–176, or in those lay ministries authorized by provinces or dioceses (cf. chapter 4 above).

Fenhagen's vision of "mutual ministry" is predicated upon the church as "enabling the enabler," inspiring, supporting, and coordinating an individual's ministries. Stewart Zabriskie, writing of "total ministry" in Nevada, sees in baptism the means whereby one can "become part of the *community's* ministry"; the church as Christ's Body exercises Christ's ministry.[33] Hannaford, too, softened the boldness of his statement, though not his conviction:

> Ministry is the proper and normal expression of *charism* in the life of the Church. Indeed speaking of ministry in terms of *charism* helps to correct an impression we might have given that ministry is simply a creation of the Church. Ministry is an action on behalf of the Church, and as such must be publicly recognised and endorsed, but it has its roots in *charism*. Ministry is the public and communally recognised form of *charism*.[34]

Christ gives the gift; the church recognizes it and uses it in its fundamental purpose of ministry. The result is a ministry based not so much on baptism itself as on the charisms and gifts that Christ bestows freely among the baptized, and that the church acknowledges and celebrates.

These concessions move each side closer to the other without, however, bridging the gap between them. The result is something of a muddle. Each position ends up being unsatisfactory, as two examples will show. First, when I arrived at a new parish, a particularly thoughtful vestry member dropped by a bag full of paper towels and cleaning supplies. When I thanked him, he explained, "That is part of my ministry." But I had to wonder: is this act of bounty really what we mean by "ministry"? Second, the current Secretary of State of the United States is a regular communicant of Saint John's Church in McLean, Virginia. Though his parish prays for him, he is in no sense commissioned by the church. But do we really want to exclude international diplomacy and governmental service as a form of Christian ministry? The danger of making everything "ministry" lies in the term's losing all its meaning; the

---

[33] Fenhagen, *Mutual Ministry*, 114–124; Zabriskie, *Total Ministry*, x, emph. added.

[34] Hannaford, "Ecclesiology," in Hall and Hannaford, eds., *Order and Ministry*, 51. Fenhagen makes much the same point (*More Than Wanderers*, 27–28).

danger of reducing "ministry" to what is done only by the church or in the name of church fails to grasp the vision of ministry that Anglican leaders have long espoused.

If each baptized person represents Christ and the church, then it follows that there must be both an individual responsibility and a corporate element in that representation. Hugh Melinsky's conclusion seems to hold both elements in tension: he writes that "ministerial authority is both from above and from within; not from God without the Church, nor from the Church without God, but from God within the Church."[35] Authority to serve Christ and church springs from baptism. Authority specifically to represent the church in any official capacity must, of course, be delegated by the church, but God is always the source and the church only the medium.

How Do Laity Relate to the Church's Formal Ministry?

What, then, is the relationship of laypersons to what is done specifically in the name of the church, such as in liturgy or in social service? Is there a need to commission laity to minister in the church's name? John Halliburton, another English writer, thinks not. He contends that the paramount activities of the laity require no official recognition, given their particular roles.

> The laity have more than enough to do in fulfilling their calling. The laity firmly believe that they are the church in the front line, that they have unique opportunities that the clergy lack, and that theologically, they are as much the church as any other member.... The laity, in other words, are integral to the church's ministry; and the church has to learn that clerical leadership in certain and essential spheres of ecclesiastical life must be balanced by a proper recognition of lay leadership, lay expertise, and lay responsibility in other areas.[36]

---

[35] Melinsky, *Shape*, 267–268.

[36] Halliburton, "The Laity in the Ministry of the Church," in Hall and Hannaford, eds., *Order and Ministry*, 120–121. I want to think, however, that Halliburton would agree that any publicly representative lay pastoral ministry would warrant some form of ecclesial authorization. On his general point, note the similarity with Fenhagen, *More Than Wanderers*, 14 (q. above, chapter 5).

But Halliburton seems to refer here to the laity's general ministry. When their efforts turn specific and they officially represent the church, then the church's endorsement is appropriate and helpful for three reasons. First, it helps to define and reveal what the church is doing and who is working specifically on its behalf. While commissioning someone to teach Christian education, lead a youth mission, organize a housing effort, assist in an evangelistic crusade, or serve as warden may not constitute a sacrament, the community still gives outward and visible shape to a wider, ongoing mission and ministry that permeate the church—or should. Blessing a healing team does not replace the countless intercessions of God's people for the sick or the work of medical professionals but rather makes visible the ministry of healing as an aspect of the congregation's prayer and action. The same theory that states that ordained ministry gives focus, shape, and visibility to the ministry of the whole church applies to formal, recognized lay ministry as well.

Second, authorization clarifies the representative quality of those who minister specifically in the church's name. Certain work in the life of the church is enhanced by formal commissioning; through it, the church declares that certain laypeople are indeed authorized to "represent Christ and the church." The same act heightens both the responsibility and accountability of those who act in the church's name. As someone needs authorization to sign the church's checks, so someone may need authorization to represent the church in a prison ministry.

Finally, specifically commissioning workers serves to remind that ministry is ultimately corporate. In turn, the ministering community may celebrate and support what its people are doing, foster collegiality that helps ministers—clergy and lay—work together, and ward off the danger of ministry's becoming a personal enterprise.

But dangers persist on the other side. That is, commissioning some laity tends to elevate the few and to elevate the positions they hold as paragons of "lay ministry," at risk of "churchifying" all of ministry once more. Against these dangers, the primary purpose of the church and all its ministries must never be overlooked. It is not to serve itself but to serve its Lord in the world. Ruth Etchells suggests:

> *To be called to lay service* is to be called to live fully in
> the secular world, to be at ease in it, to know its idioms
> and its assumptions.... All such lay ministers ought to be
> commissioned by their parishes and sent out to their
> task, and then supported by weekly prayer for them in
> the parish church, by counselling, and by a support
> group within the parish/deanery. But their function is
> not to keep the Church going as an institution, but to
> draw their support, comfort, sustenance and theological
> depth from it as they work in Christ's name in their secular
> calling.[37]

The church's purpose—and thus the laity's purpose—is not
maintenance but mission.

ARE THE LAITY AN ORDER?

Recent trends have produced a second commonplace, that
laity in themselves constitute an *order*. Often it is referred to
offhandedly, as if this fact were generally assumed. A priest writing on diaconate mentions in passing that *The Book of Common
Prayer* "reminds us that there are four orders of ministers: laypersons, deacons, priests, and bishops. Each order is entrusted with
its own peculiar ministry." Yet Hannaford has written that baptism does *not* represent admission into a fixed order.[38] Retired
bishop Theodore Eastman claims that baptism is an "ordination
to the principal order of ministry," but an American House of
Bishops study asserts that it is "not an ordination."[39] Is it or isn't
it? Are laity a separate order? What difference does it make?

The language used often insinuates that they are a distinct
order. Laity have long taken a part in governance, wielding considerable power in some provinces. Many a synod or convention

---

[37] In Tiller, *Strategy*, 62. Emph. in orig.

[38] King, "A Confusing Proposal," in Hall and Hannaford, eds., *Order of Ministry*, 13; Hannaford, "Ecclesiology," in Hall and Hannaford, eds., *Order and
Ministry*, 42.

[39] Quoted in Adams, "Decoding," in Myers, ed., *Baptism and Ministry*, 4; House
of Bishops Pastoral Study, 11. Eastman's point was reiterated and extended by
Charles Miller in "The Theology of the Laity," *Anglican Theological Review*, 84,
no. 2 (Spring 2002), e.g. 223–224: "[B]aptism establishes the lay status of a
believer by ordaining that person into the lay order."

includes a "House of Laity," as in England's General Synod. In the Episcopal Church a vote "by orders" separates the House of Deputies into the clergy and the laity, and for a diocese to elect a bishop requires a majority in both the clergy and the lay "orders." This terminology appears in the prayer book's directive that "the members of each order within the Church, lay persons, bishops, priests, and deacons, fulfill the functions proper to their respective orders."[40]

But is the legislative concept of *order* the same as a more theological/sacramental one? Two considerations suggest not: the nature of "orders" and their focus.

First, an order is by definition "ordered." That is, one who is "in orders" is also "under orders." The person assumes a discipline and comes under a particular authority that one who is not "in orders" does not take on. A bishop asks someone being ordained as deacon or priest, "Will you respect and be guided by the pastoral direction and leadership of your bishop?"[41] No hands are laid on unless the ordinand agrees. As the ordinand comes under the authority of the bishop, so she or he comes under the rule of ecclesiastical canons and secular laws (especially, but not only, in England) to a vastly greater degree than laity. Regulations concerning laity are few and generic in nature;[42] those for clergy are many and specific. Moreover, becoming a member of the clergy is highly defined by what seem, to those enduring the process, as

---

[40] ECUSA, *Constitution*, Art. 1.4, 5. The Constitution (Art. II.1) and Canons (III.22.1) delegate rules for electing a bishop to the convention of the electing diocese, though generally if not universally in ECUSA, a candidate is elected by a majority (sometimes two-thirds) of each "order." Quotation is from US BCP, 13. Interestingly, the term "orders" is used here, but "ministry" is the word employed by the Catechism in relationship to laypersons and the ordained (p. 855).

[41] Canada, *Alternative Services*, 646, 655; US BCP, 532, 543; SO 11, 17; Aus. 787, 795; NZ, 894, 905 ‖ *ASB*, 345, 358. Though some, e.g. Aus. 803, NZ 917, ask the bishop about *administering* or upholding discipline, only *ASB* asks the candidate about *accepting* it for himself (389).

[42] Cf. Doe, *Canon Law*, 164–169; the exception for laity concerns primarily those who assume particular office, such as warden or reader, or employment: cf. 184–185. "Anglican canon law appears to be weak in terms of presenting a distinct common ministry of the laity in terms of their specific rights and duties; these are, rather, scattered amongst laws dealing with other discrete subjects." Laws pertaining to liturgical licenses tend to be stronger, especially in issuing them; but canons on revoking them, Doe asserts, are "inadequate" (186).

an endless series of hurdles, while lay membership involves baptism and reception of Holy Communion for a minimal number of times. Virtually unique is the United Church of South India, which

> recognizes as its members those who, being residents in its area, have been baptized...are willing to abide by the rules and customs of this Church; and are not members of any Christian body which is not in communion with this Church; and are not excommunicated by lawful excommunication; and are not members of any Christian body which is not in communion with this Church; and are not open apostates to some non-Christian religion.

With that declaration, little wonder that the UCSI's constitution provides, "It is the duty and privilege of every member of the Church to share in the Church's ministry." More common are regulations like those of the church in Korea, whereby laypeople must attend the Eucharist each Sunday and Holy Day, observe fast days, be responsible for "the expenses of evangelism and the livelihood of the clergy," and "strive to live according to Christ's teachings, to preach the gospel and to realize God's justice in society."[43]

Baptismal membership receives little canonical attention; lay offices receive more, chiefly (and tellingly) the liturgical ones, like lay eucharistic minister or lay reader. It is notable that so many offices are expected to be held by laity on every level of ecclesial life: chancellors, treasurers, registrars, diocesan secretaries (sometimes), vestries, churchwardens. It is also typical that canonical stress lies on church-oriented ministries. Australia's "Authorized Lay Ministry Canon 1992" gives a case in point. It states that "ministry is of the essence of the life of the whole body of Christ" and "all baptised persons are called to minister in the Church and in the world." But the canon then turns to such activities as reading and conducting authorized services; preaching; assisting the priest in ministration and distribution of Holy Communion; and "any other lay ministry declared by the bishop of the diocese to be an authorised lay ministry for the purposes of this canon." Other provisions in other provinces spell out ministries including visitation, catechism, and the like.[44] In some countries, the church's ministry

---

[43] Doe, *Canon Law*, 161, 167–168.

[44] Doe, *Canon Law*, 173–185 (q. on 181).

relies heavily on lay ministry. In Uganda, for example, where the Anglican Church has grown to well over six million members, a parish might cover one or two or even ten congregations, all overseen by one priest. Because directly overseeing all of these would be an impossible task for one person, a lay reader is appointed to each congregation and authorized to perform nearly all duties that the priest may do except the sacramental. The lay reader is a veritable quasi-cleric. Indeed, serving as lay reader frequently constitutes both a way-station and preparation in the journey toward ordination. The typical Ugandan diocese runs a three-year training course for readers (to be followed, for those who pursue it, by another three years in theological college before ordination).[45] After finishing that first course, the reader will go where the bishop directs. So lay readers do constitute a semi-ordered category. It is as if the minor order of Reader were brought back to serve an urgent contemporary purpose.

This sort of regulation is exceptional. Not many laypeople would wish for the bishop to assign where they work or to give permission for them to take a job in the secular world. Though many laypeople say the daily office, they might not like being expected to do so, as English clergy are. With Holy Orders come limitations that do not apply to laity, and one result is a freedom for laity that clergy rarely possess.

In the second place, besides the "ordered" nature of the person are the nature and purpose of the orders themselves. Ian Douglas contends:

> Ministry belongs to all of the baptized, whereas the orders of bishop, deacon, and priest have been established by the church to support the *laos* in their life in mission. As such, the orders of bishop, deacon, and priest are secondary to and subservient to the calling of all the baptized to participate in God's mission of reconciliation and redemption.[46]

Douglas rightly describes the aim of orders as enabling, tending, encouraging, and serving the mission of the whole church on the

---

[45] From the author's various conversations in Uganda and with the Rev. Dr. Mabel Katahweire, Cambridge, MA, May 24, 2001.

[46] Douglas, "Baptized into Mission," 437, emph. in orig.

part of the entire *laos*. Were the laity an order, they too would be subservient to the whole. In one sense they are, for a host of lay ministries serves the whole *laos*. Readers, pastoral associates, wardens, members of American vestries or English parochial church councils, ushers, acolytes, altar guild members, and hosts of others do help to sustain the operations of the Body. They also enable others through their support of worship, mission, evangelism, service, and justice. Often, however, these are ministries strictly *within* the confines of the church. No matter how important these are, they are misleading as to the true nature of ministry and diminish the urgency of its mission to and in the world. But theologians, bishops, and conferences keep pointing to the truly important work of the people of God being *beyond* the church. This is where the laity live and move and have their being and where their greatest contribution can be made.

In sum, to consider the laity as an "order" under these circumstances ends up limiting and even depriving the laity of the greater ministry that they can pursue in their communities and world, in the name of Christ and on behalf of the church. But in the process, we have further defined the relationship of support, nurture, enablement, and care that the ministries of the ordained—and those of some laity—should properly have for the work of the entire *laos*.[47]

DISCIPLESHIP AND DIAKONIA: A VISION FOR LAY MINISTRY

For all the official exhortations to the contrary, the conception of the lay role as assisting and supporting the clergy has been hard to expunge. For centuries, the clergy were seen as the paragons of

---

[47] Discussion of laity as an "order" seems to be confined to ECUSA, evidently arising from the terminology of the 1979 BCP. Such language does not seem to be used in other provinces of the Anglican Communion. I wonder if it was the intent of the revisers—eager though they were to elevate the role and rite of baptism in the church's life—to diverge from what apparently is a prevailing Anglican consensus. Proof that this was the intent rests on references to laity as an "order" on p. 13 and to the "ministry" as including "lay persons" in the catechism (p. 855); yet the terminology ("orders," "ministry") differs. Miller ("Theology of the Laity") cites a rubrical direction on p. 361 to distinguish between the laity and the ordained ("Representatives of the congregation bring the people's offerings...to the deacon or celebrant. The people stand...."). However, "people" could as easily refer to the entire "people of God" there assembled, clergy included (who presumably also stand)—what I am calling the *laos*—as to the laity alone.

ministry, the peak of the pyramid. Laity were the beneficiaries or, in a growing number of cases, assistants in their efforts. This pyramidal image persisted so stubbornly into the twentieth century that lay theologians like Anne Rowthorn began to insist that laity needed nothing less than "liberation." She and others have inverted the pyramid. The laity's role is not to support the clergy; rather, the clergy's role is to sustain and serve the laity as the "primary ministers."[48] Ian Douglas agrees, calling holy orders "subservient to the calling of all the baptized."[49]

Although I much prefer the inverted pyramid to the old hierarchical framework, this newer concept falls short of the radical equality and interrelationship that, I believe, the metaphors of the Body of Christ and the Trinity both imply. For one thing, the inversion still keeps Christians on different planes: some are still "higher" than others. For another, the idea of the clergy's support of the laity, while absolutely vital, does not account for the practical fact that clergy themselves need support. The idea of discipleship that I proposed in chapter 6, however, places all Christians on the same plane, while the idea of diaconate gives roles of servanthood to all, not only to the world, but to each other.

One element common to all Christians is discipleship. In baptismal rites throughout the Anglican Communion, each candidate pledges to follow Jesus Christ as Savior and Lord; the words may vary, but the commitment remains fundamental. Any commitment to ministry or service, no matter how defined, arises out of that more basic pledge. It is an outgrowth of one's life in Christ—a life that also includes growing in his knowledge and love, in holiness and in grace. The Christian life entails worship and prayer; as Helen Oppenheimer said, "To feed at God's table should be quite as awe-inspiring as to wait at it."[50] Moreover, discipleship unifies all Christians in a common endeavor, both individually and corporately pursued, in the common ministry of the church. All share in the priesthood of the Body. A renewed understanding of discipleship holds the potential not just of reducing tensions over who is a "minister" but also of relationships among Christians.

---

[48] Rowthorn, Liberation, 5, 123.

[49] Douglas, "Baptized into Mission," 437.

[50] Q. in Tiller, Strategy, 66.

Discipleship provides the basis, then, for the tasks and responsibilities that individuals assume. *Diakonia* provides a framework
for assuming them. Whether these are called "ministries," "forms
of Christian service," "acts of Christian charity," or anything else
is not important. What matters is that these meaningfully arise
from the church's broad mission and purpose and from the individual's discipleship. By whatever name, *diakonia* has two aspects.
One aims at serving the world; the other strives to sustain the
Christian community. Both aspects can be seen in Acts 6, in which
the diaconal seven (whether or not they were specifically ordained
as "deacons") were assigned to minister to the nascent church but
two of whom were subsequently known for their evangelism—in
Stephen's case to the Jews, in Philip's to the Ethiopian. In their tending to the concerns of the Hellenists, the seven were assisting the apostles. An element of *diakonia*, then, is support for one another within the church—support for its needy and support for its leaders,
who knew they needed the help.

In chapter 6, I also proposed that all Christians share not only
the discipleship of Christ but his *diakonia* as well. Because *diakonia* is
directed at the society beyond the church as well as at the church
itself, all Christians to some extent—and some Christians to a
large extent—will find themselves sustaining their community, the
church. The clergy may be the ones whose ministry is primarily
that of building up the Body of Christ, but laity join in their work;
to do their job, clergy need the laity just as the laity need the clergy.

My point is simply that, in the Body of Christ, one Christian
needs another. As disciples of the Lord Jesus, all stand on the same
plane; there is no pyramid to ascend or descend. If each, out of
diakonia, helps the other, then each will become both the server
and the served; as Paul envisions, "the members will have the same
care for one another." In that sense, each becomes subservient to
the other to the point that such language no longer applies, but
rather, "if one member suffers, all suffer together; if one member is
honored, all rejoice together" (1 Cor. 12:26).

Hans Rudi Weber declared that, in the mid-twentieth-century
movement to rethink the roles of laity and clergy, "The laity are
not helpers of the clergy so that the clergy can do their job, but the
clergy are helpers of the whole people of God, so that the laity can

be the Church."[51] I would amend his comment in two ways. I would rephrase it to say "so that the *laos* can be the church," for clergy, too, are the church, and that all may help each other in mutual support. That is to say, "The laity are not helpers of the clergy so that the clergy can do their job, but in the *laos*, the whole people of God, all help each other, for together, they are the church." And together, they may proclaim and serve Christ in his world as the priesthood he has called them to be.

SHOULD LAITY CELEBRATE THE EUCHARIST?

Some members cheered as they left the synod meeting of the Diocese of Sydney, Australia, on the night of October 19, 1999, while others were more "circumspect," as one journalist put it. Synod had voted by a nearly two-thirds margin in each order to endorse the administration of Holy Communion by laypeople for a five-year trial period. For the first time in Anglican history, a diocese had approved a lay celebration of the Eucharist.[52]

This idea had been around the Anglican Communion for years. William Temple at one point confessed, "I think that if a layman 'celebrates' with devout intention, he effects a real conse-cration, and any who receive devoutly at his hands receive the divine gift." He quickly added, "None the less he acts wrongly, not only because he offends against an actual rule of the Church, but because the principle of his act is destructive of the values that the ordered ministry exists to conserve, and that are an important element in a complete Christian experience."[53] The English General Synod debated lay celebration in 1976. Bishops at Lambeth 1978 discussed the topic in subcommittee, but the parent committee squelched further talk. In 1986 several dioceses in the Southern Cone of South America came within one vote of allowing its

---

[51] Q. in J. A. T. Robinson, "The Ministry and the Laity," in *Layman's Church* (London: Lutterworth Press, 1963), 17.

[52] Information on Sydney, except as noted, is from <http://www.anglicanmedia sydney.asn.au/synod1999/> (October 23, 1999).

[53] Temple, *CV*, 163 n. 1; cf. *TPD*, 110–112. Alan Hargrave (*But Who Will Preside?* [Bramcote, Notts.: Grove Books, 1990, 14]) quotes the first half of the statement from a news article of 1982—but only the first half of the statement.

provincial synod to let bishops license deacons or laypeople to
celebrate the Eucharist for an experimental period.[54] The sixth
Anglican Consultative Council favored ordaining "local priests"
rather than authorizing lay celebration, and a committee of Lambeth 1988 agreed.[55] But the 1996 ACC meeting in Panama asked
provinces "to give urgent consideration to situations where access
to sacramental ministry is limited or impossible, and in particular
to study the theological and practical questions raised by those
who advocate lay presidency or 'extended communion.'"[56]

The need can certainly be great. As a licensed lay preacher,
Alan Hargrave recalled, he and several colleagues started a small
congregation in Santa Cruz, Bolivia's second-largest city, where
the nearest Anglican priest was a five-hundred-mile drive away in
La Paz. Congregants could have the Eucharist only once every
four to six months when the bishop came from Lima, Peru, more
than a thousand miles away.[57] As Anglicanism reached isolated
areas around the globe, that predicament grew. Even in England,
with its paucity of priests, the situation was dire enough for the
catholic-leaning Church Union to advise taking the reserved sacrament to entire congregations.[58]

Four solutions were proposed to meet the eucharistic crisis:
ordain more priests, under provisions for "local ordained ministry" if necessary; bring consecrated elements into the locality
("extended communion"); hold the Eucharist less frequently; or
license deacons or laity to preside. Each option challenged the theology and practice both of Eucharist and of orders and ministry.
The option of "local priests" will be explored in the next chapter.
"Extended communion," like local clergy, was commended by
Lambeth 1988, but an earnest attempt in a Cumbria parish in the

---

[54] Trevor Lloyd, *Lay Presidency at the Eucharist?* (Bramcote, Notts.: Grove Books, 1977), 2; *Lambeth 1978*, 83; Hargrave, *Preside*, 3.

[55] Melinsky, *Shape*, 140; Hargrave, *Preside*, 13; *Lambeth 1988*, 73 (¶205). See my next chapter re "local priests."

[56] ACC, *Being Anglican*, 160. The term "lay presidency" includes authorizing deacons as well as laity to preside at Eucharist. Cf. *Eucharistic Presidency*, 3 (¶1.10–11).

[57] Hargrave, *Preside*, 5.

[58] "Lay Administration of Holy Communion" (n.p.: The Church Union, 1977).

north of England revealed both advantages and disadvantages,[59] while having fewer eucharistic celebrations flew in the face of growing sacramental practice among Anglicans. Most objectionable was the very idea of "shipping Jesus in" from afar rather than experiencing the immediacy of his eucharistic presence in a local celebration. That left lay presidency.

So the Australians acted first. The Bishop of Armidale revealed in 1996 that he had authorized deacons to preside as a better alternative to extended communion. By then, Sydney's measure for laity and deacons to preside had entered the legislative process. It would allow suitably trained laypeople and deacons, with permission from both diocesan and local levels, to "administer" Holy Communion (the word "celebrate" was never used in the legislation). In the 1999 synod debate, the Rev. John Woodhouse pointed to the array of opportunities for the laity to be involved in ministries once closed to them. "There is no sound reason to maintain the prohibition" on lay celebration, he argued, except "to protect and preserve and express an understanding of the priesthood and the sacrament that...is totally unacceptable" to the Anglican Church of Australia and "the likes of Thomas Cranmer."[60] Woodhouse summarized the reasons against the measure this way: (1) no layperson has the power to pray the prayer of consecration effectively; (2) higher qualifications are needed for the administration of the Lord's Supper than for preaching the Word of God, which laypersons can do; (3) the validity and authenticity of the Eucharist depend on having a priest administer it; (4) a priest is essential to the conduct of the Lord's Supper, although not for any other event in church life.

---

[59] *Lambeth 1988*, 73 (¶205); David Smethurst, *Extended Communion: An Experiment in Cumbria* (Bramcote, Notts.: Grove Books Ltd., 1986), *passim.* (see response by Colin Buchanan, *Modern Anglican Ordination Rites*, 20–23). "Extended Communion" requires the reservation of the sacrament, opposition to which was a factor in the second rejection of the revised prayer book in 1928. See H. Benedict Green, *Lay Presidency at the Eucharist?* (London: Darton, Longman & Todd, 1994), 1. However, the concept of bringing the sacrament to those who cannot attend the celebration, such as the ill, is mentioned as early as by Justin Martyr (*Apol.* 65, 1).

[60] A dubious proposition. Confronted in 1540 with the hypothetical question of how to provide Holy Communion where there were no clergy at all to officiate, Cranmer chose between two extremities, preferring laity's performing of ordinations to the worse alternative of their officiating at Eucharist themselves. See Lloyd, *Lay Presidency*, 5.

Woodhouse then explained the reasons to make this change. Among them are (1) preaching the Word of God and administering the sacrament should be kept in close relationship, so that only those who are mature, gifted, and trained to preach would be authorized to administer the Lord's Supper; (2) a layperson will be so authorized only by the Archbishop at the request of the minister with the agreement of the vestry; (3) lay or diaconal administration of the Lord's Supper will be introduced only to a particular congregation (say, the 7:15 p.m. Sunday congregation) with the agreement of the vestry; (4) the effect of the ordinance is not to impose a change in practice on any congregation. There is nothing wrong with preserving the status quo, only with the perceived absolute prohibition of the laity.

The Rev. Graham Crew agreed with the motion for pragmatic reasons: his parish of Springwood-Winmalee consisted of ten congregations spread over a number of centers, some of them overseen by the parish's five lay staff. These laity could administer the sacrament far more easily than he. During the debate, Bishop Paul Barnett of North Sydney, a suffragan, found no doctrinal objection but opposed "lay administration" because the rest of the Communion could not yet accept the measure, particularly the theologically conservative provinces in Asia and Africa with which Sydney had a special affinity. Anglican geopolitics was essentially his concern.[61] It was warranted, for immediately Church of England officials warned of grave ecumenical consequences if the vote were ratified. Closer to home, the Australian primate, Keith Rayner, called the Sydney vote "a fundamental break with Catholic order...and with the principles of the Anglican reformers." It set Sydney at odds with the rest of the Anglican Church of Australia, he charged, and challenged its constitution and canons.[62]

In the end, Archbishop Harry Goodhew exerted his right to veto the legislation, bowing to concerns for wider Anglican relationships. However, its supporters indicated they would return for another try.[63] The 2000 Sydney synod did not even take up the measure,

---

[61] <http://www.anglicanmediasydney.asn.au/synod1999/> (October 23, 1999).

[62] Muriel Porter, "Australian vote sets diocese at odds with rest of Anglican Communion," *Church Times*, Internet ed. [Web issue #133], October 22, 1999 <http://www.churchtimes.co.uk> (October 23, 1999).

[63] <http://www.anglicanmediasydney.asn.au/synod1999/main.html> (May 22, 2001).

dealing instead with the idea of confirmation conducted by presbyters or "appropriate lay people" and the possibility of women
bishops in Australia, which many in that diocese oppose. Seeming
not to notice the rich irony, it also called on Anglican primates to
uphold "traditional" doctrinal teachings of the church.[64] The election in 2001 of a new archbishop, Peter Jensen, who looks favor-
ably on lay administration, gave new hope to its backers but drew
another repudiation from Archbishop of Canterbury George
Carey.[65] The latter endorsed his fellow English bishops, who, in a
1996 study led by Stephen Sykes of Ely, had already spurned it as
well. Despite their rejection, a doctrinal commission in Sydney
pressed forward with two resolutions to continue weighing the
idea. Jensen concurred—so long as the provisions were legal.[66]

To say the least, the church in Sydney is dealing with diverse controversies pertaining to orders, but it is not alone. I have heard
Episcopalians occasionally suggest lay presidency as a means of
providing sacramental ministry for small congregations. The
motive is worthy, but the solution illustrates the difficulties of not
thinking carefully about the nature and purpose of each order, as
well as its effects on relationships within the *laos* in general. For
this reason, it seems to me that lay presidency of the Eucharist is
a singularly bad idea, and identifying why it is so can assist us further
in clarifying the effective relationships that can prevail.

---

[64] Jeremy Halcrow, "Sydney Anglicans to consider confirmation by clergy and
lay people," Anglican Media, Diocese of Sydney <http://www.anglicanmediasyd-
ney.asn.au/synod2000/n11_10_1.htm>; "Working within an 'impaired Communion': Sydney Anglicans discuss the 'contentious' issue of women bishops,"
<http://www.anglicanmediasydney.asn.au/synod2000/m17_10_2.htm>; "Synod
calls on Anglican Primates to affirm traditional Church doctrines,"
<http://www.anglicanmediasydney.asn.au/synod2000/n18_10_2.htm> (May 22,
2001).

[65] Anglican Media, Sydney: "Transcript of media conference for Archbishop-
elect Peter Jensen, June 7, 2001" <http://www.anglicanmediasydney.asn.au/
conf_transcript.htm> (June 16, 2001); Bill Bowder, "Lay presidency will bring
disunity, warns Dr Carey," *Church Times*, July 6, 2001 <http://www.churchtimes.
co.uk/templates/NewsTemplate_3r.asp?recid=575&table=news&bimage=news&
issue=7220&count=6> (July 8, 2001).

[66] Margaret Rodgers, "Sydney Synod moves to forward lay and diaconal presidency
at the Lord's Supper" <http://www.anglicanmediasydney.asn.au/ synod2001/
laypres_report.htm> (August 6, 2002).

Any biblical justification for lay presidency rests on shaky ground. The New Testament simply does not say who presided at the first eucharistic celebrations. The British liturgical scholar Paul Bradshaw speculates on the possibility that patterns of volunteer leadership might have been carried into the newly founded churches by converts from Judaism.[67] Sykes's 1996 study group similarly notes that while the Jewish synagogue leader could invite any competent member to lead the prayers, the key word was "competent," and that person—as Bradshaw implies—would be a leader. In the Christian assembly, the leader would likely be one considered appropriate to pronounce the blessings (by analogy with Jewish meal-blessings, the head of the household). Neither Bradshaw nor the bishops claim to find definitive proof. The same ambiguity that the English take as cause for caution, though, the Sydney commission interprets as permission for action.[68]

The history of eucharistic presidency becomes clearer in subsequent centuries. As the threefold orders of ministry took shape, the bishop and later the presbyter became the officiating celebrant of the Eucharist. So it has remained in Orthodox, Roman Catholic, and Anglican traditions. In opening sixteenth-century gates to lay participation in other spheres of Christian life, the English Reformation did not alter the matter of who presides at the altar. Yet, the Sydney commission observed, the presbyter-ate did change in scope as priests "moved from being Mass priests to ministers of the Word, from the English role of being officials of the state...to the Australian role of being paid leaders of the local branch of a voluntary organization."[69] Along the way, key functions such as preaching were delegated. In Australia, preach-ing is an important function that authorized deacons and laity may share.

As a result, the Australian commission interprets priesthood "not in terms of the particular activities of a priest, but by the respon-sibility of the office for congregational oversight or leadership." For

---

[67] Bradshaw, *Liturgical Presidency*, 6–8.

[68] *Eucharistic Presidency*, 42 (¶4.23); Sydney Diocesan Doctrine Commission 1998, "Lay and Diaconal Administration of the Lord's Supper," Diocese of Sydney, *Year Book of the Diocese of Sydney* (Sydney: 1998), 453.

[69] "Lay and Diaconal Administration," 454–457.

the 1662 Ordinal to give the priest oversight of "the people committed to your cure and charge" marks the central distinction between presbyters and deacons, as priestly assistants. The locus of priesthood, then, is not in celebrating the Eucharist but in leading and overseeing the congregation. As a result, "The Commission's view is that the validity and effectiveness of the Lord's Supper is not affected by whether the person administering it is ordained or not."[70]

In defending their point of view, the Australians quote the British statement, "The main purpose of ordination is not to provide eucharistic presidents but to provide publicly recognised oversight of a community." However, English church authorities repeatedly stress that out of this very oversight springs eucharistic leadership: "These two types of presidency ought to be integrally related."[71] The Australian emphasis on oversight recalls the evidently close connection between presbyters and bishops, while the British note the equally probable likelihood of eucharistic presidency by those who were granted communal oversight.

For the Australian church, more important is the link between Eucharist and preaching—sacrament and Word; for the British, responsibility for Word remains with "the ordained minister of a congregation." The Primate of Australia countered even more strongly, pointing out that whereas effective preaching relies on personal gifts and training, which laypeople may possess in abundance, celebrating the Eucharist is different. "It does not depend on the personal gifts of the celebrant but on the assurance that the one who has been called and ordained to do this very thing does faithfully what Christ did in taking and consecrating the bread and wine in the manner authorised by the church."[72]

In addition to those objections to lay presidency, the theology of the church and its ministry that we have been tracing also argue

---

[70] "Lay and Diaconal Administration," 454–457. The report notes one dissent from this final view.

[71] "Lay and Diaconal Administration," 456 (¶35); *Eucharistic Presidency*, 3 (¶1.12), cf. 43–44 (¶4.25–26), 51 (¶4.51).

[72] "Lay and Diaconal Administration," 458 (¶43); *Eucharistic Presidency*, 56 (¶5.13); Keith Rayner, "The Presidential Address," in Anglican Church of Australia, *Proceedings of the Eleventh Synod, 1998* (Sydney: 1998), 16, q. Article XXVI.

emphatically against it.[73] Foremost is the ministerial representative nature of the priest at the altar. The celebrant, not the "paid leaders of the local branch of a voluntary organization," has been chosen and authorized by the church (more precisely, Christ through the church) to represent both it and Christ. Insofar as the church is concerned, he or she represents not only the local congregation there assembled as the Body of Christ but also the Body of Christ throughout space and time. Jesus is present not in the person alone of either priest or people but in the dynamic of the whole *laos* together with the power of the Spirit. Without a doubt, a layperson can speak the words and raise the cup. A layperson even "represents Christ and the Church," according to the catechism of the Episcopal Church. But without the outward and visible commissioning that comes through ordination, with everything it implies, the lay president does not represent anyone beyond him- or herself even if the parish vestry and diocesan bishop give their authority. In other words, the lay president cannot be representative of the whole Body.

Nor is the lay president a ministerial president. Inherent in the priesthood is the pastoral task, although practice will vary from priest to priest. The layperson may perform pastoral duties with dignity, grace, and effectiveness, but the ministerial dimension is not granted to one of the laity as it is to an "elder," whose special quality in the Anglican presbyterate is the combination of the ministerial with the representative. In a report printed in the same ACC publication that commended giving thought to lay eucharistic presidency, a Communion-wide consultation on Eucharist cautioned, "Separating liturgical function and pastoral oversight tends to reduce liturgical presidency to an isolated ritual function."[74] That is precisely what lay presidency inevitably would do.[75]

---

[73] Robert Taft: "From the fourth century we see a growing consciousness that presbyters celebrating the eucharist together with the bishop are doing something that the laity cannot do, something only they have the mandate to perform." This also marks the beginning of a further shift in the whole understanding of the liturgical role of bishop and presbyters, away from the notion of presiding over a rite celebrated corporately by the whole church to the idea of their doing something for and on behalf of the people (Bradshaw, *Liturgical Presidency*, 27).

[74] ACC, *Being Anglican*, 297.

[75] The next chapter cites experiences of "Canon 9" priests in the US accumulating pastoral tasks, even though not part of their mandate, as a result of their priestly/sacramental activity.

In keeping with the diocese's Evangelical heritage, proponents of the Sydney measure linked eucharistic presidency with preaching. As laity in Sydney are allowed by the bishop to preach—and can excel at the task—so the thinking goes they can also "administer" the Eucharist. But preaching and celebrating have not been invariably connected, either in pre-Reformation history or in Anglican tradition, certainly not so closely as celebrating and pastoral work. There is, however, a longstanding bias against clergy who confine their ministry to celebrating the Eucharist, as the pejorative phrase "mass priest" used to imply.

The sense of the ministerial representation exists largely in the realm of symbol. The eucharistic celebration lies in the realm of sign and symbol, of mystery beyond this world's ability to comprehend. The priest is a "sacramental" person in a triple sense: first, as the recipient of the "sacramental rite" of ordination, which many count as a sacrament in itself; second, as the presider over the sacraments of Eucharist and, normally, of baptism; third, as one who portrays outwardly and visibly another inward and spiritual reality, which is that connection with the greater church and with Christ himself and, through Christ, the fullness of a Trinitarian God. For a layperson to officiate will deprive the rite of this element of mystical symbolism.

Although the measure was motivated partly for the practical end of providing the sacrament more frequently, other options are available that avoid these difficulties, skirt potential divisiveness, and still meet the need. Non-stipendiary clergy, by whatever term they may be called, or priests ordained purely for local service, may achieve the same result while remaining within the tradition of presbyteral presidency. As an alternative to lay eucharistic presidency, John Tiller proposed a local priesthood as part of local "elder" teams in England.[76] (It is worth noting that, at present, Sydney does not ordain women to the priesthood.[77])

---

[76] Tiller, *Strategy*, 120–122. Two English dioceses experimented with schemes for local "elders" to be appointed to leadership teams within parishes. He noted, however, the etymological difficulty of using "elder," given its association with "presbyter" (119).

[77] Trevor Lloyd calls this a "side-step" (cf. his brief discussion, *Lay Presidency*, 7). It would seem crucial for those who favor lay presidency of the Eucharist but not the ordination of women to clarify whether only lay *men* would preside, and if so, why not women; and if lay *women* could preside, why not open ordination to them? I do not see how the argument could successfully be made.

Finally, the argument for lay eucharistic presidency—because of its nonrepresentative nature—restricts the very notion of Eucharist to a certain locality. But Eucharist is never just a celebration of the congregation alone. As Melinsky explains:

> There is no practical reason why an intelligent lay person in good standing could not be taught in a couple of hours how to go through the motions of presiding. The eucharist, however, is not just a local celebration and the minister is not just a local minister. Both service and minister are local manifestations of something, or someone, much greater, spanning the centuries and the continents.[78]

Although to me the thinking behind the concept of lay presidency is theologically muddled, the imperative out of which it arises remains the pastorally sensitive matter of far-flung congregations served by too few priests. To survey the other options—such as fewer eucharistic celebrations—will be unwelcome to those for whom it is infrequent to begin with. The option of bringing in the previously consecrated elements, as a kind of sacramental "take-away," deprives the local congregation of sharing in the eucharistic act of consecration itself. Ordaining local priests takes time and holds certain disadvantages. The use of non-parochial clergy works only if they can be found; moreover, the important theological connection between leadership of a congregation and leadership at the Eucharist may undermine the rationale for presbyters who are not parish priests. That is a question for the next chapter.

The solution, then, of lay presidency makes a degree of pastoral sense: if the sheep are starving, the good shepherd gets them food by whatever means necessary. Who actually feeds them matters less than that they are fed. However, one must ask whether, in the end, the medium is part of the message—whether the person appointed as an ordained representative of Christ and church to preside at the Eucharist is a necessary and inherent component of the process of spiritual nourishment. Anglicans have always maintained that this is precisely the case. As one priest, who had considered the issue of lay-led Eucharist and lay-distributed extended communion concluded, "Probably only the provision of local priests will resolve the problem."[79] Roland Allen would undoubtedly agree.

---

[78] Melinsky, *Shape*, 140.

[79] Phillip Tovey, *Communion Outside the Eucharist* (Bramcote, Notts.: Grove Books, 1993), 46.

PEOPLE FOR MAINTENANCE OR PEOPLE FOR MISSION?

Lay-eucharistic presidency illustrates one further difficulty. It does serve the church, but—to return to a question posed in this chapter's first section—whose primary task is it to serve the church and whose primary task is it to minister to the world? The answer, of course, is *both*: clergy and laity all have the mutual responsibility for the totality of the church's mission. Still, a division of labor allows for effectively pursuing that mission. But overemphasizing the *internal* needs of the church can undermine that mission. It can focus, instead, on maintaining the institution.

Over the past century, Anglican opinion generally has held that the lay role is above all to serve God in the world. According to William Temple, "The priest will stand for the things of God before the laity—who seek the help that a religious specialist can give them, while the laity stand for the things of God before the world."[80] Yet that is not how "lay ministry" is generally understood. Instead, writes one Generation X priest, "parochial activities constitute what is most frequently considered to be ministry," at least in the United States (and probably throughout the developed world). While Anglicans pride themselves on lay participation at all levels of governance, the effort can take enormous energy, as another young priest writes: "It is crucial to get off the governance treadmill. Apart from a small group genuinely needed (and, one hopes, spiritually gifted and called) for administration, why can't the majority of lay energy be plugged into encountering the living God and doing ministry where it's needed most?"[81] One reason, as the Anglican Consultative Council's tenth meeting identified, is the "tendency today to start with the ordained ministry and to see lay ministry as in some way derived. Our assertion is that the opposite is the better approach, with the ministry of the whole body coming first."

To start with clerical ministry virtually assures a *church-centered* ministry. Priestly eldership is a critical role, to be sure. But one as committed to the ministry of all as Stewart Zabriskie has

---

[80] Temple, *RSJG*, 163; cf. *HNW*, 106, in virtually the same words.

[81] Daniel Emerson Hall, "Stole and Stethoscope," and Beth Maynard, "ISO Peer Group: Episcopal Culture through an Xer Lens," both in Humphrey, ed., *Gathering the NeXt Generation*, 66, 90.

identified the presbyter as the "maintenance person," who gathers the community together to nurture and nourish it for its work beyond. To base a model of ministry upon the role of the "temple person"[82] virtually guarantees that maintenance will take priority over mission.

As long as clergy remain the models for ministry, whatever the laity does will go unnoticed and underappreciated. I have served two congregations as rector. In each case, laity were involved in myriad ways, from pastoral care, to missions and evangelism, to community involvement of every sort. Some pursued these through their employment, some through voluntary activity, friendships, family—in short, through their lives. In my second parish, a large church in a small town, wherever something worthwhile was happening in the community, our people were involved. Ironically, trying to get them to see that they were doing the work of the church was like squeezing that camel through the eye of a needle, as if the ministry that "counts" is ministry within the church's walls. It is telling, I think, that the rise of "lay ministry" is charted by milestones such as becoming readers, aiding in the Eucharist, bringing the sacrament to the sick—all of which are worthwhile. But to consider such work the epitome or sum total of the ministry of all the baptized leaves a church that is impoverished and fraught with tension. Those exhausted by the governance of the church may have no energy left for the real work of ministry. As one senior warden quipped, "The problem isn't that we have too many Episcopal priests. The problem is that we have too few Episcopal laity!"[83]

Those places where the church expands combine energetic, visionary clergy with energetic laity who have caught the vision and help to spread it. With evangelism as its organizing principle, the Diocese of Sabah in the Province of South East Asia adopted the "1–1–3 method." This formula encourages each member to commit to bring one person to Christ every three years. Sustained by work and prayer, this simple approach has caused the Diocese

---

[82] Zabriskie, *Total Ministry*, 48; see chapter 5, above. The deacon, by contrast, is the "mission" person.

[83] J. Scott Barker, "The Future of Our Generation in the Church," in Humphrey, ed., *Gathering the NeXt Generation*, 137.

of Sabah to grow more than ten percent annually[84]—and it must be primarily because of laity who take on an evangelistic task. By no means is this the only form of service: Kofi Annan of Ghana, Secretary-General of the United Nations, is an Anglican communicant. Devoting one's life to bringing peace in the world must count for something in the panoply of lay ministries. (Of course, Annan's highly visible efforts internationally betokens countless parallels on local and even personal levels.)

The people of God can influence those about them, indeed the entire world, especially as they move beyond the church to "penetrate society" with the gospel. Imagining the clergy at the church door bidding farewell to the congregation, the ordained largely remain behind, tending to the concerns of the altar and word and pastoral care, assisted invaluably by others in the congregation, who are not ordained. But their role ties clergy largely to the church, in ways that laity are not. We must not understate the degree to which clergy can become significantly active in their communities, nor miss the special role of diaconal service. Nor should we wish to diminish lay involvement in the internal life of the church. It reinvigorates local congregations, keeping clergy in touch with the community, breaking down barriers, and giving a renewed sense of participation by all the *laos*. Much less should anyone argue *against* lay ministry, at risk of assuming, in N. T. Wright's phrase, the "Canute-like" role of ordering the tide to ebb.[85] On the contrary, understanding the opportunities, gifts, roles, and functions of laity *and* clergy, in mutual respect, cooperation, and occasionally forbearance too, gives hope for a renewed mission of Christ to the world.

---

[84] Kew and Okorocha, *Vision Bearers*, 44–45.

[85] Wright, *New Tasks*, 119.

X
Old Challenges, New Forms

For as long as anyone can remember, Anglicans have cherished a certain ideal of priesthood. The image of George Herbert ringing his church bell and saying his prayers might no longer fit the realities of industrialized Britain, suburban Chicago, a Central American barrio, or a Ugandan village. Still, it has retained a hold on Anglican imaginations to the extent that, although the "parson" was gone, the "five marks" of the priesthood live on. They are enshrined in the 1662 Ordinal that until recently had been used, with little variation, for centuries in England and wherever *The Book of Common Prayer* was found.

In the first place, the priest is *parochial*. The bishop authorizes new priests to minister "in the Congregation, where thou shalt be lawfully appointed thereunto." Ordained ministry means parish ministry, and that principle infuses all other priestly roles.

Second, the priest is *pastoral*. "Have always...printed in your remembrance," the bishop exhorted the ordinands, "how great a treasure is committed to your charge. For they are the sheep of Christ.... The Church and Congregation whom you must serve, is his spouse and his body." In his writings Moberly also conjoined priesthood and pastorate, claiming that at priestly ordinations the church "stamps with so solemn an emphasis the 'pastoral' aspect of their 'priesthood.'"[1]

---

[1] Moberly, *MP*, 293. He notes the connection, in this light, of "priest" and "presbyter."

Third, the priest is a *person of the Word*. "Take thou authority to preach the Word of God," said the bishop as he handed the newly ordained priests a Bible. After communion, the bishop would pray on behalf of all, "Grant also that we may have grace to hear and receive what they shall deliver out of thy most holy Word, or agreeable to the same, as the means of our salvation." The priest is a preacher.

Fourth, the priest is a *sacramental person*. The bishop bestowed authority to preach the Word and also "to minister the holy Sacraments in the Congregation."

Finally, the priest is *full-time*. "To give yourselves wholly to this office" is what the bishop expected the candidates to do, "so that, as much as lieth in you, you will apply yourselves wholly to this one thing, and draw all your cares and studies this way."[2] Canon law and English civil legislation made the exhortation mandatory. And, though the liturgy was too discreet to mention it, the requirement obliged another mark: the priest is paid by the church.

These attributes varied in how they were practiced and what priority they received, but none of them could stand apart from the rest. The "mass priest," whose sole responsibility was sacramental, was generally scorned; instead, the pastoral and, often, the preaching responsibilities were to extend the sacramental role. To be sure, deviations from the norm could readily be found. Still, these marks constituted an ideal that the vast majority of Anglican priests strove to uphold.

In the twentieth century, however, the normative image began to hold less sway. Practical difficulties experienced in overseas churches came home to roost in the English churchyard, as throughout the Anglican Communion old tensions returned and new ones appeared. Together, the varieties of ministerial experience forced renewed thinking on the nature of priesthood.

If the standard image of the Anglican priest is a person of the parish, how then would one classify my friend Ernest Katahweire, a priest who teaches at Makerere University in Kampala? What of his wife, Mabel Katahweire, one of the first women ordained as priest in Uganda, whose vocation has led her to teach at a theological

---

[2] "The Ordering of Priests," 1662 BCP, 562–583 (cp. US 1928 BCP, 539–547).

college, then to head her church's provincial education office, and now to develop a theological education by extension program in South Africa? In what sense is Mauricio Andrade, who works as general secretary for the Igreja Episcopal Anglicana do Brasil, a priest? And what about Montagu Pearse, who as a secular employee labored for years as a substance abuse counselor in Massachusetts prisons, helped out in parishes, and was later appointed as archdeacon? Where does this leave Holmes Irving, my now-retired predecessor as rector of R. E. Lee Memorial Church, Lexington?

Some of these roles have been traditionally accepted in Anglicanism as priestly. In medieval days, some monks were ordained, giving precedent to non-parochial clergy in a specialized ministry that returned with the revival of Anglican monasticism in the nineteenth century. Because monastics had been the teachers at universities, the precedent was accepted for ordained academic ministries to such an extent that "fellows" were required to receive Holy Orders in order to teach, a requirement that remains in force for certain positions at the universities of Oxford and Durham. Life in the colonies necessitated exceptions to this norm: before he became the first American bishop, Samuel Seabury, Doctor of Divinity, made ends meet as a doctor of medicine. Diocesan officers, teachers, and chaplains of prisons, schools, or institutions of healing were all recognized as duly presbyteral, so long as the bishop assented. Although the traditional pastoral image still remained the norm, there were a number of such exceptions to the rule even though the prayer book rites did not recognize them.

Nowadays, the realities of ordained ministries are even more complex. The church itself sponsors clergy in all kinds of ministries, including education and social care. "Non-stipendiary ministers" (NSMs) include deacons along with priests. Clergy ordained under special provision to serve a particular community—"Canon 9" clergy in the United States; "local ordained ministry" (LOM) or "ordained local ministry" (OLM) in the United Kingdom; "ministers of the people" (*minita-a-iwi*) or "community priests" in New Zealand—are usually not paid for their church work. As a group they may be called "ministers in secular employment" ("MSE"), "voluntary clergy" (as Roland Allen called them), "worker priests," or "tentmaking," "sector," "honorary," "supplementary," or "auxiliary" ministers. All these terms describe clergy whose full-time employment does not come from the institutional church. Not only has the prayer book largely avoided embracing them, so has the church's thinking until quite recently.

NON-STIPENDIARY MINISTRY: "A NEW TYPE OF PRIESTHOOD"

Secular employment for clergy was not even legal in England until 1970. In 1529 Parliament passed a law designed to resolve abuses of absentee clergy holding multiple benefices who were seldom in residence to fulfill their duties. The act declared that "no spiritual Persons, secular or regular, of what Degree soever he or they be, shall from henceforth take to ferm to himself...any Manors, Lands, Tenements...upon Pain of forfeit Ten Pounds for every Month that he shall occupy such Ferm." Another clause forbade the clergy from commercial trade, lest they be fined triple their proceeds. An 1817 act clarified that the parson could legally buy items for his home and then sell what he did not want, farm up to eighty acres (more with episcopal permission), and, under certain limitations, be a shareholder or even limited partner in a company. But it did not lift the ecclesiastical canons of 1603–04 forbidding clergy to "resort to any taverns or ale-houses."[3] Until *The Alternative Service Book* became available in 1979–80, the Ordinal instructed the bishop to remind each ordinand, "Ye ought to forsake and set aside (as much as you may) all worldly cares and studies" in order "to give yourselves wholly to this office."[4] The priest was a man apart—commercially, socially, and spiritually.

Canons, laws, and liturgies like these dampened interest in— and receptivity to—other forms of ministry, such as those proposed by Roland Allen. They reflected and fostered an image of who clergy are and what they should do. As Patrick Vaughan

---

[3] Vaughan, *Non-Stipendiary Ministry*, 9–13 (q. on 9–10). However, F. R. Barry cites the Reformation-era Bishops of Lichfield and Coventry ordaining in one day seventy men who were tailors, shoemakers and other craftsmen; and two priests were reported in Devon as keeping alehouses (Barry, *Vocation*, 181–182).

[4] 1662 BCP, 574.

describes in his study of non-stipendiary ministry, the perspective was particularly English. It assumed that the class distinction between high and low, rich and poor, is divinely ordained. Society as a whole is divided into sacred and secular. The church itself is likewise segregated into clergy and laity. These three factors effectively removed the priest from the realm of other mortals and insisted that the cure of souls—the preeminent task of the priest— must be full-time. They also militated against any deviation from the traditional standard, even though the church's "livings" did not always support a clergy family such that some clerics were forced to supplement their incomes on the side and on the sly.[5]

Nineteenth-century suggestions got nowhere, especially given the urge to "professionalize" the clergy. Thomas Arnold, the Rugby headmaster who proposed revivifying the diaconate,[6] also commended a non-stipendiary ministry. One idea got no further than the other, nor did subsequent suggestions by the Archdeacon of London, William Hale, or the noted vicar of Leeds, Walter Hook. Roland Allen hardly succeeded any better, but in his fervor he developed the concept of an alternative ministry. Given overwhelming demands from overseas missionary areas and a desperate lack of clergy at home in England, in the 1920s Allen advised a system of "voluntary clergy." He claimed that the dearth of candidates for full-time ordained work must be "God's Providence...that we may learn that this type is not the only type" of ministry. Indeed, "Divine Truth," "because it is in itself right and wise to do so" and not because of a scarcity of clergy, should motivate ordaining "men in Full Orders, exercising their ministry but not dependent upon it for their livelihood." These clergy might reveal the spiritual motive of priesthood, he wrote; and placing them in the "world of work" could help to bridge the gulf between a paid clergy and working people. This latter conviction was echoed in word by the English bishop F. R. Barry and in deed by French Roman Catholic "worker priests" of the postwar era. Allen was ecstatic that an American businessman, the Rev. van Tassel Sutphen, was ordained on July 7, 1923, in the Diocese of Newark, followed

[5] Vaughan, *Non-Stipendiary Ministry*, 60–62, 18–22; Barry, *Relevance*, 172.

[6] See above, chapter 8.

in 1925 by the Rev. Ralfe Davies, an actor.[7]

As the clergy shortage continued through the 1920s, so did conversations in England about different forms of ministry. The Diocese of Southwark discussed a secularly employed diaconate in 1919, as did the London Diocesan Conference two years later. An archbishops' committee explored Allen's case for voluntary clergy but deemed it "fraught with difficulties" over conflicts with the Ordinal, with secular work, and with professional clergy. With the 1930 Lambeth Conference approaching, Australians broached the topic out of the usual motive, a shortage of clergy. English bishops talked over the Australians' proposal but scorned the idea of "Laymen in Priests Orders" and "setting up a new type of Priest-hood." Surprisingly, the idea found its way into a "Provisional Committee for Voluntary Clergy" of England's Church Assembly in 1928 and also into a Lambeth Conference preparatory memo-randum in 1930.[8] But the Lambeth Conference itself "damned it with faint praise," as Barry charged. A committee reiterated the prayer book line that "the Priesthood demands the whole of life" and is "not to be made subservient to any other interests." They feared that non-stipendiary ministers, being men of lesser education (or so they thought), might perform a purely sacramental role divorced from a wider ministry. In the end, the committee advised licensing lay readers to ease the burden of administering communion but saw "no insuperable objection," where need is great, to care-fully safeguarded experiments in "Auxiliary Priests." The positive presumption of a close link between sacrament and pastoral care prevailed, alongside the negative perception that a voluntary clergy would be inferior in learning and authority. By then, too, rising num-bers of ordinands in England lessened the urgency of alternatives.[9]

The concept lived on, however. Barry joined Allen in pushing the Church of England and the Communion as a whole to see min-istry in different forms. "Can we not conceive an ordained Ministry

---

[7] Q. from *Case for Voluntary Clergy* (1923) in Vaughan, *Non-Stipendiary Ministry*, 80, 81, 86; cf. 74–83. On the French "worker priests," see Desmond Fisher, "Worker Priests Once More," in Francis and Francis, eds., *Tentmaking*, 136–140.

[8] Q. in Vaughan, 106; cf. 98–111.

[9] Barry, *Vocation*, 157; *Lambeth 1930*, 175–177, 60 (Res. #65); Vaughan, *Non-Stipendiary Ministry*, 129–135, 139.

other than that of Rectors and Curates?" Barry asked. Some demonstration of ministry "by all its members" would make clear "that essential priesthood of all believers...embraces every legitimate vocation. It would thus help to save Christianity from becoming a caricature of itself as something that people do after working hours." The point applied to laity but also to clergy in experimental ministries, like chaplains in business firms. He saw such people bringing church to world and world to church (a subsequent justification for the diaconate). Though his lectures generated discussion, his arguments went ignored until World War II revealed—as World War I had done earlier—exactly what Barry had feared: a breach between church and people.[10]

With that great divide in mind, still yet another English commission then proposed that ordained priests might become manual laborers, and laborers might become priests. As the Industrial Christian Fellowship had involved laity in a workplace mission since 1919, so too in 1944 the Sheffield Industrial Mission placed selected clergy into the steel works, where they met with the workers and helped them think about the theological and social implications of their work. Several clergy left parochial ministry for an industrial mission all on their own.[11] Numbers were always few, but at least the ministry was legal: revisions of English canon law in the late 1940s eased prohibitions on outside work.

Meanwhile, stories arrived of successful experiments in overseas churches. Taking advantage of Lambeth's meager permission from 1930, Hong Kong ordained an auxiliary deacon in 1934. By 1960 thirteen of its thirty priests were non-stipendiary. That ten of these held university degrees demonstrated a certain appeal of church and priesthood to the educated but also showed the lack of appeal to those who were not—which was one of the aims of non-stipendiary arrangements.[12] The Church of India, Pakistan, Burma, and Ceylon modeled a permissive canon on Hong Kong's, and by 1956 the Diocese of Nagpur had ordained six non-parochial

---

[10] Barry, *Relevance*, 210, 213; cf. Vaughan, *Non-Stipendiary Ministry*, 145–148.

[11] Vaughan, *Non-Stipendiary Ministry*, 148–152; Welsby, *History*, 36.

[12] Welsby, *History*, 41–44; Vaughan, *Non-Stipendiary Ministry*, 168–180; cf. *Lambeth 1958*, 2.108–109.

presbyters including a doctor, a government inspector of education, and two schoolmasters.[13] With those examples, Barry added a fresh reminder that non-stipendiary ministers offered the chance to "emphasise the sacramental nature of daily life [and] to make for the sanctification of the secular [through] doing the world's work, and thereby serving the Creator's will."[14] All that, along with an endorsement from Michael Ramsey (then Archbishop of York), led a 1958 Lambeth committee cautiously to recommend

> that where conditions make it desirable, and in particular where political emergency threatens, provinces of the Anglican Communion should be encouraged to make provision upon these lines. The Committee, however, wishes to state its view quite clearly that such a supplementary ministry must never be regarded as a permanent substitute for the fully-trained and full-time priesthood which is essential to the continuing life of the Church.

The entire conference agreed.[15]

The Bishop of Hong Kong at that moment raised a critical question: What were such individuals to be called? "Auxiliary," he advised, suggests "a lower grade of ordination."[16] This linguistic problem persists to the present. "Honorary," as in "honorary curate," in British English connotes unpaid service, whereas in American usage it generally implies "given as an honor." "Non-stipendiary" and "non-parochial" define a positive in negative terms—one who is not paid or who is not in a parish, which in the latter case may not be correct. "Non-professional ordained ministry" sounds even more negative. Lambeth 1958 employed the term "supplementary ministry," which has a more positive tone yet retains an air of subordination—and an assistant or curate also shares that ancillary role. "Ministers in Secular Employment" (MSE), or more precisely, "Priests/Deacons in Secular Employment," is precise but plodding; "tentmaker" is more biblical, but

---

[13] Vaughan, *Non-Stipendiary Ministry*, 180; cf. *Lambeth 1958*, 2.109–110.

[14] Barry, *Vocation*, 159.

[15] *Lambeth 1958*, 2.108 (cf. Res. #89, 1.51).

[16] Appendix 1: Memorandum on "Auxiliary Priests," *Lambeth 1958*, 2.108.

sounds antiquated. Our language has yet to produce a felicitous option.

Whatever the terminology, Lambeth 1958 opened wide the door to new possibilities. Roland Allen's works were reissued. Then the Southwark Ordination Course opened in 1960, with thirty-one men preparing for orders on a part-time basis. Striving to avoid the harm done to families by uprooting married men for a residential course of several years, this program expected participants to live at home, work their jobs, and attend twice-weekly lectures plus seven weekend events and a two-week summer school. Its plan was to base theology in the realities of the working world. As in Hong Kong, though, hopes for broadening the social class of clergy ran up against the surprisingly high level of education of the students, since twenty-three percent of the first group were university graduates. In due course, fourteen SOC deacons were ordained in 1963. By 1969 ninety-four clergy had been trained by the program, which was deemed successful enough to copy. The North West Ordination Course (later Northern Ordination Course) was initiated in 1970 for stipendiary and non-stipendiary ministry alike, so by 1989 England had as many of these courses as it had colleges, fourteen of each, covering the land.[17]

Meanwhile, support for varying forms of ordained ministry increased throughout the Anglican Communion and across denominational lines. South American Anglican missions relied on unpaid ministers, clergy and lay. A World Council of Churches' conference in 1963 argued for ordaining secularly employed pastors to assist in local congregations and to witness to the gospel in sectors of society otherwise "impenetrable to existing forms of ministry" or in frontier situations.[18] Vatican II blessed alternative forms of ministry with a sentence in a decree promulgated the day before it adjourned that reinforced the French "worker priest" initiative, so that by 1970 the movement involved around two hundred clergy.[19]

---

[17] Vaughan, *Non-Stipendiary Ministry*, 186–197; Melinksy, *Shape*, 253–254.

[18] Peter Dawson, "Holy Orders in Unholy Places," in Francis and Francis, eds., *Tentmaking*, 150, re the Fourth World Conference on Faith and Order, Montreal, 1963.

[19] "On the Ministry and Life of Priests," *Presbyterorum Ordinis*, q. in Vaughan, *Non-Stipendiary Ministry*; cf. 212–219. Cf. Fisher, "Worker Priests," in Francis and Francis, eds., *Tentmaking*, 136–140.

By 1968 Lambeth bishops were convinced. "In order that the Church may be continually renewed for mission, there is need for a greater diversity in the exercise of the ordained ministry. Parochial and non-parochial, full- and part-time, stipendiary and honorary clergy are all needed." In that constellation, "the part-time non-stipendiary priest is in no way inferior to his full-time stipendiary brother." The church needs both, but in some areas the part-time non-stipendiary minister "could become the norm." Far from contravening doctrine, the bishops said, this form ministry is consistent with Scripture and early church tradition and should not undermine full-time ministries. Non-stipendiary ministers might be particularly needed where existing ministries are inadequate for proper care; in new communities beyond the reach of present parochial structures; to start new work; to strengthen team ministries; or to provide ministry where finances do not otherwise permit. Candidates would have to be experienced in the faith, mature in outlook, acceptable to church authorities and the communities they serve, and trained with care so that they may balance demands of secular work, church work, and family.[20] With that, by 1972 at least 174 diocesan clergy in England were earning their living in secular employment. Wales, faced with a sharp drop in clergy numbers, decided to foster non-stipendiary ministers, and in just five years, eight percent of the parochial clergy—55 in all—had taken on this role. Their ministry in the workplace had multiple aspects: interpreter of church to world and world to church; as informal teacher, counselor, confessor, comforter, reconciler, and intercessor. Scotland, with its sparse church population, ordained more non-stipendiary clergy than stipendiary—55 to 44—in the first decade after adopting the policy.[21]

Non-stipendiary ministry clearly is becoming an important element in the church's work. In dioceses like Colombia, the bishop is the only paid cleric; all others are tentmakers. Its new bishop, Francisco Duque Gomez, is a lawyer who received no pay at all from the parish he served as priest. In developed countries, people may prefer small churches of two hundred members that are

---

[20] *Lambeth 1968*, 102–103 (cf. Res. #33, p. 39).

[21] Vaughan, *Non-Stipendiary Ministry*, 257, 294–295.

pastor-centered, reports Barbara Brown Zikmund, head of the Association of Theological Schools, "but fewer and fewer can afford to pay what a well-trained clergy person ought to get."[22] Financial necessity may breed innovation whether the church wishes it or not. Moreover, signs indicate increasing acceptance. The Diocese of Caledonia, in British Columbia, elected a non-stipendiary minister as its bishop in 2001. In England, the idea of bus drivers, accountants, and refuse collectors also functioning as priests has grown to the point of receiving notice in *The Daily Telegraph*.[23]

The tentmaking model does, however, transgress traditional assumptions about what a priest should be and calls into question the nature of priest as "elder" of the community. Since this role is largely shared by another example of auxiliary cleric, we will consider that before contemplating its presbyteral nature.

LOCAL ORDAINED MINISTRY

Roland Allen's work was behind a second, related phenomenon: the growth of an ordained ministry serving a particular locality. The Church of England's "local ordained ministry" or "ordained local ministry"[24] and the Episcopal Church's "Canon 9" clergy are variations on the effort to provide ordained and sacramental leadership for a local community, which is generally limited to that one community. Allen, abetted by Herbert Kelly, initially provided the rationale for ordaining local indigenous leadership. The "total ministry" concept used by Bishops Gordon in Alaska and Frensdorff and Zabriskie in Nevada relied heavily on Allen's ideas for raising up out of a community leaders whom that community identifies. This too would likely be a non-stipendiary ministry, so it shares

---

[22] Larry Whitham, "Flocks in need of shepherds," *Washington Times*, July 2, 2001 <http://www.washtimes.com/national/20010702-475926.htm (July 20, 2001).

[23] Pat Ashworth, "NSM becomes bishop," *Church Times*, 26 October 2001; Chris Hastings, "Dustman by day, vicar by night," *The Daily Telegraph*, 11 August 2002 <http://www.telegraph.co.uk/news/main/jhtml?xml=%2Fnews%2F2002/2F08%2F11%Fnvicar//xml> (August 18, 2002).

[24] [Church of England,] Advisory Board of Ministry, *Stranger in the Wings* (Policy Paper No. 8) (London: Church House, 1998), 26.

many of the characteristics and much of the history of that form of service. But the idea of a *local* presbyterate, confined to a specified community, was a derivation from Lambeths 1958 and 1968 that the bishops seemed not to have anticipated.

The Diocese of Idaho experimented about that same time with training carefully selected men for non-stipendiary ministry. William Gordon applied the idea to those wishing to serve their home congregations, which made good sense in his Alaskan diocese of widely scattered churches. He proposed to the 1969 Special General Convention that "Dioceses with Congregations or missionary opportunities in communities which are small, isolated, remote, or distinct in respect of ethnic composition, language or culture" that cannot be provided for by clergy ordained under more traditional circumstances may be allowed to ordain "local Priests and Deacons," who are licensed to serve those congregations or the communities from which they come. His original language remains the basic authorization more than thirty years later.[25]

In England, both non-stipendiary ministry and local ordained ministry were limited by the politics surrounding their introduction. Despite Lambeth's nod, a 1968 report on non-stipendiary ministry assumed that any threat to current clerical professional standards would have little chance of success, so passage was won at the loss of considering any indigenous working-class candidates. As the 1970s progressed, the new movement for local ordained ministers bolstered the older case for non-stipendiary ministers, as both slowly won adherents. In 1969 a vicar in East London invited several working-class parishioners to consider ordination. Four responded and were ordained deacons in 1972 and priests in 1974. Though resembling non-stipendiary ministers, local ordained ministers differed in several ways. The latter would be part of an intentional team ministry; they were called out of a local church rather than by external appointment and were permanently attached to their own communities; they received locally

---

[25] Report of the Standing Commission on the Church in Small Communities, *The Blue Book* (2000), 39; cf. Title III, Canon 9.1(a) (ECUSA *Canons* 2000, p. 76–78). I do not agree with the commission that Lambeth 1958 "called for the ordination of local, self-supporting clergy" (*Blue Book*, 38) in the restricted sense that Canon 9 came to be understood, though that Lambeth resolution (#89, p. 1.51) undoubtedly opened the way for its development.

based, highly practical training. They were to be licensed for seven years, with renewal of the license dependent upon review; and like non-stipendiary ministers, theirs would be unpaid, voluntary ministry. Although the experiment did not flourish, it set some guideposts for what would soon follow.[26]

Thanks perhaps to theories of non-stipendiary ministry paving their way, local ordained ministers were accepted more quickly. An official paper of 1974 projected three areas where local ministry would work well: a remote rural team, an inner-city parish, and a "divided" parish with disparate ethnic or sociological segments within the congregation. A revolutionary suggestion was emerging: to abandon England's long-cherished commitment to a single standard for priestly training. A General Synod report echoed the idea in 1975, and supportive scholars like John Macquarrie served to amplify it. In part, the committee was refuting the proposal to authorize laity to preside at the Eucharist, though at the risk of ordaining "sacramentalists" and thus breaking the equally strong Anglican tradition of ministering both word and sacrament. Synod bestowed its approval in early 1976.[27]

Lincolnshire was next to instigate a "local" ministry. Its rural diocese carefully worked out a proposal much along the lines of the East London attempt. Asked for its consent, the English House of Bishops deemed that the scheme should be understood not as a new category of ministry but as a local manifestation of non-stipendiary ministry. Since non-stipendiary ministry had already been approved, local ordained ministers instantly became an option for any diocese in England. "At one stroke the long-standing tradition of a unitary standard for ordination was broken; the Church of England as a whole had made available to it a pattern of local ministry," writes Vaughan. Though the sudden, sweeping act caused confusion, it may have manifested the bishops' alarm over a potential breakdown of pastoral ministration in rural areas. By 1986 ten dioceses had ordained twenty local ordained ministers.

---

[26] Vaughan, *Non-Stipendiary Ministry*, 272–273. Some of the difficulties appear to have been that parishioners treated LOMs as they would full-time stipendiaries and laid substantial burdens upon them and that the initiating vicar departed for other work.

[27] Vaughan, *Non-Stipendiary Ministry*, 275–277.

By contrast, thirty-four dioceses had ordained eighty as non-stipendiary ministers by the same year, with ninety candidates recommended for training per year and eight courses established to cover most of the country. Thus locally ordained ministry seemed to be a small movement within the larger whole but one that appealed especially to older candidates, often with weaker educational background, who were perhaps more willing to undertake the less arduous training. At the same time, the acceptance rate of applicants was higher for this group than for non-stipendiary ministers.[28]

"Local" ministries appear to be growing in the United States and the Church of England and are likely to increase elsewhere in the Anglican Communion. The models differ in one respect: the English local ordained minister will invariably be part of a ministerial team headed by an incumbent priest (of more accustomed ordination and training), whereas his or her American counterpart might not be.[29] After Alaska and Nevada pioneered the practice of locally ordained ministeries, the concept spread to less remote areas such as Southwestern Virginia. That diocese is not nearly as large as Nevada or Alaska, but its rural congregations, small in numbers and with little or no chance of affording full-time clergy, can rarely find secularly employed priests. A case in point is Christ Church in Big Stone Gap, a tiny town in the far southwestern tip of the state about four hours' drive from the see city of Roanoke. After its last full-time priest left in the 1960s, the church tried a yoked ministry with neighboring parishes, and later someone read for orders as a non-stipendiary minister. In the 1990s, under Bishop Heath Light, Christ Church took a different direction. It adapted a plan of "total ministry" in which one of the congregation's leaders would be ordained to provide sacramental leadership while laypersons would oversee Christian education, administration, and pastoral care for its membership of about fifty-five. Several would rotate in preaching, using prepared sermon texts. In 1994 Raymond Moore was ordained its deacon and priest within the team of local members.

---

[28] Vaughan, *Non-Stipendiary Ministry*, 278–279, 282–283.

[29] *Stranger in the Wings*, 24; ECUSA, *Constitution and Canons* (2000), III.9.6(a) (p. 78), though it is presumed that the local priest or deacon will be part of a team.

A "cluster" of three congregations in Tazewell County under its full-time rector, Thomas Mustard, modified the idea for its own situation, which more closely resembled the English model of an incumbent with assistants. Two leading laity, Norman Desrosiers and Russell Hatfield, prepared for orders and were ordained by Light's successor, Neff Powell, in 1997. With a priest of the "old" model overseeing the congregations, the two Canon 9 clergy provided sacramental ministry on Sundays and preached "canned" sermons. When Thomas Mustard accepted a call elsewhere, Russell Hatfield took on added duties, retiring in 2001 from his secular job to devote himself to presbyterate. With additional training, including pursuing a doctorate of ministry from Sewanee, he assumed the title "priest and pastor" of the cluster.

All agree that their situations work effectively because of strong lay participation. The three clergy brought extensive experience as active laity to their new roles. Lay readers share in officiating and in preaching. Other laypeople take on administrative duties. The area where lay involvement is less than expected is that of pastoral care; both Russell Hatfield and Raymond Moore found themselves more in demand, and the laypeople providing pastoral care less so. As a local priest, with less training, Hatfield would often refer people to the rector (Thomas Mustard) until he departed, but, even beforehand, he was able to assist some people himself. Adequate training still remains a concern. Russell Hatfield declares he received "not nearly enough." Of his current summertime study on a seminary campus, he reports, "I could tell a difference in spending those five weeks with other clergy and professors, and my parishioners could. They could tell a difference in how I did things."

Both of these models raise questions about priesthood, but ordaining local clergy prompts one in particular: How can the adage "A priest is a priest for the whole church" apply to them? "Just as baptism by incorporating believers into Christ makes them members of the whole Church," reports an English study, "so too ordination by setting particular persons aside as ministers of Christ, makes them bishops or presbyters of the whole Church."[30] On the surface, Canon 9 clergy seem to contradict this norm. For one thing, they are limited—by canon, license, or mutual

---

[30] Q. from *The Priesthood of the Ordained Ministry* (1986) in *The Ordination of Women to the Priesthood: A Digest of the Second Report by the House of Bishops* (London: Church House Publishing, 1990 [GS Misc. 337], 27.

agreement—to service in that community, however it is specified, and lack authorization to function elsewhere. For another, they are chosen from out of a particular congregation, which can exert an "ownership" over the cleric. They can too easily be seen as a priest *only* for that community and thus *not* representative of the whole church, foregoing one of the most powerful if mysterious aspects of the presbyteral nature.

In practice, the problems appear more conceptual than real. At the outset, these clergy were ordained by a bishop in apostolic succession representing Christ and the whole church. That in itself is of note.[31] It holds several further implications. Though emerging from specific communities, the apostolic representative of the whole church—the bishop—assigned them to serve there. They function by episcopal license, as to some degree does any deacon or priest under canon or custom; theirs happens to be a bit more stringent. For Canon 9 clergy in Tazewell County to serve multiple congregations adds depth and breadth to how they are perceived. All these clergy are active in diocesan events; all are priests who received their orders like any other presbyter of the Episcopal Church. Only the terms of licensing differ, but even those terms of restriction—insofar as they attempt to curtail the usual extent of priesthood—quickly erode in most people's hearts and minds as the supposedly restricted priest begins to go about the nurturing daily occupations of ordained ministry. When the Bishop of Lincoln was about to initiate a scheme of local ordained ministers, his legal officer raised objections and concerns:

> Once a man is ordained he is ordained and I do not think as a matter of law any restrictions could be placed on the exercising of his ministry.... I think it would be perfectly valid in law if a bishop were to institute a local ordained minister to a benefice or re-license him to an area other than his original one.... This does seem to put the Local Ordained Minister in much the same position as any other member of the clergy.

---

[31] "Since the one who ordains is a bishop, representing the college of bishops, ordination is not simply ordination to the ministry of a local congregation or even of a particular diocese. It is ordination to priesthood within the whole body of Christ" ("Priesthood and the Eucharist: A Common Statement by the Joint Study Group of Representatives of the Roman Catholic Church in Scotland and the Scottish Episcopal Church," in Joseph W. Witmer and J. Robert Wright, eds., *Called to Full Unity: Documents on Anglican-Roman Catholic Relations 1966–1983* [Washington, D.C.: Office of Publications and Promotion Services, US Catholic Conference, c. 1986], 206).

A "gentleman's agreement" for them not to move seems to prevail in England.[32] In the Episcopal Church the canons generally limit the movement of local ordained ministers: they may relocate within the diocese but may function there only if requested by the congregation and licensed by the bishop, so they would need to garner the trust of the new congregation. The expectation remains that such clergy will "not move from the Congregation and Diocese in which they were ordained." Switching dioceses requires the request by the bishop of the diocese to which the deacon or priest wishes to move.[33] To perform the wedding of a niece, Hatfield had to obtain the permission of his own bishop and that of the bishop in the diocese where the ceremony occurred. How a concept designed for remote dioceses such as Alaska's with little mobility will govern situations of increasing mobility remains to be seen.[34]

That such ministers are indeed priests and deacons, however, no one really doubts. The priests in Tazewell County, for example, have noticed laity and fellow clergy treating them as such, regardless of the provisions by which they were ordained, which counters a major worry. Bishop Light reported an early conversation with a potential Canon 9 congregation in which one laywoman made clear her distress at being treated as a second-class parish. The idea died on the spot (and, years later, the congregation remains without a priest). Where it has worked, the issue has not been a problem, nor has there been evident discrimination aimed at Canon 9 clergy by laity or other clergy. "No one has looked down on me as a second-class priest," Russell Hatfield states. "I am a priest. Period. Canon 9 doesn't have anything to do with it." His perception coincides with English statistics indicating broad levels of acceptance by other clergy, congregations, and the communities at large.[35]

---

[32] Q. in Vaughan, *Non-Stipendiary Ministry,* 278 (letter from Derek Wellman to the Bishop of Lincoln, 12 January 1979, reprinted as an appendix in House of Bishops 1979 [Lincoln Diocesan Scheme for LOM]).

[33] ECUSA, *Canons* (2000), III.9.7–8 (p. 78).

[34] A deacon, later priest, who served as my assistant for four years was ordained under Canon 9 provisions in Nevada, went to serve a national church office in New York, came to two congregations in Virginia, then to placements in Maryland and Georgia.

[35] *Stranger in the Wings,* 58. US data from 1990–93 were not quite so rosy, however. Non-parochial clergy participating in the Clergy Family Project agreed

Thomas Mustard sees Canon 9 clergy effectively providing ministry to geographically or sociologically isolated congregations. But, he adds, the church needs

> much more thinking and study so that we're clear about what we're communicating to everybody, and what our expectations are of what we want this to do for us, and how we can get there given the understandings and expectations of the priesthood and what that means.

Given economic stringencies and, at least in ECUSA, the high cost of educating and maintaining seminary-trained clergy, Heath Light concludes, "My sense is that [Canon 9] is going to be an increasingly viable option philosophically. Not everyone agrees with that; but maybe we will rediscover our energy for witness and fundamental community."[36]

THE QUESTION OF AUXILIARY MINISTRIES

The question of whether local ordained ministers represent the whole church is only one part of a larger issue that was raised in 2000 by the Episcopal Church's Standing Commission on the Church in Small Communities:

---

strongly, by 40%, with the statement, "Priests in alternate ministries (e.g., chaplains, interims) are not given recognition equal to that given full-time parochial clergy" (compared with only 16% of parochial clergy strongly concurring). The two groups were alike in how supported they felt by their bishops. Roberta Chapin Walmsley and Adair T. Lummis, *Healthy Clergy, Wounded Healers: Their Families and Their Ministries* (New York: Church Publishing, 1997), 81.

[36] Telephone interviews with the Rev. G. Thomas Mustard, Bedford, VA, June 3, 2001; the Rev. Russell Hatfield, Tazewell, VA, June 11, 2001; the Rev. R. Raymond Moore, Big Stone Gap, VA, June 11, 2001; the Rt. Rev. A. Heath Light, retired Bishop of Southwestern Virginia, Roanoke, VA, June 28, 2001. On financial stringencies contributing to further LOM situations, cf. *Stranger in the Wings*, 3.

Shortly before this book went to press, the 2003 General Convention of the Episcopal Church revised its canons on ministry in ways that would incorporate "local" ministries into provisions regarding the ordained in general. It thereby ended any distinction of "locally ordained clergy." http://submitresolution.dfms. org/view_leg_detail.aspx?id=A111&type=FINAL> (August 20 2003).

> Current church practice raises questions concerning
> whether the local priesthood, essentially confined to cel-
> ebrating the sacraments, is an adequate expression of
> the church's understanding of what it means to be a
> priest. Is a local priesthood with limited responsibilities
> truly compatible with Episcopal polity and tradition?[37]

Hovering over supplementary ministry, in any of its variants, are three of the traditional assumptions about presbyterate: it is full-time; it links word and sacrament; and it is at heart pastoral. As our historical survey has indicated, non-stipendiary ministry was inconceivable as long as canons and national laws forbade secular employment for priests. Those restrictions themselves embodied an understanding of priesthood that entails total dedication to the task. It must be full-time and paid. That understanding accompanied English emigrants to the colonies they populated. Yet in vast continents like Australia, the rugged terrain of South America, or sparsely populated regions of the western United States, the demands of pastoral care and the imperatives of mission could not be met with techniques of the old country. Even there, as England watched the number of its clergy diminish, the care of souls became ever more problematic. Must a priest always be full-time, stipendiary, and in a parish? Supplementary ministry challenged those assumptions, along with two others: that ministry of word and ministry of sacrament must always be connected, and that the ministry of the altar would be linked with ministry at large.[38] Exceptions to these assumptions have always abounded. Clergy teachers and scholars, diocesan officers, and institutional or military chaplains did not necessarily combine ministries of word, sacrament, and pastoral care, yet never was their role questioned or denied. Nor, as retirement became an option for older priests, did anyone suggest that those who retired were no longer priests; instead, theirs is a form of non-stipendiary ministry.[39] From that

---

[37] ECUSA, *Blue Book* (2000), 37.

[38] Cf. Vaughan, *Non-Stipendiary Ministry*, 276.

[39] For more than twenty years, retired clergy have enriched the life of the parishes I have served, functioning faithfully as celebrants, homilists, parish visitors, counselors, and generally as active, genuine "elders" of the congregation, usually in voluntary capacities.

model to a priest's working in a factory or bank is not a huge theoretical leap after all.

What, then, of these links? A "total ministry" concept may preclude the one at the altar from serving in the pulpit. Yet while Anglicanism has historically enshrined the word-sacrament connection in its ordinals, it has never maintained an absolute bond; in some areas, preaching is a ministry licensed by the bishop, and clergy not qualified to preach read homilies instead.[40] Ray Moore preaches, but so do laypeople in the congregation as part of a shared responsibility. We saw in the previous chapter that Australians in Sydney prize the preaching of the laity, which has led them to propose extending the further sacramental role of lay-celebrant. As for pastoral care, for a time the Canon 9 clergy in Tazewell were initially expected not to perform any pastoral ministrations. The danger in each case is in their being defined totally by their sacerdotal role so that they become "mass priests." Local ordained ministers are sometimes called "sacramentalists" in witness to their chief function, and a community committed to total ministry may institutionalize that division and exclude them from ministries of word and pastoral care. Non-stipendiary ministers may find themselves with a ministry in the secular world but not necessarily with a ministry at the altar or in the pulpit.

Again, these dangers may be more theoretical than real. Hatfield and Moore both report pastoral work arising from their priesthood. Says Moore:

> I quickly began to realize that people who found themselves or a child in the hospital or who were looking at a difficult divorce didn't readily call a member of the congregation who happened to be chairman of the pastoral care committee. They wanted to talk with the priest. Rightly or wrongly, for deeply spiritual issues, they wanted the priest to be there.

Although the reality would seem to question how thoroughly lay ministry has been accepted, his experience at least shows that priests will find a pastoral ministry coming their way regardless of the provisions by which they were ordained. Likewise, duties of

---

[40] *Stranger in the Wings*, 21.

preaching were shared, with the clergy taking their part. So it would be important for the community—the parish, diocese, or whatever—to recognize and uphold these alternative ministries and to draw connections between what they do during the week and their functions at the altar. It can become a creative dynamic that expands the church's ministry as priests and deacons take on tasks outside the liturgy in ways specific to their order.

The Rev. Richard Payne, for example, after leading an Oregon parish, became a school psychologist in Massachusetts. Though serving in a non-clerical role, he found that neither the representative quality of his priestly life nor the ministerial functioning of that life was lost on co-workers. "There was an awareness, he says,

> that I was somehow different from others, some added dimension. The way it showed itself was in that I was asked to do some altar-related tasks in people's lives, such as weddings or funerals, and that I was someone to talk to who would keep his mouth shut. That can be connected back to the altar, to absolution and confidentiality of confession.[41]

Throughout his years with the school, and also since his retirement, Payne has remained active in his local parish. Sometimes he celebrates or preaches, sometimes he serves in the lay capacity of usher with his wife, Joan. Of vital importance is the connection between the presbyter and the church: For the priest to be an "elder" presumes an affiliation with others, in this case with the community of faith. Within that relationship, other issues will probably work themselves out depending on local circumstances and personalities involved. The keynotes must be collegiality, cooperation, and mutuality—clergy with clergy, laity with laity, laity with clergy—as the *laos* labors together, mindful of the imagery of a Body and of the Trinity.

Payne illustrates another growing phenomenon: understanding the diversities of vocations that may also be "priestly." In days when presbyterate was all but equated with parish priesthood, sometimes with the force of law, a vocation to Holy Orders meant virtually one career. No longer. Bishop Martineau summarizes a typically Anglican perspective:

---

[41] Interview with the Rev. Richard L. Payne, Brewster, MA, July 25, 2000.

Every Christian has a vocation. A man cannot expect to follow Christ and not be given something to do for him and to become for him. Within the great variety of service to which God calls, the life and work of a priest has a particular place; it represents to the Church itself and to the world outside one special aspect of the life and work of the Church as a whole. But...every honourable trade or profession can be the way in which a man fulfils his vocation.[42]

But "vocation" and "occupation" are no longer coterminus for clerics; instead, what one does to earn a living becomes set within the larger framework of one's vocation as a disciple of Christ. The varieties of patterns evolving for clergy mark an openness for each of the *laos* more generally to find ways of coordinating employment with discipleship and their involvement with the church integrated into the whole of their lives.

The same phenomenon, however, holds implications for the clergy as "professional" people.

PROFESSIONALISM

Theologian Urban Holmes was disgusted when he heard of someone referring to a priest as a "professional Christian." That, he flatly declared, should be "offensive to every baptized person." Holmes went on to conjure a Victorian-style image of a cleric who is "predictably 'straight,' conservatively dressed in neat, good-quality black suits," who never takes more than two drinks at a party and who speaks with authority in all matters of religion.[43] Richard Kew, born in England but now a priest in Tennessee, is more restrained but no less critical.

One of the tragedies of the late-twentieth-century church has been a "professionalization" of the ministry that has raised up managers rather than leaders, therapists rather than pastors, maintainers rather than missioners. The modern church tends to be led by those who see

---

[42] Martineau, *Office and Work of a Priest*, 9–10.

[43] Holmes, *Priest in Community*, 136–137.

ministry in terms of career rather than lifelong selfless
abandonment to Jesus Christ.[44]

The word "professional" and its cognates evoke heated passions.

Scholars like Anthony Russell and Rosemary O'Day debate
when clerical professionalism came about—whether it emerged in
the nineteenth century for the first time, as Russell argues, or
whether the phenomenon restores a status that had somehow lost
its luster, which is O'Day's thesis.[45] Both, however, presume that
clergy are "professional" people. A General Synod paper from
England took the same view. Within the ministry of the whole
laos, "accredited ministers" responsible for teaching, pastoral
care, and serving as a focus for the church and gospel

> are professionals and comparable with members of
> other professions.... The life of a professional is chiefly
> characterised by the way in which the person himself
> and the institution he represents interact. As medicine is
> often discovered through an encounter with a doctor, or
> the law through an encounter with a lawyer or police-
> man, so too the minister embodies the institution he rep-
> resents. He invests himself personally in his work. For
> many the church and the gospel are what he is. What-
> ever his personal abilities or attractiveness, these cannot
> release him from taking public responsibility for the
> church. Equally his role will not wholly obscure any
> personal deficiencies he may have.[46]

Ordained ministry, Hensley Henson told his ordinands, is in part
a profession, as it has been for centuries. It therefore requires a
proficiency equal in its way to that of a doctor, lawyer, or teacher,
and entails adequate education, practical knowledge, the ability to
win public confidence, a sense of the discipline of the office, and
avoidance of unprofessional conduct. Yet ordination also represents a response to a divine summons and the gift of a divine commission. It requires the willingness to accept "the doctrine and discipline

---

[44] Richard Kew, "Tomorrow's World, Tomorrow's Church, Tomorrow's Leaders,"
in Humphrey, ed., *Gathering the NeXt Generation*, 5

[45] Russell, *Clerical Profession*, 6; O'Day, "The Clerical Renaissance," 184–212
(see chapter 1, n. 9, above).

[46] Q. in Carr, *Priestlike Task*, 38–39.

of the Church" from which the ordinand seeks the commission.[47]
A Catholic-minded priest reflected much the same thought, within
the Ordinal's mindset of priesthood as sole occupation.

> The priesthood is not a profession in the ordinary use of
> that word. Priests must be professional and not ama-
> teurish in their work, but they are not pursuing a pro-
> fession nor earning a living. They are concerned only
> with the service of God—the sole ambition which
> should inspire them is the spiritual ambition to live ever
> more fully in their priesthood and be more worthy min-
> isters of the Gospel of God. Like Christ they are "to be
> married to the Church" and serve her in any place and
> in any sphere to which they may be called.[48]

Being "married" to one's life's labors goes beyond the realm of the
professional and—as many a clergy spouse, congregation, and
priest have discovered—can exceed the limits of what is healthy.
The question becomes all the more problematic when clergy,
placed on the Victorian-style perch of "holiness" along with fulfilling a diversity of roles and meeting even more diverse expectations,
are also supposed to have "perfect" families.[49]

Is "professionalism" a blessing or a curse? On the one hand,
vast resources of money and time are spent in training, in seminaries and theological colleges and hosts of programs, to provide
for an educated, well-equipped corps of clergy who would constitute, along with teaching, law, and medicine, one of the "learned
professions." Not all clergy are paid by the church, as we have
seen, but all are expected to perform their tasks to the best of their
ability, not amateurishly, but with the ability to do competently
what they are supposed to do. As Raynes hinted, the opposite of
"professional" as both noun and adjective is "amateur"; if "professional" has its negative tones, its antonym in the context of official responsibilities sounds even worse.

On the other hand, inappropriate attitudes or unprofessional
conduct can harm the very goal of effective ministry that clergy

---

[47] Carr, *Priestlike Task*, 144–145 (cf. 165), 153, 157.

[48] Raynes, *Called By God*, 17.

[49] Cf. Walmsley and Loomis, *Healthy Clergy*, esp. 49–61.

and laity alike supposedly aim at providing. Incompetence is not the only gremlin, for distorted models can also subtly pervert effective ministry. For instance, in the postwar period, churches in consumerist societies tended to become known as service providers, which could make the priest into something of an employee or salesperson. The management model did just the opposite, construing the rector/vicar as administrator and employer who would consider laity the equivalents of employees. The therapeutic model channeled the clergy-lay psyches along the lines of a counselor and a client.[50] All of these images contradict the nature of relationships implied in the theologies of the church as Trinity and Body alike. Each, too, underplays the spiritual dimension of the enterprise. In 1985 the Bishop of Oxford meditated on the tension of professionalism:

> Laypeople seldom want the ordained simply to be undifferentiated. Approachable and human, yes; incompetent and apologetic, no. There is a professionalism that can repel by its air of condescension or its combination of hardness and frivolity.... Surely, however, there is also a priestly and pastoral professionalism to be valued and guarded: if the clergy do not teach, do not pray, do not love and endure, do not recall Christ, what are they there for? And there is a fear evident among laypeople— a godly fear—that bishops and clergy may lose those particular marks of their calling and become largely confined to the managerial and bureaucratic roles of contemporary society, rather as head teachers cease to teach and doctors are too busy for proper healing.[51]

"Professionalism" used to have three further sociological dimensions. It distinguished those who are full-time and/or paid from those who are not, like a "professional" athlete as opposed to an "amateur." It marked those who rendered sound advice or good service. It also influenced the sense of "class," for better or worse, which clergy have of themselves. As clergy developed an

---

[50] Cf. Melinsky, *Shape*, 162; Countryman, *Border*, 165; House of Bishops Pastoral Study, 5.

[51] Patrick Rodger, in Church of England, Board of Education, *All Are Called: Towards a Theology of the Laity. Essays from a Working Party of the General Synod Board of Education under the chairmanship of the Bishop of Oxford* (London: CIO, 1985), 35.

understanding of themselves as "professional," their own esteem (if not that of society) tended to increase; as it diminishes, the "esprit de corps" also seems to change.[52] But each of these distinctions has broken down. Supposedly "amateur" athletes who win Olympic medals reap princely rewards along with their gold. Clergy do not, to say the least. In fact, several sorts of clergy receive no earnings from their labors, so pay does not define the role. Nor can they be understood as the sole providers of pastoral counsel or spiritual direction, for laity can perform these roles with ability and grace. Nor does society bestow on the clergy the automatic respect that it may once have done (and still may to law and medicine, jokes notwithstanding). Yet the church does demand at least basic standards of behavior and practice. At certain points society expects no less, for instance with regard to boundaries involving sexual behavior or the abuse of children, to cite two important examples. The ordained cannot afford to be "amateurish" with people's souls.

The concept of "elder" may assist us here. An elder is not primarily one who is paid for services rendered, nor even for advice bestowed. The role of gathering the community is not a "professional" one. Yet the elder gives focus to the community and helps to shape its self-understanding in light of its shared past within its own life and that of the wider world and community of which it is a part. Thinking of the theological role of the ordained, Stephen M. Kelsey proposes a "radical shift in the roles of the 'professional theologian' and 'the people' in the life of the church. Rather than being seen as the primary source of theological information or authority, the professional theologian serves as an important resource" to the local community to which she or he belongs, "creating bonds of mutual accountability between local and global church." "Professionalism," Wesley Carr avers, "describes the skill and competence with which the minister embodies the church's task."[53] In that sense at least, professionalism is a quality worth nurturing.

---

[52] Robert Towler and A. P. M. Coxon, *Fate of the Anglican Clergy* (London: Macmillan, 1979), *passim*. Walmsley and Loomis, *Healthy Clergy*, 47–48.

[53] Kelsey, "Celebrating Baptismal Ministry," in Meyers, ed., *Baptism and Ministry*, 28; Carr, *Priestlike Task*, 39.

CHARACTER

Does ordination bestow some special "character"?

On learning what I was writing about, a priest asked—or rather, told—me, "You aren't going to say there's a priestly 'character,' are you?" If the term "professional" raises hackles, "indelible character" strikes an even more sensitive nerve. The latter term carries moral overtones: clergy are "different" and "better" than the average Christian, certainly holier than the laity, which is precisely what the Victorians had in mind. This concept of "character" was part and parcel of the nineteenth-century image of the cleric as "professional." Where doctors or lawyers offered their skill, clergy—who presumably had some skills in their hip pockets just in case, thanks to the practical training that became mandatory for the emerging "professional"—had holiness. They were set apart by their "consecrated character" and by the same total commitment, articulated in the Ordinal, that made auxiliary ministry so hard for the ecclesial mind to absorb. Moberly typified the appeal of his era to this "dedication of the inner life to Godward."[54]

That picture of the cleric now hangs on the musty walls of old sacristies, having been lambasted by theologians and scholars like Urban Holmes. But although the men in the portraits are forgotten, neither the dedication nor the "character" should be. For "character" *is* a part of ordination. It has been for nearly two millennia. The church could hardly say otherwise, given the nature of God's action—though not as the Victorians defined it.

What is this "character"? The English word can be deceptive because it would appear to refer to the marrow of the soul, as in Martin Luther King, Jr.'s phrase, "the content of his character." This is a figurative sense, however, and more literal meanings in English derive from that Greek impression of the stamping of the seal. My computer's word-processing program contains a bevy of attractive "characters," each one distinctive, each useful in its way, although I still do not know what each one symbolizes. That same, literal, graphic sense marks a "character" upon the stage at a play I attend, or in a novel I read.[55]

---

[54] Heeney, *Gentleman*, 92, 12–34; Moberly, *MP*, 293–294.

[55] Cf. *OED*, s.v. "character."

The germ of the idea is ancient. Hippolytus distinguished between the "Spirit" that a deacon receives and that which is "possessed by the presbytery." "Character" as a mark of priesthood made its theological debut in the controversies surrounding the Donatists, fourth-century rigorists, who believed that the clergy, who in self-defense had handed over sacred books to their Roman persecutors, had betrayed the church so completely that any subsequent sacraments they celebrated must be ineffective. Augustine retorted that sacraments functioned *ex opere operato*, "by the work itself": that is, since sacraments are instruments of God, so long as its conditions are adequately fulfilled, God's grace results. The human agent's moral condition matters little when compared with divine action. Eleven hundred years later, Anglican reformers enshrined in their Articles of Religion the statement that the worthiness of the ministers "hinders not the effect of the Sacraments" (Article XXVI). Around the same time, the Roman Catholic Council of Trent defined that "character" is conveyed in baptism, confirmation, and ordination. William Temple's Doctrinal Commission and F. J. Hall each repeated the idea.[56]

They all describe a conviction that something *happens* when God acts. To take baptism at all seriously means recognizing that the person baptized is different as a result. It is like being imprinted, as wax is impressed by a seal. Greeks called this χαρακτήρ, *charaktēr*, and used it to describe the impression made by a die upon a stamp, as in the making of coins, or that mark on the seal of a document.[57] Its only New Testament usage appears in Hebrews 1:3 to describe Christ, who "is the very reflection of God's glory and the *exact imprint* of God's very being" (NRSV). Other translations call it the "express image" (KJV), "very stamp" (RSV, ǁ NEB/REB "stamp"), "exact representation" (NIV), "very imprint" (NAB), or "impress" (JB). As it passed into theology, this "character" suggested instead an objective reality that results from the grace of God. Moberly, as quoted at the chapter's start, used

---

[56] Hippolytus, *Apostolic Tradition*, 9.4; Cross, *Oxford Dictionary*, s.vv. "Donatism," "Ex Opere Operato"; Holmes, *Priest in Community*, 156. The doctrine does not deny that the right disposition of the recipient is essential for grace to have effect. The state of the recipient matters greatly; the condition of the one who ministers the sacrament does not, at least for the recipient. See chp. 2, above.

[57] Cf. *TDNT*, IX, 418–423, s.v. χαρακτήρ; Holmes, *Priest in Community*, 156.

this meaning when he stated that ordination "stamps with so solemn an emphasis the 'pastoral' aspect of their 'priesthood.'"[58] It does not bestow a moral superiority by which one may function on God's behalf; in fact, the epistle to the Hebrews lengthily describes what the high priest must go through to cleanse himself to represent the people before God. The personal state of the presbyter has little (though not nothing) to do with the sacrament and everything to do with how the priest is empowered to act. As a result of ordination, the presbyter may officiate at the Eucharist, bless marriages, pronounce forgiveness, and perform all other functions a presbyter exercises on behalf of and with the church, with the assurance for priest and church alike that these functions accomplish the results intended by God. Should the priest descend from the inevitably sinful to the intolerably scandalous, the sacraments over which the priest officiates are no less valid because they depend upon the grace that infuses these acts of Christ and church. Character, in short, empowers the priest to act both *in persona Christi* and *in persona ecclesiae*.

However, the functioning cannot be completely segregated from the being. Because God's grace *works*, and something *happens*, people are changed. Baptism, when faithfully administered, makes a difference in the life of the candidate. Ordination likewise causes some new phenomenon for the person being ordained. As Scottish Episcopalians and Roman Catholics agreed:

> The gift of the Holy Spirit conferred in ordination is a new gift of the Spirit for a new function in the Church, a gift conferred on the individual for the sake of the Church. This new gift of the Spirit constitutes a new and special relationship with Christ and is manifested by the special role which the ordained minister has in representing Christ to his brethren within the Church. It is this gift which marks the essential difference between the ministerial priesthood and the priesthood of the faithful.

For this reason, like baptism and confirmation, ordination is permanent. It is not repeated. Should someone renounce these ordination vows or be defrocked because of scandalous behavior,

---

[58] Moberly, *MP*, 293. He notes the connection in this light of "priest" and "presbyter."

he or she can conceivably be readmitted to the office—but without being "re-ordained." It is a "consecration to the whole of life."[59] Likewise, to receive Anglican orders, a deacon or priest ordained within the historic episcopate of another denomination is not ordained again but accepted or received in some other manner.[60]

The nature of the "indelible character" holds several ramifications for the ordinand. For one thing, the cleric is a marked person. A new deacon commented on what a difference wearing a clerical collar makes on those who see him in public. Some of those differences are positive; the "parson's" role is one of becoming the identifiable "person" of the parish, and he or she may be cherished as a result. But some are negative; scandal seems to be heightened when it involves a member of the clergy.

For another, "character" plays a role within the life of the church, and for that role, the ordained receive the grace requisite for the task. Archbishop of Canterbury William Wake gave a classic Anglican expression of the point at the end of the seventeenth century.

> We do not at all doubt but that the grace of God accompanies this ordinance and the discharges of those ministers which are performed in consequences of it. But then this grace is only the blessing of God upon a particular employ; and is given to such persons rather for the benefit of others than for the furtherance of their own salvation.[61]

More lately, the Scots maintained that ordination "effects a permanent consecration of the individual with the promise of special help for fulfiling his ministry." It is meant not to exclude others from ministry but to allow ministry to be possible. A recently-ordained English priest says, "I'm enabled to do what I have to do. I don't get stage fright as I would if I were to give a talk. I'm very aware of enabling grace that allows me to lead the Eucharist; in

[59] "Priesthood and the Eucharist," in Witmer and Wright, eds., *Called to Full Unity*, 205–206.

[60] E.g., ECUSA, *Constitution and Canons* (2000), III.11.5(a) [p. 81].

[61] Q. in Stuhlman, *Occasions of Grace*, 288, emph. in orig.

community that is the only outward and visible moment when I'm tested if I can do this."[62]

This particular priest speaks as a nun. For religious communities of men or women, divisions between lay and clergy members are of exceptional concern, lest the unity of the brotherhood or sisterhood be compromised. Every monastic with whom I spoke attested to that unity that orders assist but do not undermine. For women's orders, priesthood for a member of the community is a totally new experience but not necessarily a divisive one. On the contrary, this sister confirms that her ordination "effected something, but not a separation. It has been an *enabling* as far as my vocation goes, but it is an expression of what is present in our community. For our community whose vocation is prayer, it is an appropriate one. But," she added, as far as her sisters and she were concerned, "I'm not a fish of a different species."[63]

Function, then, does have something to do with this sacramental character, as does ontology: The person does become different, as Sr. Barbara June was changed, if only in specific ways. So a dilemma become evident. On the one hand, functionally, an ordained person is authorized and commissioned to perform certain tasks, and to be a particular kind of person—a "representative." In that sense, the very being—the "ontology"—of the person is affected, *and affected it must be* if we understand God's sacramental grace to have power. This in itself removes the person from the ordinary experience of others. A certain "character" is bestowed. There is another sense in which function relates to "character" and that is in the sense of an attribute that is characteristic of a certain office. Writes H. J. M. Turner:

> The functions or duties of the ordained flow from what they are, through the "character" bestowed in ordination. And Anglicans should have no doubt that ordination, whether it is or is not reckoned as a sacrament, bestows power and authority as well as "character," for

---

[62] "Priesthood and the Eucharist," in Witmer and Wright, eds., *Called to Full Unity*, 205–206; interview with Sr. Barbara June of the Lamb of God, SLG, Convent of the Incarnation, Fairacres, Oxford, January 20, 2001.

[63] Interview with Sr. Barbara June. The Rev. Brian Bostwick, SSJE, makes the same point regarding ordained and lay brothers of the Society of St. John the Evangelist (interview, Cambridge, MA, May 15, 2001).

> our liturgy assumes that these have been conveyed to
> those ordained to the priesthood.[64]

The ordained become "signs" of the church's ministry. There is a graphic quality to this "character" after all.

On the other hand, theologically speaking, the person remains very much at one with all other Christians. No ontological alteration removes the person from the community of faith. As a result, the ordained brother in a monastery or the priestly sister in a convent is not considered any different from any other member. Ray Moore and Russell Hatfield noted the same phenomenon, even as they noticed a shift both in their role and in others' perceptions of it. As a result their congregations treated them somewhat differently. Ordination creates an order, but it does not create a status.

So "character" is as objective as a graphic sign. Roland Allen conveyed this understanding in writing, "A minister of Christ is one whom God has called to bear in his person the character of a man called by God to minister always under all circumstances."[65] At the same time, it is subjective, psychological, and spiritual, as it operates on the ordained person and through him or her on the Christian community. (That the Spirit also works through others is an important proviso of the "whole body" theology.) In this aspect, the ordained changes, as does the congregation, in part in response to the even more important reality of objective sacramental action. After all, are not the people of God supposed to be changed, to become more Christlike? And are not the sacraments supposed to help them to do just this? Because the presbyter is part of the laos, then of course the presbyter's character is affected by sacraments.

But in no sense, ideally, should this "character" separate the elder from the people. Sacraments do not do that. To draw a comparison, Holy Matrimony is a ceremony that profoundly affects two people, their families, and the community of faith. It bestows a "character" and effects a change: for two to become one can hardly be a greater ontological shift. But apart from some altered

---

[64] H. J. M. Turner, "Ordination and Vocation," in Hall and Hannaford, eds., *Order and Ministry*, 132.

[65] Allen, in Paton, ed., *Compulsion*, 105.

relationships, this change is not divisive. On the contrary, a wedding usually brings people together not just in a ceremony but also in the new interconnections of families and friends. Moreover, the husband and wife ideally change and grow in fulfillment of their vows so that they become more than they were as single people. Similarly, in Sr. Barbara June's words, ordination "changes you *into* all recognition, into what you are. It is a kind of parallel of what Paul says of putting on the full stature of Christ."

Because ordination, like any sacramental rite, is an act of divine grace, it inevitably changes a person and, depending on the rite, bestows some kind of "character." But it should never be divisive. If it is, the reason lies not with the sacrament but with how human beings respond to it. One way, too often, has been through what is commonly called "clericalism."

CLERICALISM AND ITS COROLLARIES

For centuries, tensions have pervaded, and often perverted, the relationship between clergy and laity. Both face the reality that some are ordained to various specific forms of ministry and leadership, but most are not. Wesley Carr observes the impact of this:

> To some degree people define themselves by what they are not as much as by what they profess to be. In the church, with its distinction between laity and clergy (a division which does not disappear, however the different ministries of each other are regarded as complementary), lay is not-ordained and *vice versa*.[66]

This difference was intensified by clergy's becoming virtually a separate caste from laity. Before the Reformation, clerics were exempt from many of the laws and duties of other folk. They even had their own court system. Although the image of a George Herbert evokes a placid scene of unity, realities may have been different, especially as clergy held responsibilities to state and church that could put them at odds with laity. Collecting tithes was as unpopular a process as collecting taxes. As the Victorian cleric became more "professional," he gave up certain duties like that of magis-

[66] Carr, *Priestlike Task*, 89.

trate that might set him against his people, and his support was received in less confrontative ways. Yet all that made him "professional" also set him apart. An odor of sanctity came to surround the priest, whether he be an Anglo-Catholic or an Evangelical, somewhat less so if he were Broad Church.[67] Missionaries were even further set apart from the indigenous laity by their race, nationality, or status.

In fact, tensions were guaranteed to arise as the church lived out the implications of the 1662 Ordinal. Its very language created a disparity: "They are the sheep of Christ," it says of the people committed to the priest's charge, not really mentioning that the priest is also one of the flock. Hensley Henson remembered a layman sputtering over a cleric's calling him

> one of his sheep. I am not a sheep relatively to him. I am at least his equal in knowledge, and greatly his superior in experience. Nobody but a parson would venture to compare me to an animal (such a stupid animal too!) and himself to that animal's master.

Henson conceded there is something to the "layperson's repugnance. The monopoly of education and even of power that once belonged to the clergy gave a meaning to the high-sounding titles by which Christ's ministers are conventionally described, which they no longer carry." Henson's solution was "to win men's respect by our service; we cannot any more claim it for our recognised superiority. Humility rooted in penitence and sustained by discipline will secure you against this particular fault of arrogance."[68]

Henson also implied several reasons that underlay clericalist attitudes and the resentments they spawned. One is power. Clergy have had it, wielded it, and often hoarded it; laity generally have not, and some have coveted it. A second reason is superiority, either claimed or presumed. The old ideal of "an educated gentleman in every parish" distinguished the cleric from the mass of laity on the basis of schooling. When in Southwestern Virginia the question arose of whether to send Raymond Moore to seminary

---

[67] Broad Churchmen were sometimes more skeptical of the value of "professionalism" and of a separation from the laity (Heeney, *Gentleman*, 64–65, 33).

[68] Henson, *Ad Clerum*, 185.

for a year, the answer was no, lest an innate inequality be created by a disparity of education that would frustrate the intent of Canon 9.[69] Although Liberal Catholics like Moberly and Ramsey strongly disclaimed innate priestly preeminence, the radical theologies of a Carter or Baverstock fed attitudes of sanctimoniousness and a sense of being chosen—attitudes shared by other members of the clerical establishment and by those laity who for their own reasons placed priests on pedestals.

A third reason is money. Many clergy labored unnoticed, underpaid, and in the harshest conditions, and prelates and senior clergy who were visibly wealthy sometimes paid their curates scandalously low wages. But even a presbyter maintained on a middle-class income could appear rich to low-wage workers, giving rise to resentments that separated the elder economically from his neighbors. Tithes were not abolished as one of England's ways of paying for its church until 1886. Until then, tensions rose around collecting the church's tenth of the produce, causing resentment in those who had to pay and overzealousness on the part of those who collected them: one priest was garnering his share of the 1824 barley harvest when an argument broke out, whereupon the rector gave the farmer a bloody nose.[70] Then there was the raising of funds; some vicars went door to door soliciting for church projects like schools.[71] On the whole, as one observer said,

> Most clergy carry out their tasks from day to day conscientiously and with humanity. Unfortunately some do not; they are engaged in a self-created drama which gives meaning to their own lives while at the same time exploiting the laity who form their congregations as mere objects for their own gratification. Often they do not realize this and would be shocked if it were drawn to their attention. But anyone who has had contact with the Catholic movement is forced to suspect the motives of some clergy, mainly because their behaviour seems so at odds with the values for which they ostensibly stand.[72]

---

[69] Interview with Bishop A. Heath Light.

[70] Peter C. Hammond, *The Parson and the Victorian Parish* (London: Hodder and Stoughton, 1977), 30.

[71] Heeney, *Gentleman*, 88.

[72] Penhale, *Anglican Church Today*, 146.

But the Anglo-Catholics were not the only ones with these problems; the entire church faced them, without always facing up to them. Some causes for resentment (by laity or clergy or both) were built into the system of the day. Archbishop Harcourt, who ordained his nephew as deacon and priest all at once, finally died in his ninety-second year (1842), still in office though he had ceased to function years before, because no scheme for retirement was arranged until efforts began in 1871—curiously, and problematically, with the retiree's successor paying the retiree's pension. Clerics might be absent from their parishes for long periods because of ill health, prolonged holidays, or a lack of provision for housing. B. J. Armstrong, vicar of East Dereham, was accustomed to taking a two- or three-week holiday in May or June and a month around August; those with other responsibilities might need longer periods, for residentiary canons were required to spend three months of the year at their cathedrals, with even more time for professors. But Bartholomew Edwards, rector of Ashill in Norfolk, a great horseman and rider to hounds, came to feel that hunting was unsuitable for a clergyman and gave it up. He was absent from his parish church on only three Sundays in the thirty years before 1886, when he died within nine days of his hundredth birthday.[73]

By the twentieth century some of these problems had been cleared up, but memories were long. The unique role of the clergy of the Church of England added further pungency to the already potent brew of potential resentments. Anticlericalism on the continent, meanwhile, was fueled by the fact of churches' being established.

Clericalism also has its less evident, less discussed opposite. "Laicism" has taken on shape as laity have assumed new roles, authority, energy, and power. The overweening cleric is a staple of ecclesiastical lore, but so is the stereotypical "lay pope" who rules the parish as it cycles through one priest after another. For all the advantages of lay involvement, it too can become distorted. A recent Episcopal Church study of ministry defines the syndrome this way:

---

[73] Hammond, *Parson*, 68, 44.

In the case of an inappropriate sense of lay authority, laity conceive of the church as their "property" and the clergy their "employees." In such circumstances, lay persons commit abuses as well—undermining clerical ministries, refusing financially to support the church, forcing clergy from positions. In either case, clericalism or laicism, the church becomes a battle ground for power issues and any real sense of the mission of church is lost.

The two phenomena, the American bishops noted, "have a relationship not unlike that of chicken and egg."[74]

In the midst of expending vast amounts of effort and funds to recruit people for ministry (clergy or lay), training them, and then with often enormous difficulty hiring them for parish and other ministries, such divisiveness between clergy and laity seems contrary to the ideal of the Body and counterproductive to its mission. The report from the Episcopal Church Foundation's Zacchaeus Project concluded that conflicts with clergy rank among the most difficult of all congregational challenges.[75] Hosts of issues may be involved in any given situation, including personality, vision, leadership styles, internal tensions, or simple misunderstandings. Inevitably, clericalism and laicism are both realities of church life.[76]

Both of these distortions of healthy relationships within the church can be addressed through a radical mutuality inherent in the concepts of both the Body and the Trinity. Overemphasizing either clergy or laity at the other's expense is tantamount to the one saying to the other, "I have no need of you." It violates the

---

[74] SCMD, "Toward a Theology of Ministry," 10, n. 12; House of Bishops Pastoral Study, 19.

[75] Episcopal Church Foundation, *Zacchaeus Project*, 10.

[76] It may be coincidental, and perhaps not, that about the same time that laity were emerging with new energy, such organizations as the National Network of Episcopal Clergy Associations was founded in the US (1970). Its website carefully avoids assigning anything but positive motives, but it does list as accomplishments such items as protecting the clergy housing exclusion from taxable income; encouraging professional standards; helping to shape revision of the ministry canons; promoting adequate compensation/benefits for clergy; pressing for due process in clergy dissolutions; advocating for clergy sabbaticals, collegiality, ministry reviews, and accountability; and other efforts to promote clergy and clergy-family health and well-being. <http://www.nneca.org/> (June 26, 2001).

essential vision of the whole functioning together. On the contrary, as the Zacchaeus Project report comments in its reflections on congregational life, "'Pulling together' at its deepest level entails seeking and finding a deep sense of common purpose and mutual support." The House of Bishops study reiterated the thought in imagining a situation in which "community and pastor are in each other's service."[77] Conversation and honest dialogue; mutual respect, service, and commitment to a common cause; and a conviction that the mission at hand arises from and contributes to the building up of the Body of Christ are ways by which the *laos* may work together—paid and volunteer, clergy and laity. As Stephen Kelsey observes:

> Many seem to have the impression that the professional church leader is somehow diminished when all the baptized are empowered to share more powerfully in the leadership of the church. The mystery of mutuality is that the opposite is the case. For whenever anyone in the Body of Christ is empowered to act more boldly, with more personal authority, every member is honored and strengthened.[78]

The growth of varieties of ministry—presbyteral, diaconal, and lay—together with the changing realities of the church's life and dynamics, all underscore an overriding reality: Presbyteral work in the present day must occur within the team. The English bishops' survey of the church's history, *Eucharistic Presidency*, concludes:

> A basic pattern of a pastor, a collegial association for the pastor, and pastoral assistants to carry out ministry in the world is one that has been adopted by the large majority of Churches in one form or another to the present day. In recent ecumenical discussion this has been expressed in terms of three dimensions of ministry: the personal, collegial and communal (synodical), exercised at the local, regional and universal levels of the Church's life.[79]

---

[77] Episcopal Church Foundation, *Zacchaeus Project*, 21; House of Bishops Pastoral Study, 14.

[78] Kelsey, "Celebrating Baptismal Ministry," in Meyers, ed., *Baptism and Ministry*, 30.

[79] *Eucharistic Presidency*, 3.16, q. in *Stranger in the Wings*, 19.

Given the growing involvement of laity, this vision may be too small and too pastor-centered. The trend toward collaboration among the *laos* in all its variety is likely to continue, as the vision likewise widens. And this is a development devoutly to be wished.

XI

Entering a New Millennium

As the church of Christ begins its third millennium, what will be the future of those commissioned to lead Anglican Christians as "presbyters"? In another millennium the Anglican Communion may have long disappeared, but the awareness of God, the search for a divine connection, and the presence of a community of faith, however reconfigured, will endure. Therefore the need for a few human beings to lead that community and assist others in their quest for the living God will also continue. The church as we know it may long have passed away, but presbyters—"elders"—will remain. It is even more likely that the body of the faithful will stand together as a corporate priesthood before God and humanity.

Several trends that have been long evident are likely to continue. These will doubtlessly revise the practice of presbyterate, as changes in the world have clearly done in recent centuries. They also will influence the shape of presbyterate, and the life of the corporate priesthood of all the faithful.

CHANGING WORLD, CHANGING CHURCH

When my son and I visited Uganda in 1998, Mabel Katahweire invited us to her home village deep in the Ankole countryside.

Although the village had no electricity, there was no way that the family was going to miss the chance to cheer for the Cameroons in their soccer match in the World Cup, so they wired a small television to a truck battery and we watched the whole game.

The same medium that transmits sports to pre-electrified Ugandan villagers also brings them American televangelists. As a result, I was told, broadcasts of Pentecostal services are inserting different music, forms of preaching, and ideas into a church whose culture has largely maintained a fervent but conservative Evangelical style. When clergy assembled for a continuing-education class, they would usually sing a hymn straight out of Victorian England. Yet their archbishop's sermon at the Martyrs' Day remembrance, before a huge gathering at the site where in 1886 thirty-two Anglican and Roman Catholic youths were slaughtered for their faith, would have done the Pentecostalists proud.

The church of Christ invariably exists within a wider context. Theologians Hatch and Hort made the point more than a century ago as they speculated on how the church adapted the institutions and ideas of the wider society and consecrated them for its own use. Some of their claims may have been proven false by later scholarship, but their more fundamental point cannot be denied. The example of Uganda shows how wide that context has become. Global economic and environmental trends have both direct and indirect repercussions on all Ugandans and their churches. The growth of technology affects not only how Christians live on a daily basis but also how they think and act, what they know, and what they have come to expect. As television has powerfully affected life in the twentieth century, so will the computer and the Internet influence the twenty-first.[1]

Less tangible forces also sway the mind and soul, such as the evident end of Enlightenment thinking and the demise of "Christendom" as a viable description of the western world as a religious unity. A predominately scientific and secular worldview has looked on in amazement as religious fundamentalism has become a force to be reckoned with. After Islamic fundamentalists led an entire revolution in Iran in 1979, one American official wanted to know, "Whoever took religion seriously?"[2] Apparently more and

---

[1] Cf. Kew, *Brave New Church*, 3–15.

[2] Q. in Karen Armstrong, *The Battle for God* (New York: Knopf, 2000), 317.

more people do. Interest in religion and spirituality is alive and well, although not necessarily the Christian religion: even the city of Bradford in England abounds with the mosques and temples of recent immigrants. "Church-shoppers" who would try out the Episcopal parish I served in the western reaches of Virginia, might also experiment with Presbyterians, Quakers, Buddhists, or New Age cults. That western societies are automatically "Christian" can no longer be assumed. What we can assume instead is that wide varieties of religious expression compete with each other everywhere—and sometimes aggressively. Nigeria may be among the largest and fastest-growing provinces of the Anglican Communion, but in several of its dioceses Christians have faced severe persecution from an aggressive form of Islam. Nor is Islam the only religion to see a rise in a conservative and energetic orthodoxy characterized as "fundamentalist." Christianity has as well, in various forms, but so have Judaism, Hinduism, and others.[3] All these phenomena affect Anglicans to some degree.

Meanwhile, certain developments within the Anglican Communion are likely to continue, one of which is the increasing prominence of Anglicans in the global South and East. As numbers of Anglicans have declined and now leveled off in Britain and the United States, the Asian, African, and Latin American provinces continue their remarkable growth. They are also beginning to exercise power within the Communion, as when the Archbishops of Rwanda and Singapore consecrated American bishops in defiance of the Archbishop of Canterbury and the Presiding Bishop of the Episcopal Church.[4] As they produce more theologians and evangelists,

---

[3] See Armstrong, *Battle for God*, on fundamentalism in the three great monotheistic faiths—Christianity, Judaism, and Islam—though she acknowledges its presence in every major religious tradition (xi).

[4] Archbishop Moses Tay of Singapore and Archbishop Emmanuel Kolini of Rwanda, and others, made John Rodgers and Charles Murphy "missionary bishops to the United States" on January 30, 2000, in Singapore. On June 24, 2001, Kolini and the new Archbishop of the Province of South East Asia, Datuk Yong Ping Chung, led in consecrating four other American clergy in Denver, Colorado, over the protests of the Archbishop of Canterbury and others, "to minister in the United States of America." Cf. "Two American Priests Become Bishops in Singapore, Then Return to US," *The Living Church*, 220, no. 8 (February 20, 2000), 6–8; and Jan Nunley, "AMiA consecrates four new bishops," Anglican Communion News Service (June 27, 2001) <http://www.anglicancommunion.org/acns/acns archive/acns2500/acns2512.html> (July 1, 2001), or Schuyler Totman, "AMiA Consecrates Four More Bishops," *The Living Church*, 223, no. 3 (July 15, 2001), 6–7.

moreover, these newer corners of Anglicanism will develop a vigorous voice in the Communion's affairs that will assert itself in the decades to come.

A second development likely to continue is the increasingly visible role of laity. The Zacchaeus Project report found that "many Episcopalians today link the exercise of leadership to an overall sense of spiritual community rather than to particular functions reserved for formally defined offices....The idea of the ministry of all baptized persons has become a widely accepted ideal."[5] This ideal may not have been accepted throughout the Communion, especially in provinces that still vest substantial authority in the bishop and other clergy. But in each province, as we saw in chapter 4, provisions for lay involvement are present. The seeds are sown. The plants will follow.

In addition to promoting the role of laity, an increased sense of community may also intensify the authority of the local and the personal at the expense of the distant and hierarchical. Congregations will, accordingly, pay less attention to dioceses and bishops even as their own local clergy exercise authority not so much because of their office, but through their community role—not because they are ordained, but because in function and essence they are "elders."

A third continuing development is the ever-growing influence of women in relationship to Holy Orders. Their effect extends beyond how many provinces ordain women or how many women are being ordained, both of which statistics are likely to continue to grow. More basically, women's ordination has been shaping how the *laos* understands the very nature of ordained ministry. Prior to the 1970s, priesthood was a masculine preserve. Diaconate was slightly more complex; those ordained were male, but deaconesses filled a quasi-ordained capacity. Religious orders and communities for women frequently pursued diaconal ministries of social care. These factors shaped images: Priesthood—and episcopate—were for men. Diaconate—the role if not the order—was for women. Beginning in the 1970s, these images broadened in two directions. The entrance of women into the priesthood and

---

[5] Episcopal Church Foundation, *Zacchaeus Project*, 28–29.

subsequently into the episcopate began to allow the concept of presbyterate to move beyond its male orientation into one that embraced male and female alike. At the same time, the very idea of diaconate turned from being associated with "women's work" performed by deaconesses to one that engaged both men and women, as deaconesses were incorporated into the ranks of the ordained and as men and women were ordained for the purpose of service. The trend has begun, then, of priesthood and diaconate (and episcopate, too) transcending gender altogether. The opportunity lies before us of orders' being increasingly understood in nature and function as truly reflective and representative of the entire Body of Christ.

A fourth continuing development is the ecumenical impulse, although in this instance there are continuing counterforces as well. Relationships with Lutherans have become closer as Anglican churches in England signed the Porvoo Declaration with Baltic Lutherans, while the Episcopal Church and the Evangelical Lutheran Church in America (ELCA) agreed in *Called to Common Mission* (CCM) to share ministries and orders. As one result, a Lutheran pastor may be called to serve an Episcopal congregation or vice versa, and bishops of one denomination share in the ordinations of the other. The 2000 General Convention that ratified the agreement also approved opening discussions with Presbyterians, Pentecostalists, the National Association of Evangelicals, and groups that had earlier left the Episcopal Church.[6] Discussions with Roman Catholics, unfortunately, took an uncertain turn.

A different force, however, threatens to splinter denominations and cause them to realign along doctrinal lines rather than those of liturgy, ethnicity, or tradition. "Political groups adhering to theologies deeply at variance with each other are tearing at the fabric of the church," notes Richard Kew, with human sexuality one urgent issue among many. "There are deep tensions," he writes, "...within each of the old-line denominations, with breakaways, particularly among conservative Christians, being threatened against Methodists and Presbyterians, for example."[7] Some of

---

[6] Cf. the report of the Standing Commission on Ecumenical Relations to the 73rd General Convention, *Blue Book* (2000), 81–118; and General Convention (2000) resolutions A039–042, D051, D047, D105.

[7] Kew, *Brave New Church*, 19.

these dissidents are finding common ground with like-minded people across denominational lines. Within Anglicanism, geographic lines are already being crossed. By mid-2001, about a dozen American congregations had affiliated with either the Province of Rwanda or the Province of South East Asia. To what degree these new alignments occur, and what effect they will have—especially in light of the controversy over the consecration of V. Gene Robinson, a non-celibate homosexual, as Bishop Coadjutor of New Hampshire in 2003—remains to be seen. The influence of major denominations on each other, however, is likely to continue.

THE ABIDING PRIESTHOOD AND ITS PRESBYTERS

Priests, then, are not likely to disappear, but other changes are in store. For one, there may be *fewer* clergy, in absolute numbers in certain provinces and on a per capita basis in others. Some areas of the Communion face the situation of more clergy retirements than ordinations, and those who are ordained are often older or second-career people whose years of service will naturally be fewer.[8] On the other hand, there may be *more* clergy as the renaissance of spirituality and prayer leads others to pursue religious vocations. Growing churches, such as in Africa, often cannot find enough places in institutions to train those who wish to attend. Renewed Episcopal recruitment aims at inspiring younger men and women to consider orders (and, occasionally, other forms of ministry).[9] The need is definitely present. For the Episcopal Church to meet the goal its 2000 General Convention set of doubling its average Sunday attendance in twenty years, some 5,000

---

[8] The *Zacchaeus Project* (59) indicates that in 1960, the average age of the 126 Episcopal ordinands was 27.53 years. In 1985 the number had increased to 434, but so had the average age, to 41.24 years. In 1998, numbers of new clergy had decreased to 264, but the age soared to 46.35 years. The difficulty is not limited to Anglicanism, according to two articles appearing in summer 2001 regarding clergy shortages and a dearth of younger clerics in various American denominations: Larry Whitham, "Flocks in Need of Shepherds," *The Washington Times*, July 2, 2001; Jane Lampman, "Where Are the Young Clergy?" *Christian Science Monitor*, July 19, 2001 <http://www.csmonitor.com/durable/2001/07/19/fp15s1 csm.shtml> (July 20, 2001).

[9] "Gathering the NeXt Generation" was an effort in this regard. See Humphrey, ed., *Gathering the NeXt Generation, passim.* "Older" candidates are not excluded, however.

to 7,500 new clergy will be needed, along with at least 2,500 to 3,000 new congregations.[10]

There will also be *different sorts* of clergy. Of all possibilities this is the most assured, especially as the variety of ministries grows, as different opportunities for ministry are recognized, and as people are encouraged to pursue them. The abundant growth of models that the twentieth century has produced is likely to continue. A menu of ministries may attract people to serve in ways that suit their particular vocational callings and their practical needs. The variety may also reflect the church's circumstances. For instance, affording a full-time clergyperson can already be difficult for congregations, so clergy and congregations alike may seek alternative models to the traditional full-time, seminary-trained priest. Rather than posing a problem, the high cost could become an opportunity to finding new ways of doing the church's work, using non-stipendiary ministers, team ministries, ecumenical partnerships, lay and ordained members involved in total ministry—or models yet to be devised.

The church, however, must be in a position to respond positively if the church will outfit itself for mission. There is some doubt that it will. "For many churches today the mood is one of maintenance and survival, not mission and advance," argues Richard Kew.

> Huge numbers of our ecclesiastical institutions seem totally unable or unwilling to accept the reality of what is going on and are refusing to face up to the flood of changing circumstances that is shaping their world.[11]

He speaks of places where the church is struggling, but in other places around the Communion the church is expanding rapidly. For example, the Diocese of Bradford, England, and the Diocese of Southwestern Virginia share a partnership with each other and with the Episcopal Church of the Sudan. In February 2001, Bishop Neff Powell ordained three deacons (three more than the previous year) in Southwestern Virginia. At the Petertide ordinations that June, Bishop David Smith ordained three deacons and four priests

---

[10] Kew, *Brave New Church*, 27, 41.

[11] Kew, *Brave New Church*, 24.

in Bradford. That same day, the Bishop of Khartoum ordained thirty-five new deacons and priests from at least ten different Sudanese tribes.[12]

Whether the situation is one of coping with growth or of moving beyond stability, a revitalized understanding of the ministry of the church may contribute to its mission. Where the church strives to rejuvenate, for the *laos* of the church to know their purpose and role as an integral part of that mission is an essential element in pursuing what the Holy Spirit sends them to do and to be. It is no less important for those where the church is expanding, in order for it to grow effectively into ever-deepening maturity. In neither case does confusion benefit the church of God.

The Anglican heritage as we have traced it shows considerable clarity about who this *laos* is and what its components may do and be. The picture may not be a simple one, but it holds significant implications for how the church may better serve its Lord. It is based on a series of metaphors. First, the church is the "Body of Christ," the *whole* people of God, the *laos* who are joined to Christ and each other through baptism and who share in the divine life of the Trinity. As a "royal priesthood," to use a second metaphor, it stands before the Godhead on behalf of all the world and before the world in the name of God. This priesthood is corporate, not limited to some but incorporating all the baptized. Third, as a "holy nation," it is consecrated to God—dedicated to divine purpose and use and also inspired by the Holy Spirit. While it may be too much to say that the church's role is to "restore all people to unity with God and each other in Christ,"[13] it certainly plays a role in that effort as one of the tools of the Holy Spirit.

As one means of fulfilling this purpose, Christians believe that, under the Spirit's guidance, a particular organization emerged out of the apostolic era. We do not know precisely how it emerged; the basic statement of faith called the Nicene Creed did not take formal

---

[12] Diocese of Bradford <http://www.bradford.anglican.org/features /010701ordain. html> (July 2, 2001); "Many Tribes, One Lord," press release from the Episcopal Church of the Sudan, July 2, 2001 [Bridgett Rees, e-mail to the author, July 2, 2001].

[13] I have suggested earlier (chapter 4) that the US BCP catechism (p. 855) overstates the point.

shape until the fourth century. Sometime in the second century, a pattern of ordered ministry appeared, consisting of bishops, priests, and deacons, and this became the normative model of ordained ministry for well over a thousand years. The Anglican Communion has continued in that model, emphasizing the following principles that we have been tracing:

Bishops have an apostolic role of oversight, grounded in witness to the resurrection and intimately connected to priesthood of which they are a part.

Priests or presbyters have a sacramental focus that takes its fullest meaning from evangelism (a ministry of the Word) and from pastoral care for the people of the church, which is part of the leadership of an "elder."

Deacons are focused on serving the needs of the church and calling forth the church's response to the needs of the world. They act as go-betweens, linking church and world, with service in word and deed their primary concern.

Laity are full participants in the ministry of the church, sharing in the church's service to the needs of body and soul both within the Christian community and in the world at large. As active participants in the priestly ministry of worship and mediation, they strive for the reconciliation and unity of all people with God and each other in Christ. As important as their involvement in the Christian community is, their much greater contribution to the mission of the church lies beyond the church itself, as they take the gospel to the worlds of family, work, and community they inhabit day by day.

A radical understanding of the images of Body and Trinity puts all Christians—lay and ordained—on the same plane before God. In our day the truths these images convey are only gradually being perceived. No Christian is superior to another by virtue of a sacramental rite; each is as important to the effective workings of the whole as a leg or spleen is to a human body. Some may be called and appointed by God and church to be "shepherds," but they are also part of the flock. Centuries of hierarchical attitudes take a long time to unlearn, and this process of change risks throwing out the essential along with the obsolete. The line can be fine between the exercise of authority and the wielding of power. Moreover, the ramifications are enormous for how clergy are paid, housed, considered, called, and treated—as also for lay workers in the life of the church. But the trend toward a greater egalitarianism continues.

These observations hold several implications for a new century in certain aspects of the church's life. If the ministry of the church is to be open to all, fostering inclusion requires mutual respect for the insights and gifts of others. It also demands an added measure of cooperation, a radical mutuality that embraces the gifts each has to offer, regardless of order. As a result, power can have no legitimate place within the Body of Christ, except the power of the Spirit shown in ways like word, sacrament, and gifts. "Clericalism" as a form of clergy control, as well as "laicism," which is the lay equivalent, are inappropriate to Christians—divisive in nature, counterproductive to mission, and contrary to the example of Jesus, who in the gospel accounts never exerts his power to coerce other people. While the functions of the ordained inevitably place them in positions of prominence within the community, they have no justification for lordship over others. Positions of responsibility may hold authority of supervision, but any authority in the church of Christ derives from Jesus as Lord, who emptied himself and took the form of a slave (Phil. 2:7). For this reason if no other, I am convinced that all orders should base themselves in a serious exercise of discipleship and *diakonia*.

Ministry is a gift. It is based in charisms from God. The community has the responsibility of discerning, respecting, and utilizing those gifts. Yet that is a communal enterprise; as Roland Allen emphasized, individuals alone cannot decide what those gifts are or how to utilize them. Through various rites—not only ordination but also commissioning for service and the rite of confirmation[14]—the community authorizes its people to function and serve in specific ways. I wince whenever someone refers to "my"

---

[14] See, for example, "A Form of Commitment to Christian Service" in the US BCP, 420–421, and the section of "Commissioning for Lay Ministries" in *BOS*, 160–176. Substantial reconsideration of the rite of confirmation remains necessary in light of the emphasis upon baptism as full initiation into the Body of Christ.

ministry, as some kind of personal possession. Christian ministry is always corporate—"our" ministry, shared with all Christians, shared ultimately by Christ.

Meanwhile, countless forms of service and ministry occur day by day, usually unseen and only "authorized" on the basis of baptism. What is commissioned is public; it also often serves the church itself, "to equip the saints for the work of ministry."[15] These ministries are never ends in themselves but invariably serve the greater mission that is the church's. They are never the sum total of what the church offers to its Lord in the world but can at best symbolize, as outward and visible signs, a vastly wider effort. This is why clearly understanding the ministry of the entire *laos*, clerical and lay, is so important.

Collegiality, then, must be a priority, given the abundance of forms of ministry and of people engaged in them. Clergy working together with laity and with each other may become the increasing norm, as it should in light of an Anglican theology of the church. Given that interdependence, collaborative ministry among laity, deacons, priests, and bishops (and with other denominations) is crucial, a point that is now well-established in governance procedures.[16] More important will be the infusion of collegiality in the everyday practices of the Body of Christ. "Effective congregations take seriously the concept that every member of the Body of Christ is called to be a minister," write authors Kew and Okorocha, whose passion is evangelism. "It ought to be obvious to everyone who has eyes to see, that there isn't a member of the clergy alive today who has a compendium of all the gifts for ministry God has poured out!"[17]

Discerning the nature of a person's ministry as part of the *laos* involves more than ordained ministry. The lay theologian Kathleen

---

[15] Eph. 4:12 (NRSV). Whether a comma should appear between "saints" and "for" is a hotly contested matter, on which rests the issue of whether the purpose of those listed in 4:11 is to equip saints *and* do the work of ministry or whether they equip the saints who then do ministry. The 1946 edition of the RSV included the comma, implying the former; the 1971 edition did not, implying the latter. For one opinionated view, cf. Collins, *Are All Christians Ministers?*, 17–22.

[16] *Lambeth 1988* (section I report, ¶154–7), 61–63.

[17] Kew and Okorocha, *Vision Bearers*, 105–106.

Staudt writes of how much easier it is to recommend someone for a vocational track leading to ordained ministry than for a track leading to lay service. When committees designed to help discern vocational calling determine that ordination is not the answer, they often stop there rather than assisting the seeker in finding what a particular *lay* ministry may be. "Though it is surely right for the church to select, ordain, and support its leaders," she continues,

> it may well be that the Holy Spirit is calling the church of our time to send out many more persons as missionaries, teachers, and healers, serving the world both visibly and invisibly in the name of Christ and his Church. We do not have a well-thought-out system for understanding or supporting these ministries.[18]

A further problem is that discernment to ordination is usually focused on ordination to the priesthood, not to the diaconate. A thoroughgoing process of discernment to Christian vocation ought to consider possibilities for service as a layperson, deacon, or priest.[19]

Such a system of vocational discernment is precisely what the church needs, first to explore possibilities, then to train, then to sustain the *laos*—all its members, not just the ordained ones. After several visits, my impression is that the English church is several paces ahead of ECUSA in equipping and supporting lay ministries within the church, like that of lay reader, while the Episcopal Church remains ahead in adult education generally.[20] The University of the South, for example, has pioneered programs like "Theological Education by Extension" (TEE), renamed "Education for Ministry" (EFM), and "Disciples of Christ in Community" (DOCC).

---

[18] Kathleen Henderson Staudt, "Annunciations in Most Lives: Vocational Discernment and the Work of the Church," *Sewanee Theological Review*, 43, no. 2 (Easter 2000), 130–131, 133.

[19] A strong theoretical case could be made for including episcopate among the ministries to be considered in the initial processes of pondering Christian vocations. However, many practical objections, and some theoretical ones, stand in the way of this occurring. Each Anglican province has determined some other means of discerning potential calls to episcopate.

[20] Several US dioceses, however, have developed well-established programs for specific training for lay ministries.

These in turn are being exported to other parts of the Communion; Mabel Katahweire has left Uganda to begin a TEE program in the Province of Southern Africa. But these programs can only begin to address the challenge of continually preparing the *laos* to exercise its priesthood.

THE GREATER CHRISTIAN CHURCH

This entire work has focused almost exclusively on Anglican thought and practice, with very little emphasis on ecumenical influences despite their impact on Anglicans from the late nineteenth century onwards. My purpose has been to clarify what Anglicanism itself believes both for the sake of Anglican self-awareness and for discussions with others, so that Anglicans know what they hold, and others may, too. Four areas that might be pursued beyond this work occur to me.

First, the World Council of Churches, meeting in Lima, Peru, in 1982, issued a significant manifesto entitled *Baptism, Eucharist and Ministry*, often called the "Lima Statement." This document is so outwardly compatible with Anglican thinking that Lambeth Conferences and other authorities frequently refer to it. It makes much of baptism and of the ministry in which all the baptized share. These words should sound familiar:

> All members of the believing community, ordained and lay, are interrelated. On the one hand, the community needs ordained ministers.... They serve to build up the community in Christ and to strengthen its witness.... On the other hand, the ordained ministry has no existence apart from their community. Ordained ministers can fulfil their call only in and for the community.[21]

Baptism, Eucharist and Ministry not only recognizes the historic threefold pattern of bishop, priest, and deacon but also acknowledges the obscurity in which that pattern evolved. It seriously considers apostolic succession and ministry but observes that "the reality and function of the episcopal ministry have been preserved in many...churches, with or without the title 'bishop.'" It upholds

---

[21] *BEM*, (¶12) 21–22.

a concept of ordination in which Jesus is the one who truly ordains, through "an action by God and the community" that strengthens the ordained for their task and gives the acknowledgment and prayers of the congregation. It thereby tries to open the way for mutual recognition by churches of each others' orders.[22] Precisely what is meant by the "threefold orders" varies considerably among denominations. Many, like Methodists and Moravians, have bishops, "elders," and deacons, but how they function, how they are understood, and what jurisdiction and authority their bishops, in particular, may hold vary substantially. Opportunities for continued ecumenical discussions abound.

Second, if a dialogue is pursued between Episcopalians and Presbyterians, the concept of bishops may be an alien one but that of "elders"—"presbyters"—may offer some common ground. In Presbyterian polity, the ordained clergy are called "teaching elders" and the local church's governing body, the session, is composed of "ruling elders"—laity who are understood to be ordained to that office. While the polity of the two denominations differs, contemporary scholarship has made it impossible for any denomination to call its own orders *authoritatively* biblical to the exclusion of all others and so opens the way to mutual recognition. Moreover, each denomination does give to some a ministry of oversight, understanding that ministry in different ways according to the tradition of each. So despite significant disparities between the Reformed and Anglican traditions, there are potentially fruitful topics for exploration.

Third, *Called to Common Mission* heralds a strong link between Lutherans and Anglicans in the United States, as did the earlier "Porvoo Declaration" for their counterparts in Northern Europe. One goal is "to work towards a common understanding of diaconal ministry."[23] The episcopate was of the greatest concern for many when church leaders celebrated their new relationship at Washington National Cathedral in January 2001. When the General Convention approved *Called to Common Mission* in 2000—in the very same convention room where the Lutherans had passed the proposal the year before—some in the Episcopal Church resisted the participation in episcopal ordinations of those

---

[22] BEM, (¶19–22) 24, (¶34, 37) 28–29, (¶39–40) 30, (¶51–55) 32.

[23] "Porvoo Declaration," §b.vii, in *Being Anglican*, 352.

who were not themselves episcopally ordained. Opponents within the Lutheran church, furthermore, resented the imposition of the historic episcopate—some fearing the increased authority that might devolve—and others resisting what seemed to them the imposition of an additional article of faith.[24] Apart from the fact that bishops in the Episcopal Church exert far less power than their colleagues in many other provinces, the vision of servant-bishops in collegial relationships, which I have attempted to define and document, may relieve some anxieties. Furthermore, the emphasis upon the pastoral nature of the order of "elder" finds deep roots in each tradition, to the extent that Lutherans customarily call their ordained minister "pastor."

Finally, the relationship with Roman Catholics regarding orders in general and priesthood in particular is more complex, given a long history of controversy and one specific papal statement. In 1896, Pope Leo XIII issued an encyclical, *Apostolicae Curae*, which condemned Anglican orders as invalid. He faulted the Ordinal for insufficiently emphasizing the sacrificial nature of Anglican priesthood. In consequence, he declared in a famous phrase, Anglican orders are "absolutely null and utterly void." The contrast is evident in *Apostolicae Curae* when Leo stressed the power "of consecrating and of offering the true body and blood of the Lord," tying that power with an individual rather than with the corporate Body, as Anglicans are wont to do.[25]

The Archbishops of York and Canterbury retorted that, in the long if stormy relationship between Roman Catholics and Anglicans, this had never been a problem before.[26] For his part, Moberly

---

[24] Steve Waring, "One Common Lord" and "Some Expect More Opposition," *The Living Church*, 233, no. 4 (January 28, 2001), 6–7; cf. David Dennison Daubert, "The Historic Episcopate for North American Lutherans: Lessons from Tanzania in a Historical Context" (Unpubl. Ph.D. thesis, The Graduate Theological Foundation, May 2000), 152.

[25] Franklin, ed., *Anglican Orders*, 134 (Leo used language from the Council of Trent).

[26] The official response of Anglicans came in the form of a letter from the Archbishops of Canterbury and York entitled *Saepius Officio* (1897), which refutes the papal assertions, asking why, if Anglican orders were null, it took more than three hundred years for Rome to say so, and asserting that it is the *Roman* rites that are questionable. Excerpts of the text can be found in Franklin, ed., *Anglican Orders*, 138–149 or completely in *Answer of the Archbishops of England to the Apostolic Letter of Pope Leo XIII on English Ordinations*, trans. John Wordsworth (London: Longmans, Green, 1912).

upheld the sacrificial nature of the priesthood of which all were a part, not merely presbyters.[27] Along the same line, the English doctrinal commission of the 1930s deftly avoided refuting Pope Leo while questioning "whether the priesthood of the Anglican or of any other communion is properly a sacrificing priesthood." All depends on what one means by a term whose meaning evolved over the ages, from the earliest times when "sacerdotal terms were not at first applied freely to the Christian Ministry" to the Reformation, when many desired "to dissociate the office of the presbyter who celebrated the Eucharist from the sacrificial interpretation of his function." The doctrinal commission did not settle that point of contention. Instead, it asserted "the priestly character implicit in the celebration of the Eucharist from the beginning," which only gradually produced "a formally sacerdotal interpretation of the functions of the celebrant.[28] So the Anglican answer is generally that the sacrifical/sacerdotal character is found primarily in the *church*, which is then reflected in its presbyterate.

Following Vatican II, dialogues of the Anglican and Roman Catholic International Consultation (ARCIC) produced a series of documents showing considerable agreement on Eucharist, ministry, and authority. These boded well for future rapprochement, as did the visit in 1982 to Canterbury by Pope John Paul II, and continued discussions in various parts of the world. However, the declaration *Dominus Iesus* issued in 2000 by the Congregation for the Doctrine of the Faith, chaired by Cardinal Joseph Ratzinger, seems to reassert *Apostolicae Curae* and ignore the ecumenical gains of the past thirty years, as Archbishop George Carey was quick to point out:

> The idea that Anglican and other churches are not "proper churches" seems to question the considerable ecumenical gains we have made.... Of course, the Church of England, and the world-wide Anglican Communion, does not for one moment accept that its orders of ministry and Eucharist are deficient in any way. It

---

[27] *MP*, 257–258, 285–289.

[28] *Doctrine in the Church of England*, 158–159.

believes itself to be a part of the one, holy, catholic and apostolic church of Christ, in whose name it serves and bears witness, here and round the world.[29]

Ratzinger's letter does make clear that significant differences remain between Anglican and Roman Catholic understandings. *Apostolicae Curae* has not been revoked or repudiated (an unlikely event in any case) and, moreover, the pastoral ethos of Anglican priesthood would seem to contrast with the eucharistic emphasis of Roman Catholic priesthood. The cultural assumptions of local clerics differ as much as the perspectives of archbishops and prelates. A survey of English clergy published in 1977 asked respondents to rank the priority of various roles. "Pastor" topped the Anglican list followed by "Celebrant," whereas the Roman Catholic respondents reversed the order. The study is now dated, but I suspect not much has changed.[30] Not only, then, are the denominations separated by the fact that Anglicans have largely determined that women can be "elders" and Roman Catholics have not. So also does the degree to which the history, theology, and ethos run deep and differently within the soul of each tradition.

THE PARADOXES OF PRESBYTERATE

These ecumenical differences—and at times similarities—shed new light on the fundamental paradoxes of Anglican priesthood. Does the priest function *in persona Christi* or *in persona ecclesaie*? Is the ordained priesthood sacrificial or pastoral? Is it a ministry of word or of sacrament? Does it represent Christ or the church? Is the priest one of the *laos* or set apart? Does the priest belong to the local church or to a wider ecclesial body?

In each case, the classic Anglican answer has been, "both." Finding, expressing, and living out this balance have been the

---

[29] [Roman Catholic Church,] Congregation for the Doctrine of the Faith, *"Dominus Iesus": On the Unicity and Salvific Universality of Jesus Christ and the Church* (London: Catholic Truth Society, 2000); "Canterbury concerning the Roman Catholic Document 'Dominus Iesus'," ACNS release #2219, September 5, 2001 <http://www.anglicancommunion.org/acns/acnsarchive/acns2200/acns2219.html> (July 2, 2001).

[30] Stewart Ranson, Alan Bryman, and Bob Hinings, *Clergy, Ministers and Priests* (London: Routledge & Kegan Paul, 1977), 63 (Table 4.1).

challenges for Anglicanism, and so they will remain. For at the heart of presbyterate is an entire range of seeming contradictions, which in themselves reflect a faith full of enigmas: God is three persons yet one being; Christ is fully human yet fully divine. The church is incongruously at once a human institution and a divine entity, namely, the Body of Christ. Can it be any wonder, then, that a priesthood representing a paradoxical Christ and a paradoxical church should itself be paradoxical? However, as with all orders, as indeed with the church, the paradox of presbyterate serves in its way to reveal the nature of God, the workings of Christ, and the phenomenon of the church.

The priest is a human being, yet divinely commissioned. Though Paul never called himself a "presbyter," he never ceased to marvel at the improbability at the center of his life. "We have this treasure in earthen vessels, to show that the transcendent power belongs to God and not to us" (2 Cor. 4:7 RSV). Underlying the reality that God uses human beings for divine purposes is the concept of Incarnation itself: In the person of Jesus, God took on earthen nature, and chose to work with mortals as a mortal. Jesus included human beings in his mission, gathering the disciples, sending out the seventy, ultimately instructing the apostles to go, baptize, and teach (Mt. 28:19–20). The Acts of the Apostles can be seen as a continuation of Jesus' proclamation.[31] Anglicans generally believe that the church perpetuates that mission and does so with divine appointment as the Body of the One who is its Lord. Baptism, Eucharist and Ministry reached a similar conclusion: "The Church needs persons who are publicly and continually responsible for pointing to its fundamental dependence on Jesus Christ, and thereby provide, within a multiplicity of its gifts, a focus of its unity."[32]

The very humanity of the priest, then, becomes an integral part of the message that priesthood proclaims. Henri Nouwen encouraged plumbing the depths of the human life so that the minister could become the "wounded healer."[33] Rowan Williams, preaching on

---

[31] Cf. e.g., Luke Timothy Johnson, *The Acts of the Apostles* (Collegeville, MN: The Liturgical Press, 1992), 1, 14–18.

[32] *BEM*, 21.

[33] Henri J. M. Nouwen, *The Wounded Healer: Ministry in Contemporary Society* (Garden City, NY: Doubleday, 1972).

the saintliness of a French priest afflicted by gout, migraines, depression, and suicidal obsessions, reflected that despite the Abbé Huvelin's brokenness,

> [t]here is another kind of wholeness—a wholeness of identification with the needs of the world, the self-generated and self-perpetuating tortures of the human race—a wholeness of compassion, a catholicity of sympathy, knowing one's own incompleteness in a way that reaches out to the incompleteness of others.

In another sermon, Archbishop Williams discerned vocation revealing the true self:

> Vocation is not something that obliterates the self "in God," however much it may, at times, *feel* like a violence done to our nature. The Holy Ghost calls us to be more, not less, ourselves—teaching Peter to be more Peter, John to be more John.[34]

Human personhood is of the essence of divine commission.

The priest, too, is both a pastor and a shepherd, yet as a baptized human being is also one of the sheep. Humanity makes the priest one with the world; baptism unites the priest with all Christians—in each case long before ordination. Yet the presbyter has been set apart, with the responsibility to act in the name of Jesus Christ. Paradoxically, then, the priest is one with his or her people, yet set apart by the commission and responsibility that ordination bestows.

In perhaps the most important paradox of all, the priest exists and acts *in persona Christi* and at the same time *in persona ecclesiae*, representing both Christ and church. To celebrate the Eucharist has no meaning apart from Jesus—his incarnation, life, death, resurrection, and ultimate return. But eucharistic presidency also has no significance apart from the community that gathers around Jesus: Anglicans have always insisted that at least two or three must gather for Christ to be sacramentally present, and one of those must be a priest. In the liturgy, the priest gives voice to the congregation (as in the collect) and to Christ himself through

---

[34] Williams, *Ray of Darkness*, 182–183, 166.

preaching, in giving absolution and blessing, and in saying the words of institution, "This is my body," "This is my blood." The priest offers eucharistic prayers but only together with the congregation; the priest presides, yet Christ is always the unseen host, who through the Spirit blesses and sanctifies.

Every Eucharist is at once local yet universal. Each celebration occurs in a given place and time with a certain people. Few or many, they may kneel before the altar of a great cathedral or stand around a makeshift table on a battlefield. Wherever they are, they join "with angels and archangels and all the company of heaven." In a similar way the priestly celebrant of that particular Eucharist reflects a wider focus and commitment. Ordained by a bishop who represents the wider church, canonically responsible to a given diocese, the presbyter holds a greater purview than the congregation at hand. As a representative of Christ and church, furthermore, the priest embodies the Body of Christ. Joined with the people of God in a specific locale, the priest also exists within a greater context of diocese, province, Communion, indeed, the whole church throughout time and space.[35]

The priest is sacramental both in function and in being. Anglicanism vests the presybter with authority to preside as the ordinary minister of the sacrament, understanding that it is Christ who ultimately is the minister of all sacraments. So the priest presides at Eucharist. Yet, as Gordon Lathrop observes, "the leadership of the liturgy is part of the liturgy." The clergy "are a living part of the assembly's collection of symbols." In diverse ways, they symbolize the communities that called them to be its "parsons." They symbolize Christ as well, acting in the liturgy *in persona Christi* especially in preaching the Word and presiding at the Eucharist, also thereby acting *in persona ecclesiae*.[36] They symbolize, even as they share in, the mystery that surrounds the liturgy itself.

---

[35] Not only in the Eucharist but in preaching is this personification significant, in that the sermon applies universal truths contained in Scripture to a local congregation. This sense of the universal focused upon and through the individual preacher is implied, too, I think, through the authority to preach granted by the bishop in ordination or in special license (to clergy or laity), as the case may be.

[36] Gordon Lathrop, *Holy Things: A Liturgical Theology* (Minneapolis: Fortress Press, 1993), 190, 192.

The paradoxes of priesthood, then, are emblematic of the church and its practices. The church as the Body of Christ is in, yet not really of, the world. An all-too-human institution is at the same time divine. It is as local as the nearest congregation, yet as universal as Christian history. As the two British authors of *Being a Priest Today* reflect, in this new century the priestly vocation is a paradox:

> It is a calling to *indicate* the identity of the Church by embodying the characteristics of the Church. It is a calling to live out the way of being to which the Church is called. The Church is called to be a holy priesthood. The presbyter is called to signify this priestly calling.[37]

With paradox comes tension. Priesthood may reflect a universal quality in a local way and vice versa. The presbyter may represent Christ and church, but explicating a biblical text that condemns a local practice could land the preacher in the modern-day equivalent of Jeremiah's cistern. And while the humanity of the ordained reflects the Incarnation—and human personality with all its gifts and woundedness may become a genuine asset to ministry—human sinfulness and folly can ruin the endeavor altogether. The priest lives always with the tension that the sinful act or the foolish word can wreak enormous harm, not only to one's career, but to the Body of Christ and the work of the gospel.

With the tension also comes a creative dynamic. I often find the congregation to have keen insights into the "word of the Lord," more sometimes than their seminary-trained ordained "elder." The sheep can be more on target than their shepherd. But that possibility should be expected to arise, given the limits and fallibility of the preacher's human nature and the corporate nature of the Body of Christ, along with the divine giftedness of individuals regardless of order. And because the shepherd is one of the flock, the congregation may also care pastorally for the shepherd in times of personal need. Role reversal accompanies paradox. In the process, priest and people build each other up in blessing.

In the end, paradox, tension, and a living dynamic all help to

---

[37] Christopher Cocksworth and Rosalind Brown, *Being a Priest Today* (Norwich: Canterbury Press, 2002), 24.

unveil the mystery surrounding God's message, grace, methods, and love.

THE EUCHARISTIC SHAPE OF PRIESTHOOD

As sacramental beings, presbyters take on some of the qualities of the Eucharist at which they preside, including its very shape. They reflect the way God works, one of those ways being through sacrament. In this sense, along with many others, priests are genuinely "sacramental beings."

At the heart of the eucharistic sacrament, as Dom Gregory Dix lustrously explained, is the fourfold liturgical action, "a thing of an absolute simplicity—the taking, blessing, breaking and giving" of bread and of a cup of wine and water. Jesus told his friends to "do this" in remembrance (*anamnesis*) of him; "and they have done it always since."[38] If not at the very beginning, then soon after, the nascent church commissioned and authorized in the name of Jesus some of its number to take, bless, break and give the eucharistic bread and cup. Ever since, century upon century, presbyters who in the name of Jesus literally take in their hands, bless, break, and give the elements, themselves are taken, blessed, broken, and given, in the name of Jesus.

They are taken. In an Orthodox ordination, the ordinand is escorted by two others, one at each arm, as if to signify that a greater authority is summoning, even compelling him to service, whether the ordinand wills it or not. Roland Allen urged the local community to identify those with gifts for God's service and, if not to compel them, to instill in them a vocation that the community perceives before they do. Even if ordinands first offer themselves to the church, the result is the same: The church, in Jesus' name, takes their lives and, laying episcopal hands upon their heads, consecrates them to become something different than they were before. They are taken, set apart, and dedicated to special work, in the name of Jesus.

They are blessed. The ordinand is given grace to do what he or she could not do before, to speak and act in the name of Jesus and

---

[38] Gregory Dix, *The Shape of the Liturgy* (2nd ed., London: Dacre Press, 1945), 743–744.

his church. The speaking and acting have no meaning apart from Jesus or his church; the power received is always a derived power, always serving a greater authority. But the power is there and the "character" imposed is an ability to fulfill the purpose for which the ordinand is blessed with the order received.

Blessing is inherent in the liturgy itself, too. Gordon Lathrop cites a Gallic explanation of the liturgy from around the year 700: "The bishop, addressing the people, blesses them, saying: 'The Lord be with you always.' The blessing is returned, 'And with your spirit.' He receives a blessing from the mouths of all the people so that he may be more worthy to bless them in return."[39] Celebrant and congregation build each other up in blessing.

They are broken. As the eucharistic bread cannot be shared unless it is broken, so the priest cannot serve effectively until he or she is broken and able to say what Jesus said in the garden: "Yet, not my will but yours be done" (Luke 22:42). This, too, is a paradox of priesthood, that the earthly vessel can truly function only if the vessel is broken. The preacher is not free to express his own thoughts or choose her own texts and arbitrarily classify the result as "the word of the Lord," any more than a celebrant may recite nursery rhymes over milk and cookies and call it Eucharist. The Body of Christ has determined otherwise. As for pastoral care, Henri Nouwen observes in *The Wounded Healer* that "no God can save us except a suffering God, and…no man can lead his people except the man who is crushed by its sins." Yet, he goes on, "ministry can indeed be a witness to the living truth that the wound, which causes us to suffer now, will be revealed to us later as the place where God intimated his new creation."[40]

They are given. That point of brokenness is when the priest can truly be given—to Christ, to the church and its people, to the world. Lathrop writes, "A ritual presider does not, *in se*, look like God any more than the bread looks like Christ. A preacher's words are not the word of God any more than bread, by itself, is the body of Christ, except that both bread and ritual speaker, together, are broken to the assembly's purpose."[41] In the dynamic

---

[39] Lathrop, *Holy Things*, 194, citing *Expositio antiquae liturgiae gallicanae,* found in *Patrologia Latina* 72.89–98.

[40] Nouwen, *Wounded Healer,* 73, 98.

[41] Lathrop, *Holy Things*, 193.

of being taken and blessed, broken and given, Jesus becomes present. In that dynamic, too, the priesthood becomes sacrificial. Moberly referred to the church's "intense 'for-other-ness'" as the eucharistic sacrifice takes practical form, adding that, like the good shepherd who gives his life for the sheep, "there is no pastoral love without sacrifice."[42]

The Anglican vision of the church remains pastoral. As an inseparable component of its ecclesial ideal, its ministerial priesthood exudes the pastoral aura that surrounds the image of George Herbert. It is the coda with which Moberly concluded, citing the "utterly loving pastor."[43] When the archbishops responded to Leo XIII, they cited the pastoral nature of Anglican priesthood in contradistinction to the sacramental and sacrificial approach taken, as they saw it, by Roman Catholics. The English reformers

> saw that the duties of the pastoral office had but little place in the Pontifical, although the Gospel speaks out fully upon them. For this reason, then, they especially set before our Priests the pastoral office, which is particularly that of Messenger, Watchman, and Steward of the Lord.... They entrusted to our Priests all "the mysteries of the Sacraments anciently instituted"...and did not exalt one aspect of one of them and neglect the others.[44]

Though priesthood no longer means parish ministry alone—if it ever did—the pastoral element remains central to the Anglican understanding of presbyterate. The pastoral vision endures. But, for all its continuing appeal to the *laos* of clergy and laity, Anglicanism cannot limit itself to its pastoral dimension alone. No matter how costly or sacrificial, if "pastoral" in any sense confines the church to caring for its own, without a mission that takes it to those who do not know Christ or who desperately need what Christ can offer, then the church will fail in its purpose as the Body of Christ.

The harvest is plentiful but the laborers few. The missionary vision is pastoral, even as the pastoral vision is missionary. Some

---

[42] Moberly, *MP*, 257.

[43] Moberly, *MP*, 285.

[44] *Answer of the Archbishops*, 36–37.

are chosen as deacons, some as bishops, and some as presbyters. The presbyterate remains an essentially pastoral office within the priesthood of all Christians, for teaching, for nourishing the community of faith through word and sacrament, and for leading the community as an elder. A vocation to the priesthood will take twists and turns as the needs of the community, the personal sense of call, and the guidance of the Spirit may beckon. The priest may not necessarily be a *parish* priest. But regardless of the specific way in which priesthood is personified, we indeed know who our priests are, because the link with Christ and the church abides. God can operate without benefit of clergy but, as with sacrament, seems to choose to use them still. As long as God does so, the presbyter will remains a ministerial representative of the Lord and of his Body, a living symbol of God's love and the community of grace.

Bibliography

Abbreviations:

CUP: Cambridge University Press

OUP: Oxford University Press

A. General Reference Works

Cross, F. L. *The Oxford Dictionary of the Christian Church*. Oxford: OUP, 1977.

Dictionary of National Biography. London: OUP, 1882–1982.

Oxford English Dictionary. 2nd ed. Oxford: Clarendon, 1989.

Kittel, Gerhard, ed. *Theological Dictionary of the New Testament*. Geoffrey W. Bromiley, ed. and trans. 10 vols. Grand Rapids, MI: Eerdmans, c. 1964–c. 1976.

B. Lambeth Conference Reports:

Lambeth Conference 1930. London: SPCK, 1930.

Lambeth Conference 1948. London: SPCK, 1948.

The Lambeth Conference 1958. London and Greenwich, CT: SPCK and Seabury, 1958.

The Lambeth Conference 1968: Resolutions and Reports. London and New York: SPCK and Seabury, 1968.

The Report of the Lambeth Conference 1978. London: CIO, 1978.

The Truth Shall Make You Free: The Lambeth Conference 1988. London: Anglican Consultative Council, 1988.

The Official Report of the Lambeth Conference 1998: Transformation and Renewal. Harrisburg, PA: Morehouse. 1999.

C. Other Official Documents and Reports

Anglican Consultative Council. *Anglican Cycle of Prayer*. Cincinnati, OH: Forward Movement, 2000/1.

———. *Being Anglican in the Third Millennium: The Official Report of the 10th Meeting of the Anglican Consultative Council.* James Rosenthal and Nicola Currie, eds. Harrisburg, PA: Morehouse, 1996.

———. *The Communion We Share: The Official Report of the 11th Meeting of the Anglican Consultative Council, Scotland, 1999.* James Rosenthal, ed. Harrisburg, PA: Morehouse, 2000.

Anglican-Roman Catholic International Commission. *Agreed Statements on Eucharistic Doctrine and Ministry and Ordination with Elucidations.* Cincinnati, OH: Forward Movement Publications, 1980.

———. *The Final Report.* London: SPCK and Catholic Truth Society, 1981.

———. *Church As Communion: An Agreed Statement by the Second Anglican-Roman Catholic International Commission.* London and Vatican City: ACC/Pontifical Council for Promoting Christian Unity, 1991.

Answer of the Archbishops of England to the Apostolic Letter of Pope Leo XIII on English Ordinations. John Wordsworth, trans. London: Longmans, Green, 1912.

Australia, Anglican Church of. *A Prayer Book for Australia.* Alexandria, NSW: Broughton Books, 1995.

———. *Proceedings of the Eleventh Synod, 1998.* Sydney: 1998.

———. Diocese of Canberra and Goulburn. *Administration of Parishes and Special Districts Ordinance 1957.* Canberra, NSW: 1996.

———. Diocese of Sydney. *The 7th Handbook.* Sydney: 1994.

———. Diocese of Sydney. *Year Book of the Diocese of Sydney.* Sydney: 1998.

Canada, Anglican Church of. *The Book of Alternative Services for the Anglican Church of Canada.* Toronto: Anglican Book Centre, 1985.

———. *Handbook of the General Synod of the Anglican Church of Canada.* 11th ed. Toronto: 1996.

———. Diocese of Athabasca. *Handbook.* Alberta: 1994.

———. Diocese of Caledonia. *Constitution, Canons, Policy and Procedures Manual.* British Columbia: 1994.

———. Diocese of Huron. *Constitution and Canons.* Ontario: 1990.

Central Africa, Church in the Province of. *Constitution and Canons.* N.p.: 1996.

England, The Church of. *The Alternative Service Book 1980*. London: Clowes, SPCK, CUP, 1980.

————. *The Book of Common Prayer*. 1662. Cambridge: CUP, c. 1968.

————. *Common Worship: Services and Prayers for the Church of England*. London: Church House, 2000.

————. *Deacons in the Ministry of the Church*. London: Church House, c.1988.

[————.] Advisory Board of Ministry. *Ordination and the Church's Ministry: An Interim Evaluation of College and Course Responses to ACCM Paper No. 22*. London: ABM, 1991.

————. Advisory Board of Ministry. *Stranger in the Wings* (Policy Paper No. 8). London: Church House, 1998.

————. Advisory Council for the Church's Ministry. *Call to Order: Vocation and Ministry in the Church of England*. London: ACCM, 1989.

————. Advisory Council for the Church's Ministry, Ministry Committee. *Ordained Ministry Today: A Discussion of its Nature and Role*. Westminster: Church Information Office, 1969.

[————.] ACCM, "Ordained Ministry in Secular Employment: Reflections on the History and Theology." Occasional paper No. 31 (February 1989).

————. Archbishops' Commission on Doctrine. *Doctrine in the Church of England: The Report of the Commission on Christian Doctrine Appointed by the Archbishops of Canterbury and York in 1922*. 1938. London: SPCK, 1982.

————. Board of Education. *All Are Called: Towards a Theology of the Laity. Essays from a Working Party of the General Synod Board of Education under the chairmanship of the Bishop of Oxford*. London: CIO, 1985.

[————. General Synod.] *Eucharistic Presidency*. London: Church House, 1997.

[————.] General Synod. *The Liturgical Ministry of Deacons: A Discussion Document*. N.d. (c. 1999).

[————.] *The Ordination of Women to the Priesthood: A Digest of the Second Report by the House of Bishops*. London: Church House Publishing, 1990 (GS Misc. 337).

Episcopal Church, The. *The Blue Book: Reports of the Committees, Commissions, Boards and Agencies of The General Convention of the Episcopal Church Seventy-Third General Convention, Denver, Colorado, July 2000.* New York: Church Publishing, 2000.

———. *The Book of Common Prayer.* New York: Seabury, 1928.

———. *The Book of Common Prayer.* New York: Church Hymnal, 1979.

———. *The Book of Occasional Services, 1994.* New York: Church Hymnal, c. 1995.

———. *Constitution and Canons.* New York: Church Publishing, 2000.

[———.] "House of Bishops Pastoral Study on Priesthood: The Priest in the Gathered Community," 2000.

———. *The Hymnal 1982.* New York: Church Hymnal, 1982.

———. *Lesser Feasts and Fasts.* New York: Church Publishing, 2000.

[———. Permanent Diaconate Evaluation Committee.] *Raising Up Servant Ministry: Eight Dioceses Work Toward the Future of the Diaconate and the Enablement of Servant Ministry.* Foreword by Timothy Sedgwick. New York: 1985.

[———.] Standing Commission on Ministry Development. "Toward a Theology of Ministry." May 2000.

———. Standing Liturgical Commission. *The Ordination of Bishops, Priests, and Deacons: Prayer Book Studies 20.* New York: Church Hymnal, c. 1971.

Episcopal Church Foundation, The. *The Zacchaeus Project: Discerning Episcopal Identity at the Dawn of the New Millennium.* N.p.: 1999.

Fairweather, E. R., ed. *Anglican Congress 1963: Report of Proceedings.* Toronto: 1963.

[Ireland, The Church of.] *Alternative Prayer Book 1984.* Dublin: Collins, 1984.

———. General Synod. *The Constitution of the Church of Ireland.* Dublin: 1988.

Indian Ocean, Church of the Province of. Diocese of Mauritius. *Constitution.* Mauritius: 1983.

Johnson, Eleanor, and John Clark, eds. *Anglicans in Mission: A Transforming Journey* [Report of MISSIO, the Mission Commission of the Anglican Communion, to the Anglican Consultative Council, meeting in Edinburgh, Scotland, September 1999]. London: SPCK, 2000.

Kenya, Church of the Province of. *Constitution*. Nairobi: 1992.

———. Diocese of Mount Kenya Central. *Constitution*. N.p.: 1990.

New Zealand, Church of the Province of. *A New Zealand Prayer Book: He Karakia Mihinare o Aotearoa*. Aukland: Collins, 1989.

Nigeria, Church of. Diocese of Akure. *Constitution*. Ajure, Nigeria: Hope Printer, 1989.

[Roman Catholic Church.] Congregation for the Doctrine of the Faith, *"Dominus Iesus": On the Unicity and Salvific Universality of Jesus Christ and the Church*. London: Catholic Truth Society, 2000.

Scotland, Episcopal Church in. *Scottish Ordinal 1984*. Edinburgh: General Synod of the Scottish Episcopal Church, 1984.

Southern Africa, Church of the Province of. Diocese of Johannesburg. *Parish Guide*. Johannesburg: 1997.

Sudan, Episcopal Church of. Diocese of Mundri/Lui. *The Constitution of the Diocese of Mundri/Lui, The Province of the Episcopal Church of the Sudan*. Khartoum: ECS/New Day, 1997.

[Wales, The Church in.] *The Book of Common Prayer for Use in The Church in Wales*. Vol. 2. Penarth: Church in Wales Publications, 1984.

West Africa, Church of the Province of. *Constitution and Canons*. Accra, Ghana:1990.

West Indies, Church in the Province of the. Diocese of Belize. *The Constitution and Regulations of the Church in the Diocese of Belize*. Belize City: 1995.

Witmer, Joseph W., and J. Robert Wright, eds. *Called to Full Unity: Documents on Anglican-Roman Catholic Relations 1966–1983*. Washington, D.C.: Office of Publications and Promotion Services, U.S. Catholic Conference, c. 1986.

World Council of Churches. Faith and Order Commission. *Baptism, Eucharist and Ministry*. Geneva: World Council of Churches, 1982.

———. *The Ministry of Deacons*. World Council Studies No. 2. Geneva: World Council of Churches, 1965.

D. Books and Monographs

Acheson, Alan. *A History of the Church of Ireland 1691–1996*. Dublin: Columba, 1997.

Ahlstrom, Sydney E. *A Religious History of the American People.* New Haven and London: Yale University Press, 1972.

Allen, Roland. *The Compulsion of the Spirit.* David Paton and Charles Long, eds. Grand Rapids, MI: Eerdmans, 1983.

————. *Missionary Methods: St. Paul's or Ours?* 2nd ed., 1927. Reprint, with a foreword by Lesslie Newbigin. Grand Rapids, MI: Eerdmans, 1962.

————. *The Spontaneous Expansion of the Church.* 1927. Reprint, with forewords by Lesslie Newbigin and Kenneth Grubb. Grand Rapids, MI: Eerdmans, 1984.

Architectural Record, editors of. *Religious Buildings: An Architectural Record Book.* New York: McGraw-Hill, 1979.

Armstrong, Karen. *The Battle for God.* New York: Knopf, 2000.

Barnett, James Monroe. *The Diaconate: A Full and Equal Order.* New York: Seabury, 1981.

Barry, F. R. *The Relevance of the Church.* London: Nisbet, 1935.

————. *Vocation and Ministry.* Welwyn: James Nisbet, 1958.

Bartlett, David L. *Ministry in the New Testament.* Minneapolis: Fortress Press, 1993.

Baverstock, A. H. *Priesthood in Liturgy and Life.* London: Faith Press, 1917.

Booty, John E. *The Servant Church: Diaconal Ministry and the Episcopal Church.* Wilton, CT: Morehouse Publishing, 1982.

Bowering, Michael, ed. *Priesthood Here and Now: Reflections on the ASB Ordinal by Priests Serving in the Diocese of Newcastle.* N.p.: Diocese of Newcastle, 1994.

Box, Hubert S., ed. *Priesthood.* London: SPCK, 1937.

Bradshaw, Paul. *Liturgical Presidency in the Early Church.* Liturgical Study No. 36. Bramcote, Notts.: Grove Books, 1983.

Bradshaw, Tim. *The Olive Branch: An Evangelical Anglican Doctrine of the Church.* Carlisle: Paternoster, 1992.

Brent, Charles H. *The Inspiration of Responsibility.* New York: Longmans, Green, 1915.

————. *Prisoners of Hope, and Other Sermons.* New York: Longmans, Green, 1915.

————. *With God in the World*. New York: Longmans, Green, 1908.

Brown, C. K. Francis. *A History of the English Clergy, 1800–1900*. London: Faith Press, 1953.

Brown, Raymond. *Priest and Bishop: Biblical Reflections*. London: Geoffrey Chapman, 1970.

Buchanan, Colin, ed. *Modern Anglican Ordination Rites*. Bramcote, Notts: Grove Books, 1987.

Bullock, F. W. B. *A History of Training for the Ministry of the Church of England in England and Wales from 1800 to 1874*. St. Leonards-on-Sea: Budd and Gillatt, 1955.

————. *A History of Training for the Ministry of the Church of England in England and Wales from 1875 to 1974*. London: Home Words, 1976.

Carpenter, James. *Gore: A Study in Liberal Catholic Thought*. London: Faith Press, 1960.

Carr, Wesley. *The Priestlike Task: A Model for Developing and Training the Church's Ministry*. London: SPCK, 1985.

Carter, T. T. *The Doctrine of the Priesthood in the Church of England*. 1857. 3rd ed. London: J. Masters, 1876.

Chadwick, Owen. *Michael Ramsey: A Life*. Oxford: OUP, 1991.

————. *The Spirit of the Oxford Movement: Tractarian Essays*. Cambridge: CUP, 1990.

————. *The Victorian Church*. 2nd ed., Part II. London: Adam and Charles Black, 1972.

Childs, Brevard S. *The New Testament as Canon: An Introduction*. Philadelphia: Fortress Press, 1984.

————. *Biblical Theology of the Old and New Testaments*. Minneapolis: Fortress Press, 1993.

Cocksworth, Christopher, and Rosalind Brown. *Being a Priest Today*. Norwich: Canterbury Press, 2002.

Collins, John N. *Are All Christians Ministers?* Collegeville, MN: Liturgical Press, 1992.

————. *Diakonia: Re-interpreting the Ancient Sources*. New York and Oxford: OUP, 1990.

Collins, William Edward. *The Study of Ecclesiastical History*. London: Longmans, Green, 1903.

Countryman, L. William. *The Language of Ordination: Ministry in an Ecumenical Context*. Philadelphia: Trinity Press International, 1992.

———. *Living on the Border of the Holy: Renewing the Priesthood of All*. Harrisburg, PA: Morehouse, 1999.

Cox, Harvey. *Fire from Heaven: The Rise of Pentecostal Spirituality and the Reshaping of Religion in the Twenty-first Century*. Reading, MA: Addison-Wesley, 1995.

Craighill, Peyton G., ed. *Diaconal Ministry: Past, Present and Future: Essays from the Philadelphia Symposium, 1992*. Providence, RI: North American Association for the Diaconate, c. 1994.

Daubert, David Dennison. "The Historic Episcopate for North American Lutherans: Lessons from Tanzania in a Historical Context." Ph.D. thesis. The Graduate Theological Foundation, May 2000.

Davie, Grace. *Religion in Britain Since 1945: Believing Without Belonging*. Oxford: Blackwell, 1994.

Davies, S. J. G., ed. *A New Dictionary of Liturgy and Worship*. London: SCM, 1986.

Davies, W. D. *Paul and Rabbinic Judaism: Some Rabbinic Elements in Pauline Theology*. London: SPCK, 1958.

Davis, Gerald Charles, ed. *Setting Free the Ministry of the People of God*. Cincinnati, OH: Forward Movement, 1984.

Dix, Gregory. *The Shape of the Liturgy*. 2nd ed. London: Dacre Press, 1945.

Doe, Norman. *Canon Law in the Anglican Communion: A Worldwide Perspective*. Oxford: Clarendon, 1998.

Douglas, Ian T., and Kwok Pui-lan, eds. *Beyond Colonial Anglicanism: The Anglican Communion in the 21st Century*. New York: Church Publishing, 2001.

Douglas, Ian. *Fling Out the Banner!: The National Church Ideal and the Foreign Mission of the Episcopal Church*. New York: Church Hymnal, 1996.

Dowland, David. *Nineteenth-Century Anglican Theological Training*. Oxford: Clarendon, 1997.

Edwards, David. *Christian England*. Vol 3. Grand Rapids, MI: Eerdmans, 1984.

Ehrman, Bart D. *After the New Testament: A Reader in Early Christianity*. New York: OUP, 1999.

Fenhagen, James C. *More Than Wanderers: Spiritual Disciplines for Christian Ministry*. New York: Seabury, 1978.

———. *Mutual Ministry: New Vitality for the Local Church*. New York: Seabury, 1977.

Field-Bibb, Jacqueline. *Women Towards Priesthood: Ministerial Politics and Feminist Praxis*. Cambridge: CUP, 1991.

Francis, James M. M., and Leslie J. Francis, eds. *Tentmaking: Perspectives on Self-Supporting Ministry*. Leominster: Gracewing, 1998.

Franklin, R. William, ed. *Anglican Orders: Essays on the Centenary of Apostolicae Curae, 1896–1996*. Harrisburg, PA: Morehouse, 1996.

Furlong, Monica. *The C of E: The State It's In*. London: Hodder and Stoughton, 2000.

Gassmann, Günther. *Historical Dictionary of Lutheranism*. Lanham, MD: Scarecrow, 2001.

Gieselmann, Reinhold. *Contemporary Church Architecture*. London: Thames and Hudson, 1972.

Gibaut, John St. H. *The Cursus Honorum: A Study of the Origins and Evolution of Sequential Ordination*. New York: Peter Lang, 2000.

Gibbs, Mark, and T. Ralph Morton. *God's Frozen People*. Philadelphia: Westminster Press, 1964.

Gibbs, Mark. *Christians with Secular Power*. Philadelphia: Fortress Press, 1981.

Giles, Richard. *Re-Pitching the Tent: Re-ordering the Church Building for Worship and Mission in the New Millennium*. Norwich: Canterbury, 1997.

Gill, Robin. *The Myth of the Empty Church*. London: SPCK, 1993.

Goodenough, Simon. *The Country Parson*. Newton Abbot, London and North Pomfret, VT: David and Charles, 1983.

Gore, Charles. *The Incarnation of the Son of God*. Bampton Lectures for 1891. New York: Charles Scribner's Sons, 1891.

———. *The Ministry of the Christian Church*. 2nd ed. London: Rivingtons, 1889.

———. *Orders and Unity*. New York: E. P. Dutton, 1909.

———, ed. *Lux Mundi: A Series of Studies in the Religion of the Incarnation*. London: John Murray, 1904.

Green, H. Benedict. *Lay Presidency at the Eucharist?* London: Darton, Longman and Todd, 1994.

Greenwood, Robin. *Transforming Priesthood: A New Theology of Mission and Ministry*. London: SPCK, 1994.

Grubb, Kenneth G. *A Layman Looks at the Church*. London: Hodder and Stoughton, 1964.

Guiver, George, et al. *The Fire and the Clay: The Priest in Today's Church*. London: SPCK, 1999.

Hall, Christine, ed. *The Deacon's Ministry*. Leominster: Gracewing, 1992.

———, and Robert Hannaford, eds. *Order and Ministry*. Leominster: Gracewing, 1996.

Hall, Francis J. *The Church and the Sacramental System*. 1920. Reprint, Pelham Manor, NY: American Church Union, 1967.

———. *Introduction to Dogmatic Theology*. 1912. Reprint, Pelham Manor, NY: American Church Publications, 1970.

———. *The Sacraments*. 1921. Reprint, Pelham Manor, NY: American Church Union, 1969.

Hall, J. R. Clark. *A Concise Anglo Saxon Dictionary*. 4th ed. Toronto: University of Toronto Press, 1984.

Hallenback, Edwin F., ed. *The Orders of Ministry: Reflections on Direct Ordination, 1996*. Providence, RI: North American Association for the Diaconate, 1996.

Hammond, Peter. *Liturgy and Architecture*. London: Barrie and Rockliff, 1960.

Hammond, Peter C. *The Parson and the Victorian Parish*. London: Hodder and Stoughton, 1977.

Hanson, A. T. and R. P. C. Hanson. *The Identity of the Church: A Guide to Recognizing the Contemporary Church*. London: SCM, 1987.

Hanson, Anthony Tyrrell. *The Pioneer Ministry*. London: SCM, 1961.

Hanson, R. P. C. *Christian Priesthood Examined*. Guildford and London: Lutterworth Press, 1979.

Hargrave, Alan. *But Who Will Preside?* Bramcote, Notts.: Grove Books, 1990.

Hastings, Adrian. *A History of English Christianity 1920–1990*. London: SCM, 1991.

Hatch, Edwin. *The Growth of Church Institutions*. New York: Thomas Whittaker, 1887.

———. *Memorials of Edwin Hatch*. London: Hodder and Stoughton, 1890.

———. *The Organization of the Early Christian Churches*. Bampton Lectures for 1880. London: Longmans, Green, 1918.

Heathcote, Edwin, and Iona Spens. *Church Builders*. London: Academy Editions, 1997.

Hebert, A. G. *The Form of the Church*. Rev. ed. London: Faber and Faber, 1947.

———. *Liturgy and Society*. 1935. Rev. ed. London: Faber and Faber, 1966.

Heeney, Brian. *A Different Kind of Gentleman: Parish Clergy as Professional Men in Early and Mid-Victorian England*. Hamden, CT: Archon, 1976.

Henson, Herbert Hensley. *Ad Clerum*. London: Hodder and Stoughton, 1937.

Herbert, George. *The Country Parson, The Temple*. John N. Wall, Jr., ed. New York: Paulist, 1981.

Hewitt, Emily C., and Suzanne R. Hiatt. *Women Priests: Yes or No?* New York: Seabury Press, 1973.

Hinton, Michael. *The Anglican Parochial Clergy: A Celebration*. London: SCM, 1994.

Holmes, David. *A Brief History of the Episcopal Church*. Valley Forge, PA: Trinity Press International, 1993.

Holmes III, Urban T. *The Future Shape of Ministry*. New York: Seabury, 1971.

———. *The Priest in Community: Exploring the Roots of Ministry*. New York: Seabury, 1978.

———. *Spirituality for Ministry*. New York: Harper and Row, 1982.

Hort, Arthur Fenton. *Life and Letters of Fenton John Anthony Hort*. Vol. 2. London: Macmillan, 1896.

Hort, Fenton John Anthony. *The Christian Ecclesia*. London: Macmillan, 1908.

Humphrey, Nathan, ed. *Gathering the NeXt Generation: Essays on the Formation and Ministry of GenX Priests*. Harrisburg, PA: Morehouse, 2000.

Hunt, Allen Rhea. *The Inspired Body: Paul, the Corinthians, and Divine Inspiration*. Macon, GA: Mercer University Press, 1996.

Hunter, A. M. *Interpreting the New Testament 1900–1950*. London: SCM, 1958.

Iremonger, F. A. *William Temple: Archbishop of Canterbury*. London: OUP, 1948.

Irvine, Christopher. *Worship, Church and Society*. Norwich: Canterbury Press, 1993.

James, Eric. *Stewards of the Mysteries of God*. London: Darton, Longman and Todd, 1979.

Jasper, Ronald C. D., ed. *The Renewal of Worship: Essays by Members of the Joint Liturgical Group*. London: OUP, 1965.

Jasper, R. C. D., and Paul F. Bradshaw. *A Companion to the Alternative Service Book*. London: SPCK, 1986.

Jenkins, Daniel. *The Gift of Ministry*. London: Faber and Faber, 1952.

Jenkins, Philip. *The Next Christendom*. Oxford: OUP, 2002.

Johnson, Luke Timothy. *The Acts of the Apostles*. Collegeville, MN: The Liturgical Press, 1992.

———. *The Writings of the New Testament: An Interpretation*. Rev. ed. Minneapolis: Fortress, 1999.

Johnston, John Octavius. *Life and Letters of Henry Parry Liddon*. London: Longmans, Green, 1904.

Kelly, J. N. D. *Early Christian Creeds*. 3rd ed. London, Longman, 1972.

Kew, Richard. *Brave New Church: What the Future Holds*. Harrisburg, PA: Morehouse, 2001.

———, and Cyril Okorocha. *Vision Bearers: Dynamic Evangelism in the 21st Century*. Harrisburg, PA: Morehouse, 1996.

Kirk, Kenneth Escott. *Beauty and Bands*. London: Hodder and Stoughton, 1955.

————, ed. *The Apostolic Ministry*. London: Hodder and Stoughton, 1946.

Kraemer, Hendrik. *A Theology of the Laity*. London: Lutterworth Press, 1958.

Kuhrt, Gordon. *An Introduction to Christian Ministry*. London: Church House Publishing, 2000.

Larson, Duane H., ed. *From Word and Sacrament: Renewed Vision for Diaconal Ministry*. Chicago: Evangelical Lutheran Church in America, 1999.

Lathrop, Gordon. *Holy Things: A Liturgical Theology*. Minneapolis: Fortress Press, 1993.

Leech, Kenneth. *Soul Friend: A Study of Spirituality*. London: Sheldon Press, 1977.

Liddon, Henry Parry. *Clerical Life and Work*. London: Longmans, Green, 1903.

————. *Sermons Preached Before the University of Oxford*. 2nd ser. London: Rivingtons, 1879.

Lightfoot, J. B. *The Christian Ministry*. London: Chas. J. Thynne and Jarvis, 1927.

————. *Dissertations on the Apostolic Age*. London: Macmillan, 1892.

————. *Ordination Addresses and Counsels to Clergy*. London: Macmillan, 1891.

————. *Sermons Preached on Special Occasions*. Vol. 13 of *Works*. London: Macmillan, 1891.

Lloyd, Roger. *The Church of England 1900–1965*. London: SCM, 1966.

Lloyd, Trevor. *Lay Presidency at the Eucharist?* Bramcote, Notts.: Grove Books, 1977.

Lowrie, Walter. *Ministers of Christ*. Louisville: Cloister, 1946.

Macquarrie, John. *A Guide to the Sacraments*. New York: Continuum, 1997.

Martin, Dale B. *The Corinthian Body*. New Haven and London: Yale University Press, 1995.

Martineau, Robert. *The Office and Work of a Priest*. Rev. ed. London: Mowbray, 1981.

Mascall, Eric, ed. *The Church of God: An Anglo-Russian Symposium*. London: SPCK, 1934.

Maurice, Frederick Denison. *The Kingdom of Christ*. Alec R. Vidler, ed. London: SCM, 1958.

McGrath, Alister E. *The Renewal of Anglicanism*. Harrisburg, PA: Morehouse, 1993.

McKee, Elsie Anne. *Diakonia in the Classical Reformed Tradition and Today*. Grand Rapids, MI: Eerdmans, 1989.

Melinsky, M. A. H. *The Shape of the Ministry*. Norwich: Canterbury, 1992.

Meyers, Ruth A., ed. *A Prayer Book for the 21st Century*. New York: Church Hymnal, 1996.

————. *Baptism and Ministry*. Liturgical Studies One. New York: Church Hymnal, 1994.

Middleton, Arthur. *Towards a Renewed Priesthood*. Leominster: Gracewing, 1995.

Minear, Paul S. *Images of the Church in the New Testament*. Philadelphia: Westminster, 1960.

Mitchell, Leonel L. *Praying Shapes Believing: A Theological Commentary on the Book of Common Prayer*. Minneapolis: Winston Press, 1985.

Moberly, George. *The Administration of the Holy Spirit in the Body of Christ*. 2nd ed. Oxford and London: James Parker, 1870.

Moberly, Robert Campbell. *Ministerial Priesthood: Chapters (Preliminary to a Study of the Ordinal) on the Rationale of Ministry and the Meaning of Christian Priesthood*. 2nd ed. London: John Murray, 1899.

Morgan, John H. *The Diaconate Today: A Study of Clergy Attitudes in the Episcopal Church*. Notre Dame, IN: Parish Life Institute, 1979.

Moyes, John Stoward. *America Revisited*. Sydney: Church Publishing, 1955.

Mutrux, Robert. *Great New England Churches*. Chester, CT: Globe Pequot, 1982.

Neill, Stephen. *A History of Christian Missions*. New York: Penguin Books, 1964.

————, and Hans-Ruedi Weber, eds. *The Layman in Christian History: A Project of the Department on the Laity of the World Council of Churches*. Philadelphia: Westminster Press, 1963.

New Churches Research Group. *Church Buildings: A Guide to Planning and Design*. London: Architectural Press, 1967.

Nolan, Richard T., ed. *The Diaconate Now*. Washington: Corpus Books, 1968.

Nouwen, Henri J. M. *The Wounded Healer: Ministry in Contemporary Society*. Garden City, N.Y.: Doubleday, 1972.

Paton, David, ed. *Reform of the Ministry: A Study in the Work of Roland Allen*. London: Lutterworth, 1968.

Paton, David M. *R.O.:The Life and Times of Bishop Ronald Hall of Hong Kong*. Hong Kong: Diocese of Hong Kong and Macao, 1985.

Penhale, Francis. *The Anglican Church Today: Catholics in Crisis*. London: Mowbray, 1986.

Perham, Michael, ed. *Liturgy for a New Century*. London: SPCK/Alcuin Club, 1991.

Plater, Ormonde, ed., *Deacons in the Episcopal Church: Guidelines on their Selection, Training and Ministry*. Providence, RI: North American Association for the Diaconate, 1991.

Prestige, G. L. *The Life of Charles Gore*. London: William Heinemann, 1935.

Quick, Oliver Chase. *The Christian Sacraments*. London: Nisbet, 1948.

———. *Doctrines of the Creed: Their Basis in Scripture and Their Meaning To-Day*. New York: Charles Scribner's Sons, 1951.

———. *The Testing of Church Principles*. London : John Murray, 1919.

Ramsey, A. Michael. *The Anglican Spirit*. Dale Coleman, ed. London: SPCK, 1991.

———. *The Christian Priest Today*. Rev. ed. London: SPCK, 1987.

———. *An Era in Anglican Theology: From Gore to Temple*. New York: Charles Scribner's Sons, 1960.

———. *The Gospel and the Catholic Church*. 1936. Reprint, Cambridge, MA: Cowley, 1990.

———. *Holy Spirit: A Biblical Study*. Reprint, Cambridge, MA: Cowley, 1992.

Ranson, Stewart, Alan Bryman and Bob Hinings. *Clergy, Ministers and Priests*. London: Routledge and Kegan Paul, 1977.

Raynes, Raymond. *Called By God (What It Means to be a Priest)*. London: Church Literature Association, c. 1945.

Redfern, Alastair. *Ministry and Priesthood*. London: Darton, Longman and Todd, 1999.

Reed, John Shelton. *Glorious Battle: The Cultural Politics of Victorian Anglo-Catholicism*. Nashville, TN: Vanderbilt University Press, 1996.

Richardson, Cyril C., ed. *Early Christian Fathers*. Philadelphia: Westminster, 1953.

Rock, Daniel. *The Church of Our Fathers*. London: John Hodges, 1903.

Rowthorn, Anne W. *The Liberation of the Laity*. Wilton, CT: Morehouse-Barlow, 1986.

Russell, Anthony. *The Clerical Profession*. London: SPCK, 1980.

Russell, Keith A. *In Search of the Church: New Testament Images for Tomorrow's Congregations*. Bethesda, MD: Alban Institute, 1994.

Sachs, William L. *The Transformation of Anglicanism*. Cambridge: CUP, 1993.

Sanday, W[illiam]. *The Conception of Priesthood in the Early Church and in the Church of England*. London: Longmans Green, 1898.

Schweizer, Eduard. *The Letter to the Colossians*. Andrew Chester, trans. Minneapolis: Augsburg, 1982.

Sedgwick, Timothy F. *The Making of Ministry*. Cambridge, MA: Cowley, 1993.

Shea, Victor, and William Whitla, eds. *Essays and Reviews: The 1860 Text and Its Reading*. Charlottesville: University Press of Virginia, 2000.

Sims, Bennett J. *Servanthood: Leadership for the Third Millennium*. Cambridge, MA: Cowley, 1997.

Smethurst, David. *Extended Communion: An Experiment in Cumbria*. Bramcote, Notts.: Grove Books, 1986.

Smith, Peter F. *Third Millennium Churches*. London: Galliard, 1972.

Smith, William, and Samuel Cheetham, eds. *A Dictionary of Christian Antiquities*. Hartford, CT: J. B. Burr, 1880.

Snow, John. *The Impossible Vocation: Ministry in the Mean Time*. Cambridge, MA: Cowley, 1988.

Stanley, Arthur Penrhyn. *Christian Institutions*. New York: Charles Scribner's Sons, 1881.

Stone, Lawrence. *The Family, Sex and Marriage in England 1500–1800*. New York: Harper and Row, 1977.

Streeter, B. H. *The Primitive Church*. London: Macmillan, 1929.

Strudwick, Vincent. *Christopher Wordsworth, Bishop of Lincoln 1869–1885*. Lincoln: Honywood Press, 1987.

Stuhlman, Byron David. *Occasions of Grace: An Historical and Theological Study of the Pastoral Offices and Episcopal Services in the Book of Common Prayer*. New York: Church Hymnal, 1995.

Sumner, David E. *The Episcopal Church's History: 1945–1958*. Wilton, CT: Morehouse-Barlow, 1987.

Sykes, Stephen, and John Booty, eds. *The Study of Anglicanism*. Minneapolis: Fortress, 1988.

Sykes, Stephen. *Unashamed Anglicanism*. Nashville: Abingdon Press, 1975.

Temple, William. *Christ In His Church*. London: Macmillan, 1925.

———. *Christian Faith and Life*. New York: Macmillan, 1931.

———. *Christus Veritas*. 1924. London: Macmillan, 1949.

———. *Church and Nation*. London, Macmillan, 1915.

———. *The Church Looks Forward*. New York: Macmillan, 1944.

———. *Fellowship with God*. London: Macmillan, 1920.

———. *The Hope of a New World*. New York: Macmillan, 1942.

———. *Nature, Man and God*. London: Macmillan, 1934.

———. *Readings in St. John's Gospel*. London: Macmillan, 1940.

———. *Thoughts on Some Problems of the Day*. London: Macmillan, 1931.

———. *William Temple's Teaching*. A. E. Baker, ed. Philadelphia: Westminster, 1951.

Terwilliger, Robert, and Urban T. Holmes, III, eds. *To Be a Priest: Perspectives on Vocation and Ordination*. New York: Seabury, 1975.

Thomas, W. H. Griffith. *The Catholic Faith*. London: Longmans, 1911.

———. *The Principles of Theology*. London: Church Book Room, 1956.

Tiller, John. *A Strategy for the Church's Ministry*. London: CIO, 1983.

Tovey, Phillip. *Communion Outside the Eucharist*. Bramcote, Notts.: Grove Books, 1993.

Towler, Robert, and A. P. M. Coxon. *Fate of the Anglican Clergy*. London: Macmillan, 1979.

Turner, Philip, and Frank Sugeno, eds. *Crossroads Are For Meeting: Essays on the Mission and Common Life of the Church in a Global Society*. Sewanee, TN: SPCK/USA, 1986.

Underhill, Evelyn. *The Ways of the Spirit*. New York: Crossroad, 1990.

Vaughan, Patrick H. *Non-Stipendiary Ministry in the Church of England: A History of the Development of an Idea*. San Francisco: Mellen Research University Press, 1990.

Walmsley, Roberta Chapin, and Adair T. Lummis. *Healthy Clergy, Wounded Healers: Their Families and Their Ministries*. New York: Church Publishing, 1997.

Webb, Val. *Florence Nightingale: The Making of a Radical Theologian*. St. Louis, MO: Chalice Press, 2002.

Welch, Claude. *Protestant Thought in the Nineteenth Century*. Vol. 2, 1870–1914. New Haven and London: Yale University Press, 1985.

Welsby, Paul A. *A History of the Church of England 1945-1980*. London: OUP, 1984.

White, Alison, and Di Williams. *Deacons at Your Service*. Bramcote, Notts: Grove Books, 1987.

Williams, Rowan. *A Ray of Darkness*. Cambridge, MA: Cowley Publications, 1995.

Wingate, Andrew, et al., eds., *Anglicanism: A Global Communion*. New York: Church Publishing, 1998.

Wright, N. T. *Evangelical Anglican Identity: The Connection Between Bible, Gospel and Church*. Oxford: Latimer House, 1980.

———. *New Tasks for a Renewed Church*. London: Hodder and Stoughton, 1992.

Wybrew, Hugh. *Called to be Priests*. Oxford: SLG Press, 1989.

Zabriskie, Stewart C. *Total Ministry: Reclaiming the Ministry of All God's People*. Bethesda, MD: Alban Institute, 1995.

E. ARTICLES, PAMPHLETS, AND PAPERS

1. *Regarding R. C. Moberly:*

Holland, Henry Scott. "Robert Campbell Moberly," in *Personal Studies*. London: Wells Gardner, Darton and Co., Ltd., n.d. [1905], 272–279.

"Robert Campbell Moberly." *Church Quarterly Review*, 58, no. 115 (1904), 74–93.

"Moberly, Robert Campbell."*Dictionary of National Biography*. 1912, 2nd suppl., s.v. "Moberly, Robert Campbell."

Moberly, W. H. "Robert Campbell Moberly." *Journal of Theological Studies* 6 (1905), 1–19.

Sanday, William. "Robert Campbell Moberly." *Journal of Theological Studies* 4 (1903), 481–499.

2. *Regarding Ministerial Priesthood:*

"Apostolical Succession: The Latest Nonconformist Manifesto." *London Quarterly Review*, 30, no. 60 (July 1898), 289–302.

Bascom, John. "Reason and Faith." *The Dial*, 24, no. 284 (April 16, 1898), 261–263.

"Moberly's *Ministerial Priesthood*." *Church Quarterly Review*, 46 (April 1898), 1–23.

Monnier, Jean. [review of *MP*] *Revue de L'Histoire des Religions*, 54 (1906), 141.

3. *Other:*

Alexander, John D. "Rethinking 'Ministry of All the Baptized'." *The Living Church*, vol. 226, no. 2 (January 12, 2003), 23–24.

Ashworth, Pat. "NSM becomes bishop." *Church Times* (October 26, 2001).

Baverstock, A. H. "The Theology of Priesthood," in Herbert S. Box, ed. *Priesthood*. London: SPCK, 1937.

Berndt, Ronald M. "Australian Religions: An Overview." *Encyclopedia of Religion*. Mircea Eliade, ed. New York: Macmillan, 1987, I, 529–547.

———. "Law and Order in Aboriginal Australia," in *Aboriginal Man in Australia*. Ronald M. Berndt and Catherine H. Berndt, eds. Sydney: Angus and Robertson, 1965.

"Christian Athiesm: The 'God Is Dead' Movement." *TIME*, vol. 86, no. 17 (October 22, 1965), 61–62.

"Concerns of Ordained Ministry Highlighted in Recent Statistics." *The Living Church*, 211, no. 26 (December 24, 1995), 6.

Doss, Joe Morris. "The Unified Symbol of Ministry: Sacramental Orders." *Anglican Theological Review*, 71, no. 1 (January 1980), 20–36.

Douglas, Ian T. "Authority After Colonialism: Power, Privilege and Primacy in the Anglican Communion." *The Witness*, vol. 83, no. 3 (March 2000), 10–14.

———. "Baptized into Mission: Ministry and Holy Orders Reconsidered." *Sewanee Theological Review* 40, no. 4 (1997), 431–443.

Firminger, W. K.. "The Ordinal," in *Liturgy and Worship: A Companion to the Prayer Books of the Anglican Communion*. W. K. Lowther Clarke, ed. London: SPCK, 1950, 626–682.

Gore, Charles. "Hatch's Bampton Lectures." *Church Quarterly Review*, 12 (1881), 409–452.

Harding, Leander S. "What Have We Been Telling Ourselves About the Priesthood?" *Sewanee Theological Review*, 43, no. 2 (Easter 2000), 144–166.

Hardy, Jr., Edward Rochie. "Priestly Ministries in the Modern Church," in *The Ministry in Historical Perspectives*. H. Richard Niebuhr and Daniel D. Williams, eds. New York: Harper and Brothers, 1956, 149–179.

Hein, David. "Hugh Lister (1901–1944): Priest, Labor Leader, and Combatant Officer." *Anglican and Episcopal History* 70, no. 3 (September 2001), 353–374.

Hinchcliff, P. "Deacon." *A New Dictionary of Liturgy and Worship*. J. G. Davies, ed. London: SCM Press, 1986, 208.

Hollis, Michael. "A Doctrine of the Church." *International Review of Mission*, 39 (1950), 461–464.

Kaye, Bruce. "The 1850 Bishops Conference and the Strange Birth of Australian Synods." The Sydney Smith Lecture, Melbourne, Australia. Unpubl. paper (15 November 2000).

Lambert III, Lake. "Called to Serve: Diaconal Ministry in the ELCA," Division for Ministry, Evangelical Lutheran Church in America (July 2001).

"Lay Administration of Holy Communion." N.p.: The Church Union, 1977.

"Looking at the Age Gap: Now and Then." *Congregations*, 27, no. 2 (March/April 2001), 9.

Miller, Charles. "The Theology of the Laity: Description and Construction with Reference to the American Book of Common Prayer." *Anglican Theological Review*, 84, no. 2 (Spring 2002), 219–238.

"Moberly, George." *Dictionary of National Biography*. Oxford: OUP, n.d. XIII, 535.

Moorman, John R. H. "Charles Gore and the Doctrine of the Church." *Church Quarterly Review*, 158 (1957), 128–140.

O'Day, Rosemary. "The Clerical Renaissance in Victorian England and Wales," in *Religion in Victorian Britain*. Gerald Parsons, ed. Manchester: Manchester University Press, 1988. I, 184–212.

Oxtoby, Willard G., et al. "Priesthood," in *Encyclopedia of Religion*. Mircea Eliade, ed. New York: Macmillan, 1987. XI, 528–534.

Presler, Titus. "Old and New in Worship and Community: Culture's Pressure in Global Anglicanism." *Anglican Theological Review*, 82, no. 4 (Fall 2000), 709–723.

Preston, Ronald. "William Temple: The Man and his Impact on Church and Society," in *Archbishop William Temple: Issues in Church and Society 50 Years On*. Manchester: William Temple Foundation, 1994, 4–15.

Ray, Thomas K. "The Small Church: Radical Reformation and Renewal of Ministry." *Anglican Theological Review*, 78, no. 4 (Fall 1996), 615–627.

Robinson, J. A. T. "The Ministry and the Laity," in *Layman's Church*. London: Lutterworth Press, 1963, 9–22.

Staudt, Kathleen Henderson. "Annunciations in Most Lives: Vocational Discernment and the Work of the Church." *Sewanee Theological Review*, 43, no. 2 (Easter 2000), 130–143.

Sykes, Stephen W. "The Theology of Priesthood." *Sewanee Theological Review*, 43, no. 2 (Easter 2000), 121–129.

Temple, William. "The Church," in *Foundations*. B. H. Streeter, ed. London: Macmillan and Co., 1914.

Totman, Schuyler, "AMiA Consecrates Four More Bishops," *The Living Church*, 223, no. 3 (July 15, 2001), 6–7.

"Toward a Hidden God." *TIME*, vol. 87, no. 14 (April 8, 1966), 82-87.

"Two American Priests Become Bishops in Singapore, Then Return to US." *The Living Church*, 220, no. 8 (February 20, 2000), 6–8.

Waring, Steve. "One Common Lord" and "Some Expect More Opposition." *The Living Church*, 233, no. 4 (January 28, 2001), 6–7.

Wical, Hillary. "Clergy by the Numbers." *Congregations*, 27, no. 2 (March/April 2001), 6–9.

Winter, Mildred. "Deaconess," in *The Encyclopedia of the Lutheran Church.* Julius Bodensieck, ed. Minneapolis: Augsburg, 1965, 660–664.

Wright, J. Robert. "Sequential or Cumulative Orders vs. Direct Ordination." *Anglican Theological Review*, 75, no. 2 (Spring 1993), 246–251.

Young, Frances. "A Cloud of Witnesses," in John Hick, ed. *The Myth of God Incarnate*. Philadelphia: Westminster Press, 1977, 13–47.

F. WEBSITES AND INTERNET RESOURCES

Alpha North America <http://www.alphana.org>, The Official Website from the Headquarters of Alpha <http://www.alpha.org.uk/> (April 27, 2001).

Anglican Communion News Service. "Canterbury concerning the Roman Catholic Document 'Dominus Iesus'." ACNS release #2219 (September 5, 2000), <http://www.anglicancommunion.org/acns/ acsarchive/ acns2200/acns2219.html> (July 2, 2001).

[Australia, Anglican Church of.] Anglican Media, Sydney. "Synod calls on Anglican Primates to affirm traditional Church doctrines," <http://www.anglicanmediasydney.asn.au/synod2000/n18_10_2.htm> (May 22, 2001).

———. "Transcript of media conference for Archbishop-elect Peter Jensen, June 7, 2001" <http://www.anglicanmediasydney.asn.au/ conf_transcript.htm> (June 16, 2001).

———. "Working within an 'impaired Communion': Sydney Anglicans discuss the 'contentious' issue of women bishops." <http://www.angl canmediasydney.asn.au/synod2000/m17_10_2.htm> (May 22, 2001).

Blaikie, Andrew. "Ageing: Old visions, new times?" *The Lancet*. (December 18, 1999) <http://proquest.umi.com/pqdweb?TS=98684...1&Dtp= 00000007412342&Mtd=1&Fmt=4> (April 9, 2001), 2.

Bowder, Bill. "Lay presidency will bring disunity, warns Dr Carey." *Church Times* (6 July 2001) <http://www.churchtimes.co. uk/templates /NewsTemplate_3r.asp?recid=575&table=news&bimage=news&issue=7 220&count=6> (July 8, 2001).

Church of England. "Petertide sees a further rise in ordinations— 26/06/1999" <http://www.cofe.anglican.org/cgi-bin/news/item_frame.pl?id=41> (April 26, 2001).

————. Diocese of Bradford. [The General Ordination] <http://www.bradford.anglican.org/features/010701ordain.html> (July 2, 2001).

Halcrow, Jeremy. "Sydney Anglicans to consider confirmation by clergy and lay people." Anglican Media, Diocese of Sydney <http://www.angli canmediasydney.asn.au/ synod2000/n11_10_1.htm> (May 22, 2001).

Hastings, Chris. "Dustman by day, vicar by night." *The Daily Telegraph* (11 August 2002) <http://www.telegraph.co.uk/news/main/jhtml?xml= %2Fnews%2F2002/2F08%2F11%Fnvicar//xml> (August 18, 2002).

Lampman, Jane. "Where Are the Young Clergy?" *Christian Science Monitor* (July 19, 2001) <http://www.csmonitor.com/durable/2001 /07/19/fp15s1-csm.shtml> (July 20, 2001).

Infoplease Almanac. "Life Expectancy at Birth for Selected Countries, 1950–1998" <http://www.infoplease.com/ipa/A0774532.html> (April 10, 2001).

————. "Life Expectancy by Age, 1850–1998" <http://www.info please.com/ipa/A0005140.html> (April 9, 2001).

North American Association for the Diaconate. "History of NAAD and the North American Diaconate" <http://www.diakonoi.org/naadhist. htm> (April 13, 2001).

National Network of Episcopal Clergy Associations. <http://www.nneca.org/> (June 26, 2001).

Nunley, Jan. "AMiA consecrates four new bishops." Anglican Communion News Service (June 27, 2001) <http://www.anglicancommunion. org/acns/acnsarchive/acns2500/acns2512.html> (July 1, 2001).

Porter, Muriel. "Australian vote sets diocese at odds with rest of Anglican Communion." *Church Times*, Internet ed. [Web issue #133] (October 22, 1999) <http://www.churchtimes.co.uk> (October 23, 1999).

Pulford, Cedric. "English ordination figures surge higher." *World* (September 1999) <http://www.anglicanjournal.com/1225/07/world02. html> (June 3, 2003).

Rodgers, Margaret. "Sydney Synod moves to forward lay and diaconal presidency at the Lord's Supper" <http://www.anglicanmediasydney .asn.au/synod2001/laypres_report.htm> (August 6, 2002).

Stannard, Ed. "Lay professionals urged to feel their authority, given in baptism." *Episcopal Life* (July 20, 2001) <http://www.ecusa.anglican. org/ens/2001-190.html> (July 21, 2001).

Sudan, Episcopal Church of the. "Many Tribes, One Lord." Press release (July 2, 2001). From Bridgett Rees, e-mail to the author (July 2, 2001).

Whitham, Larry. "Flocks In Need of Shepherds." *Washington Times* (July 2, 2001) <http://www.washtimes.com/national/20010702 475926. htm (July 20, 2001).

G. INTERVIEWS AND CONVERSATIONS

In addition to these printed and electronic resources, I have relied extensively on conversations and interviews with more people than I can possibly enumerate. Some of them include:

In England: The Reverend Canon Vincent Strudwick, the Reverend Dr. John Macquarrie, the Reverend Dr. Jane Shaw, the Very Reverend Robert M. C. Jeffery, Sarah Ogilvie, Sr. Barbara June SLG, Sr. Eve of the Promise of God n/SLG (Oxford); the Reverend Stephen and Heather Treasure, the Reverend Adrian Botwright, the Reverend Canon Christopher Lewis, Christopher and Jill Wright (Diocese of Bradford).

In or from Uganda: The Reverend Canon Mabel Katahweire, the Reverend Canon Ernest Katahweire, the Reverend Jonathan Byamugishu, the faculties of Bishop Tucker Theological College at the Uganda Christian University, Mukono, and Bishop Barham Theological College, Kabale; clergy participating in conferences in Namugongo and Kabale in June, 1998.

At Virginia Theological Seminary, Alexandria: The Reverend Dr. Robert Prichard, Dr. Timothy Sedgwick, the Reverend Dr. Richard Jones, Dr. Kathleen Staudt, Glenda McQueen (Diocese of Panama), the Reverend Samuel Mweve (Province of Tanzania), the Reverend Boanerges Rosa (Diocese of Honduras), and countless seminarians.

In Cambridge, Massachusetts: The Reverend Brian Bostwick SSJE, the Reverend Gift Makwasha (Zimbabwe), the Reverend Dr. Ian Douglas; the Reverend Jean Larson-Hurd, the Reverend George Thomas, the Reverend Peter Laarman, the Reverend Dudley Rose; the Reverend Dr. R. Scott Nash (Mercer University); the Reverend Dr. Carl Daw; seminarians of Harvard Divinity School and Episcopal Divinity School.

Others: The Reverend Dr. Jackson Hershbell, The Reverend Tad deBordenave (Richmond, VA), the Reverend Dr. John Martiner (Wilmington, DE); Lomole James Simeon (Diocese of Khartoum, Sudan), the Rev. Melford E. Holland, Jr. (Coordinator for Ministry Development, the Episcopal Church, New York, NY), and a wide variety of clergy of the Diocese of Southwestern Virginia, among them Raymond Moore, G. Thomas Mustard, Russell Hatfield, the Right Reverend A. Heath Light, John Runkle on architecture, and clergy of the Augusta Convocation.

Index

1978 Lambeth ; each province decides
         yes/no on ordn. of ♀ to P

1988 ~~others~~ joined ECUSA in ordng ♀
         (along @ canada, NZ, & HonaKong
↓CofE

Laos Greek
     people whole peopls

     1966 Time Is god dead? 195
214 Countis man on priest dly.

22⊖ Mutual ministry Total min.

     Bible - church as comm imge
              "creative energy of God
                                         232
       Fernhagen quote: all life
245 priest -sacramental

246 presg. is diaconal